Typography
on the Web

Typography
on the Web

Joseph T. Sinclair

AP PROFESSIONAL

An imprint of Academic Press

San Diego London Boston
New York Sydney Tokyo Toronto

Quotation in Chapter 1 by Esther Dyson from *Release 2.0* by Esther Dyson (Broadway Books, 1997).

Quotation from *A History of Reading* (Alfred A. Knopf, 1996, and Penguin, 1997) © 1996 Alberto Manguel in Chapter 1 used with permission of the author Alberto Manguel and by permission of Penguin, a division of Penguin Putnam Inc.

Quotation in Chapter 7 is from *Cold Mountain* by Charles Frazier (Grove Atlantic, 1997).

Figure 17.7 used with permission of WebTV Networks, Inc.

Academic Press
A division of Harcourt Brace & Company
525 B Street, Suite 1900, San Diego, CA 92101-4495
WorldWideWeb site at http://www.apnet.com

Academic Press
24–28 Oval Road, London NW1 7DX, UK
http://www.hbuk.co.uk/ap/

Library of Congress Cataloging-in-Publication Data
Sinclair, Joseph T.
     Typography on the Web / Joseph T. Sinclair
          p. cm.
     Includes index.
     ISBN 0-12-645545-7 (acid-free paper)
     1. Web sites—Design. 2. Computer fonts. 3. Typesetting.
  I. Title.
  TK5105.888.S58   1998
  686.2'25445276--dc21   98-22952
                                                                      CIP

Printed in the United States of America
98 99 00 01 02 IP 9 8 7 6 5 4 3 2 1

Contents

Chapter 21 What's Your Type? *429*

Foreword

Times New Roman and Times are enjoyable fonts; that is, if you don't have to look at them all the time. Unfortunately, even as recently as a few months ago, they were all that was available on the Web. Even with all the graphic and multimedia options available, someone apparently forgot to give you realistic control for the type in your designs. Recently new capability to choose from a wide variety of typefaces for your Web typography has brought a new range of aesthetic appeal and professionalism to your Web pages. Cascading Style Sheets provide you with precise layout. Indeed, it's an exciting time in Web publishing. Knowing that you have the options available to finally make type really work for you will bring the Web as a publishing medium a long step forward.

An exciting new age of typography started in 1984 with the desktop publishing revolution. The Web has only poured fuel on the fire, and today the publishing world is ablaze with new technology, new economics, new talent, and new type designs, all coming together to provide you with a fresh way of expressing yourself in words—and by publishing. Moreover, the Web itself has outdone even desktop publishing in bringing unlimited publishing capabilities to a broad base of people. We have come to a time when anyone with a PC, a modem, good taste, and something to say can publish inexpensively, yet professionally. Surely this will have profound consequences for our society. The press is finally the property of the common man.

But there is a dark side to the Web too. Font designers as well as writers, artists, photographers, and other creative people struggle to protect their work products— their life sustenance—from those who casually appropriate it online without compensation. Specifically, I question whether Microsoft's font embedding goes far enough to protect the products of hard-working font designers. Better protection is needed against Web font piracy. Nothing will dry up this marvelous new golden age of typography faster than the inability of creative people to derive compensation from their work.

But let me step down off my soapbox long enough to compliment Mr. Sinclair for providing us with a book that helps us put this new technology to work. The technology isn't much good if no one understands how to use it, and this book will help you play a part in this amazing new world of online publishing. It doesn't matter whether you're publishing on the Web for your family, on the Internet, or on your company's intranet: good typography makes a difference. It's the bread and butter as well as the spice of reading. The digital engineers and programmers have provided you with astonishing new tools. The font designers have provided you with a scope of choice and creativity unavailable a generation ago. Now it's up to you to use them well, and Mr. Sinclair's book will help.

Don Synstelien
Font Designer

Acknowledgments

My thanks to Brad Chase at Bitstream who was helpful in discussing many typographical issues regarding TrueDoc as well as non-TrueDoc technology, and to Mike Brown of SoftQuad and Daniel Will-Harris who both made helpful suggestions for the book. As always, my thanks to my spouse, Lani, and my daughter, Brook, for being so supportive during the time it took to complete the book, and to my literary agent, Carole McClendon. Finally, thanks to the nice people at AP Professional, including Thomas Park and Julie Champagne.

Introduction

My interest in typography predates my first use of a computer for word processing in 1981, and certainly that first computer fueled my yearning for more typographical control. One of my early (1989) attempts at writing was a book on typography for the office, although the prospects of office personnel using good typography *easily* with DOS were not encouraging. I had great fun later with Windows desktop publishing and laser printers. Then in 1994 I built my first Web site, a gourmet food store, with considerable typographical appeal in the heading GIFs. But I had given up on competent typography for the Web. When, in the spring of 1997, I suddenly became aware of Bitstream's TrueDoc, the prospects for Web typography suddenly looked more encouraging. With Cascading Style Sheets, I realized that competent Web typography would soon become not only possible but a normal feature of the Web.

Most webmasters—the term I use throughout the book to include Web developers, Web site operators, and other Web workers—are not programmers, nor am I. Most are not graphic designers or professional typographers, nor am I. Yet we all have to display text competently. We publish to an unlimited audience, potentially reaching many thousands of people. We can substantially improve our chances of making a good impression or making money by using good typographical techniques. In other words, presumably our efforts will be more favorably received if people can easily read what we have to say on the Web than if they can't. Consequently, a book covering all the bases on how to use typography on the Web is a useful addition to our information resources. I include myself in this statement, because just organizing the information for this book has helped me considerably as a webmaster.

This book does not cover graphic design, font design, digital font technology, or other professional skills that webmasters in general do not have. There have been plenty of good books written on those subjects already, and I encourage people to read such books as far as their interests take them. This book sticks to knowledge and technologies that webmasters should use, indeed must use, to successfully publish on the Web text that people can read. Topics include:

- The influence of 500 years of typography technology
- An overview of digital typography
- HTML typography
- Cascading Style Sheets (CSS)
- Web font display technology (i.e., TrueDoc, font embedding, NetTV)
- The SGML system (e.g., HTML, DHTML, XML, and XSL)

The book briefly covers XML and XSL because they represent the future of the Web and understanding them enables one to better comprehend HTML, CSS, and Web typography. The book also provides information on typography for NetTV (e.g., WebTV), an overview of Dynamic HTML as it relates to typography, a summary of Java typography for Java documents, and some thoughts about cross-media publishing.

We have experienced a revolution in typography that will result in a new kind of reading: networked, immediate, interactive, and garnished with all the digital multimedia that the Web has to offer. The revolution in typography is part of a widespread information revolution that blurs the line between local and global, author and publisher, bureaucracy and individual. Web typography and publishing technology compose the nuts and bolts of the information revolution. This typography revolution is about to make reading respectable online. Make no mistake: This book is not about Web glitz, dancing headlines, marquee banners, or blinking words. It's about readable text and how to create it.

For the first time, via TrueDoc, font embedding, and style sheets, we can control and professionally display text online. In addition, digital online technology brings new capabilities to typography that were undreamed of by leading typographers just a short quarter-century ago. But this revolution creates a quandary.

We have already seen that online typography as practiced by technical people has resulted mostly in unreadable text. Content people have gradually taken over Web development and have been more sensitive to Web site visitors' need for readable text. As a consequence, the 500-year-old typography technology has taken hold on the Web and is now influencing the current and future course of Web technologies. This must be considered a commendable development. However, the quandary is that Web typography must take a radical departure from print typography, because the Web is a nonpaper medium that is different from print, and it has expanded capabilities. Yet traditional typography must guide that radical departure if text is to remain readable and useful. Webmasters will play a major role in resolving the problems inherent in this quandary.

This book is written from the webmaster's point of view. What works? How does it work? And how do I do it on the Web? These are the questions that this book attempts to answer in terms that nonprogrammers, nondesigners, and nontypographers can understand. Nonetheless, the book is not just for webmasters. Others who want or need to learn the ABCs of Web typography will also find the book useful. Because so much of Web typography is so new, a broad range of people may find the book useful.

I use Windows NT 4.0, and this book reflects that fact. I have never used a Mac, although I'm sure it would be preferable if Apple had enough market share to generate the breadth and scope of the Windows programs now available. Even though the programs I use run in Windows, the Web remains a cross-platform medium that works much the same for all computers. Consequently, everything that the book covers applies equally

Style This book is about *style*, a euphemism for digital typography on the Web. Typography concerns the use of type and space on the page (typesetting and layout) with the end of providing readable text. Thus, a style sheet is essentially a specification sheet for Web typography (i.e., a specification sheet for typesetting and layout).

to Mac as well as Windows. Some of the authoring programs I mention may not be available in Mac versions, but comparable Mac programs provide the features needed. Most of the typeface examples included come from either the Adobe Type Library or the Bitstream type catalog.

As Paul Levinson, author of *The Soft Edge: A Natural History and Future of the Information Revolution*, has indicated, the information revolution is primarily about the written word—text—and not necessarily about other media. If he is right, the other shoe is about to drop. Text and nice color images got millions of users online, yet most people find it difficult to read comfortably on the Web. Now with CSS to provide professional layout, TrueDoc and font embedding to provide professional typesetting, and active matrix LCD flat panel monitors to provide a better reading environment, comfortable reading online will soon become a fact of life. Comfortable reading on the Web will carry the information revolution forward another big lurch, and this book provides the nuts and bolts.

Fundamentals of Typography

Readability: The Historical Objective

Typography is about aesthetics, elegance, and function, but most importantly it is about *readability*. The new Web typography excites us foremost because, for the first time, Web developers have control over typesetting, and Web site visitors can now read comfortably at Web sites that pay attention to good typesetting and design practices.

"Ah ha," some people would say, "Text is dead. Long live multimedia. Go for the glitz. That's where the action is on the Web." And it has certainly seemed that way until now. Nonetheless, text is not dead. Quite the contrary: For most Web sites, text remains the most important medium of the multimedia Web.

Text is a very efficient medium from a number of points of view. First, people can read fast. They can read a transcribed panel discussion on national defense policy, for instance, much faster than they can listen to a radio broadcast or an audio recording of it. Second, a writer can produce text quickly. One writer can crank out a lot of polished text in a reasonably short time. Other media often take longer to produce a polished product. For example, creating a commercial-quality audio recording of a seminar usually requires making a composite of segments of the seminar clipped from three or four recorded performances and then edited together in a sound studio. Some mediums even require teams to produce a presentation (e.g., a television production), adding a bureaucratic overhead to the process. Third, text remains inexpensive. Writers are a dime a dozen (I speak from firsthand experience). Production personnel in other media cost real money, especially when teams are required. Fourth, digital text is lightweight; that is, you can transmit a lot of text in a small file in contrast to audio, video, and even graphics files which are often huge.

Touting text is not to say that other media are less important. On the contrary, text combined with other media brings to the Web the richness and color of a fine magazine, and more. Clearly, the combination of text and color graphics has driven the popularity of the Web. Esoteric media such as RealAudio have created a lot of excitement and provided a lot of utility. But for most, text is the real work horse, and it will be with us for a long time. As Esther Dyson points out in *Release 2.0*, a stream of multimedia is nice, but what have you learned at the end of the experience? "Do you want an enjoyable experience that flows through your head, or something more interactive in the truest sense of the word—that is, a book or an essay that makes you think? You have to think to absorb words and transform them into ideas and arguments. You have to change the model with which you view the world, rather than just add some images to a large store of pictures, factoids, emotional responses, and sound bites that don't support any structure. But if all you do is watch, you'll have a hard time formulating what you learned when it's over."

Words are powerful. Read what Alberto Manguel has to say in *A History of Reading* about one of the first evidences of human reading: two tiny Sumerian tablets.

> They are simple, unimpressive objects, each bearing a few discreet markings: a small indentation near the top and some sort of stick-drawn animal in the center. One of the animals may be a goat, in which case the other is probably a sheep. The indentation, archeologists say, represents the number ten. All our history begins with these two modest tablets. They are . . . among the oldest examples of writing we know.
>
> There is something intensely moving in these tablets. Perhaps, when we stare at these pieces of clay carried by a river which no longer exists, observing the delicate incisions portraying animals turned to dust thousands and thousands of years ago, a voice is conjured up, a thought, a message that tells us, 'Here were ten goats,' 'Here were ten sheep,' something spoken by a careful farmer in the days when the deserts were green. By the mere fact of looking at these tablets we have prolonged

a memory from the beginning of our time, preserved a thought long after the thinker stopped thinking, and made ourselves participants in an act of creation that remains open for as long as the incised images are seen, deciphered, read.

Words are evocative. No need to provide examples here. Reread your favorite novel or a stirring speech by Winston Churchill. Words are also utilitarian. Remember the Sears catalog? Visit the Sparco Web site (http://www.sparco.com), and have a look at their mundane catalog of computer parts, peripherals, and supplies. Not very evocative, but very useful when you need an inexpensive thingamajig for your computer in a hurry.

Interestingly, Paul Levinson, author of *The Soft Edge: A Natural History and Future of the Information Revolution*, sees the information revolution as essentially the third revolution for the written word. The first was the graduation from hieroglyphics to the alphabet. The second was Gutenberg's printing press. And the third is word processing and the Web (digital text authoring and publishing). The telegraph, telephone, movies, radio, and television are not necessarily the main attractions of the third revolution. Digital text is.

But after all that one might say about text and reading, the text isn't much good unless it's readable. Indeed, the Web's history of text-handling practices has not brought about widespread comfortable reading for Web site visitors. But all that can now change. Professional typography has arrived, and Web developers that don't pay attention and revamp their Web sites accordingly will find their Web sites beginning to look outdated. Even worse, their Web sites will disappoint visitors expecting easy reading.

Aesthetics

Typography has a long tradition of aesthetic appeal as well as functionality. Claude Garamond crafted type within a century after Gutenberg's time and was followed in later centuries by such typographers as William Caslon, John Baskerville, and

Giambattista Bodoni. Their typefaces remain popular to this day, with Garamond currently perhaps the most popular of all. If you look at typefaces by these typographers in 60-point sizes or above, you can easily see the elegant beauty of their designs. Fine typography has captured the artistic souls of many writers, publishers, printers, and readers over the centuries and continues to do so. It's addictive. Look too closely, and you succumb to the addiction.

Function

It isn't enough for type to be beautiful, however; it must also serve the reader. It must retain its aesthetic appeal when printed in text sizes but must also look appealing in words and groups of words, flow well, and carry the reader along tirelessly. If it isn't readable, it's not much use except perhaps as display type (i.e., type for titles).

Sharpness and Clarity

A well-designed typeface generates well-defined individual characters that display in such a way as to be easily seen and identified. The letters display sharply and clearly. This is one design aspect of a typeface, but even sharp and clear letters must have other qualities.

Legibility

Assuming the characters have sharpness and clarity, they must also support smooth and easy reading. This has to do with the design of the typeface as a whole rather than how well defined the individual characters are. A competent typeface enables unrestrained reading. People can read the characters easily in groups (words) and in text blocks (sentences and paragraphs). The type design must maintain a transparency; that is, if a reader notices the typeface while reading, the typeface is probably not legible.

Readability

Readability goes a step beyond legibility. It has to do with the total reading environment. Such factors as type combinations, layout design, and background and foreground (text) colors make the most legible typefaces either effortless to read or difficult and sometimes impossible to read. As a Web developer, you cannot be satisfied with clear and sharp legible text. You need readable text. This is especially important on the Web where the conditions for readability remain minimal. It is important for you to take every opportunity to improve readability.

Digital Irony

Ironically, after the long history of an evolution toward more efficient readability, we have returned to the starting gate in the new electronic media. Computer monitors offer low resolution barely adequate for prolonged reading. Online media (i.e., the Web), which have risen meteorically to prominence in publishing, have offered inadequate typesetting and layout capabilities and have even provided user control over typesetting and formatting, a questionable practice for most publishing situations. Digital technologies have focused on desktop publishing and prepress activities, skewing the capabilities of digital typography to serve printing. Digital technicians with little appreciation for typography as a craft have proscribed online typesetting practices that have favored a neat, clean look over readability. What it all boils down to is that reading on the Web isn't as easy as it should be and can be.

Digital Future

But things change. The new active matrix LCD flat panel computer monitors offer the potential for higher resolution than the cathode ray tube (CRT) monitors that most people now use, and flat panel monitors have started to sell well in the market after substantial price drops. The Web Consortium has created Cascading Style Sheets (CSS), a typesetting and layout system for HTML typography. And two new digital typesetting technologies, Bitstream's TrueDoc and Microsoft's font embedding, compete to provide competent typesetting capabilities for online publishing. Creative online typography and comfortable reading online are finally here.

NCs

In September, 1997, WebTV announced a new model of its pioneering network computer (NC) for television viewers that had been introduced just a year earlier. The WebTV Plus replaced the WebTV "Classic." The very small Sony and Phillips WebTV Classic set-tops, which are powerful computers with built-in modems, went on sale nationally for $99. Two years earlier, digital pundits had proclaimed that an NC at the projected cost of $500 was impossible. The new $299 WebTV Plus offers amazing new capabilities, including a 1.1 GB hard drive onto which WebTV pushes select Web sites in the middle of each night using the wide bandwidth vertical blanking interval of broadcast and cable television. Indeed, I hate to be the one to break it to you, but your grandmother accesses the Web with her WebTV Plus about eight times faster than you do with your PC and a 56K modem. Hey, don't try to sell Granny a PC.

Flat Panel Monitors

The new active matrix LCD flat panel monitors (see Chapter 5) will eventually provide resolution in color that's over twice that of the best CRTs. In 1995, you could buy one of these new flat panels for $11,000, if you could find one. In 1996, the price descended to about $6,000. By the end of 1997, you could buy active matrix LCD monitors for less than $2,000. In the first quarter of 1998, you could buy one for under $1,200. How soon will the $150 high-resolution active matrix LCD flat panel arrive?

Readers

Put the NC, the active matrix LCD flat panel, and a small hard disk into a *reader* about the size, thickness, and weight of a hardcover book, and sell it for $250. Now you've got something that together with the Web will cause a real publishing revolution. And how many years away is it? Not many. This small device even strikes down the last-resort argument of those who claim that a digital device will never replace the book: the *bathroom* argument. "But can I take it to the bathroom and read it?" For the NC reader described above, the answer is yes, you can take it into the bathroom and read it. Keep in mind that this reader can be manufactured today. It just can't be sold for $250 yet.

You can't do much about the prices of NCs and flat panel monitors unless you are a manufacturer. But you can do something today to advance comfortable online reading by aggressively experimenting with CSS, TrueDoc, and font embedding and by becoming proficient with these new technologies that enable professional typography on the Web.

Parallel?

Between 1450 and 1455, Johannes Gensfleisch zur Laden zum Gutenberg published his famous bible, the first book ever printed in Western civilization. He had already experimented for about ten years, borrowing large sums of money. By inventing molded metal type, a press, and an oil-based ink, he had solved three important problems for printing with moveable type. What he apparently did not anticipate was the size of book which we use today. Books were much bigger then and were usually displayed on a lectern and read aloud to others. By the turn of the century (i.e., 1500), however, printers proliferated widely in Europe and decreased the cost of books considerably. With book publishing booming, printers started printing small books that a person could hold in his or her hand and read privately and silently. Thus, in just a few decades the reading technology evolved from one paradigm (large book, public, primarily aural, limited market) to the beginning of another (small book, private, silent, mass market) which remains with us even today.

There is, perhaps, a bit of a parallel today. We sit at desks with big-box PCs and huge CRT monitors. We read on such monitors in order to do work or otherwise use PCs for various activities. We often share PCs with coworkers or family members. But for the most part, most of us don't use PCs to just read. We would rather use books or magazines. Even laptops are somewhat awkward with their hinged screens and keyboards. But the small book-size reader with the high-resolution screen promises to be as comfortable for reading as a book. Yet, it presents interactive digital multimedia with almost unlimited capacity. It makes a better book than a book. And because text remains the most important medium, this revolutionary new digital reader—revolutionary as a reading paradigm, not as a computer—requires capable online digital typography to become popular and thrive. Such typography has already arrived with the multimedia Web, CSS, TrueDoc, and font embedding. The digital reader will certainly follow.

The New Web Typography

Will books become obsolete? Books continued to thrive following the invention of television. Bookstores sell more books today than ever before. The Web will probably boost the sales of printed books too, particularly if you include books that publishers publish on the Web but that readers print on a laser printer before reading. Nonetheless, publishing books to be read solely on digital devices will soon emerge as a substantial growth industry regardless of the success of print or other information technologies.

Monomedia (print only) printing—and occasionally duomedia when illustrations are used—has been the basis of reading technology for 500 years. We now stand at the threshold of interactive multimedia online publishing that will change reading forever. The new reading technology will require typography of the same high quality that we have come to take for granted in print technology. With the great traditions of fine typography behind us and the new innovative digital typography crafted by ingenious professional typographers proliferating around us, we can surely look forward to a new golden age of typography.

But enough of romanticizing typography. It is readability that we chase after; and the new Web technologies covered by this book enable a giant step forward in online readability. You can now provide readable documents for your Web site visitors or your intranet colleagues—actual professional quality publishing.

Summary

Remember, it's *readability* that's important. You only have to ask one question: Can you read it easily? If the answer is *yes*, you've done your job. If *no*, perhaps this book can help you. In any event, once you know the basics of typography, this book can carry you forward into the digital online world of the Web.

It's All in the Face

T ype is the flower of typography, and surveying type provides a fertile subject for beginning this book. If you're an accomplished typographer already, you'll find this information old hat. If not, this chapter may clarify some things you've heard about type.

Typefaces

A typeface is a distinctive design of type. Typefaces range from the contorted to the elegant. Look over the four typefaces below.

Mezz

Humanist

Univers

Adobe Garamond

Although the above typefaces differ from one another, two typefaces can look similar to each other yet convey a very different gestalt (feeling). You can recognize typeface names because they are capitalized. The following list provides some familiar examples: Palatino, Century Schoolbook, Times New Roman, Bookman, and Helvetica. Although one cannot copyright typeface designs in the United States, one can copyright the names; so, as a legal matter, no two names should be exactly the same. Typefaces include variations called typestyles.

Typestyles

Each typeface design includes different typestyles, that is, variations within the design. Typestyles follow traditional formats of which at least four have become common: regular (roman), italic, bold, and bold italic. See four of the typestyles of Adobe Garamond below:

Adobe Garamond regular
Adobe Garamond italic
Adobe Garamond bold
Adobe Garamond bold italic

The typestyles of the Adobe Garamond typeface have certain unifying characteristics even though they differ. They look well together. Typestyles are not names, just generic descriptions; therefore, they are not capitalized: italic, bold, bold italic.

Some additional typestyles that you will see less often can add a special appeal to your typesetting in appropriate situations: *light*, *book*, *medium*, *demi*, *ultra*, *black*, *heavy*, and *heavyface*. The differences primarily involve weight (e.g., light is a little lighter than regular). For sans serif type, you may see *oblique* or *slanted* substituted for italics. A *condensed* type might be a separate typeface or a typestyle within an existing typeface. Condensed type has narrow widths. An *expanded* type has wide widths. The many typestyles attest to the ingenuity of typographers, but such creativity presents a problem.

No industry coordinating committee approves names for typefaces or typestyles. The U.S. Copyright Office has copyright procedures for the *names* of typefaces, but nothing more. Additionally, no official guidelines for classifying and naming typefaces or typestyles exist. Consequently, you may not be able to tell much from names. In addition, two typefaces can be almost identical and have very different names. The most reliable way to evaluate a typeface or typestyle is to use it or look at some content typeset in it. This lack of an official nomenclature system creates problems for digital typography. See Chapter 10 for more details.

Fonts

The word *font* originated in the print industry. A font is simply one size of a specific typestyle of a specific typeface as manifested in lead type. The 14-point font of Baskerville italic was used to print the following line.

Baskerville italic 14 points, a font

This definition came from traditional print shop usage. When a document called for 14-point Baskerville italic, a journeyman printer reached for a set of lead type that was all 14-point Baskerville italic. Printers called that set a *font*.

Today, in the digital world, the word *font* means something different. A digital font is a computer program that generates characters. Because a font program generates *all* sizes for a specific typestyle of a specific typeface, size no longer defines a font. A digital font is simply a specific typestyle of a specific typeface. For instance, the digital font Century Schoolbook italic will generate all sizes of Century Schoolbook italic type.

The word *font* in digital terms has also come to be used as a substitute for the word *typeface*. Unfortunately, this causes much confusion when discussing digital typography, for example, with vendors. If the understood meaning of *font* differs between customers and vendors, customers may not get what they think they have purchased.

Anatomy of Type

A little anatomy will prove helpful to you in understanding the terminology of typography in this book. The graphics in the figures illustrate the components that make up type (component parts of letters, Figure 2.1) and how type sets on a line

What Is a Font? In regard to digital publishing, when someone specifies the Minion font, they might mean a software package of four separate font programs, each a digital font: Minion regular, Minion italic, Minion bold, and Minion bold italic. However, the person may be referring instead to the full set of Minion typestyles, which has many more typestyles. Or, the person may mean simply Minion regular.

Copyright Although one cannot copyright a typeface design, one can copyright the program that constitutes a digital font. Consequently, you cannot distribute a digital font (the program) without licensing it first and presumably paying a royalty on each copy of the font program distributed. Once you have licensed a digital font for your own use (not for distribution), you can of course distribute the type produced by the digital font, either on the printed page or in a digital document, without further licensing or payment of royalties.

(dimensions of type in a line, Figure 2.2). The figures do a better job than words can of defining such components and the position of letters on a line. Note, however, that there is no accepted world standard for naming the parts of letters.

Characteristics of Typefaces

Typefaces have two basic attributes directly related to appearance and readability: character spacing and serif design.

Letter Spacing

The space that characters occupy directly affects readability. This section covers the inherent horizontal spacing of characters, monospacing and proportional spacing.

Monospacing

If each character takes the same amount of horizontal space, it is called monospaced type. Monospacing originated with typewriters. Courier is a popular monospaced typeface.

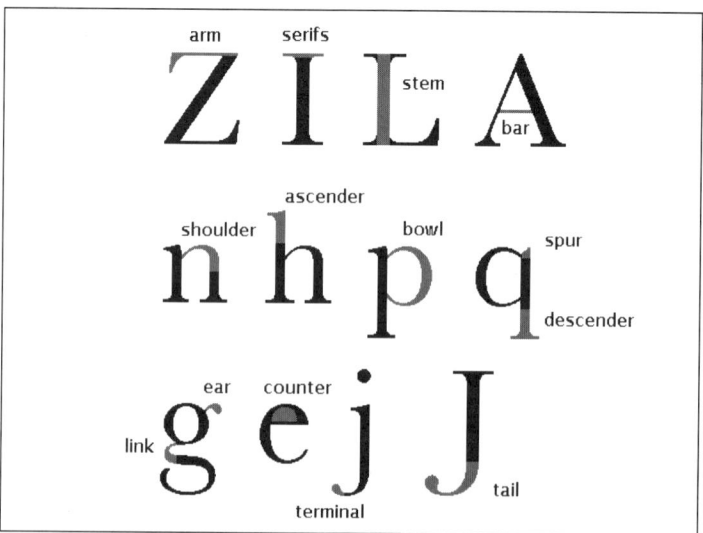

Figure 2.1 *Component parts of letters.*

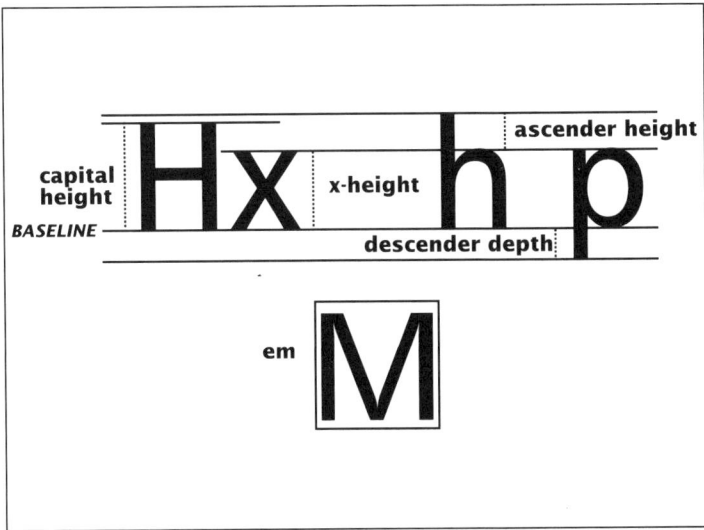

Figure 2.2 *Dimensions of type in a line.*

```
Courier 12-point is a popular
monospaced font for typewriters
```

You can read proportionally spaced type much more easily than monospaced type. Nonetheless, many people in the digital world use monospaced type to indicate programming code. They also use it to show precisely positioned text on the Web using the *<pre>* HTML markup (see Figure 2.3).

Fortunately, the Web now offers more layout controls than it did just a few years ago, and you do not have to resort to using preformatted text for precise text layout. See Chapter 10 on Cascading Style Sheets (CSS).

Proportional Spacing

Proportional spacing gives each character an amount of horizontal space appropriate to its width. Thus, an *m* takes more space than an *i*, because an *m* is wider. Publishers print books in proportional type. Today, word processors typeset (desktop

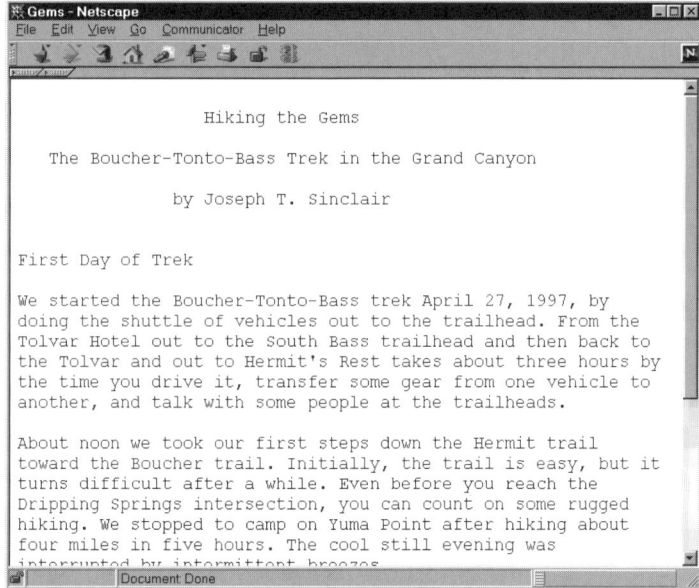

Typewriters Due to mechanical limitations, most typewriters such as the IBM Selectric use monospaced type. A few typewriters such as the IBM Executive use proportionally spaced type, but such typewriters are more expensive and more difficult to use. They have never become popular except in the upper echelons of the corporate world.

Figure 2.3 *Monospaced text (preformatted) on the Web, already passé.*

publish) documents in proportional type, even for correspondence. This book is typeset in proportionally spaced type. The default type in Web browsers is proportional type.

Serif Design

Serif design is simply a classification as to whether the letters include serifs. Most typefaces either do or do not include serifs. A few fall in between.

Serif

Serif type has tiny horizontal lines attached to it that form parts of the characters. The serifs enhance readability by assisting your eyes to keep on track more easily as you read. It works very subtly, but well. Publishers prefer serif type for its readability and hence use it for text. This book is typeset in a serif typeface.

Perpetua, the serif typeface of this book

Most Web browsers use serif type as the default. PCs use Times New Roman. Macs use Times. Users, however, can change the default.

Old Style

Old style serif designs come from the 15th and 16th centuries (e.g., Garamond, by Claude Garamond, 1480–1561, see Figure 2.4). They have a distinct difference between thick and thin strokes, having been modeled on script. They work well for long reading formats such as books. They also make elegant display typefaces in large type sizes.

Garamond, an old style typeface
Bembo, an old style typeface

Transitional

Transitional type designs come from the 17th and 18th centuries (e.g., Baskerville, by John Baskerville, 1706–1775, see Figure 2.5). Because traditional type designs are further away from the days of hand drawing than the old style designs, they have a more geometric or abstract look, with less differentiation between thick and thin strokes. The x-height (height of lowercase) for transitional designs is greater in relation to the capital height than it is for the old style designs.

Baskerville, a transitional typeface
Bulmer, a transitional typeface

Like the old style designs, transitional designs work well for extensive reading and look good as display type. They are also popular for signage and advertising. They look good together with well-matched sans serif designs. The term *transitional*

ftin demande aux Donatiftes en vne fem-
blable occurrence : *Quoy donc ? lors que*
nous lifons , oublions nous comment nous auons
accouftumé de parler? l'efcriture du grand Dieu
deuoit-elle vfer auec nous d'autre langage que
le noftre?
Puis que Iefus Chrift dit clairement

Figure 2.4 *Garamond's roman and italic types used in Richelieu's* Les
Principaux Poincts de la Foy Catholique Defendus: *Imprimerie*
Royale, Paris, 1642. From Printing Types Vol. I, *Daniel Berkeley Updike,*
Harvard University Press, 1927. (Hand scanning distorted original.)

indicates a period between the old style and the modern, but in
fact most typefaces widely used today also fall into the transitional category.

Moderns

Modern type designs come from the late 18th and the 19th
centuries (e.g., Bodoni, by Giambattista Bodoni, 1740–1813,

Double Pica Roman.
TANDEM aliquando, Quirites!
L. Catilinam furentem audacia,
fcelus anhelantem, peftem patriæ nefa-
rie molientem, vobis atque huic urbi fer-
rum flammamque minitantem, ex urbe
A B C D E F G H I J K L M N O P.

Figure 2.5 *Baskerville's Broadside Specimen, Birmingham, 1762. From*
Printing Types Vol. II, *Daniel Berkeley Updike, Harvard University Press,*
1927. (Hand scanning distorted original.)

see Figure 2.6). They tend to be refined and stylized, with a larger x-height, and more distinct differences between thick and thin strokes compared with the old style designs. In fact, some designs have hairline strokes and serifs.

Didot, a modern typeface
Bodoni, a modern typeface

These designs may prove too fancy for some applications, although contemporary interpretations of some modern designs have resulted in typefaces that work well in a wide variety of applications. Moderns are, perhaps, the least legible on the screen.

Slab Serifs

Slab serif type designs come from the 19th century. They have some similarities to moderns, coming from the same time

ottimamente fatte. Che però la grazia della scrittura forse più che in altro sta in certa disinvoltura di tratti franchi, risoluti, spediti, e nondimeno così nelle forme esatti, così degradati ne' pieni, *che non trova l'invidia ove gli emende.* Ma forse più sicuro è ristringerci a dire che han grazia le lettere, quando sembrano scritte

Figure 2.6 *Bodoni's Prefazione: Manuale Tipografico, Parma, 1818. From Printing Types Vol. II, Daniel Berkeley Updike, Harvard University Press, 1927. (Hand scanning distorted original.)*

period. But they are distinctive. With thick serifs, they offer high legibility for short lines of text. Some slab serifs even make good general text typefaces. They are, perhaps, the most readable on the screen.

Clarendon, a slab serif typeface

Contemporary

Contemporary is not a classification. In the 20th century, printing and typography have erupted into a whirlwind of innovation and creativity. Digital typography has accelerated that whirlwind. Attempting to classify what has been created in the 20th century is beyond the scope of this book, and there is no one typeface or typographer that defines the contemporary period. Moreover, it is interesting to note that whatever typographers do that's newly invented, they also never seem to tire of going back and resurrecting the old typefaces to modernize them. Consequently, such classifications as *old style, traditional,* and *modern* remain in use today.

If future typography historians find one category of type that defines the 20th century, that category will probably be sans serif.

Sans serif

Sans serif type first appeared early in the 19th century but became popular later. It is plainer but more difficult to read. This paragraph is typeset in Syntax, sans serif type. If you use sans serif type rather than serif type, you should have a specific reason for doing so that makes sense. For instance, you might typeset short documents that people don't read quickly, such as forms, in sans serif type. To add variety to documents, a sans serif typeface may be used for headings, but it should match well with the serif text typeface.

Geometric

Geometric sans serif type designs have a distinct abstract look, with little or no variation between thick and thin strokes. The individual letters look round, giving them an exaggerated circular appearance.

Futura, a geometric typeface
Eurostile, a geometric typeface

Grotesque

Grotesque sans serif type designs look less circular and more like traditional serif type than geometrics, but like geometrics they have an abstract look. Some grotesque designs have variation in the strokes.

Helvetica, a grotesque typeface
Univers, a grotesque typeface

Humanist

These designs, based on the old style designs but without the serifs, may have variations in their strokes. They are not as abstract as other sans serif designs.

Gill Sans, a humanist typeface

Hybrid

Hybrid is not a classification, but encompasses typefaces intended to combine designs. A few sans serif typeface designs have strokes that flare out at the ends, creating a subtle serif effect. Some typographers have created hybrid designs to enhance readability but at the same time retain the contemporary look of sans serif designs. In fact, you can read hybrid typefaces faster and more easily than sans serif typefaces—but not quite as fast as you can read serif typefaces. A good example of a hybrid is the humanist typeface Optima.

Optima, a humanist typeface

Display Typefaces

This designation simply indicates a type that catches attention. Use display typefaces for headlines, headings, titles, banners, advertising, posters, and other attention-getting uses. Any typeface can act as a display face in large sizes or in bold. In fact, old style, transitional, and modern type designs all work well as display type in large sizes or in bold. Many sans serif types also work well as display typefaces in large sizes and in bold, but because sans serif types contrast with serif text blocks, they work well as display typefaces even in small sizes.

Univers Extra Black, a display typeface

Generally, you can read display type in text blocks, although many have only marginal readability. The major difference between display type and decorative type is that you cannot read decorative type easily in text blocks.

Other Typeface Classifications

A few other classifications are worth mentioning, although their use is specialized. Use such type only in situations for which they are intended.

Scripts

Scripts simulate hand-drawn letters or handwriting. They are often very beautiful in small sizes as well as large. You will find their use limited, however, as they are difficult to read in text blocks and as display typefaces too, particularly on the screen. Use a script for formal printed correspondence such as invitations. You can also use one to simulate handwriting or as a decorative face.

Shelley, a script typeface

The lowercase letters usually link to each other to simulate handwriting. The uppercase letters also link with lowercase letters but not with other uppercase letters. Therefore, all caps for a script doesn't work very well and is difficult to read even in large sizes.

Swashes

Swashes are flourishes on all or a portion of the characters in a typeface. Swashes usually come in a separate font. Used sparingly, they bring elegance. Overused, they distract. Usually, you set the first letter of the first word in a paragraph or phrase with a swash. Placement after that is a matter of aesthetics.

Minion, with a swash for the M

Decorative Typefaces

Decorative type designs generally serve the same purpose as display type. They get attention. In contrast to display types, people have a lot of trouble reading decorative type in small sizes or in text blocks. That makes them single-purpose designs, and they often come in only one typestyle. Use them only for headlines, headings, titles, banners, advertising, posters, and the like, but not for text blocks. They also tend to be fashionable: popular today, forgotten tomorrow. Indeed, the creation of interesting and bizarre "designer" digital fonts has emerged as a growth industry in the last few years. Decorative typefaces can be exciting, innovative, and aesthetically appealing, but restrain yourself from using them in text blocks.

Madrone, a decorative typeface
Badger Fatboy, a decorative typeface

Blackletters

Blackletters became popular in the 12th century for a period, and they continue to exist today for limited uses. They have a Germanic or liturgical quality to them. Most people find blackletter type difficult to read either in text blocks or as a display face.

Linotext, a blackletter typeface

Special Symbols

Look at the character set window (which shows the extended character set) for each font to determine what you will get when you use the font. You will find some of the extended characters handy, and they can do a lot to dress up your typesetting.

- § © ® ± $^1/_4$ $^1/_2$ $^3/_4$ é ÷ ™ ¢

To get additional characters, use a special symbol or pi font such as Symbol or Wingdings. With both the regular character set and the extended character set for these fonts, you'll get a generous assortment of familiar and exotic graphic symbols and characters.

Gestalt

Typefaces carry with them a certain gestalt. They evoke certain feelings and perceptions that are often difficult to define and are sometimes interpreted by writers, designers, and type foundries with misleading or inane descriptions. The use of typefaces is an art and a matter of taste. Look at the following identical texts set in different typefaces. Do they convey the same gestalt?

Adobe Garamond

The Secretary of State anticipated the danger to the population in revising the policy. Many lives were at stake. The dire alternative had its risks too, risks that the coalition had assessed in great detail prior to the incident. The situation was not black and white. It was many shades of gray, and the Secretary moved skillfully and swiftly to ameliorate the setback. In Cairo he spoke to the British envoy only one day after the receiving the first draft.

ITC Benguiat

The Secretary of State anticipated the danger to the population in revising the policy. Many lives were at stake. The dire alternative had its risks too, risks that the coalition had assessed in great detail prior to the incident. The situation was not black and white. It was many shades of gray, and the Secretary moved skillfully and swiftly to ameliorate the setback. In Cairo he spoke to the British envoy only one day after the receiving the first draft.

In large sizes (e.g., 60 points and above), the characters for almost all high-quality typefaces and typestyles look like the beautifully crafted works of art that they are. Looking at large sizes makes it difficult to choose a typeface for a project because they all look so good! This increases the chances of

Windows Boredom The Windows operating system comes with Times New Roman, Courier, and Arial (a variation of Helvetica) typefaces. The Mac operating system provides the corresponding Times, Courier, and Helvetica. Virtually all of your Web site visitors will have these fonts installed in their software. Without TrueDoc or font embedding, your text will be displayed in these typefaces to most Web site visitors regardless of what you do. Boring! That's why TrueDoc and font embedding excite Web developers. These new technologies provide variety and lay a foundation for greatly expanded creativity.

making a poor choice. When choosing a typeface, look instead at type in the size that matches the requirements of your project. You will make a better decision.

In choosing a typeface for text, look at blocks of text typeset in the typefaces you want to consider. The text blocks will convey a feeling that the typical alphabet type samples do not capture. Even typefaces with similar names may convey different feelings. For instance, variations of Garamond include ITC Garamond, Sabon, Simoncini Garamond, Berthold Garamond, Stempel Garamond, and Adobe Garamond, each different in its gestalt from the others. Be sure to see the text-block samples of classic typefaces and not-so-classic typefaces in Chapter 21. They will enrich your appreciation of readability and give you a better understanding of how different typefaces feel. Try Esperfonto (http://www.will-harris.com) to assist you in choosing fonts by impression and to choose a serif and sans serif that have the same gestalt.

Combinations

Can you use both serifs and sans serifs, as well as multiple typefaces and typestyles? Yes, if you mix and match with care.

1. Choose a serif and sans serif that go well together. This is a matter of taste and aesthetic inclination. Two serifs or two sans serifs may clash.

2. Choose only one typeface for the general text (body) type. That will most often be a serif type.

3. Use a well-matched sans serif type for tables, captions, titles, headings, and the like. This can add variety and interest to documents, but setting tables, captions, titles, and headings in the primary typeface always works well too.

4. Don't mix serifs and sans serifs together in the same text block.

5. When you mix serifs, sans serifs, and their typestyles, be careful not to cause clutter by using too much variety. See Chapter 4 for specific quantitative guidelines on keeping your typesetting readable.

Summary

Defining some of the basic terminology is a simple and useful way to begin a book. In this case, digital technology—the desktop publishing revolution—has already changed the meanings of some of the traditional terms. But rely on the traditional terminology as much as possible for accuracy, and use ambiguous words like *font* carefully. The book has much more to say about readability, but first it makes sense to survey common typesetting practices in the next chapter.

Three

Typesetting Practices

This chapter covers the typesetting and layout basics that you will find helpful to make your text presentations look good. In addition, intermittent comments explain how the basics relate to making Web pages look good. The comments also serve as a preview to the remainder of the book. Most typesetting practices for print carry over to text presentations via an electronic device such as a computer monitor.

Using Characters

Using characters (letters and numbers) in ways that enhance readability, rather than impair it, makes sense. As you will see, however, these decisions do not rest completely in the hands of typesetters (desktop publishers). They also require attention from writers and editors.

Regular Type

Regular type is the workhorse of civilization. Use it generously. Nothing that can be typeset in regular type should be typeset any other way except for a specific purpose. In a serif typeface, regular might have the name *roman*, *book*, or *light*. You can read the following text block set in Adobe Garamond regular quickly, easily, and comfortably.

Regular type
The Tonto was surprisingly devoid of visible animal life. Lizards, of course, were abundant. An occasional soaring raptor was visible in the distance,

usually quite large. From more than one of the trickling creeks came a morose loonlike bird call. There were tadpoles in every pool, no matter how small. We saw one small Kingsnake. And there were a few bats at night. But small birds were absent most places, and we saw no mammals other than the bats.

Italics

Use italics for emphasis in print just as people use underlining on the typewriter, but use them sparingly. Emphasis should be a factor of good writing, not of heavy-handed typesetting. Where someone has used a lot of italics for emphasis, the writing is probably poor. Don't fall into the trap of using italics generously. The following block of text disobeys the rule and contains busy and gratuitous emphasis—but it shows you that italics still read more smoothly than text using other emphasis techniques.

Italics for emphasis

The Tonto was *surprisingly* devoid of *visible* animal life. Lizards, of course, were abundant. An occasional soaring raptor was visible in the distance, usually *quite* large. From more than one of the trickling creeks came a morose *loonlike* bird call. There were tadpoles in *every* pool, no matter how small. We saw one small Kingsnake. And there were a few bats at night. But small birds were *absent* most places, and we saw no *mammals* other than the bats.

Keep in mind the common uses of italics. You can find the rules for such usage in some dictionaries, *The Chicago Manual of Style*, and other reference publications. For example, book titles should be italicized. Look up these rules in your favorite reference book, and keep them handy. Note that there are different style guidelines for typewritten material than for printed material, because typewriters have inherent limitations. With computers, we must all adhere to print style guidelines.

Within text, you can always use italics as a substitute for bold. For blocks of text, italics sometimes do not work well. Italic type that is fancy and has a lot of flourishes may be difficult to read as text. Italic type that is not so fancy may read just as well as regular type. Nonetheless, italics are more difficult to read on a screen because the PC cannot render them with as much definition as regular type (see Chapter 18 for further information).

Italic type

The Tonto was surprisingly devoid of visible animal life. Lizards, of course, were abundant. An occasional soaring raptor was visible in the distance, usually quite large. From more than one of the trickling creeks came a morose loon-like bird call. There were tadpoles in every pool, no matter how small. We saw one small Kingsnake. And there were a few bats at night. But small birds were absent most places, and we saw no mammals other than the bats.

Bold

Bold type has its place, but that place is not for emphasis within text. Do not use bold in place of italics or as some kind of super italic for added emphasis. Bold gets in the way. It confuses and slows down readers when used incorrectly. It accomplishes just the opposite effect of what was intended.

Bold for emphasis

The Tonto was **surprisingly** devoid of visible animal life. Lizards, of course, were abundant. An occasional soaring raptor was visible in the distance, usually quite large. From more than one of the trickling creeks came a morose **loonlike** bird call. There were tadpoles in every pool, no matter how small. We saw one small Kingsnake. And there were a few bats at night. But small birds were absent most places, and we saw no **mammals** other than the bats.

Emphasis for HTML
HTML provides an emphasis markup <*em*> and a stronger emphasis <*strong*> markup which supposedly replace italics. Fortunately, HTML also supports italics with the <*i*> markup. Use the <*i*> markup, and ignore the <*em*> markup and the <*strong*> markup unless you find some special use for them.

Instead, use bold for titles, headlines, headings, subheadings, and the like. Use it for emphasizing entire sentences and paragraphs in forms, legal documents, and legally required warnings or disclaimers. Use it in manuals to warn of life-threatening or equipment-threatening situations. Because bold is used this way, it is often used with a larger type size than the text. You can also use bold in place of underlined words in column headings for charts and tabulations.

Trekking the Grand Canyon

Keep in mind that you do not have to use bold for headings and headlines. For instance, simply using a larger type size of regular type for headings and subheadings can often work just as effectively. Larger type naturally has more weight and differentiates itself from the text, thereby performing well as a heading.

Trekking the Grand Canyon

Bold Italic

Bold italic is never a substitute for italic. You can use it as a substitute for bold type, and that's its only use. Don't use bold italic within a bold headline or heading.

Trekking the Grand Canyon

Underlining

Underlining is used in place of italics for typewriters. Don't use underlining for typesetting. It distracts. The one possible exception is for headings in tabulations and charts. Even for these, however, bold headings can be used instead. The following text block provides disruptive reading. Would you like to read a long document like this?

Underlines for emphasis

The Tonto was <u>surprisingly</u> devoid of <u>visible</u> animal life. Lizards, of course, were abundant. An occasional soaring raptor was visible in the distance, usually <u>quite</u> large. From more than one of the trickling creeks came a morose <u>loonlike</u> bird call. There were tadpoles in <u>every</u> pool, no matter how small. We saw one small Kingsnake. And there were a few bats at night. But small birds were <u>absent</u> most places, and we saw no <u>mammals</u> other than the bats.

Hyperlinks on the Web

Keep in mind that, on the Web, an underlined word indicates a hyperlink. Using underlining for other purposes will surely cause confusion.

All Caps

All capitals is another faux pas of the typewriting world. People find all caps (all uppercase) difficult to read quickly, even in headlines. You don't need to use this archaic typewriting practice any longer for either emphasis or headings. But do use capitals, of course, where English grammar and usage require them. Capitalize the first letter of each word in a title, heading (optional), or subheading (optional), but not in a headline. You will find the following text blocks difficult to read quickly.

All caps

THE TONTO WAS SURPRISINGLY DEVOID OF VISIBLE ANIMAL LIFE. LIZARDS, OF COURSE, WERE ABUNDANT. AN OCCASIONAL SOARING RAPTOR WAS VISIBLE IN THE DISTANCE, USUALLY QUITE LARGE. FROM MORE THAN ONE OF THE TRICKLING CREEKS CAME A MOROSE LOONLIKE BIRD CALL. THERE WERE TADPOLES IN EVERY POOL, NO MATTER HOW SMALL. WE SAW ONE SMALL KINGSNAKE. AND THERE WERE A FEW BATS

AT NIGHT. BUT SMALL BIRDS WERE ABSENT MOST PLACES, AND WE SAW NO MAMMALS OTHER THAN THE BATS.

Small Caps in HTML

With HTML, you can reduce the size of the caps using the font markup: *<font size= -1>*. Although far from perfect, it may be acceptable. It's better to use TrueDoc or font embedding with a small caps font.

Caps for emphasis

The Tonto was SURPRISINGLY devoid of VISIBLE animal life. Lizards, of course, were abundant. An occasional soaring raptor was visible in the distance, usually QUITE large. From more than one of the trickling creeks came a morose LOONLIKE bird call. There were tadpoles in EVERY pool, no matter how small. We saw one small Kingsnake. And there were a few bats at night. But small birds were ABSENT most places, and we saw no MAMMALS other than the bats.

Small Caps

As you can see in the preceding example, capitals impair readability as they tower above the rest of the text. Nonetheless, usage calls for certain expressions to be capitalized. For instance, AFL-CIO stands for a labor union with a rather long name. You wouldn't want to repeat the name over and over again in a long document. Yet, the acronym itself tends to tower above the remainder of the text, causing a distraction. To solve this dilemma, use small caps for AFL-CIO, thus making it blend better into the line of text. In order to use small caps, however, you need a small caps font for the typeface/typestyle you use for the text. Simply reducing the point size of the capital letters does not work well.

Raised Caps and Drop Caps

Use large capital initials to start text at the beginning of formal writing such as book chapters. They break the monotony of the normal text and invite the reader in. Sometimes a drop cap initial appears bounded (inside a box) with a different background color or with a special background design.

Locate a raised cap like the one that begins this paragraph on the same line as the first line of text. The raised cap initial projects above the line. Never use a bounded initial as a raised cap.

Place a drop cap initial inside the corner of the text block, and flow the text around it. The top of the drop cap initial is flush with the top of the first line. The bottom of the drop cap initial rests on the same baseline as one of the lines of text. A drop cap initial usually takes three to four lines. Bounded initials make appropriate drop caps.

Because an initial is larger than normal text, the space below the line that the initial is on will be greater than the space for normal text. Browsers don't make an adjustment for this, and the extra space will look awkward. Therefore, make an adjustment with Cascading Style Sheets (see Chapter 10), or use GIF initials instead of making initials with fonts (see Figure 8.8 in Chapter 8 for a GIF initial example).

Super/Subscripts in HTML HTML enables superscripts and subscripts. Take advantage of this capability when you need it. It will give your Web documents a polished look.

Superscripts and Subscripts

This typesetting capability simply raises or lowers the characters a bit while still keeping them on the same line. Use a superscript as the exponent for a number (e.g., 10^7) or as a footnote mark. Use a subscript for math and chemical formula notation and the like. Create a fraction by the use of a superscript and a slant (e.g., $^{39}/_{53}$). As you have observed, superscript and subscript characters usually appear in a type size smaller than the text.

Numbers

Numbers come in two typestyles: old style (nonaligning) and modern (lining). The old style numbers blend well with lowercase letters and have a lot of personality. When you use them with capital letters, however, they don't fit well because some have descenders (extensions below the baseline). Lining numbers, which are full height and more abstract, fit well with capital letters and stay sharp when used in small sizes. Use

Ligatures on the Web
While ligatures remain important for print, with the low resolution of computer monitor displays, you don't need them as much for Web text. Still, you can use them via TrueDoc or font embedding if you have the requisite ligature font to accompany the typeface and typestyle that you use.

them for tabulations. Generally, typefaces (even old style typefaces) come with a set of lining numbers. If a typeface has old style numbers, they will usually come in a separate font.

Old style numbers: 1 2 3 4 5 6 7 8 9 0
Modern numbers: 1 2 3 4 5 6 7 8 9 0

Strikethrough

Words typeset with strikethrough characters simulate the editing process. Word processors and editing groupware use strikethroughs for editing. The relevance of strikethroughs to normal typesetting is specialized. Use strikethroughs only to simulate editing.

> The Tonto was surprisingly devoid of visible animal life. ~~Lizards, of course, were abundant.~~ An occasional soaring raptor was visible in the distance, usually quite large.

Ligatures

A ligature consists of two or more characters joined together. Why use ligatures? It makes certain combinations of letters look better in text under 15 points. For instance, the following combinations of letters are examples of common ligatures:

Characters:

ff fi fl ffi ffl

Ligatures:

ff fi fl ffi ffl

Display and Decorative Typefaces

Outline typefaces, display typefaces, decorative typefaces, shadowed type, and glowing type are appropriate for advertising, commercial art, and graphic design, although not for text documents except as titles or headings. Many so-called display or decorative typefaces include only one typestyle (i.e., one font).

Trekking the Grand Canyon

TREKKING THE GRAND CANYON

Always be aware of a typeface's gestalt. You don't want the display typeface to send the wrong message or convey the wrong feeling. For instance, the first of the following decorative typefaces seems better suited to a topic regarding the history of the Grand Canyon. The second display typeface is perhaps better suited to a contemporary account of a trek in the Grand Canyon.

Prospecting in the Grand Canyon

Trekking the Grand Canyon

Bullets

Remember the following ideas in regard to bulleted text:

- Bullets highlight the lines of text in an unnumbered list, just as numbers do in a numbered list.
- Bullets and numbers are a type of emphasis. Use them sparingly under the theory that if everything is emphasized, nothing is emphasized.
- Bulleted or numbered lines arc often indented.
- In instructional and technical books, use bulleted and numbered lists to organize information and to break up otherwise monotonous text.

Borders

You can make borders using border fonts. Some are very fancy. A border font has a vertical element, a horizontal element, corner elements, and other variations. Naturally, using fonts to make borders requires precise placement around a page or around a box of text. Borders can overwhelm text quite easily. Make sure that any borders you use add to the design of the page and do not cause clutter or otherwise impair readability. For instance, a recipe book with bordered pages might be very attractive, but a novel with bordered pages might seem a little claustrophobic. Unfortunately, border fonts do not work well for the Web except with fixed-width, fixed-height page elements for which no text wrapping is permitted.

Web Points Even though the point is not an accurate physical measurement in the digital world, it still makes a handy traditional measurement. Desktop publishers use and understand it. Use it for typesetting on the Web if you feel comfortable with it. However, an *em* is a better measurement for Web typesetting. See Chapter 10 for more information on using the em.

Measurement

A point is $1/72$ of an inch. You measure type size in points. Normal book type is 9 to 12 points high. Normal correspondence type is 11 or 12 points. Each typeface differs. In one typeface, 12-point type might look about the same size as 10-point type in another typeface. The point remains an important measurement in the world of type.

Type Sizes

Determining what type size to use requires good judgment and a sense of what purpose the document serves. Determine size in context with other factors. Are you using columns or the full width of the page? What typeface are you using? How long is the document? What is the purpose of the document?

Because you need to consider a number of factors, you will find it time consuming to reinvent the wheel on every occasion—that is, to repeatedly make decisions about type size. Predetermined standards for various kinds of Web documents can help you make these decisions much more quickly and easily. There are other reasons for Web document standards. A uniform look for all documents gives an impression of a well-organized Web site. You can incorporate type size into templates or style sheets. You can then use templates or style sheets to completely format and control the look of Web documents with speed and ease.

Keep in mind that readability should be a primary factor in every decision you make about text. For instance, newspapers facilitate very quick reading even though they have relatively small print, because newspapers print narrow columns. Books usually have 9- to 11-point type. Correspondence usually looks good at about 11 points. Typeset your superscripts and footnotes with about a 2-point difference from the text type. Note, however, that the foregoing observations are based on Times New Roman; every typeface is different (see Table 3.1). Look at magazines, newspapers, books, and other widely circulated printed documents to help you determine what you want to do. Alas, then you have to translate what you want to do into the Web, which is not always an easy task.

Your inclinations might be different, but a typical size chart (in points) for Times New Roman on the Web, as compared to print, follows:

Table 3.1 *Type Sizes for the Web (Based on Times New Roman)*

	Web	Print
General text documents	12	11
Very short correspondence	13	12
Book pages	12	10
Small print and footnotes	11	9
Report title	18	same
Headlines	16	same
Subheadings	14	same
Sub-subheadings	13	same

Note: Subtitle type size within two points of text type size should be bold or italic to help differentiate it from the text.

As you can observe, the sizes for the Web need to be a little larger. The type will appear a little large on 640 x 480 screens and a little small on 1024 x 768 screens. The book covers these considerations more in Chapter 5.

Remember that one typeface can seem large or small compared with another typeface of the same point size. However, within a typeface, no apparent size difference should show between the typestyles of the same point size. If it does, it's a poorly designed typeface.

Kerning

Even with proportional spacing some characters in combination with certain other characters do not look right. For instance, an A next to a V looks funny without kerning. Kerning will fit these two characters a little closer together than they would otherwise be placed: AV. Notice how they overlap. Thus, words look better, and people can read them faster and more easily. Fonts usually handle kerning automatically. Unless you know what you're doing, don't change the spacing between letters. You are more likely to impair readability than enhance it.

Expanding

Occasionally, you will want to add extra space between letters (uppercase) for a heading or title. Such a use can give your heading an attractive spread-out, attention-getting look. Expanding is otherwise a highly specialized technique used only to solve specific problems.

TREKKING

Hyphenation

The capability to easily hyphenate a word at the end of a line remains important for efficient typesetting. Hyphenation is

Typesetting on the Web

Typesetting in print is only the starting point for determining what to use on the Web. You must take into consideration a new range of factors on the Web.

• Web site visitors view the Web in resolutions of 640 x 480, 800 x 600, and 1024 x 768, all of which display the same type differently. Set-tops (e.g., WebTV) generally use a resolution of 544 x 420 and increase the size of the type after converting it to sans serif.

• Web site visitors use 14-, 15-, 17-, 19- and 21-inch computer monitors or 14- to 30-inch televisions.

• Web site visitors sit 20 to 35 inches or more away from their monitors, and 8 to 10 feet away from their televisions.

• Web site visitors can adjust the font settings in their browsers to their own preference to show type bigger or smaller than you have typeset it (unless you set it in an absolute size—see Chapter 10).

All these factors have an effect on how Web site visitors see your Web site. These considerations are covered in greater detail in Chapter 5.

crucial for justification (see the following Justification section). Moreover, hyphenation makes left justification (ragged right) look much better too. Do not hyphenate the last word of a paragraph, thus leaving only a portion of the word on the last line.

Extended Character Set

A character set is the collection of characters that make up a font. There are many different character sets (e.g., standard PostScript). Usually, you use the standard character set provided by your operating system such as the character set for Windows. Make use of some of the extra characters available in the extended character set window (see Figure 3.1). Yes, it's a little awkward to use them. But then, you probably won't use them often. Have some fun with them. Also note that many characters in a character set are not cross-platform (see Appendix 1 for comparisons).

Standard character sets have the upper- and lowercase letters, the numbers, and the punctuation marks you find on a typewriter. They also have a few things you find only on a PC keyboard, such as the back slash or back slant (\). But also keep in mind the hidden and mysterious extended character set. What you don't see is what you get. There are no single keys for the extended character set. You must use the extended character set window in your operating system or word processor, or you can use a special combination of keystrokes to generate a desired extended character.

Languages

Typography for languages other than English is beyond the scope of this book. Nonetheless, keep in mind that the standard extended character set contains additional characters necessary for certain foreign languages such as French and Spanish (see Figure 3.1). You can find these by using the extended character set window in Windows programs, and HTML also provides them.

Hyphenation Not Supported Hyphenation has little relevance to the Web now. Maybe someday soon it will. HTML wraps text in different places depending on the size of the display, the size of the Web browser window, and the resizing of the type by the browser, but it does not enable hyphenation.

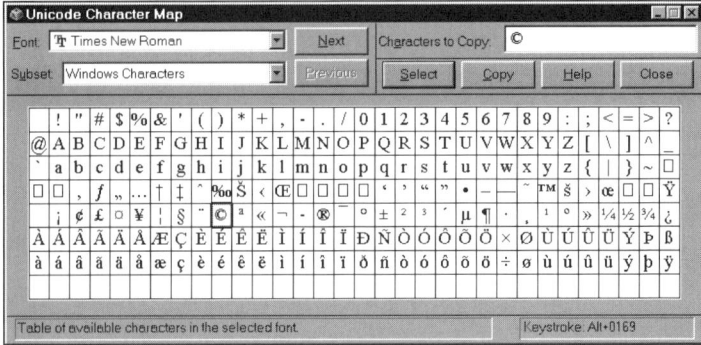

Figure 3.1 *Windows NT extended character window.*

Sometimes you use foreign characters in English. For instance, my Spanish name José requires an accent é. But don't use the accent é for San Jose, home of Silicon Valley. Do use the accent é for San José, Costa Rica. With the use of foreign characters now made more convenient by digital typography, expect the correct typesetting of foreign words used in English to become customary over the next decade in business documents as well as online publishing.

Layout

The way that you arrange text on the page determines the layout. Layout is an important factor in readability and an important aspect of typography. For large blocks of text, a book like *Book Design & Production for the Small Publisher*, by Malcolm E. Barker (San Francisco: Londonborn Publications, 1990) is a useful guide for designing layout.

Grids

Traditionally, typographers have used grids for layout (see Figure 3.2). A grid makes the placement of text blocks and graphics easy to organize. A grid also enables standard page templates with preset margins and other preset spacing. For Web publishing, grids make sense too. For normal HTML, you

Figure 3.2 *Simple layout grid.*

can use tables for grids (see Figure 3.3). For CSS and Java text authoring programs, you can use grids to assist your precise placement of page elements.

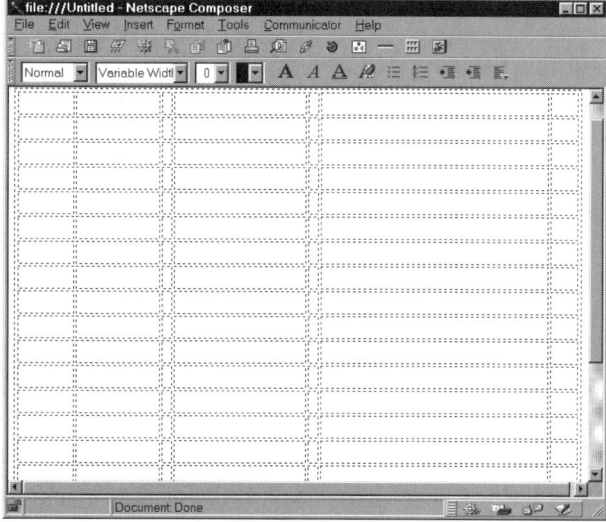

Figure 3.3 *HTML table used as a grid.*

Text

Add a touch of elegance to your typesetting. Digital technology enables a full range of typesetting techniques. Use them. For instance, you can typeset a long quotation in a slightly smaller type size in its own indented paragraph. It will look like a book, and you can do it quite easily with word processors and desktop publishers. With the *<blockquote>* markup, HTML enables indentation too. The *<blockquote>* markup will indent the paragraph on the left and right sides.

Justification

You normally align only to the left for most documents (flush left, left justified, ragged right). That means that all the text aligns in a nice vertical line on the left and ends up ragged on the right. Flush right (right justified, ragged left) is the opposite. You normally use flush right only in special situations such as for artistic effect or for creating columns of numbers in charts and tabulations. Flush left reads considerably easier than flush right.

Flush left (ragged right)

Tourist access to the Grand Canyon on the South Rim goes west from Desert View to Hermits Rest with the historic Tolvar Hotel a few miles east of Hermits Rest. From the trailhead at Hermits Rest you hike into the canyon in a generally northwesterly direction to eventually get to Boucher creek. Continuing in a northwesterly direction along the Tonto bench about 800 feet above the Colorado River you cross a number of rugged and isolated canyons. The "Gems" going from southeast to northwest are Topaz (Boucher Creek), Slate, Agate, Sapphire, Turquoise, Jasper, Jade, Ruby, Quartz, and Emerald followed by Serpentine and Bass. The topo map does not name Jasper, Jade, Quartz, or Emerald. In fact, the topo map names another canyon *on the other side of the river*, Emerald.

Flush right (ragged left)

Tourist access to the Grand Canyon on the South
Rim goes west from Desert View to Hermits Rest
with the historic Tolvar Hotel a few miles east of
Hermits Rest. From the trailhead at Hermits Rest you
hike into the canyon in a generally northwesterly
direction to eventually get to Boucher creek.
Continuing in a northwesterly direction along the
Tonto bench about 800 feet above the Colorado River
you cross a number of rugged and isolated canyons.
The "Gems" going from southeast to northwest are
Topaz (Boucher Creek), Slate, Agate, Sapphire,
Turquoise, Jasper, Jade, Ruby, Quartz, and Emerald
followed by Serpentine and Bass. The topo map does
not name Jasper, Jade, Quartz, or Emerald. In fact,
the topo map names another canyon *on the other side
of the river*, Emerald.

You can use justification, both left and right, for a neat and
symmetrical appearance (justified text). Be careful, though,
when using this technique. If the width of the text column is
too narrow, unseemly gaps may appear on many lines.
Newspapers, magazines, and newsletters use justified text a
great deal. Currently, HTML by itself does not support justified text, but you can now use CSS to justify text for potentially easier reading.

Justified

Tourist access to the Grand Canyon on the South Rim
goes west from Desert View to Hermits Rest with the
historic Tolvar Hotel a few miles east of Hermits Rest.
From the trailhead at Hermits Rest you hike into the
canyon in a generally northwesterly direction to eventually get to Boucher Creek. Continuing in a northwesterly direction along the Tonto bench about 800
feet above the Colorado River, you cross a number of
rugged and isolated canyons. The "Gems" going from
southeast to northwest are Topaz (Boucher Creek),
Slate, Agate, Sapphire, Turquoise, Jasper, Jade, Ruby,

Quartz, and Emerald followed by Serpentine and Bass. The topo map does not name Jasper, Jade, Quartz, or Emerald. In fact, the topo map names another canyon *on the other side of the river*, Emerald.

Columns on the Web

Unlike print, on a Web page you do not have to do layout with multiple columns. You can create one column as a continuous scroll using a simple layout. Take care to use wide enough columns and large enough type so that Web site visitors can read easily. Place large blocks of text on the Web in columns rather than have them occupy the full width of the Web page. Remember that people with high-resolution monitors will have extremely long lines of text to read if you do not place your text in a column.

You can create multiple (side by side) columns with HTML, but don't make them longer than about a half-screen. Otherwise, a Web site visitor will have to scroll up and down to read them.

Note that the party line for typographers for a number of years has been that flush left is more readable than justified. That now seems dubious (see Chapter 16). Nonetheless, you want to make sure that your columns are not so narrow that large gaps appear between words as a result of the justification process. Such gaps impair readability.

Because HTML and CSS cannot do automatic hyphenation, you may find that justified text will never be spaced properly, even for wide columns. Without tight word spacing, even wide columns will be more difficult to read with justification than with flush left. Therefore, the use of justification may not be appropriate for the Web. And because browsers window sizes vary greatly, automatic hyphenation may not be a feature of Web typography for a while.

Columns

The capability to create columns can be very useful. Lines longer than 60 characters are difficult to read. Up to a point, people can read narrower columns more quickly. That's why magazines and newspapers use columns extensively. The narrower the column, the smaller the appropriate type size. With columns and smaller type you can get more on a printed page and still maintain readability.

Boxed Text

Reserve the use of boxed text for text blocks that you want to set apart from the regular text. Some people call these sidebars. They can be as short as one sentence or one paragraph, or as long as several pages. They can be vertical rectangles or horizontal rectangles. Usually, the shorter they are, the more effectively they draw attention. A three-page sidebar loses some of its separateness by being so long. If it's that long, why not integrate it into the text? You can also use boxes for tables and illustrations.

Headlines and Headings

Set headlines in bold. Write headlines as sentences with a verb but without a period. Capitalize headlines as you would capitalize normal text; that is, do not use all caps, and do not capitalize the first letter of each word.

Trekkers find Tonto devoid of life

Set titles and headings the same as headlines, with or without the verb. In the alternative, capitalize the first letter of each word except for prepositions and articles. For titles and headings, you do not necessarily have to use bold type, but use a significantly larger type than the text if you do not use bold. Indeed, titles and headings in regular type often look very elegant. Bear in mind that often headings have a hierarchy. Always set the higher-level headings in larger type.

Title: **Trekking the Grand Canyon**

Heading: **Four Days on the Tonto**

Subheading: **Animal Life on the Tonto**

Titles and headings do not necessarily have to be in serif typefaces. Sans serif typefaces for titles and headings go well with serif text, too.

Title: **Trekking the Grand Canyon**

HTML Substitutes HTML offers a variety of boxed text treatments, such as separate hyperlinked Web pages, Java applets with floating frames, and the border formatting offered by CSS, all of which are covered in later chapters.

Heading: **Four Days on the Tonto**

Subheading: **Animal Life on the Tonto**

One problem with headlines and headings occurs when they pour over onto a second line. Make a break where it makes sense and looks good. Do not leave this task to digital automation.

Hiking the Grand Canyon's Tonto Trail in Mid-Spring

Hiking the Grand Canyon's Tonto Trail in Mid-Spring

The second of the preceding examples looks better than the first but still needs a little work. Headings require care. The placement of headings is an art and an important part of the page layout design (see the *
* tag in Chapter 7).

You can have great fun using GIFs made from text characters for headings (see Figure 3.4) But if you need a lot of headings, it amounts to a lot of work. Do you really need heading GIFs? With TrueDoc and font embedding, you can use any typeface in any size and color that you desire. Who needs GIFs? When everyone uses the 4.0 browsers, you won't need GIFs any longer.

Space

Space is as important as type. Your arrangement of space and type constitutes your layout. For instance, traditionally you set a margin of at least one inch on the left and right, and top and bottom, of each page of a business document. You handle other documents differently, and the margins might be greater or smaller depending on the use. Plenty of options exist; layout is

Hiking the Gems

Figure 3.4 *Heading GIF.*

a creative endeavor. Remember, however, you can easily darken the page with type using the capability of digital type-setting (see Figure 3.5), but readability and attractiveness require space (see Figure 3.6).

Space can also present problems. For instance, once typeset, a text block might show rivers: spaces that run from line to line between words appearing to be a river of space running through the text block. Justified text in particular tends to show rivers. Rivers can distract readers, and you need to eliminate them. But because Web browsers create line breaks unpre-dictably, you cannot anticipate or control rivers in Web pages.

Always include margins for text. Text flush up against the left side of the screen, or the right side, is not as easy to read as text with margins on the left and right.

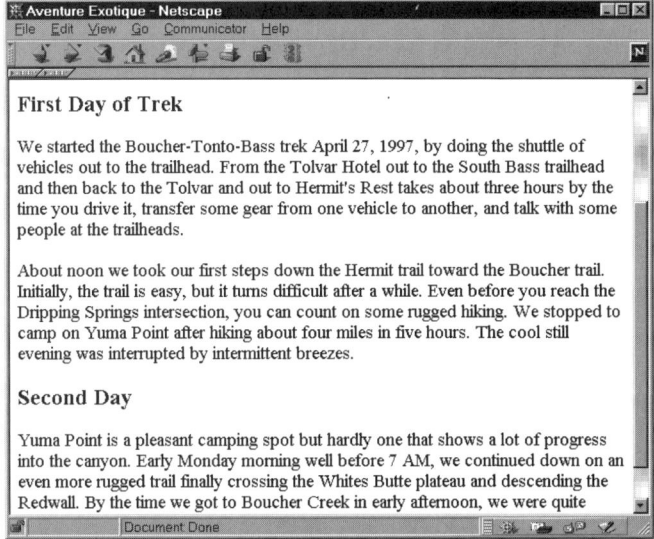

Figure 3.5 *Web page loaded with text.*

Give Your Web site Visitors a Break Space is particularly important to type-setting for the Web because the continuous scroll feature of Web pages can create an endless car-pet of text. Without the page breaks inherent in printed text, you need to create some relief for your Web site visitors. You can do this with headings, inline graphics, and other Web multi-media objects, many of which naturally create space and break up the text flow.

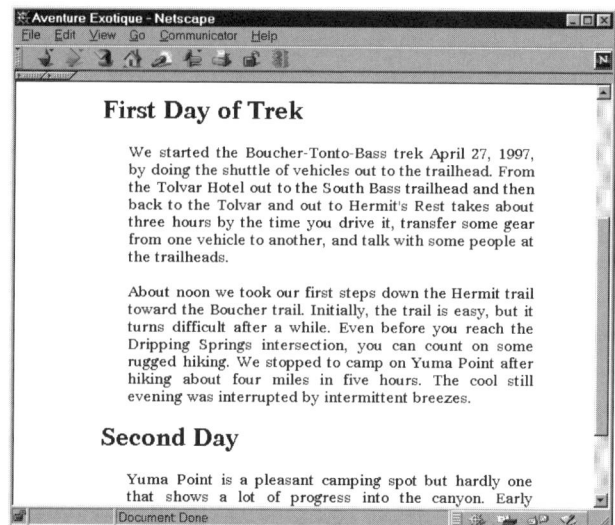

Figure 3.6 *Web page with plenty of space in the layout.*

Leading (Line Spacing)

The vertical space is the distance from the baseline of one line of text to the baseline of the next line of text. Leading is the vertical distance of space between each line of text. Thus, if a 10-point font has an 11-point vertical space, there is 1 point of leading. Traditionally, the process of setting the line spacing was called leading, because printers changed the line spacing by inserting lead strips between the lines of type. Generally, up to about 12-point type, the leading should be at least 1 point. Thus, for 8-point type, the line height should be set at 9 points. For 12-point type and above, the line height should be set 1.5 points larger than the type size (1.5-point leading). Thus, for 14-point type, the line height should be set at 15.5 points. As you progress even higher in type size, you should add additional increments of leading except for headings and headlines which may require special treatment. On the other hand, some typographers recommend as much as 20 percent leading. That would suggest 2 points of leading for 10-point type; that is, a 12-point line height.

Normal leading

The Tonto was surprisingly devoid of visible animal life. Lizards, of course, were abundant. An occasional soaring raptor was visible in the distance, usually quite large. From more than one of the trickling creeks came a morose loonlike bird call. There were tadpoles in every pool, no matter how small. We saw one small Kingsnake. And there were a few bats at night. But small birds were absent most places, and we saw no mammals other than the bats.

Negative leading (negative two points)

The Tonto was surprisingly devoid of visible animal life. Lizards, of course, were abundant. An occasional soaring raptor was visible in the distance, usually quite large. From more than one of the trickling creeks came a morose loonlike bird call. There were tadpoles in every pool, no matter how small. We saw one small Kingsnake. And there were a few bats at night. But small birds were absent most places, and we saw no mammals other than the bats.

Four-point leading

The Tonto was surprisingly devoid of visible animal life. Lizards, of course, were abundant. An occasional soaring raptor was visible in the distance, usually quite large. From more than one of the trickling creeks came a morose loonlike bird call. There were tadpoles in every pool, no matter how small. We saw one small Kingsnake. And there were a few bats at night. But small birds were absent most places, and we saw no mammals other than the bats.

Most software automatically adjusts the leading for page composition. Automatic leading features don't always work properly, however, and you will have to check the leading when it doesn't seem right. Different typefaces require different leading, and the leading recommended in this section is only a general guideline. Too little leading makes text difficult to read. Too much leading makes the eye jump around the page.

You can add a substantial amount of leading, say 80 percent, to text to give it an elegant look for a promotional piece. This works well and is readable for short blocks of text such as are found in brochures. For normal reading of long passages of text, however, excess leading doesn't work well.

Realistically, some fonts require more leading than others. A typeface with a small x-height (lowercase character height), such as an old style, requires less leading than a typeface with a large x-height. The smaller x-height creates the illusion of more space between the lines. In contrast, a typeface with a large x-height, such as a modern, creates the illusion of less space between the lines and requires more leading. Sans serif typefaces require more leading than serif typefaces. Some typographers suggest as much as double the leading for sans serif as for serif (i.e., as much as 40 percent leading).

Double Line Spacing

Double line spacing is more difficult to read. There is seldom any reason for using it. Proofreading remains the exception where an editor uses the space between the printed lines for adding proof marks. Yet, extra space between the lines—somewhere short of double spacing—can give a more elegant look to certain kinds of short documents as mentioned in the preceding section, but such documents are more difficult to read.

Horizontal Rules

Don't use horizontal rules except where appropriate. Even though they're popular on the Web, use them only for situations where you want to signal a significant change in the subject matter of the text. Don't use them to create space. Even if a rule is appropriate, consider using a printer's mark or ornament instead. Such ornaments are usually more elegant. Keep in mind also that you may find it appropriate to switch to another Web page via a hyperlink rather than use an ornament to signal a change in the subject matter of the text.

HTML Leading To increase the leading in a Web documents, you add spacer GIFs (see Chapter 8). If needed, this technique can give your Web pages a more polished look. Web browsers, however, provide automatic leading which is adequate for most situations. CSS also provides leading controls.

Widows and Orphans

A widow is a single line at the top of the page which is the last line of a carry-over paragraph. If a widow is a full line, it's OK. If it's a partial line, reformat to add a preceding line (a full line) at the top of the page. An orphan is a single line of a new paragraph at the bottom of the page. If an orphan is a full line, leave it be. If it is shorter than a full line, reformat to get it on the next page. On the Web, continuous scrolling eliminates widows and orphans. Nonetheless, widows and orphans can present a problem when attempting to create fixed-length Web page segments that act like printed pages.

Paragraphs

Laying out paragraphs entails making design decisions. You can indent the first word of a paragraph and forgo using a blank line between paragraphs. You can use a blank line between paragraphs and make the first word of the paragraph flush left. Paragraphs break up the text into logical information blocks. The point is to make the readers aware of the blocks without interrupting the flow of their reading.

Indented paragraphs

We started the Boucher-Tonto-Bass trek by doing the shuttle of vehicles out to the trailhead. From the Tolvar Hotel out to the South Bass trailhead and then back to the Tolvar and out to Hermit's Rest takes about 3 hours by the time you drive it, transfer some gear from one vehicle to another, and talk with some people at the trailheads. Then we started hiking.

About noon we took our first steps down the Hermit trail toward the Boucher trail. Initially, the trail is easy, but it turns difficult after a while. Even before you reach the Dripping Springs intersection, you can count on some rugged hiking. We stopped to camp on Yuma Point after hiking about 4 miles in 5 hours. The cool still evening was interrupted by intermittent breezes.

Paragraphs with line spacing

We started the Boucher-Tonto-Bass trek by doing the shuttle of vehicles out to the trailhead. From the Tolvar Hotel out to the South Bass trailhead and then back to the Tolvar and out to Hermit's Rest takes about 3 hours by the time you drive it, transfer some gear from one vehicle to another, and talk with some people at the trailheads. Then we started hiking.

About noon we took our first steps down the Hermit trail toward the Boucher trail. Initially, the trail is easy, but it turns difficult after a while. Even before you reach the Dripping Springs intersection, you can count on some rugged hiking. We stopped to camp on Yuma Point after hiking about 4 miles in 5 hours. The cool still evening was interrupted by intermittent breezes.

Within paragraphs, don't use more than one space after a period at the end of a sentence. The space around the period combined with the space between sentences provides enough space for the requisite break. The old typewriter practice of using two spaces after a period is not appropriate. Regardless, a browser will not recognize more than one space anyway.

Running Heads and Foots

Make running heads (headers) and foots (footers) transparent, in effect, or they will interfere with reading. Better they be light than heavy. Headers and footers can be an art form; that is, they can carry a logo, a name, or even a message. If you make them promotional, take care in their preparation so as to make them unobtrusive. HTML frames without the borders showing (see Figure 3.7) provide a mechanism for creating a running head or foot, in effect. Use the *<frame>* and *<frameset>* markups (see Chapter 7).

Footnotes

When printed on the same page as text, footnotes look attractive with type about two points smaller than the text type size.

When printed on a separate page at the end of the document, smaller print is traditional but not necessary. In fact, readers will read normal size text more easily.

Reverse Type

Reverse type (white type on a black background) is very difficult to read in print in most situations. Color type on a color background doesn't work well in print either, because readability suffers. Black on white is best (see Chapter 18). On a cathode ray tube (CRT) monitor, however, this may not hold as true. Color type can be viable for readability. Many contrasting combinations of light type on dark backgrounds are readable. Light colors on a black background seem to be popular for Net TV (see Chapter 17).

Graphics

Graphics affect layout. Text must flow around them or otherwise make space for them. You should caption graphics, and position them so as to give the page a balanced and appealing look (see Figure 3.8). Treat tables, sidebars, Java applets, and other Web objects analogously to graphics.

Automation

Templates can enable many of the typesetting techniques covered without much effort on your part. The idea of being able to automatically format documents according to predetermined standards can make your typesetting more efficient. With a template, you can determine the type characteristics and other formatting attributes of a set of documents. Then, just fill in the content.

For the Web, you can use precoded Web page templates that require you to add content and little more. You can also use Cascading Style Sheets. Soon you will be able to use Extensible Markup Language (XML) and Extensible Style Language (XSL) style sheets to create Web page templates.

Paragraphs on the Web

David Siegel, an accomplished typographer, in his book *Creating Killer Web Sites*, Hayden, Indianapolis, 1996, advocates using indents and forgoing line spacing between paragraphs. Is he right? This works well for many printed documents and is widely used in books, but the technique may have less value for long documents on the Web. The lower resolution of the Web and the seemingly endless scroll of a long Web page argues in favor of using a blank line between paragraphs. Unfortunately, using a full blank line between paragraphs does not look as good in print or on the Web as using a half-line of space. Therefore, use CSS (to control line height) or a spacer GIF about 6 points (0.5 em) in height to create a half-line space.

Footnotes on the Web

On the Web, you can use a hyperlink to pop up a footnote. Make a standard template for footnotes so that the reader recognizes them as such. Of course, one of the great benefits of the Web is that you can often use a variety of original reference resources in place of footnotes. When such references are available someplace on the Web in their own format, it doesn't make sense to attempt to make them look like footnotes.

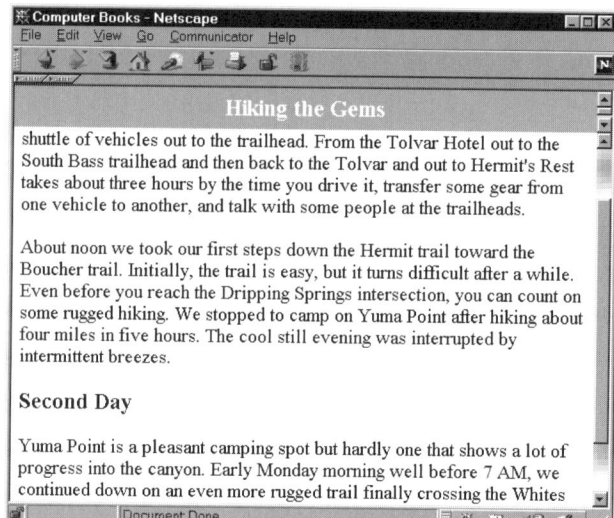

Figure 3.7 *Web page with a running head (done with frames). The running head has a different color background for purposes of illustration, but it will normally have the same color background as the text.*

Creativity

This chapter focuses on typesetting and layout for text. It does not purport to cover the use of typography for aesthetic, promotional, or decorative uses. Nothing in this chapter rules out the imaginative use of text for creating dazzling Web pages. Many other books provide the design guidelines for doing so. Now, with the advent of TrueDoc and font embedding, you can substitute typesetting for heading graphics (heading GIFs) and potentially reduce the size of your Web pages (i.e., fewer graphics to download) while saving time and energy as well.

When you're ready to provide a lot of content in the form of text, however, stick to the basic guidelines in this chapter. Remember, readability is the goal.

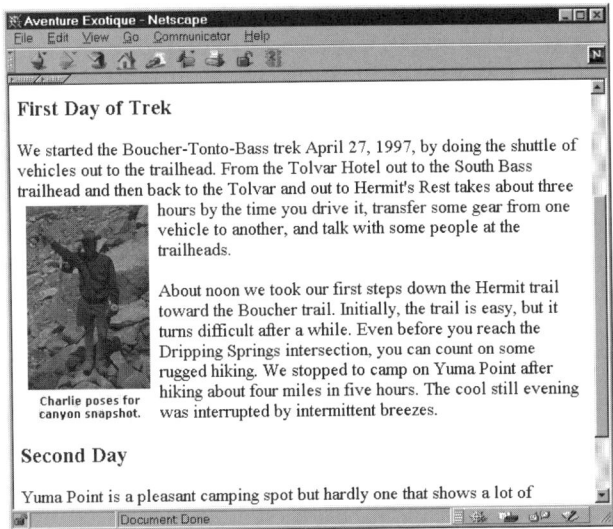

Figure 3.8 *Web page with a graphic.*

Inline Graphics Inline graphics in Web pages affect the layout directly, and HTML provides a number of possible formats for using graphics in your layout (e.g., left flush, centered, right flush). Be sure to create a space around your graphics so that text doesn't butt up against a graphic and become difficult to read. Keep in mind too that other multimedia objects, such as Java applets, often take up space on Web pages, and you need to treat them like graphics in relation to the text.

Summary

This chapter serves as an introduction to the typesetting portion of the art of typography. Most typesetting practices carry over directly to digital presentations of text. Starting with Chapter 7, the remainder of the book shows you how to incorporate these typesetting practices into your Web pages, with the result of more effective communication and a more polished look. Bitstream's TrueDoc (Netscape 4.0 browser, Chapter 12) and Microsoft's font embedding technology (Microsoft 4.0 browser, Chapter 14), together with CSS (4.0 browsers, Chapter 10), bring exciting new capability that enables you for the first time to realize the incorporation of professional typesetting practices at your Web site. The next chapter provides a short and simple means of measuring your typesetting for the purpose of creating simple, but forceful and elegant text documents.

The Rating System

You will find it easy to clutter Web pages with a mishmash of different type-faces, typestyles, and type sizes. Such clutter reduces readability, conveys a sense of disorganization, and generally makes a bad impression. To instill some discipline into my work and to establish some easy-to-use and easy-to-remember guidelines, I have made up a rating system which I have found handy from time to time. Even if you're not a novice, you may find it useful on occasion.

Rating

Use a simple five-step process to rate your text:

1. Use the rating system as expressed in a simple table (see Table 4.1). Use this table as a guideline for your typesetting.

Table 4.1 *Rating System for Type Elements*

Type	Rating
Normal text—regular	None
Normal text—italic	50
Different size	50
Different typestyle	75
Different typeface	100

(continued)

61

Table 4.1 *Rating System for Type Elements (continued)*

Type	Rating
Underlining (except for column heads)	300
All caps for emphasis	300
Bold (except for headings)	300
Monospaced type (except for code)	300
Script (except for special uses)	300
Page limit	300

2. Start with one size of one typestyle of one typeface as a base, but do not assign it a rating. This will usually be the normal text.

3. Give any additional typeface, typestyle, or type size you use that differs from the beginning base the highest rating for which it qualifies. But apply no more than one assignment of rating. For example, suppose your base font is 12-point Times New Roman regular. Give a 75 rating for the addition to the page of 18-point Times New Roman bold for being a different typestyle, but no rating for being a different type size.

4. Check to see that you don't give a Web page a rating more than twice for the same typestyle used in different sizes. For example, give 50 for one different size of regular type (e.g., 10-point Times New Roman regular), 100 for two different sizes of type (e.g., 10-point and 14-point Times New Roman regular), but no more than 100 for three or more different sizes of regular type (e.g., 10-point, 14-point, 16-point, and 20-point).

5. Allow each Web page no more than a rating of 300.

Note that the rating system is for the *addition of different type*, not for the addition of text. Thus, for the preceding example, the addition of one word in 12-point Times New Roman italic warrants a rating of 75. However, as additional words are set in 12-point Times Roman italic throughout the text, no additional rating is applied.

Sample Document

Apply the rating system to the following sample document:

The Beginning

We started the Boucher-Tonto-Bass trek by doing the *shuttle of vehicles* out to the trailhead. From the Tolvar Hotel out to the South Bass trailhead and then back to the Tolvar and out to Hermit's Rest takes about 3 hours by the time you drive it, transfer some gear from one vehicle to another, and talk with some people at the trailheads. Then we started hiking.

First Steps

About noon we took our first steps down the Hermit trail toward the Boucher Trail. Initially, the trail is easy, but it turns difficult after a while. Even before you reach the Dripping Springs intersection, you can count on some rugged hiking. We stopped to camp on Yuma Point after hiking about 4 miles in 5 hours. The cool still evening was interrupted by intermittent breezes.

For basic formatting, the document uses an italic, a bold heading in a different typeface larger than the text, and a bold subheading in the same typeface as the text but larger than the text. The assigned rating is in Table 4.2. (Note that normally you don't mix serif and sans serif headings. The example uses them for the purposes of clearly illustrating the rating system.)

Table 4.2 *Rating for the Sample Document*

Type	Rating	Reason
Serif text—regular	None	
Serif text—italic	50	Used for emphasis
Headings: sans serif bold	100	Different typeface

(continued)

Special Text When you provide lines or blocks of programming code for a computer book, you don't expect readers to read through it at normal speeds. You expect them to consider the code carefully. Setting it in a different typeface (e.g., monospaced) and running up the rating over 300, therefore, does not necessarily defeat the expected degree of readability for the chapter.

There are parallels to this example in other kinds of writing. For instance, you might want to typeset occasional short correspondence that supposedly has been republished from the handwritten original, in a readable script typeface when it appears in a chapter of a book. Although the script disrupts readability, it adds an authentic flavor to those passages and encourages readers to slow down and consider them carefully. Therefore, to run up the rating over 300 by using a readable script typeface does not necessarily impair the readability expected for the particular design of that chapter. Nonetheless, if all chapters of the book were loaded with such correspondence, it would make tedious reading.

Table 4.2 *Rating for the Sample Document (continued)*

Type	Rating	Reason
Different size from text	None	No rating assigned*
Subheadings: serif bold	75	Different typestyle
Different size from text	None	No rating assigned*
Total	225	

*No rating assigned for size because higher rating assigned for being a different typeface or typestyle.

Well! It looks like things are under control. But what about abnormal pages such as a chapter that opens with a title?

Abnormal Page

An example of an abnormal page for the sample document is the first page of the chapter with the chapter title.

Chapter 6
Hiking the Gems

Tourist access to the Grand Canyon on the South Rim goes west from Desert View to Hermit's Rest with the historic Tolvar Hotel a few miles east of Hermit's Rest. From the trailhead at Hermit's Rest you hike into the canyon in a generally northwesterly direction to eventually get to Boucher Creek. Continuing in a northwesterly direction along the Tonto bench about 800 feet above the Colorado River, you cross a number of rugged and isolated canyons. The "Gems" going from southeast to northwest are Topaz (Boucher Creek), Slate, Agate, Sapphire, Turquoise, Jasper, Jade, Ruby, Quartz, and Emerald followed by Serpentine and Bass. The topo map does not name Jasper, Jade, Quartz, or Emerald. In fact, the topo map names another canyon on the other side of the river, Emerald.

The Beginning

We started the Boucher-Tonto-Bass trek by doing the *shuttle of vehicles* out to the trailhead. From the Tolvar Hotel out to the South Bass trailhead and then back to the Tolvar and out to Hermit's Rest takes about 3 hours by the time you drive it, transfer some gear from one vehicle to another, and talk with some people at the trailheads. Then we started hiking.

First Steps

About noon we took our first steps down the Hermit trail toward the Boucher trail. Initially, the trail is easy, but it turns difficult after a while. Even before you reach the Dripping Springs intersection, you can count on some rugged hiking. We stopped to camp on Yuma Point after hiking about 4 miles in 5 hours. The cool, still evening was interrupted by intermittent breezes.

This requires an additional rating to adjust for the added type elements (see Table 4.3).

Table 4.3 *Additional Rating for Added Type Elements*

Type	Rating	Reason
Basic page format	225	From Table 4.2
Chapter number: serif bold	None	Rating assigned previously
Different size of bold	50	
Chapter title: sans serif bold	None	Rating assigned previously
Different size of bold	50	
New Total	325	

What about Special Sections? You can typeset special text sections—such as sidebars that disrupt the flow of the text and call aside the reader's attention to special information—in a different typeface. As long as the special sections occur only occasionally, don't worry about running up your rating over 300. If they occur frequently, however, you should revise the sidebar formatting to keep almost all of your pages under 300.

If you take everything into consideration, it looks a little busy. The only thing that saves the document is the fact that all of these different type characters are unlikely to appear in the same page (screen) often; that is, the chapter number and the chapter title appear only at the beginning of a chapter. For an entire Web page (or an entire chapter), you can make a good argument for not including the chapter number and the chapter title in the rating, because they don't occur frequently. This approach probably makes sense in many cases, but use care when you bend the rules.

Most of the time, you are concerned with much shorter documents than a book. If your standard print formatting makes it likely that you will regularly exceed a 300 rating on a page (screen), you should revise the standard formatting to keep almost all of your screens under 300.

What about special typesetting for the text? You normally typeset a long quotation in a separate indented paragraph in a smaller size type. You typeset footnotes in a smaller size type. And you sometimes typeset special sections of text differently than the normal text (e.g., a table typeset in smaller size and in a different typeface than the text). These all have the potential for causing clutter. If you use these sparingly, don't worry about it. Simply be as careful as you can. If, however, you use these special sections extensively in your documents, you should make your typesetting scheme as simple as possible. For instance, make your headings the same typeface and typestyle as the text (but larger size).

The Web

How does the information in this chapter apply to Web pages? First, you can think of a Web page (HTML document) as a printed chapter or report. Second, you can think of a Web page screen (that portion of a Web page appearing on the monitor) as a printed page in a chapter or report. With this comparison in mind, you can apply the rating system easily and successfully.

The Web is no different than print when considering clutter and readability except for one thing. The Web is in color, and you must manage foreground (text) and background colors. Color doesn't necessarily have an effect on the rating system that this chapter proposes. It is difficult to rate a color scheme. You have to use your own judgment to be sure that the text and background colors are tasteful and comfortable and have enough contrast to read easily. *But certainly, when you start using multiple colors for text, you will generate the same sort of reading disruption as you do using multiple typefaces, and such a practice is not advisable.* In fact, hyperlinks (both unvisited and visited) should be colors close enough to the text color to read through easily but different enough from the text color to notice easily. More specifically, a charcoal hyperlink in black text is probably not sufficiently different enough from the text to adequately signal a hyperlink for all situations, but a dark blue hyperlink probably is; and a dark blue hyperlink is still easy to read through. The point is that you don't have to make a hyperlink red for black text to have readers perceive it as being a hyperlink, and a red hyperlink in black text is difficult to read through.

Other Than Text Blocks

The rating system does not necessarily apply to text that is not meant to be read as text blocks. For instance, many Web pages have indexes (lists of hyperlinks) arranged in a graphic design. No rating system should hamper a designer's creativity. Nonetheless, indexes and lists must be read, even if incorporated into a graphic design. When it comes to reading, the characteristics of simplicity, clarity, and elegance always seem to be more effective than clutter.

No Substitute

This rating scheme is not a substitute for good taste and design. It merely provides you with a quantitative measurement for gauging clutter. Although design is beyond the scope of this book, the typesetting guidelines mentioned from time to time (including this rating scheme) will give you a good start on refining your Web page designs.

Usually, as a tenet of sound design, you will have one typeface for text and perhaps a second typeface for headings. If you have two typefaces, they will probably constitute a serif–sans serif combination, with the serif used for text and the sans serif used for headings and perhaps special text treatments. You will find that two serif typefaces or two sans serif typefaces used together usually clash. When you include code on a page as this book must (because it's a computer book), you will probably use a third monospaced typeface to set the code. It may look awkward, but it's important to distinguish the code from other text treatments. See Chapter 2 for a few more design guidelines in the section on combinations.

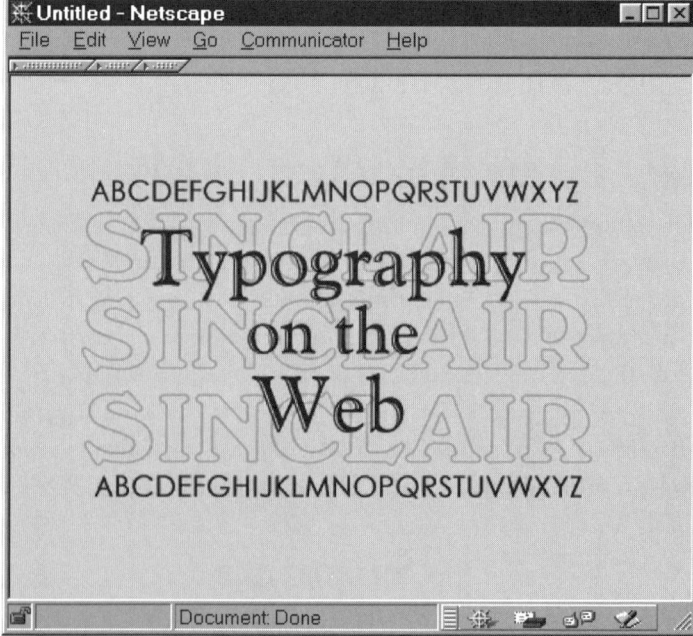

Figure 4.1 *Page head design that includes type.*

Page Head Designs

Don't confuse ordinary typesetting with promotional or aesthetic designs that happen to use type. Such designs, which appear at the head of a magazine article or at the head of a Web page, are often freestanding designs even though they have been integrated into the page (see Figure 4.1). Often the type used is in a graphical format rather than normally typeset. The type in such heading designs in most cases does not have to be rated according to this chapter. In other words, this chapter is not meant to hamper a designer's creativity.

Summary

Do you have to use this rating system all the time? The answer is no. Use it for a few weeks or a few months. Pretty soon you will get a feeling for when you are running up a rating too high. Once you get a feeling for too much clutter, you won't need the rating system any longer. The rating system only provides a guideline, but it's a pretty realistic one. Abuse it at the risk of publishing cluttered Web pages that are difficult to read.

Part Two

Digital Typography

How Typography Works on a Computer

This is not a book about digital typography. Books on desktop publishing have covered that topic adequately. But unfortunately, many readers who have not read a desktop publishing book will not be able to progress beyond this point intelligently without some basics on digital typography. Additionally, desktop publishing books focus on the computer system as a sophisticated printing system, not as an online publishing system. Consequently, this chapter addresses these two issues: Digital typography for those who are not desktop publishers and digital typography in an online publishing system.

Display Realities

Cathode ray tubes (CRTs—computer monitors) provide an inherently low-resolution publishing medium and blast light at readers as well. In contrast, ink and paper are high resolution and use reflected light—quite a difference.

Resolution

Resolution takes on different meanings in the electronic world than it does in the physical world.

CRT Physical Resolution

One kind of resolution measures physical resolution in dots per inch (dpi). Tiny dots make up the reproduction of images like photographs and even type. The dpi measurement is two dimesional. A measurement of 300 dpi (e.g., original laser printer resolution) is really a square: $300 \times 300 = 90{,}000$ dots packed into 1 square inch. A measurement of 600 dpi (e.g., high-resolution laser printer) is: $600 \times 600 = 360{,}000$ dots packed into 1 square inch. As you can see, 600 dpi has four times the resolution of 300 dpi.

Beyond 600 dpi, the human eye does not perceive greater resolution for text without conscious concentration. This means that, unless you look closely, all text over 600 dpi looks the same. Images require higher resolution than text to look sharp. Service bureaus typically compose masters for printing at 1200 to 4000 dpi, and printers use the masters to print at a slightly lower resolution. Today, most laser, ink jet, and press printing produces text of at least 600 dpi or more. Indeed, text printed with today's equipment looks pretty sharp.

CRT displays, in contrast, have resolutions of 72 dpi to 116 dpi. You measure CRT displays by dot pitch. An aperture mask lines the inside of the CRT. It contains tiny holes designed to display glowing phosphor dots but without having the dots bleed their colors into one another. The distance between the centers of the holes (measured in millimeters) determines the dot pitch. The average CRT computer monitor has a dot pitch of .28 meaning that the holes are on .28, millimeter centers. This equates to a measurement of 92 dpi. The newest CRT monitors have a dot pitch of .22 which equates to 116 dpi (e.g., Phillips Brilliance 107 and 109). Older monitors have a dot pitch of .31 (82 dpi), while televisions have a dot pitch of .39 (65 dpi) or above.

Dot pitch is only one way of measuring sharpness in computer monitors, and certainly two monitors with a .28 dot pitch can look very different. Electronic processing is important too. But dot pitch is a physical measurement that's easy to understand and gives you an idea of how a CRT display compares with print.

Electronic Resolution

You use pixel dimensions to measure electronic resolution. The most popular resolutions are 640×480, 800×600, and 1024×768. Macs generally use 640×480. PCs generally use

800 × 600. The greatest resolution 1024 × 768 packs 786,432 pixels (electronic dots) into a CRT display, while the smallest resolution packs only 307,200 pixels into the same display (see Figure 5.1).

One interesting phenomenon is the way that type displays for different resolutions. The computer sizes type in pixels. Consequently, type is large in a 640 × 480 display. A 1024 × 768 display squeezes type down in size. Small type sizes become difficult to read in 1024 × 768. Graphics accelerators (color cards, video boards, graphics boards, etc.) usually offer a choice of *system* font sizes for different resolutions, with small fonts for 640 × 480 and either small fonts or large fonts for 800 × 600 and 1024 × 768.

Displays for NetTV are under 640 × 480. WebTV is the smallest at 560 × 420 (544 × 378 safe image). This shows that television is a comparatively low-resolution display. Keep in mind, however, that television viewers sit about five times as far away from the screen as computer users sit away from monitors. Thus, even at low resolution, television looks sharp.

Set the Resolution To set the resolution in Windows go *Control Panel*, *Display*, *Settings*, *Desktop Area*.

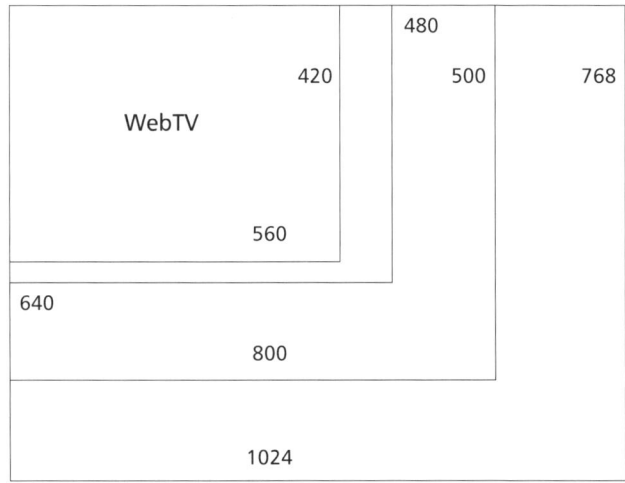

Figure 5.1 *Common digital resolutions.*

Monitor Size

Color monitor CRTs range in size from 14 to 21 inches. Occasionally, you run across a 13-inch monitor, and there are even some larger than 21 inches. It makes sense to use 640 × 480 on a 14-inch monitor. If you use 1024 × 768 instead, you might have trouble reading normal size type. On the other hand, it makes sense to use 1024 × 768 on a 21-inch monitor. If you use 640 × 480 instead, the type will be quite large.

Television CRTs vary in size from 9 to 36 inches, with some being even smaller or larger. With a 544 × 420 display on a 36-inch television, type will display comparatively large.

Put It All Together

When you put all these factors together—physical resolution (dpi), electronic resolution (pixel dimensions), viewing distances, and physical sizes of the CRTs—it's difficult to make sense of them and how they will affect type display. Perhaps the only way you can get a feeling for it is to experiment as much as possible. In any event, all these factors determine how type will look on a monitor (or television). Everybody sees the Web differently, and you must seek some common ground that works for everyone you intend to include in the market for your Web site.

Electronic Color

Electronic color is an RGB (red, green, blue) system. You specify color using an RGB number (1–255, 1–255, 1–255), with 255 designating the pure color. For instance, pure green is (0, 255, 0). You can also use hex numbers (e.g., pure green is #00ff00), as well as color names (e.g., pure green is *lime*).

Computer monitors and televisions display 16 million colors, but only if the electronics driving them can do so. For instance, the graphics accelerator for one CRT might display 8-bit color (256 colors), while another might display 16-bit color (64,000 colors). Some display 4-bit color (16 colors) or

True Color (24-bit, 16 million colors). A CRT displays only as well as the graphics accelerator driving it. Most people see the Web in 8-bit color, but the public has become more interested in more powerful graphics accelerators as prices have come down. Soon 16-bit color will be the norm. It's the norm already for PC *sales*. The question is, do people who have 16-bit capability know enough to set their color systems to use it? Color presents another dimension to the already complex character of electronic displays.

Flat-Panel Monitors

With funding from the Defense Department, Xerox PARC invented a new technology for flat panel screens which it calls active matrix LCD. Instrumentation in the cockpits of jet aircraft use it. It offers the capability for 150-dpi color displays (equivalent of .17 dot pitch), over twice the resolution of the best and most up-to-date CRT technology. In monochrome, active matrix LCD technology offers the capability of 600-dpi resolution, the same as a high-resolution laser printer (print quality!). In addition, active matrix LCD monitors use subdued light rather than blasting light at readers as do CRTs.

The prices for these new flat panel monitors come down monthly. As this book went to press, you could buy an NEC 14-inch flat panel monitor for under $1,200 street price, considerably lower than the $11,000 price for active matrix LCD monitors in late 1995. The current manufacturing of these monitors does not realize the potential of the technology, and the flat panel monitors are currently comparable in physical resolution to normal CRTs (about .28 dot pitch). But the potential for higher physical resolution is there, and eventually monitor manufacturers will undoubtedly begin to upgrade their active matrix LCD products. With a mode changing capability (from color to black and white), these monitors could display text in print resolution! As mentioned in Chapter 1, these flat panel monitors are one of the prime components that will usher in a new reading paradigm.

Meanwhile, these monitors sell well to corporations, ironically not for their superior readable displays, but for their thin size. A corporation can make an office cubical a foot smaller with a flat panel monitor than it can with a normal CRT. No doubt, Dilbert is in a dither.

Digital Font Technology

You can use several methods for digitally describing the characters that make up an alphabet. The methods represent an evolution of digital font technology that starts with bitmaps and ends with the current OpenType.

In the Beginning There Were Bitmaps

A pattern of dots in a matrix (a map) describes a character. The more densely you pack the dots into the matrix, the higher the resolution. The matrix is a square measured by one of its sides. Thus, 92 dots per inch (dpi), as mentioned earlier in this chapter, means 92 × 92 dots, or 8,464 dots per square inch (about the dpi of a common .28 dot pitch color monitor). By mapping each of those dots in the matrix—all 8,464 of them—a program can make each dot the color it must be to achieve the intended effect. Thus any image, any size is a dot map; but because bits represent color, the map becomes a *bitmap*.

Color monitors and laser printers both create bitmapped displays. Color monitors display the bitmaps (about 92 dpi) as color images on a CRT screen. Laser printers print bitmaps (at least 300 dpi) as images on paper. Bitmaps provided the original means of describing type characters digitally, and color monitors and laser printers still use them (see Figure 5.2).

Bitmaps are analogous to lead type. A font of bitmapped characters is a collection of individual bitmaps of individual characters in one size of one typestyle of one typeface. Thus, a font of 255 characters consists of a collection of 255 bitmaps of a specific size type. To use Baskerville regular in 9-point, 10-point, 11-point, 12-point, 14-point, 16-point, and 18-point, you

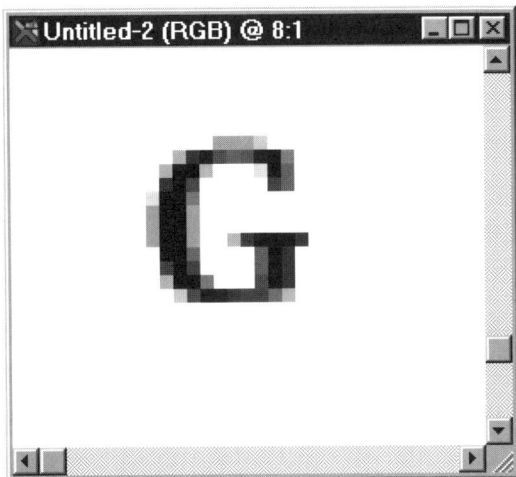

Figure 5.2 *Bitmapped character.*

will have to have 1,785 bit maps. This creates something of a burden for both memory and CPUs, and it turns out there's a better way to describe characters. You can use vector graphics.

PostScript

Adobe's PostScript uses vector graphics to describe characters. Like everything else in the physical world, you can specify the combination of straight and curved lines that make up characters in terms of mathematics. Accordingly, you can describe individual characters with a series of mathematical (vector) formulas. CPUs handle mathematics easily and quickly, and describing characters in terms of mathematical formulas is more efficient than handling huge libraries of bitmaps (see Figure 5.3). A PostScript font is a collection of 256 individual vector graphics that define characters.

Vector graphics are scalable; that is, by using a multiplier you can create larger or smaller mathematical descriptions from the same initial vector graphics. As a consequence, a

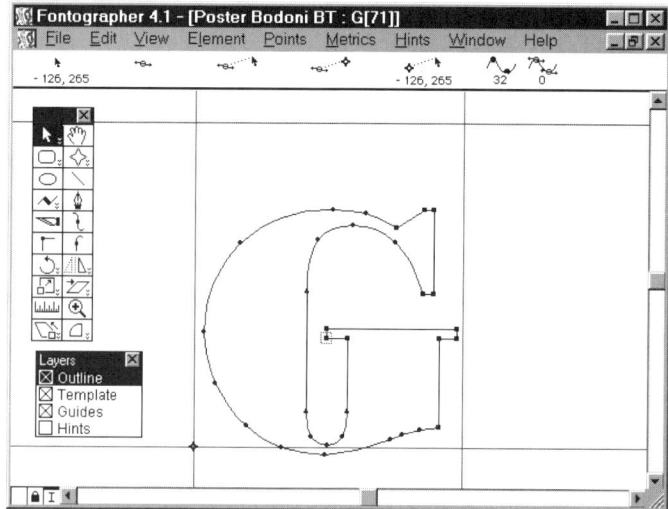

Figure 5.3 *Vector graphic character.*

PostScript font generates all type sizes of one typestyle of one typeface. The vector graphic font files are smaller than the many groups of bitmaps that make up a font collection that includes enough different type sizes to be useful.

The normal PostScript fonts are Type 1 fonts and can contain the hinting information that can make them more readable in text sizes. Type 1 fonts also can contain an estimated average of about 280 kerning pairs. Other PostScript Type designations are for special purposes, not for general use. For Windows, you must use the Adobe Type Manager (ATM) to use PostScript fonts (although you can print with a PostScript printer without ATM but also without seeing the PostScript fonts on the screen). Designers and typographers seem to prefer Type 1 fonts for prepress and printing work because the service bureaus that use Macs—and most do use Macs—have less trouble with Type 1 fonts. PostScript Type 1 Multiple Master fonts contain additional information that enables using the font in a variety of versions of different weights and widths and allows fine-tuning at a variety of type sizes as well. Adobe also offers CID-keyed fonts that contain much larger character sets, which are important for languages with a large number of characters such as Japanese Kanji.

TrueType

Like PostScript, TrueType is a vector graphic system font system. The initial improvement that TrueType provided over PostScript was more control and flexibility for hinting (see the following section on hinting). Hinting is especially important for font sizes under 15 points and for low-resolution displays. TrueType started with the Apple System 7 but was licensed to Microsoft which integrated it into Windows 3.1. PostScript, used primarily on Macs, has dominated the creative community as well as the prepress industry, while TrueType, promoted by Microsoft, has been more widely used in business and on substantially more computers due to Microsoft's domination of the market. But TrueType is native to both Windows and Mac and requires no additional software to make it work in either operating system.

TrueType also has some interesting capabilities built into it. You can actually embed fonts in a document. You can use TrueType four ways in a digital document (e.g., a word processor document):

1. **Installable embedding**. Embedding allowed. Editing and permanent installation of font on remote computer allowed.

2. **Editable embedding**. Embedding allowed. Editing and temporary installation of font on remote computer allowed.

3. **Print and preview**. Embedding allowed. Read-only and temporary installation of font on remote computer allowed.

4. **Restricted**. No embedding allowed.

It is up to the font vendor to determine what to allow. However, these capabilities are generally unperceived by consumers. If a font enables embedding, you can use Microsoft Word 7.0 (and PowerPoint 7.0) to embed the fonts you use in the Word document, attach the document to an e-mail message, and send the e-mail message to someone. The recipient will see the document just as you typeset it regardless of whether he or she has the requisite fonts installed in their computer. The fonts travel with the Word document, but the recipient cannot necessarily use the fonts except for displaying or printing that specific document. Each embedded font adds about 40–80 K to the size of the word processor file. Thus, a one-page letter of 12 K turns into a letter of 78 K with just one font embedded. The embedding system doesn't work perfectly, however, and you always need to check to catch any fonts that the embedding process may have overlooked.

Do your own experiments with font embedding in Word 7.0 or 8.0 (*Tools, Options, Save, Embed TrueType Fonts*) to see how it works. On the PC, TrueType fonts have the extension *.ttf,* while on the Mac they have the characters *SFNT*. Note that, for the Web, you will need font embedding. Make sure you have TrueType fonts with embedding enabled (see Chapter 14).

TrueType fonts contain many tables of information that enable the advanced hinting and other features that this font technology offers. In fact, a TrueType font is a small program by itself that uses the extensive information in the internal tables to render text. Microsoft provides the OpenType Font Properties Shell Extension (free download from the Microsoft Web site—http://www.microsoft.com/typography) which enables you to get information on your TrueType fonts simply by *right* clicking on the font file and choosing *Properties* (see Figure 5.4).

Keep in mind that, while Adobe makes and sells many wonderful fonts, Microsoft makes few and sells none. The standard fonts that Microsoft provides for Windows are licensed from font vendors, and Microsoft provides additional fonts free at its Web site, such as Trebuchet, Georgia, Verdana, etc. (see Chapter 21).

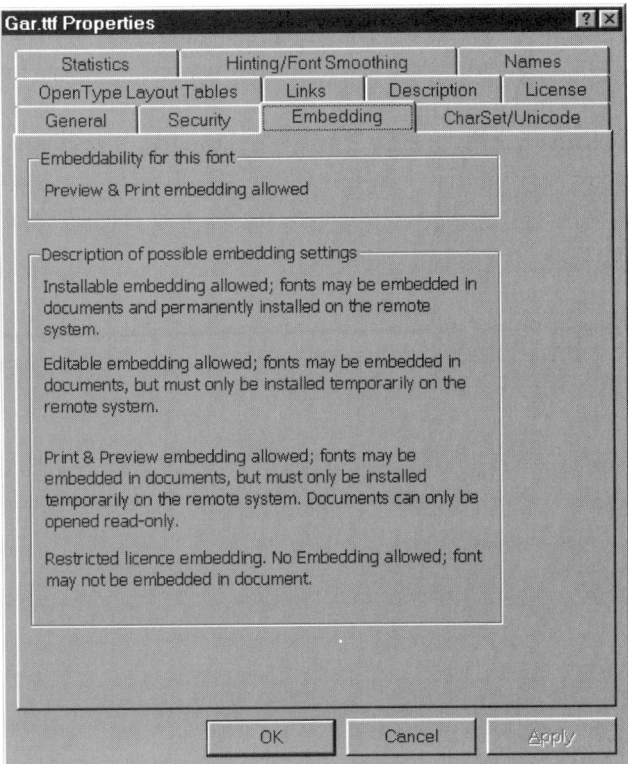

Figure 5.4 *The Microsoft OpenType Font Properties Shell Extension shows the kind of embedding that the font allows.*

Rasterizing

Computer monitors and laser printers cannot use vector graphics. They display or print only bitmaps. Vector graphics must be converted into bitmaps in order to be displayed. The computer uses a rasterizing program to rasterize the vector graphics (turn them into matrices of bitmaps). Accordingly, a rasterizer must rasterize the vector graphic characters generated by PostScript or TrueType fonts before a computer monitor can display the characters or before a laser printer can print the characters. You normally find rasterizing programs embedded in operating systems. In addition, rasterizers are specifically programmed to work with only one vector graphic system. In other words, a rasterizer that rasterizes TrueType vector graphic characters into print will not necessarily work for PostScript vector graphics. The Windows and Mac operating systems use the TrueType rasterizer. The PostScript rasterizer is in the Adobe Type Manager (see Figure 5.5) program which you can use for Windows or Mac.

Font Tuning

Mathematics does a fine job on a grand scale, and vector graphics do a mathematically perfect job of describing characters. Unfortunately, the eye doesn't necessarily cooperate. Keep in mind that most fonts look good on the screen in large sizes. In text sizes, they require tuning.

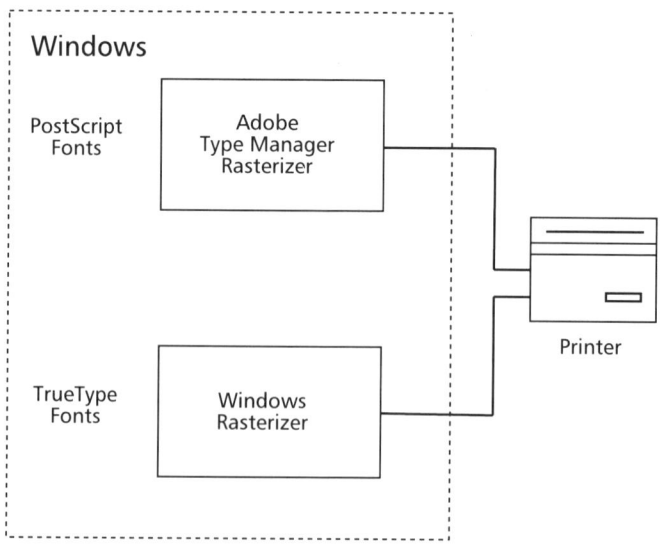

Figure 5.5 *Adobe Type Manager for Windows.*

Hinting

For small print (under 15 points), vector graphics need a little help distorting the characters to trick the eye into seeing sharper type both on the screen and in print. This is called hinting. The mathematical formulas must be massaged a little to make the characters of the font look sharper in small sizes. Since people read text in small sizes in print, hinting is quite important to desktop publishing. Unhinted fonts do not look as sharp or as good as hinted fonts, and hinting is a characteristic of high-quality fonts. PostScript hints well for print. TrueType, with its inclusion of many tables of information on how to form fonts, hints text commendably for screen display as well as for print. However, it is up to the font vendor for either PostScript or TrueType to do the hinting that creates the quality.

Screen Tuning

High-quality font vendors tune (maximize for sharpness) their PostScript and TrueType fonts for print. And why wouldn't they? After all, print was the product, whether a laser-printed letter or a printed brochure, and what was seen on the screen was not nearly as important as the printed product itself. Then came the Web and Web publishing. The CRT screen suddenly became a new and important publishing medium. Fonts tuned to the screen look better on the screen than those tuned solely to print. For a long time, font vendors did not tune many of their fonts to the screen. It's expensive to do so. But as Web commerce increased, screen-tuned fonts appeared on the market in greater numbers from the high-quality font vendors. There is still much work to be done.

Again, the small type sizes need the tuning. Screen-tuned fonts provide extra sharpness to characters on the screen, both for those who work in front of a CRT all day or for Web publishing where the final product is a Web page. Bitstream has even created one font, Prima, from scratch to be used for screen displays, as seen in Figure 5.6. Similarly, Microsoft created Trebuchet, Georgia, and Verdana and provides them free. Monotype offers its Enhanced Screen Quality (ESQ) fonts; Bitstream offers its "delta-edited" fonts; and Adobe offers its WebType fonts. Look to all the high-quality font vendors to supply screen-tuned fonts, and use such fonts with font embedding for your Web publishing.

Antialiasing

The trouble with bitmaps on the screen is that they have the jaggies; that is, they look jagged around the edges, particularly in low-resolutions. Antialiasing reduces the jagged look by smoothing the edges, but at the same time often makes the edges look a little fuzzy. It blends the edges of the type with intermediate colors. For black and white, this is called gray scaling. Antialiasing is controversial among typographers. Some claim it makes small type more readable by removing the jaggies. Others claim that the resulting fuzziness impairs reading. You have to evaluate antialiasing on a case-by-case basis.

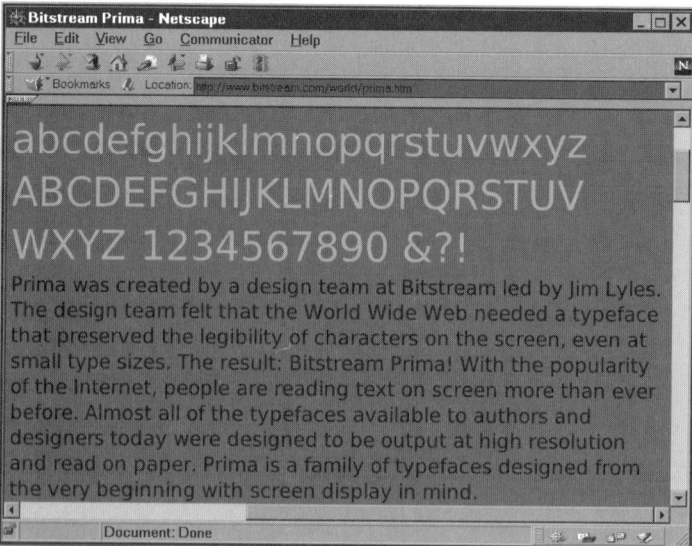

Figure 5.6 *Bitstream's Prima font.*

Windows 95 (with the font smoother available free at the Microsoft Web site or in the Plus! Pack) and Windows NT each can antialias in the 16-bit color mode (64,000 colors), but only if you select antialiasing (*Control Panel, Display, Plus!*). Try it with a wide range of text fonts and color schemes, and make up your own mind whether it helps or hinders readability. With the color schemes I use, it doesn't seem to help much. See Figures 5.7 and 5.8 for examples (unfortunately, you may not be able to see much in print). Keep in mind that Web site visitors, not you, control whether their operating systems antialias (unless they are browsing a TrueDoc Web page).

TrueDoc antialiases all the fonts that it renders for Web pages. TrueDoc does an excellent job of antialiasing, even in 8-bit color, but it's not perfect. It can improve readability, but it can impair readability too. Be particularly careful in evaluating the effect of TrueDoc on long passages of text. If the text is too fuzzy, you may need to switch to a typeface that shows less fuzziness. Again, try TrueDoc with a wide range of text fonts, and make up your own mind. Also keep in mind that Web site visitors have no control over the antialiasing in TrueDoc (see Chapter 12 for more details on TrueDoc).

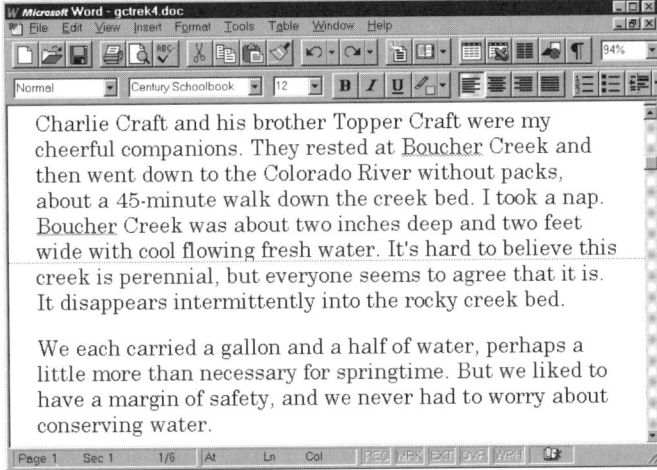

Figure 5.7 *Plus! antialiasing off.*

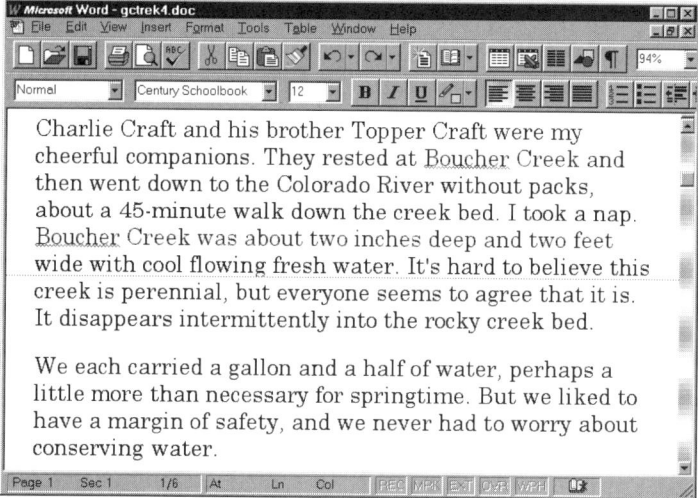

Figure 5.8 *Plus! antialiasing on.*

Other Comparisons To see an antialiased graphic, look at Figure 3.4 and compare it with Figure 2.1, which is not antialiased.

Character Set

A character set is simply the set of characters included with a font. It can be anything that a font vendor wants it to be. The standard character sets for Windows, Mac, and PostScript all have 256 possible characters. A font vendor can provide characters for all 256 possibilities or just a portion of them. You can use many of the characters via your keyboard (e.g., A through Z), but for some characters you must use the operating system character set window (character map—see Figure 5.10) or special keystrokes. Programs also provide character selection windows such as the one in Word for Windows (see Figure 5.9).

Unicode

The Latin extended character set supports about 200 characters, enough to cover European languages reasonably well, but not the rest of the languages in the world. As digital technology spreads to the far corners of the globe, an expanded character set is needed. Unicode fulfills the need by providing

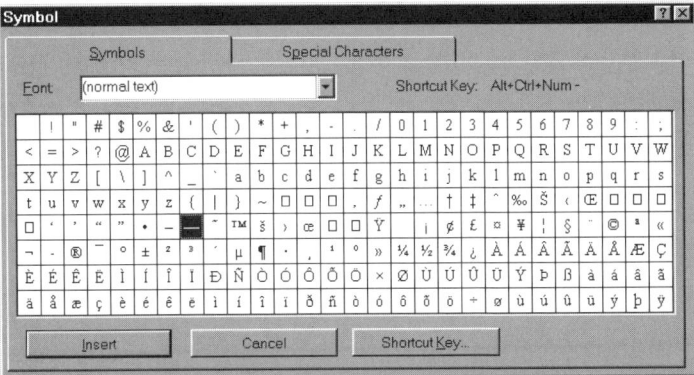

Figure 5.9 *Word for Windows character selection window (Insert, Symbol).*

65,000 characters. However, Unicode is not of much signifi-
cance to you unless you work with foreign languages.
Monotype's WorldType Unicode font includes the following
Script Modules:

Base Level: Pan-European Latin, Cyrillic, Greek, Hebrew,
Arabic

Chinese 1: Simplified Chinese

Chinese 2: Traditional Chinese

Japanese: Hiragana, Katakana, Kanji

Indic 1: Devanagari, Bengali, Tamil, Telugu

Indic 2: Gujerati, Oriya, Sinhalese

Indic 3: Gurmukhi, Malayalam, Kannada

Korean: Hangul

Thai.

Extended Arabic: Urdu, Sindhi, Pashto, Kurdish

Armenian

Georgian

Burmese

Vietnamese Latin

Extended Latin

Laotian

Cambodian

Ethiopic

International Phonetic Alphabet

Polytonic Greek

Mathematical Symbols

Technical Symbols

Dingbats

Custom Modules

But a Unicode font need not have the full 65,000-character set. It can have a partial set such as for one language. You can have Monotype custom adapt the WorldType font for you to include just the languages you need. Bitstream offers Cyberbit (free download at http://www.bitstream.com), a Unicode font that weighs in at about 6.6 MB (compressed) and has a similar character set to the one listed for Monotype WorldType. Pick your language and Cyberbit will take care of your text. And Bitstream will custom adapt Cyberbit to include just the language or languages you need (e.g., a 6.6 MB font is a little large to haul around everywhere with you). Unicode is the latest version of universal character coding after ASCII and ANSI. Windows NT 4.0 supports Unicode. You can check your fonts in the Windows Unicode Character Map (a Windows NT accessory—see Figure 5.10). All operating systems will undoubtedly support Unicode eventually.

The character set for HTML is the Universal Character Set (UCS) which is the equivalent of Unicode. You can, of course, use subsets of this character set. A common subset is the Latin-1 character set that forms the basis for the character sets in computer operating systems.

OpenType

As mentioned above, PostScript type has provided the premier typesetting technology for print, while TrueType has been used more for business documents and publishing online. PostScript

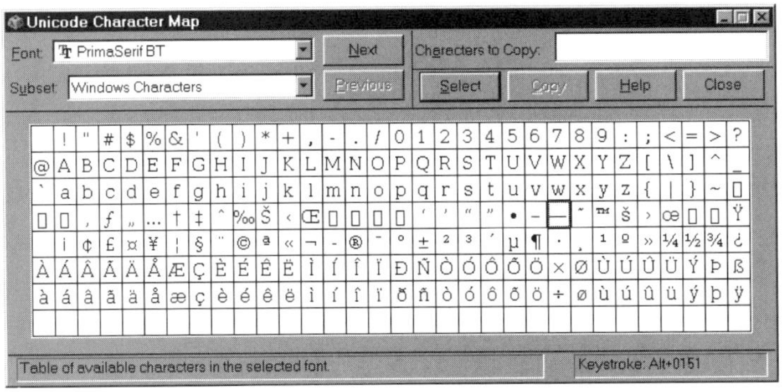

Figure 5.10 *Windows NT Unicode character map for Bitstream's Prima Serif.*

has a close association with the Apple computing platform while TrueType is the typesetting system for Windows. With the advent of the Web comes a greater need for cross-platform documents systems; that is, systems that are cross-platform in respect to computing platforms and cross-media in respect to publishing media. For instance, the TCP/IP network as a cross-platform network has engendered a new trend in cross-platform thinking and many publishers need to publish in print but also on the Web. For computer users to endure the continuation of two incompatible type systems in the face of a cross-platform world is perhaps too much to ask.

With that in mind, Adobe and Microsoft reached an agreement to create one type system called OpenType. Indeed, from a consumer's point of view, OpenType is one type system that features fonts that work the same on all platforms and in all media. In fact, Adobe, Microsoft, and font vendors can continue to compete with their own technologies, because under the hood OpenType accommodates both PostScript and TrueType fonts. Think of OpenType as a container for both technologies. Although OpenType is actually an extension of TrueType technology, it can contain either a TrueType font or a PostScript font (including Multiple Master fonts) and present it as one cross-platform font to consumers. Presumably, OpenType will work seamlessly for the Web and for print.

Although a few OpenType fonts have reached the market already, you will see OpenType fonts proliferate over the next few years. You will still be able to use your existing PostScript or TrueType fonts, but OpenType fonts will eventually provide you with extra benefits in future operating systems.

OpenType Benefits

The cross-platform benefit has been mentioned but not elaborated. Adobe believes that OpenType being included in the Windows system will bring it new business. Although Windows users can use PostScript fonts now if they install ATM, absent a PostScript rasterizer to render them to the screen, OpenType will cause the conversion and rasterization of PostScript fonts to the screen as TrueType fonts. The rastizer in a PostScript printer will rasterize the same OpenType fonts as PostScript fonts. Thus, ATM may not be needed. Or, ATM may be provided free with Windows (undecided as book went to press). Microsoft believes that OpenType will bring more prepress and publishing business to the Windows platform, via Adobe, that has traditionally gone to the Mac platform. Consumers benefit, because one font (one OpenType font) fits all.

Of course, cross-platform doesn't mean cross-browser. Netscape has adopted TrueDoc as its Web font technology. Whether it will adopt OpenType font embedding in the future remains to be seen. For now, you use TrueDoc for Netscape browsers. You will have to duplicate your efforts for Microsoft browsers by using font embedding for TrueType (now) and OpenType (soon); or, use the ActiveX control which enables the Microsoft browser to handle TrueDoc. In any event, font embedding seems to work about the same for TrueType and OpenType.

The other benefits conferred by OpenType fonts include:

• Supports both Adobe and Microsoft font compression and embedding for using fonts in Web pages.

- Supports more international character sets.
- Supports more robust subsetting of characters.
- Gives broader support for typographical controls.
- Supports PostScript Multiple Master fonts.
- Provides protection against illicit alteration or use for font vendors. (Unfortunately, this protection may not work until everyone is using Windows NT 5.0.)

The Microsoft compression technology Font Express (licensed from Agfa) compresses fonts into a smaller size for downloading into Web pages (see Chapter 14). The Adobe compression technology Compact Font Format (CFF) does the same. OpenType can be used with each of these to embed compressed fonts into Web pages for quicker downloads and better Web typography.

OpenType can include more character sets, including multiple Unicode subsets. OpenType can provide special subsets in one font. For example, a font designer can provide an expert's set of small caps and include it in an OpenType font, together with the regular characters. Perhaps more relevantly, an OpenType font can include the different weights of fonts that CSS will specify in its *font-weight* property (see Chapter 10). Similarly, OpenType supports PostScript Multiple Master fonts.

One of the payoffs of any advance in digital typography regarding fonts should be more typographical controls. TrueType already supports many tables of information that a font can use in rendering the type. OpenType provides for more tables and even broader typographical controls.

Finally, OpenType contains a digital signature, a kind of encrypted reference. By reading the signature (through appropriate software), you can ascertain the identity of the font vendor and whether the font has been altered. This offers protection to font vendors and consumers, because consumers can tell whether they have the real thing or an illicit imitation. But this won't stop pirating. If an operating system (i.e., Windows NT 5.0) accepted only fonts with valid digital signatures, that would offer sound protection to font vendors, but only OpenType fonts would work; all current TrueType and PostScript fonts would be useless.

How OpenType Works

OpenType provides a series of many tables inside a font in which the myriad of various font specifications reside. Of course, the more robust a particular font, the larger it will be. You use OpenType fonts like any other fonts, but with the appropriate software you can potentially exercise more control over your digital typography.

How OpenType Works on the Web

You use OpenType fonts for the Web by embedding them in Web pages, a technique that Chapters 14 and 15 cover. OpenType fonts are appropriate for the Web, because they accommodate the requisite compression technologies.

Designing Fonts

As mentioned above, PostScript and TrueType fonts are vector graphics. So, why not design them or alter them using draw programs like Adobe Illustrator (http://www.adobe.com), Corel Draw (http://www.corel.com), or Macromedia Freehand (http://www.macromedia.com)? That's possible. Actually, you can do better with specialized vector graphics programs dedicated to fonts such as Macromedia Fontographer or Pyrus ScanFont and FontLab (http://www.pyrus.com).

Font design programs provide various ways to create fonts. You can start from scratch. You can start from one of many generic fonts that may be provided with the design program. You can put weight on or take weight off a font; you can compress or extend a font; or you can blend fonts together. In addition, you can use dozens and dozens of controls that enable you to do detailed design work (see Figure 5.11). Note, however, that doing this with fonts designed by someone else may be a violation of their copyrights in the digital fonts. See Typeright at http://www.typeright.org for more information on font copyrights.

If, after experimenting with high-quality fonts on the CRT screen, you don't like what you've seen, design your own typefaces. How difficult is it? It's quite difficult for high-resolution media. For low-resolution media such as the CRT, however, there's a certain fuzzy factor that may favor amateurs more than for other media. In any event, the font design software now available enables almost anyone who cares enough to do some research and to spend a lot of time to design his or her own fonts with some degree of success.

Regardless of the ease-of-use of font design programs, designing high-quality fonts for text is a complex endeavor

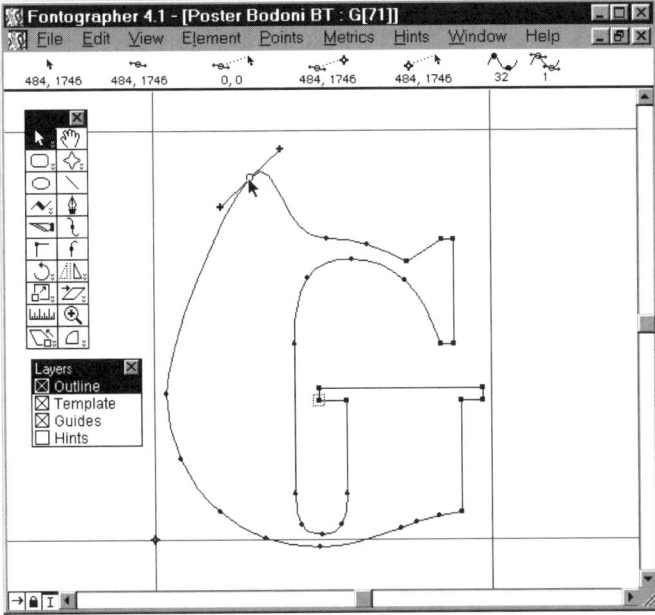

Figure 5.11 *A vector graphic display of a character being altered.*

Roll Your Own A few years back, I mentioned to Sumner Stone (designer of the Stone typefaces and proprietor of Stone Type Foundry) at a trade show that I thought designing my own typeface would require a lot of time with no hope of creating something successful. He told me that I should try it and that I might be surprised. He said it's an addictive sort of craft.

He's right. Eventually, I did try my hand at creating a typeface that would look sharp and readable on a CRT display. Using a font design program, I blended a variety of combinations of generic fonts supplied with the program until I came up with something that looked pretty good. It took a lot of time. It wasn't original design work, just a blend. And when I was done, my new typeface still needed a lot of tuning. But I could smell success at that point. Unfortunately, other priorities overtook me, and I never did complete the final tuning. And of course, when it came to printing, my new typeface was ugly. However, now that I can typeset on the Web, I hope to get back to my font designing soon, with the hope that I can create something that looks sharp on the screen in at least one type size.

requiring a high level of expertise and skill. There are many people creating fonts today, but the professionals are still a small percentage. The difference today is that a diligent and persistent amateur with competent font design software may eventually join the ranks of the professionals without working for a font foundry. But it still takes diligence, research, hard work, experimentation, and time.

Certainly, there seem to be a generous number of font designers selling their fonts on the Web. Undoubtedly, most of them are designing their fonts digitally (i.e., with a font design program). There are a lot of new typeface designs now available through recently established small digital type foundries as well as through major font vendors. It's an exciting time in the history of typography, and many of the new typefaces are great designs well worth their modest prices. Still, you will not find as many new typefaces that provide readable text as you will the decorative typefaces that now flood the market (see Figure 5.12).

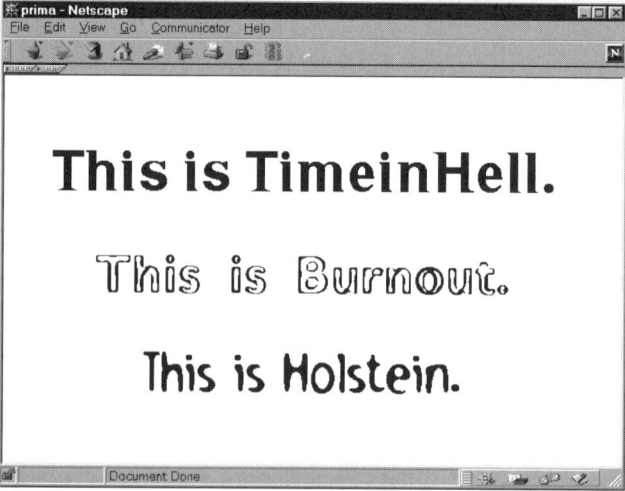

Figure 5.12 *Some contemporary typefaces.*

Designing fonts goes well beyond the scope of this book, and other authors have written books on digital font design. The aesthetics of type design are addictive, and you may want to investigate this traditional craft further.

Style

Two of the words you will see a lot in this book are *style* and *style sheets*. What do they mean? For the purposes of this book, style means typesetting and layout which add up to *typography*. Or, to state it succinctly, style is typography. A style sheet is an ASCII document that lists a set of specifications to control the style in a document. For instance, a style sheet might include specifications regarding fonts, font sizes, margins, line spacing, and the like.

Summary

It's difficult to summarize a chapter that covers so many diverse topics. This chapter is intended to provide you with a useful background in the digital aspects of typography from screen display to font design. With this chapter and Chapter 6 (basic information on the SGML document system of which HTML is a part), you will have a sound basis to understand and master HTML typography, CSS, TrueDoc, and font embedding.

SGML and XML

To understand the new Web typography, it is enlightening to go back to HTML's roots and examine how it fits into the overall scheme of publishing, particularly Standard Generalized Markup Language (SGML). Armed with the knowledge gained from that examination, you will begin to understand many of the new developments in Web document technology that may have been unclear. Accordingly, the chapter finishes with background information on Extensible Markup Language (XML) and Extensible Style Language (XSL) style sheets.

Introduction

A printed writing has content (words), structure (the organization and placement of words on the page), and style (the graphic display of the words). Consider these one at a time.

Content

A writing is a communication that uses words expressed by visual symbols either on paper or on a computer screen. An author creates (writes) the words. The author might be an attorney writing a contract for a client, a reporter writing a story for a newspaper, a business person writing a marketing report for a corporation, or a freelance writer composing a magazine article. These authors control the words and the expression of ideas and facts. They control the relationships of the words using grammar and literary devices. They control the structure of the words using such devices as headings, subheadings, and paragraphs. The words compose the content. Usually, however, the authors do not create or provide the structure *system*.

Structure

Although the writer is free to be creative with the use of words, the structure of the resulting document is usually imposed by custom or a promulgated guideline. In other words, the writer structures a document according to a preexisting structure system. The attorney writes contracts in customary form, even though that form may vary somewhat from one attorney to another or from one law office to another. A reporter writes stories in the form prescribed by the newspaper, even though that form may vary slightly from newspaper to newspaper. A business person may write a report using any form that comes to mind (usually one learned in college) or may be required to write the report according to corporate guidelines. The freelance writer must write an article according to guidelines provided by the magazine that is publishing the article.

The elements of structure take on many forms such as titles, indexes, headings, text blocks, lists, and footnotes. Within each form, there are variations. Headings include subheadings. Text blocks include paragraphs as well as sidebars. Lists include numbered lists, bulleted lists, and unnumbered lists. The variations are endless, but, in most systems, a limited number of variations enable the system to be useable for authors.

It is difficult to imagine content without structure, because authors use structure to express ideas and facts just as they use words. The outline format, which includes headings, subheadings, and text blocks (paragraphs) arranged in a hierarchical pattern, provides the basic underlying structure for most written documents (not including forms). The outline format soundly grounded in logic is one that authors learn to use as early as grammar school. Because authors use structure so fluently in their writings, many people have difficulty conceptually separating content and structure.

It is easier to conceptually separate content and structure when considering forms (e.g., the forms you fill out to get a driver's license). An author simply places the requisite word or words in the blanks provided without any thought at all for structure. The form provides the structure, which may or may not make sense to the author. (Presumably, the form makes sense to the bureaucratic promulgator of the form.) The form presents a certain convenience to authors. Which of the following structures is more convenient for applying for a driver's license, the first (Figure 6.1) or the second (Figure 6.2)?

Likewise, a specific guideline for a writing such as a corporate report presents a certain convenience to authors. An author following such a guideline does not have to worry about inventing the structure. The guideline provides the structure system. Once the author learns to comply with the guideline, he or she can concentrate on providing the words that express the ideas and facts—the content. Since most authors do repetitive work, the guideline used over and over again becomes a real time-saver.

Words are the *content*, and the organization of the words is the *structure*. But how the writing will display (be styled) so that readers can understand the structure is another matter. The content might display in 12-point Baskerville or 11-point Helvetica. Paragraphs might be set apart by extra space between them or by a small indentation of the first line.

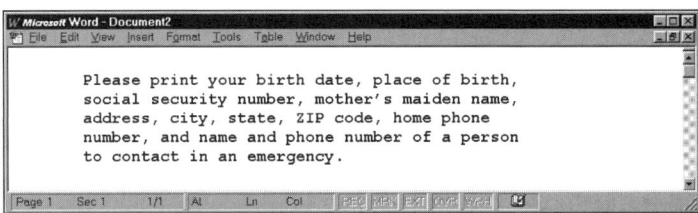

Figure 6.1 *A request for information.*

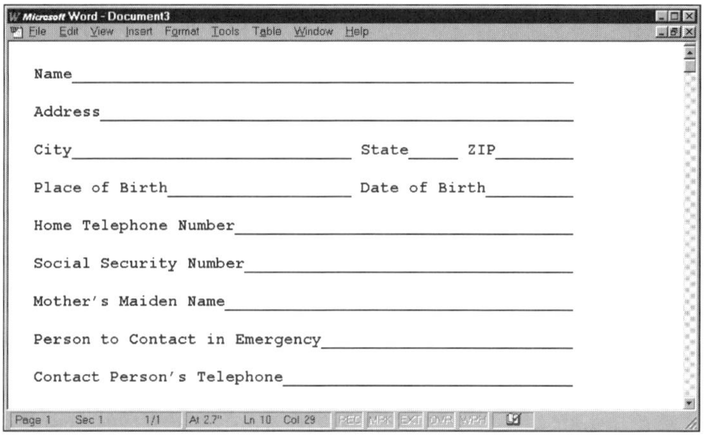

Figure 6.2 *A request for information via a form.*

Style

Virtually all online text is standard ASCII (American Standard Code for Information Interchange) text. ASCII text typically displays in the monospaced Courier typeface, has an uninteresting appearance, but is truly universal. HTML files are ASCII text files. So are e-mail files. Only when you display ASCII text with some "style" does it show some pizzazz. For instance, an attorney might take the ASCII text of a contract and, via a word processor, print it on a laser printer in Century Schoolbook with Arial headings, a solid look. A reporter sends the ASCII text of a story to the printing system which prints it in the standard type used by the newspaper. A business person takes the ASCII text of a report and, via a word processor, prints it on a laser printer in Garamond with Garamond bold headings or perhaps in a standard typeface used by the corporation. A freelance writer sends the ASCII text of an article via e-mail to a magazine which prints it in the standard typeface for the magazine.

The publisher can change the *style* without affecting the words *(content)* or their organization *(structure)*. If there is a way to always keep the content and structure separate from the style, then you can change the style of a document easily without manually changing each heading or paragraph of the content individually.

All Mixed Up

Unfortunately, content, structure, and style get all mixed up. In a word processor, you must create both the structure and style when you format the content of a document. A word processor provides this structuring and styling capability for convenience. It's great if you are doing only one document and publishing in only one medium (i.e., print).

If you do more than one document for print, a word processor template comes in handy. You can set up a template with an appropriate standard for printing, say a hierarchical outline structure that displays text in 11-point Garamond and headings in 13-point Gill Sans bold. This works well until you want to publish on the Web. You understand that, on the Web, Times New Roman text with Arial headings works best, all things considered. Consequently, you will have to restyle your content. Then you realize that part of your structure (e.g., the sidebar) is not directly translatable into HTML, and you must make a custom adjustment for that. Wouldn't it be better to keep content, structure, and style separate for multiple documents that must be published in different media? That is, structure would be generalized and not tied to any specific style. For printing, you would apply one style, and for Web publication another style.

Word Processors

Another problem is that word processors use proprietary markups to add formatting (structure and style) to text. You don't see them, but they're there. WordPerfect uses its own markup language, and Word uses its own markup language. In addition, the markups are not limited to ASCII characters, and the word processor files are not ASCII files. The files are unique,

Authoring Programs

Word processors are printed-text authoring programs. You use them to author text that you print on a computer printer and read or distribute. Although they have never been called authoring programs, if you look at them as printed-text authoring programs, you can better understand their relation to other authoring programs such as HTML authoring programs.

not universal. Consequently, to translate a WordPerfect file into a Word file, you need a translation program (conversion program, filter). Likewise, to translate a WordPerfect file into HTML or other ASCII files, you need a translation program.

One universal markup scheme that has been around for the last decade is Rich Text Format (RTF). It provides advanced formatting for ASCII characters but uses only ASCII characters for markups instead of proprietary markups. Thus, it remains an ASCII file, albeit one with rich formatting information. Most word processors have an RTF converter.

Whether with proprietary markups or RTF, word processor files have a huge overhead which adds substantially to their size over and above the content they contain. My experiments indicate that this amounts to about a 40 percent increase in size over ASCII text.

What is needed for online text is simple ASCII markups (for ASCII content) that are generalized rather than proprietary and do not add a lot of overhead to an ASCII file. SGML provides such a markup scheme.

SGML

Standard Generalize Markup Language (SGML) offers an infinite number of generalized ASCII markups for adding structure to ASCII text (content).

SGML Structure

When envisioning structure, what comes to mind first is the normal hierarchical outline structure (roman numerals, letters, and numbers) that everyone understands. SGML is quite capable of describing such structure, but it is capable of much more. It can provide any structure you want to create for a document, including any structure you can *invent* for a document. For instance, suppose you need to create a catalog with merchandise and prices. You might invent a *<price></price>* markup with which you wrap the price of each item in the catalog.

For printing, the *<price>* markup might be used to print in another typeface, or color, or even in magnetic ink. For online use, the *<price>* markup is even more versatile. For instance, a program (agent) seeking pricing information can find the prices of the merchandise quite easily in the SGML ASCII document. The program might be one provided to online customers for shopping (shopping cart); one that a volume buyer uses to seek favorable prices from multiple online catalogs; or one that personnel use in-house for informational purposes. Without the *<price>* markup, it may be difficult and haphazard for a software agent to find pricing information.

How does SGML enable you to invent your own markup system? SGML is a language that lets the user define any number of ASCII markups (tags) and provides a way to describe the tags and their organization to a computer. The user writes this description of the markups and their organization and saves it in a separate file called a Document Type Definition (DTD). An SGML authoring program uses DTDs, and you must put the document system that you invent in the form of a DTD. You create an SGML document by using an SGML authoring program together with a DTD. Since an SGML document is no more than ASCII text, it is also possible to create a an SGML document with a simple text editor using the SGML markups that you have invented. The next code section is an SGML document:

```
<article>
<source>freelance</source><date>2005
97</date><author>José Santa
Clara</author><articletitle>Hiking
the Gems</articletitle><location>
Grand Canyon</location> <subject>
trekking</subject><description>Three
backpackers take a six-day trek
through the Grand Canyon along the
Tonto trail between the Hermit and
South Bass trailheads.</description>
```

```
<body><h3>First Day of Trek</h3><p>
We started the Boucher-Tonto-Bass
trek <startdate>April 27,
1997</startdate>, by doing the
shuttle of vehicles out to the
trailhead. From the Tolvar Hotel
out to the <startplace>South Bass
trailhead</startplace> and then
back to the Tolvar and out to
Hermit's Rest takes about three
hours by the time you drive it,
transfer some gear from one vehicle
to another, and talk with some
people at the trailheads.</p>

<p>About noon we took our first
steps down the Hermit trail toward
the Boucher trail. Initially, the
trail is easy, but it turns
difficult after a while. Even
before you reach the <link
ref="waterresource.sgm">Dripping
Springs</link>intersection, you can
count on some rugged hiking. We
stopped to camp on Yuma Point after
hiking about four miles in five
hours. The cool still evening was
interrupted by intermittent
breezes.</p>

<h3>Second Day</h3>
<p>Yuma Point is a pleasant camping
spot but hardly one that shows a lot
of progress into the canyon. Early
Monday morning well before 7 AM, we
continued down on an even more
rugged trail finally crossing the
Whites Butte plateau and descending
the Redwall. By the time we got to
<link ref="waterresource.sgm">Boucher
Creek</link> in early afternoon, we
were quite tired.</p>
</body></article>
```

The preceding SGML document follows the DTD created for *Aventure Exotique Magazine*. The magazine created the DTD for its magazine articles, and it contains markups for the following:

<source>	This indicates the source (e.g., freelance, staff).
<date>	Submission date.
<author>	Writer.
<location>	Location of adventure.
<subject>	Classification of adventure.
<articletitle>	Title of article.
<description>	Short description of article.
<startdate>	Starting date of adventure.
<startplace>	Starting place of adventure.
<link ref=" ">	Link to other information sources.

Without even talking about what else SGML provides, you can see that the document has become a database. Wouldn't it be easy for a search program to find all the articles on the Grand Canyon that *Aventure Exotique* has published or all the articles it has published written by José Santa Clara? In this case, there is another article in the same magazine issue about water sources in the Grand Canyon. The links refer the readers to the other article, *waterresources.sgm*. See Figure 6.4 for an online published version of the "Hiking the Gems" article, and Chapter 20 for an SGML authoring demonstration using a different DTD.

Is writing a DTD difficult? It can be. SGML is a very robust markup language and an international standard (ISO 8879). It has a wide scope of capability. The annotated specification runs over 600 pages. Nonetheless, for straightforward documents, DTDs can also be simple in their programming. For instance, HTML is a DTD written in SGML. The HTML DTD fills only a few pages. Almost anyone can write a simple DTD. You don't have to be a programmer. To write DTDs that describe complex

HTML Authoring Program If you use an SGML authoring program with the HTML DTD, the SGML authoring program becomes an HTML authoring program.

structures, however, you will have to understand SGML more thoroughly. There are only a few development programs for creating DTDs, and most DTD programmers use simple text editors.

If DTDs are so simple, why is SGML so expensive to use? A large expense for SGML is not necessarily in coding the DTD but in agreeing on what tags to define and in what order they should appear. Corporations turn to SGML to help standardize their documents and ease the publishing in multiple media. When they set about standardizing their documents, however, every department that will use the document has a voice in creating the DTD design. This requires endless meetings of personnel that are often political rather than creative in nature. Consequently, it often takes a long time to invent a DTD. When you add up the price (as corporations do) of personnel time devoted to the creation process for the DTD, it adds up to a very expensive endeavor even without taking into account the actual coding.

Many DTDs are industrywide projects. That means that many different corporations must have a voice in the invention process, and personnel must travel to the requisite meetings necessary to create a DTD that will be useful for everyone. The personnel expense adds up quickly. Nonetheless, DTDs can enable efficiency that far outweighs their expense (see Figure 6.3 for a magazine article DTD).

An alternative to custom DTDs is off-the-shelf DTDs. An industry association might create DTDs for member firms or a software company might create DTDs to sell. For users, these might be relatively inexpensive or even free. Many users of off-the-shelf DTDs make simple alterations to them to customize them. This can make the use of SGML inexpensive. A good example is the American Association of Publishers' (AAP) book DTD. It was designed for the publishing industry to use in the publication and printing of books. Very few publishers use it as it was created. Most alter or enhance sections

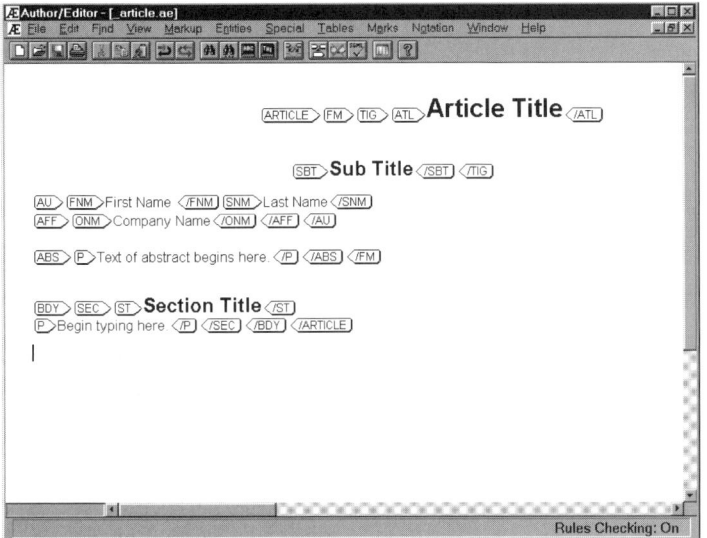

Figure 6.3 *Using SoftQuad Author/Editor, an SGML authoring program, with a magazine article DTD.*

of it to more closely match their own book organization rather than develop a book DTD from scratch.

SGML Style

Keep in mind that a DTD is just a structure system. How do you add style? You create and use a style sheet. You map the style characteristics in the style sheet to the SGML markups (see Table 6.1).

The style sheet is a separate file from the DTD and provides the typesetting and layout characteristics for a document. (See Figure 6.4 for a published version of the "Hiking the Gems" article.) Just as you can create multiple documents with diverse content but the same structure using one DTD, one style sheet can serve multiple documents. To change the style for all the documents, you simply change the one style sheet.

HTML The HTML DTD is relatively simple, and it's easy to learn the markup system, although it gets more complex with each new Web Consortium Recommendation. The latest is HTML version 4.0, created by an Internet committee, of course (Web Consortium).

Table 6.1 *Style to Structure Map*

Style Sheet	Article DTD Markup
12-point Baskerville	*<p>*
20-point Baskerville bold	*<h1>*

Style sheets have languages of their own. The style sheet language associated with SGML is the Document Style Semantics and Specification Language (DSSSL). It is also an international standard (ISO 10179) and is quite complex. Although creating *simple* DSSSL style sheets may fall within the capability of nonprogramming Web developers, it's not a coding system that many programmers have embraced. Most SGML formatting systems have their own style sheet language and offer an attractive user interface to create the styles. These are easy to use, but these style sheets cannot be shared with other SGML systems.

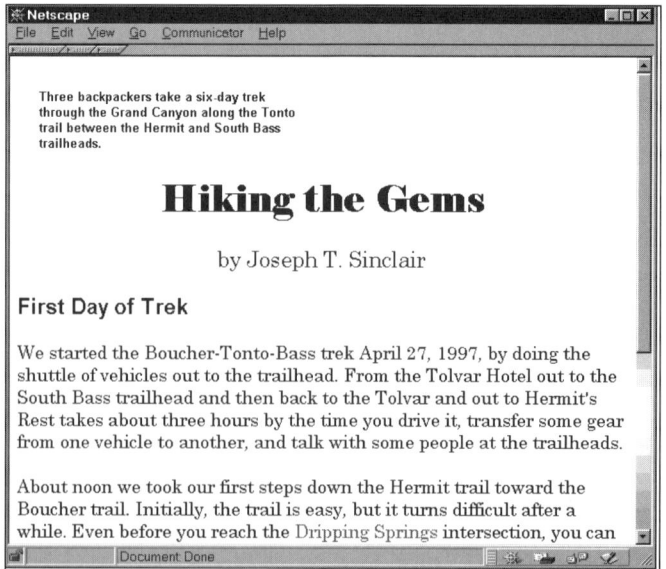

Figure 6.4 *A published version of the "Hiking the Gems" article in an SGML browser after style is applied (simulated by Web browser).*

Conversion for Publishing

The strength of SGML is that it is truly generalized. It is appropriate for all existing media and for media yet to be invented. Therein lies its complexity. It must accommodate all media from newspaper printing to Web pages. How do you go from the general (SGML) to the specific (a single media)? You map the markups.

Suppose you want to go from a word processor template to HTML. You map the word processor structures (which are also styles) to the comparable HTML markups. The structure of a word processor document will be translated by the mapping program into an HTML document. It's similar to the mapping in Table 6.1 where style specifications map to the structure, only in this case the structure maps to structure and no style information is translated (see Table 6.2).

Programs

There are a number of programs that you will use with an SGML publishing system.

- **SGML Authoring Program.** You use this with a DTD to create SGML documents, and it works similar to an HTML authoring program or a word processor.
- **SGML Development Program.** You use this to create (invent) a DTD without doing any coding. Most SGML developers, however, use a plain text editor.
- **Style Sheet Development Program.** You use this to create a style sheet without doing any coding. This is combined with the SGML development program or the SGML publishing program by most software companies.
- **Publishing Program.** You use this together with an SGML document, the DTD, and a style sheet to publish the document. The publishing program can be a program like Adobe Framemaker+SGML (printed documents) or a program like SoftQuad Panorama (an SGML Web browser).

Table 6.2 *Structure to Structure Map*

Word Processor Template	HTML
Normal	Paragraph markup: $<p>$
Heading 1	Top-level heading markup: $<h1>$
Heading 2	Second-level heading markup: $<h2>$

SGML Authoring Programs Export XML Most SGML authoring programs on the market in the future will be able to export XML documents (described in the following pages) without using supplementary translators (converters, filters). In other words, the converters will be built in.

Most SGML programs remain relatively expensive ($400 to $4,000). But with the possibility of a wider market for XML, some SGML vendors such as SoftQuad (http://www.sq.com) and Corel (http://www.corel.com) are developing SGML/XML authoring programs to sell for $300 or less. Most SGML programs come with a variety of useful DTDs.

Creativity

Although for many purposes, off-the-shelf DTDs and simple DTDs may be useful, they do not necessarily provide the range of creativity that you need to realize the full potential of SGML. Using SGML creatively requires substantial knowledge of SGML, of your documents and their sources, of how the content is to be stored and manipulated, and of available programs to process and deliver those documents in multiple formats such as paper and online. Additionally, SGML was designed to be highly generalized so as to serve *all* publishing systems (e.g., even audio). If your only concerns are print and online publishing, you can get by with a less robust markup system.

XML

Extensible Markup Language (XML) is a subset of SGML designed to simplify the creation and display of user-defined markups on the Web. Along with XML is an accompanying new style system, XSL (Extensible Style Language), which begins with Cascading Style Sheets (CSS) but goes much further in its ability to describe complex formats. Because HTML is a DTD of SGML and because XML is a subset of SGML, a good place to start in understanding XML is with the HTML that you already know.

HTML Limitations

One way to understand the need for XML is to look at the limitations of HTML, the markup language of the Web. The HTML DTD changes as the requisite Web committees add new features (markups) to it periodically. With each new version, it provides more robust capabilities, at least to those who use the latest HTML authoring programs and Web browsers. HTML enables some creativity in regard to the publication of content, but it provides no creativity in regard to altering its markup scheme. Yet, there is a widespread need for specialized markups. For instance, the *<price>* markup mentioned earlier in the chapter might be used productively for Web commerce in online merchandise catalogs. However, you cannot create such a markup within HTML. Only the Web Consortium can create such a markup—maybe next year. For the Web, there is a need for more than one DTD, but SGML itself is too complex and too difficult for nonprogrammers to use efficiently.

The Compromise

XML is the online compromise between the fixed nature of the HTML DTD and the full functionality of SGML. XML pertains to online documents and also to printed documents and databases. The World Wide Web Consortium XML Working Group's design goals for XML are:

- XML shall be straightforwardly usable over the Internet.
- XML shall support a wide variety of applications.
- XML shall be compatible with SGML.

HTML Style Cascading Style Sheets compromise the new style system for HTML (covered in Chapters 10 and 11).

HTML? HTML is not XML compatible and, therefore, will not work with XML. Until everyone uses XML-capable Web browsers, Web browsers will continue to be dual clients (HTML + XML). Presumably, a specific XML document structure designed to do so could implement documents virtually identical to HTML. The Netscape and Microsoft 5.0 browsers are XML compatible.

- It shall be easy to write programs which process XML documents.
- The number of optional features in XML is to be kept to the absolute minimum, ideally zero.
- XML documents should be human-legible and reasonably clear.
- The XML design should be prepared quickly.
- The design of XML shall be formal and concise.
- XML documents shall be easy to create.
- Terseness in XML markup is of minimal importance.

The XML specifications run about 32 pages, compared with the 600-page annotated SGML specifications. With very little adjustment, an XML document can become an SGML document, or vice versa. But unlike SGML, XML does not require a DTD, thus enabling Web developers to more easily devise new document structures for the Web. Yet, if a developer's purpose is to create many documents that can all share the same style sheet, then it facilitates that purpose if all the documents use the same markups and organization. A DTD can prove very useful for authoring consistent documents.

Think of XML as a simplified SGML created for online use that will introduce thousands of Web developers to the power of creating their own markups, encourage more software vendors to create XML tools for authoring and viewing, increase ease-of-use, and lower application costs. The 5.0 versions of the leading Web browsers will implement XML for the Web in 1998. Many expect that XML will become the dominant markup language for Web publishing.

XML Style Sheets

Style sheets for XML follow an identical development track to XML. Because DSSSL is so difficult to implement, a simplified DSSSL, known as Extensible Style Language (XSL), is being developed for XML. The Web Consortium XML Working Group's design goals for XSL are:

- XSL should be straightforwardly usable over the Internet.
- XSL should be expressed in XML syntax.
- XSL should provide a declarative language to do all common formatting tasks.
- XSL should provide an "escape" into a scripting language to accommodate more sophisticated formatting tasks and to allow for extensibility and completeness.
- XSL will be a subset of DSSSL with the proposed amendment.
- A mechanical mapping of a CSS into an XSL style sheet should be possible.
- XSL should be informed by user experience with the FOSI style sheet language.
- The number of optional features in XSL should be kept to a minimum.
- XSL style sheets should be human-legible and reasonably clear.
- The XSL design should be prepared quickly.
- XSL style sheets shall be easy to create.
- Terseness in XSL markup is of minimal importance.

Because XSL style sheets promise to have more capabilities than Cascading Style Sheets (CSS and CSS 2), they will be more difficult to code. But XSL and CSS will coexist on the Web to meet different needs. You will use XSL for complex formatting where the content of the document might be displayed in multiple places on your Web site, such as a heading that appears in the primary text window and also in a side window as a table of contents generated automatically. In contrast, CSS is intended for formatting online documents for multiple media. Although its simple nature limits its capabilities, CSS is easy to generate and modify. There will be some overlap between CSS and XSL, but don't expect XSL to be fully backward-compatible.

Authoring Programs

Just like HTML and SGML, XML will be enabled by a full assortment of authoring programs. You will not have to code XML or XSL style sheets. The software repertoire for XML will undoubted grow rapidly. Because XML is easier to use than SGML, creating ingenious new online documents (markup systems) that will work in XML-capable Web browsers will become a reality for many Web developers who take the trouble to learn this new Web technology. See Figure 6.5 and Chapter 20 for more on authoring and XML.

HTML

This chapter helps put HTML in perspective. Although HTML is a DTD of SGML, it has not made good use of SGML capabilities such as the definable style sheet. Before CSS was developed, the Web browser alone decided what HTML elements it would support and how it would display those elements (e.g.,

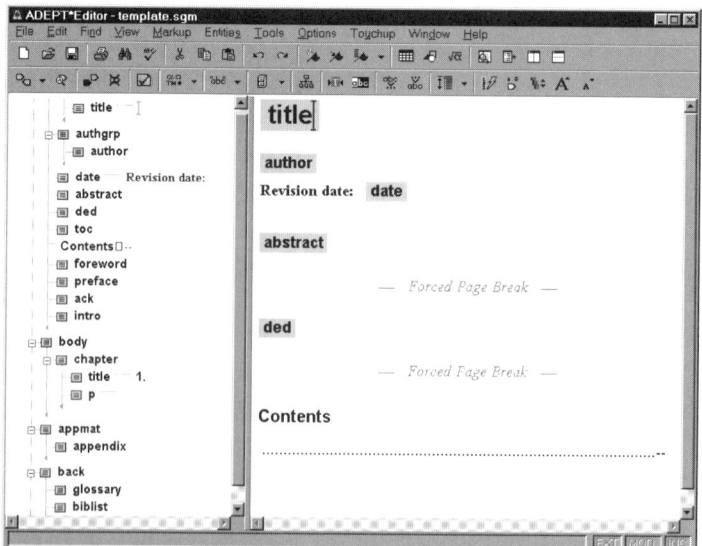

Figure 6.5 *The ArborText SGML authoring program Adept Editor using a book DTD. The program can export the document as an XML document.*

the style sheet was programmed into the browser). In later HTML versions, certain alterations of the browser style sheet are enabled through the use of additional markups and markup attributes. This is a merger of structure and style, much like a word processor, appropriate for individual Web documents, but not appropriate for Web document systems. By separating structure (HTML) and style (CSS), later versions of HTML together with CSS offer greater control over the typesetting and layout of Web pages. Chapters 10 and 11 on CSS will give you a basic understanding of how the style sheets work.

The content portion of an HTML document is the ASCII text, which, together with the ASCII markups, compose the HTML document. That text might be created in a word processor, a plain text editor, an HTML text editor, an HTML authoring program, or any other editor that processes ASCII text. Most content is created in a word processor and exported as plain (ASCII) text or otherwise converted into an HTML document. The structure provided by the HTML DTD can relieve authors of the effort to create their own structure system. They simply learn the HTML structure and use it. The separation of structure and style enabled by CSS further free authors from the task of creating style as they write content. A CSS style sheet can provide the style to multiple documents, and you can easily change it to accommodate one document, if required (see Chapter 10).

Style for HTML Cascading Style Sheets separate style from HTML structure and compose a separate code system (covered in Chapters 10 and 11). The new CSS code system is simple and enables the HTML DTD with the full style capability supported by SGML.

Structure and Style

This chapter puts forth a major effort to convince you that structure and style are completely separate things. And that's a good way to look at these two aspects of text. But structure and style go hand in hand, too. For instance, look at footnotes. Footnotes structure ancillary information or metainformation (information about information) to a place that is essentially outside of the text (i.e., at the bottom of the page or back of the book). Yet, at the same time, footnotes have very traditional styling. Inevitably, they appear in small print.

Thus, structure and style go hand in hand for footnotes, according to tradition.

Is it possible that you will create structure solely for the purpose of style? More specifically, is it possible that you will create custom markups in XML (or SGML) for the sole purpose of marking up the text for style (typesetting or layout)? The answer is an absolute yes. You use structure to communicate in a logical and orderly manner. The logic of structure, such as expressed in the traditional outline format, will stand on its own without style (e.g., typewritten outline). On the other hand, italic emphasis in text is structure expressed solely through style. Consequently, you will create markups to structure a document in such a way that added style will express the specific structure rather than place the structured text in a particular location on the page. Nonetheless, this is not a reason to merge structure and style. By keeping them separate, when it comes time to change the style, you will be able to do so easily in style sheets that serve numerous documents.

Metainformation

One of the benefits of SGML and XML is that you can create metainformation (information about content) by creating and using metamarkups (markups that designate certain content as metainformation or are themselves metainformation). You can use meta information for all sorts of purposes including the enhancement, manipulation, and accounting of content. This becomes especially relevant to Web typography when you use metainformation in conjunction with style.

For instance, suppose you write a business report in English for your international consulting company. It has 63 paragraphs. Only 41 of the paragraphs are relevant to the North American market; only 39 paragraphs are relevant to the Japanese market; and only 46 paragraphs are relevant to the French market. Your XML document has a *<lang2>* markup, a *<lang5>* markup, and a *<lang7>* markup which with corresponding input (a key) are themselves metainformation about the content that they will mark up. You create a key that determines the language for each text markup (e.g., the key might define lang1 = Korean, lang2 = English, lang3 = German, lang4 = Italian, lang5 = Japanese, lang6 = Swedish, and lang7 = French). Then you tag each paragraph in your report with the appropriate markups. A <*p*> markup means the paragraph goes in all reports.

A special program uses your XML document to publish a 41-paragraph report in English using English characters. The program translates and publishes a 39-paragraph report in Japanese using Kanji characters. Finally, the program translates and publishes a 46-paragraph report in French using French characters. For this XML document, the <*lang2*>, <*lang5*>, <*lang7*> markups and corresponding key comprise metainformation relevant to the way that the text will be published and the style in which it will be published. A portion of the report follows below.

Attributes More typically, you designate metainformation through attributes inside tags (e.g., <p lang="french">). This section uses tags instead for simplicity.

```
<p>The international auto market
continues to prosper with virtually
all auto manufacturers enjoying
healthy sales. This contrasts with
the last decade when the auto
markets endured much confusion and
realignment. Today manufacturers
have all reached a level of
efficiency and quality such that
the real competition takes place in
marketing activities, and the world
market continues to expand.</p>

<lang5>The Japanese auto market has
reached a plateau domestically, but
the continued expansion of sales in
some foreign markets have enabled
Japanese manufacturers to continue
to expand production. The
Kyoto-Osaka area, however, is one
domestic market that continues to
be strong.</lang5>
```

```
<lang7>The domestic market in the
Marseille, Toulon, and Nice areas of
the Mediterranean coast has shown
exceptional strength while other
French markets have experienced only
modest increases in auto sales.
Because France has experienced an
increased market share in interna-
tional markets, auto production con-
tinued to expand this year.</lang7>

<lang2>Although auto sales for the
year have been static domestically
with slight increases in
international markets, the West
Coast economic recovery promises to
generate increased production next
year. The manufacturers are going
into a new domestic model cycle
which historically has given a
boost to production.</lang2>
```

The metainformation provides a sort of fourth dimension to Web typography. You might think of it as dynamic Web typography, not in the sense that text moves necessarily, but in the sense that text displays differently according to its metainformation. The display scheme goes beyond normal style. It involves language translation and even different character sets.

The Future

If the HTML-CSS system is so efficient for authors, why do they need XML and XSL? The answer is that most may not need it, at least initially. XML is for creating special documents that provide special functionality, such as more intelligent searching, sorting, or other manipulation of the text or data. Most authors won't get involved in creating XML documents or XSL style sheets. But they may have to learn to use the special XML documents that others create or that software companies sell. It will be like learning a special version of HTML.

For instance, if the *<price>* markup existed in an XML online catalog document, authors writing content for the catalog documents would have to learn how to use this special markup. Eventually, software vendors will develop XML documents especially suited to your publishing activities, whatever they might be. Such XML documents will tempt you to start using this new Web technology.

Hence, XML seems destined to eventually take over the Web. With XML, you can have it both ways. It offers all authors the simple markup tags known as HTML, and it offers those who want it the added capability of creating additional markup tags.

For those who desire to create special documents with exotic functionality, XML provides the capability. How many Web developers will soon use this capability remains speculative. It seems clear that the more complex something is to use, the fewer people will use it. Nonetheless, it is likely that many Web developers will soon start trying their hands at creating special Web documents with XML. As XML authoring programs materialize to make using XML easy, more and more Web developers will migrate to XML.

Although this chapter has kept the XML examples very simple, XML can handle very powerful digital processing inside online documents. Many experts say it will rival Java and CGI scripts as a mechanism for providing computing power in Web pages. The way it will do so is with scripts (e.g., JavaScript in the Web page). It will be quite interesting to see what software vendors do with it. Expect some killer documents and XML-implemented applications to materialize before the end of the decade.

And what will happen to SGML? Remember that XML is designed specifically for more limited use. For those who need to publish online, in print, and in other diverse media, SGML will remain the preferred scheme. WordPerfect 8.0 has SGML capability, and Word has an add-on to handle SGML. Right now, the best way to create XML documents is to use an SGML authoring program and an existing SGML DTD and then export the resulting documents as XML documents (see Chapter 20).

Still, XML is robust enough to cover many publishing applications. Microsoft has announced that HTML and XML will be data formats for their future Office software (http://www. microsoft.com/corpinfo/press/1997/dec97/htmlpr.htm). WordPerfect is working on an XML addition. Will XML be the basis for future word processors? It makes sense.

If publishing shifts completely online over the next 20 years, XML may dominate. XML offers almost as much as SGML offers. Nonetheless, SGML will continue to enable cross-media publishing in diverse media outside the scope of XML. It is a possible scenario that HTML has hooked both the strong and the meek. HTML is not difficult to learn. It might be that most Webmasters—even the meek—will step up to the next level: XML. It will depend on how easy to use the XML authoring programs become. In any event, XML seems likely to be part of your future.

Summary

How far has this chapter strayed from Web typography? Not far, as you'll see from the reasons listed below.

- CSS is important today, and this book devotes two chapters to it. But XML and its corresponding XSL style sheets are close at hand. CSS may coexist with XSL and XSL for a while. If you better understand the role of style sheets in the content-structure-style paradigm as explained in this chapter, you will better understand online typography. In any event, XSL has some backward compatibility with CSS.

- Learning how SGML and HTML operate gives you insight as to how typesetting and layout can work in an online publishing environment.

- HTML is an SGML DTD. Understanding that fact enhances your capability to use the Web system productively for displaying text online.

- What XML does best is provide the capability to create enhancements to online documents such as special markups for special structures within documents. Such enhancements are often tied directly to style considerations.

- With the proliferation of digital assets online, accounting for them and manipulating them become a huge chore. XML enables metasystems with which you can keep track of images, audio bites, and other multimedia assets. Specifically, you can use metamarkups to provide the basis for enhancing, manipulating, and accounting for text. This capability is relevant to typography when the enhancing and manipulation have to do with style.

With the 5.0 browsers, XML will come into its own. The first version of XML became a Web Consortium Recommendation in February, 1998. XSL was still being reviewed as this book went to press. The Web Consortium will make it a standard soon, and you may find yourself creating XSL style sheets sooner than you think. If you learn CSS, which is easy, XSL will be an easier step up. Consequently, the final message of this chapter is that XML and XSL relate directly to Web typography because they represent the future of Web typography. And the future is close at hand.

Part Three

Typography on the Web

Seven

Using HTML for Web Typography

A word processor uses a markup language to add markups to text. The markups determine how the word processor will structure, display, and print the text. The markups stay proprietary; that is, they are invented and used only by the software vendor that develops a specific word processor. The actual markup process takes place in a WYSIWYG interface and remains transparent to users. Users simply highlight text or headings and execute simple keystrokes or mouse clicks to structure and format the text.

HTML works exactly the same way, with two historical differences. First, HTML is public, not proprietary. Internet standards committees set HTML and related standards for everyone. No one owns HTML. Second, HTML came into widespread use before there were any WYSIWYG authoring programs for it. Hundreds of thousands of people learned to code HTML directly with an ASCII text editor or a simple HTML editor. Today, HTML authoring programs with a WYSIWYG interface abound, and millions of people create HTML documents (Web pages).

A word processor is really just a printed-text *authoring* program, although it is generally not referred to as an authoring program. Thus, word processors and HTML authoring programs have many similarities. In fact, you might ask why Netscape has offered Composer as part of its Communicator suite. Composer is much less robust than HTML authoring programs such as Microsoft's FrontPage or Macromedia's Dreamweaver. Why a simple HTML authoring program instead of a robust one? The answer is that advanced HTML authoring programs are designed to build Web sites, while Composer is intended to be a *word processor* for HTML documents. After all, many Web sites are just one or a few Web pages, not huge sprawling document systems. And now HTML e-mail has appeared on the scene. A word processor approach to HTML document creation makes a lot of sense for many people.

What do you make of Composer's special e-mail version? Again, it is a word processor for HTML e-mail messages. HTML e-mail will predominate as the norm before long, and Composer's e-mail interface makes creating HTML e-mail messages very handy.

Even though Microsoft continues to offer FrontPage with its extended capability for Web site builders, it isn't to be outdone by Netscape. Therefore, Microsoft also offers FrontPage Express, a simple HTML authoring program similar to Netscape's Composer. FrontPage Express and Composer are cyber word processors. They look like word processors; they work like word processors; and they *are* word processors. This will become more apparent as HTML e-mail catches on and everyone puts a few Web pages on the Web.

Like the proprietary markup languages of word processors, HTML includes both structuring and display capabilities for formatting online text. As Chapter 6 informs you, structuring and displaying are better kept separate than rolled into one process. Regardless, structure and display have been combined in HTML, and you can use HTML to style Web pages as well as to structure them. Some examples of structure markups with corresponding style:

<p>	Defines a paragraph (normal size type).
<h3>	Defines a third-level heading (2 points larger than normal type).
<ul>	Defines an unnumbered list (normal type with bullets).

Both Composer and FrontPage Express (and many other HTML authoring programs) do an excellent of structuring, typesetting, and laying out Web pages. You can use them like word processors. They make HTML typography easy.

Who Do You Want to Satisfy Today?

Before you can do anything, you must ask yourself, "Who do I want to satisfy?" If you want to satisfy everyone, you have a big job ahead. There are still people out there using the following browsers:

Lynx (Text only)

Mosaic

Cello

Emissary

Accent (Multilanguage)

Netscape 2.0

Netscape 3.0

IE 3.0

Netscape 4.0

IE 4.0

And many more. Will you attempt to accommodate them all? It might make more sense to play the statistics; that is, cater your Web site to the majority of Web surfers. With this approach, you can limit yourself to just a few Web browsers and require other browser users to upgrade to see your Web site in all its grandeur. It seems harsh, but there's just too much divergence out there in small numbers. If you accommodate just the last five browsers listed, as many webmasters do, you'll cover probably over 90 percent of the market. In fact, some industry experts believe that the 4.0 browsers will have an 80 percent market penetration by the summer of 1998.

This book covers technology only available in the last two browsers listed, which clearly do not cover the total market yet. This might be a little misleading, however. Many corporate employees still use Netscape 2.0. As corporate software replacement cycles roll around, many corporate employees will be upgraded to Netscape 4.0 or Microsoft 4.0 which provide the capability for improved Web typography. Windows 98 includes the Microsoft 4.0 browser. Additionally, the 4.0 browsers offer many advanced capabilities that businesses will find compelling. Thus, the market share for these advanced browsers will grow quickly.

In any event, you may want to follow good typesetting practices using normal HTML as outlined in Part Three of this book. This is particularly important should you choose not to take advantage of CSS immediately. With that in mind, this book covers *only* the tags that *both* Netscape and Microsoft browsers use. It's difficult to keep track of the Netscape/Microsoft statistics regarding the respective market shares of the browsers. They come from different sources, and they conflict. Clearly, both browsers together dominate the market, and most webmasters make the effort to accommodate both.

The Markups

The HTML markups (tags) provide typesetting and layout capability that, while inadequate for topnotch publishing, are nonetheless reasonably robust. This section will comment on each tag that's significant to layout and typesetting, focusing primarily on its relationship to typography. This chapter features only characteristics common to both Netscape and Microsoft browsers. See the Netscape *HTML Reference Guide* and the Microsoft *Author's Guide and HTML Reference* for additional tags, attributes, and values unique to the respective browsers. This summary is based on the 4.0 versions of the browsers.

Keep in mind that an objective summary of HTML markups would look much different than the one offered by this chapter. This chapter is slanted toward typographic use of the markups and for the most part ignores other perfectly legitimate uses for HTML markups.

The word *Deprecated* after a markup means it is on the way out and will become obsolete soon. The word *Obsolete* means that the browsers may no longer support it. The following markups have been deprecated because CSS now replaces their

functions. Does that mean you shouldn't use them? Not necessarily. Use them as long as current browsers still support
them and as long as you want to support earlier browsers that
cannot handle CSS.

Note that the purpose of this list is not to provide an HTML
primer. It is to alert you to the HTML tags relevant to typography and to make comments regarding their use for typography. Please refer to the requisite books or HTML guides for
precise instructions on using these tags.

<!-- -->

This tag encloses text that will *not* display in the Web page. You
can use this for comments. Be generous in writing comments
for yourself for uncommon typographical arrangements that
you have created. It will help during revisions. Where you
work with others, comments can prevent wasted time and
frustration for everyone.

Talk about dynamic text! Web site visitors don't see this
text, but webmasters do (when they code).

<address>

This tag is not recommended for HTML typesetting. It displays
text in a way determined by the browser. It does nothing that
you cannot do with the *<i>* tag (italics) or *<code>* tags
(monospaced typeface). However, this makes a good structure
tag to use with CSS (see Chapter 10), where you can give it
any style and layout specifications you desire. It also acts as a
structure tag to indicate the address of the person creating the
HTML page.

<b>

This changes the text to the bold typestyle and is quite useful.

<basefont> Deprecated

This sets the default size of the base font. It overrides the size
that a browser user sets. If you do not use this tag, the default

—————◦◦◦◦◦—————

<blink> Since IE 4.0 does not recognize this unpopular tag, it does not belong in this chapter. But it provides an opportunity to philosophize. Therefore, I've included it. The question is: Does the *<blink>* tag represent a fourth dimension for typography? The first two dimensions are width and height. The third dimension is color. The fourth dimension is movement. The blink feature just turns the text on and off, but that is a kind of movement. Dynamic HTML (DHTML) with the use of scripts can create much more movement for the HTML elements in a Web page. In other words, it can animate the text. Thus, in a sense the *<blink>* tag symbolizes a fourth dimension for typography: animation (movement). Yes, *<blink>* seems to be universally unpopular, but what it symbolizes is a *new* dimension in typography. Using this fourth dimension has actually been practiced in films and on television for many years. But the Web puts it in the hands of everyone, and that is new.

size is 3 or whatever the browser user sets for the browser. This tag is now deprecated. Consider using CSS instead.

`<big>`

This increases the font size by 1. For instance, if the base font size in the text is 3, this tag increases the text that it encloses to 4.

`<blockquote>`

This tag indents a block of text on both the left and the right, nothing more. This can be handy. Traditional usage for quotes, however, may require also making the text slightly smaller as well.

`<body>`

This tag sets parameters for the visible portion of a Web page. Of particular importance for typography are the following attributes:

background	Background image (tiled).
bgcolor	Background color.
link	Unvisited hyperlink color.
text	Text (foreground) color.
vlink	Visited hyperlink color.

`<br>`

This tag creates a line break without adding a line of space.

The *clear* attribute controls the flow of text around an image:

all	Displays text at the next clear left and right margins.
left	Displays text at the next clear left margin.
right	Displays text at the next clear right margin.

Note that, absent the *clear* attribute, the text displays immediately after the image. For the *left* value, the text displays on the first line that is clear of an image on the left. For the *right* value, the text displays on the first line that is clear of an image on the right. For the *all* value, the text displays on the first line that is clear of an image on both the left and the right.

`<caption>`

This tag specifies the caption for a table. It goes inside the *<table>* tag but not inside the *<td>* or *<tr>* tags. The *align* attribute enables you to display the caption at the *bottom* or *top*. In essence, it's a cell that spans the top or bottom of the table. Where you use the *<table>* tag to actually typeset a tradition-al table (rather than using it for layout control as covered in Chapter 9), you will find the *<caption>* markup handy.

`<center>` *Deprecated*

This tag centers the text and other HTML elements. This is quite handy for titles and headings. When you apply it to a text block, all the lines in the text block become centered. In other words, the text block is ragged left *and* ragged right. If this is not the effect you intend, you might consider *<blockquote>*. Certainly, ragged left/ragged right is difficult to read. The *<center>* tag, of course, is one of the most well-used tags for Web typography, and you can use it within other tags. This tag is now deprecated. Consider using CSS instead.

`<cite>`

This tag is not recommended for HTML typesetting. It displays text in a way determined by the browser. It does nothing that you cannot do with the *<i>* tag (italics) or *<code>* tags (monospaced typeface). However, this makes a good structure tag to use with CSS (see Chapter 10), where you can give it any style and layout specifications you desire.

`<code>`

This tag sets enclosed text in a plain text monospaced typeface to simulate computer code. This is handy for use within a text block. This tag does not preserve formatting as does the *<pre>*

tag. For entire text blocks of plain text, you may find the *<pre>* tag more useful, particularly where you want to preserve spacing and line breaks. Use *<pre>* for long sections of code where you want to preserve the formatting.

<dd>

This tag specifies a glossary definition in a list of definitions. You use this with the *<dl>* and *<dt>* tags. The text marked by this tag displays in a left-indented paragraph with no line space between the preceding or succeeding *<dt>* paragraphs. See the *<dt>* tag for further information.

Use the *<dl>* and *<dd>* tags to create an unbulleted and unnumbered list. However, the list items won't have a line space between them. If you want the line space, add the *<p>* tag (see Figure 7.1).

You can also use *<dd>* to create a left margin for text. Unfortunately, there is no similar way with basic HTML to create a corresponding right margin. But one margin may be better than none. Use *<dd>* and *<blockquote>* to create a large margin on the left and a small margin on the right—not symmetrical, but appropriate for many uses (see Figure 7.2). In any event, both tables and CSS provide you with the capability to create left and right margins, too.

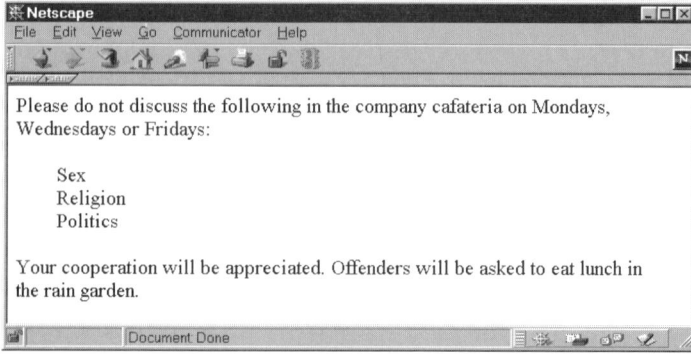

Figure 7.1 *Unbulleted and unnumbered list using the* <dl>, <dd>, *and* <p> *tags.*

`<dir>` *Deprecated*

This tag creates a bulleted directory list, supposedly with limited (20 characters) list items. You use the *<li>* tag to indicate the list items. This seems to be a redundant tag to the *<ul>* tag.

`<div>`

This tag, together with the *align* attribute, encloses a division of a Web page for the purpose of aligning the paragraphs and graphics in bulk within the division. You can use this where a division of the Web page has a different alignment for paragraphs than the main body of the Web page. It's also good for modular construction (covered in Chapter 9).

`<dl>`

This tag encloses a definition list. You use this with the *<dt>* and *<dd>* tags. The *<dl>* starts the list. The *<dt>* tag indicates the term to be defined, and the *<dd>* tag indicates the glossary definition of the term. The *<dl>* tag and the *<dt>* tag

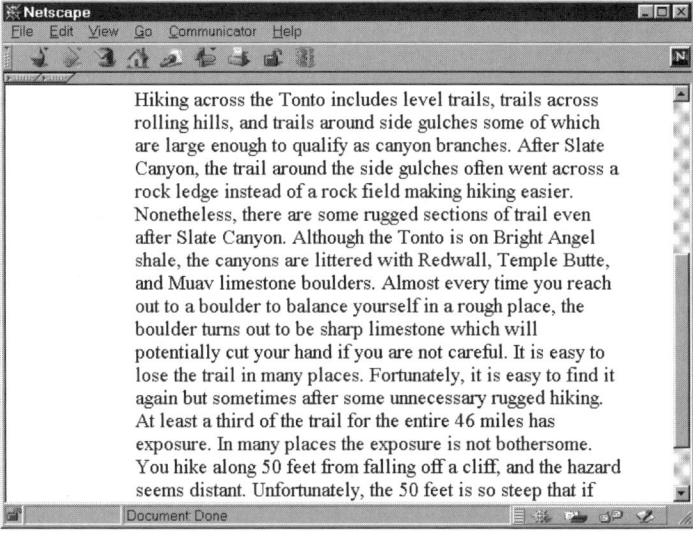

Figure 7.2 *Creating margins with* <dd> *and* <blockquote> *tags.*

used together do not display an indentation. Only the *<dd>* tag will display the text indented.

Use the *<dl>* and *<dd>* tags to create an unnumbered unbulleted list (see Figure 7.1).

The *<dl>* tag and the *<dd>* tag used together will walk an HTLM element across the Web page. This proves handy for positioning (see Figure 7.3).

<dt>

This tag designates a term to be defined. It displays flush left. Use the *<dd>* tag to indicate the glossary definition of the term which will display left-indented on the next line.

<em>

This tag is not recommended for HTML typesetting. It displays text in a way determined by the browser. It does nothing that you cannot do with the *<i>* tag (italics) or *<code>* tags (monospaced typeface). However, this makes a good structure tag to use with CSS (see Chapter 10), where you can give it any style and layout specifications you desire.

Figure 7.3 *Positioning an element with the <dl> and <dd> tags.*

`<font>` *Deprecated*

This tag enables you to change the typeface, size, and color of the enclosed text. This overrides the browser default, the *<basefont>* tag, and browser user settings. Nonetheless, if the operating system on the computer displaying the Web page does not have the requisite fonts to display the typeface specified, using this tag will have no effect for that computer. Note that you must use this tag to use TrueDoc (Netscape) or font embedding (Microsoft) covered in later chapters. The attributes for this tag are straightforward:

color	Text color. This adds a third dimension (after width and height) to typography.
face	Font expressed as a typeface and typestyle.
size	Text size on the 1–7 size scale. Place a + or - in front to change from the base font size.

This tag is now deprecated. Consider using CSS instead.

`<form>`

This tag creates a form. Creating forms is beyond the scope of this book. Many of the typography techniques work well with the general use of forms, but the text displayed when a user fills out forms that you have created or the text displayed for your form menus may be beyond your control. Also, note that forms do not nest (i.e., you can't have a form within a form), but you can place more than one form on a Web page.

`<frame>`

This tag creates an independent Web page that locates inside a framework (*frameset*) with other independent Web pages. The independent pages scroll separately. Does it add a valuable new fourth dimension to Web typography to have different portions of a Web page display acting independently? Yes and no. The answer is yes if readability is enhanced. The answer is no if the scheme that you use does not enhance readability.

Tables Many webmasters refuse to use frames. They feel they can achieve the same effect using tables instead, which makes navigation easier for webmasters and Web site visitors alike.

Frames come with default borders. However, you can render the borders invisible. A thin nonscrolling frame across the top or bottom (of the remainder of the Web page) with an invisible border makes a useful running head or running foot much like a chapter title in a book. This can be a valuable addition to a long Web page that scrolls through many screens. Think of this as a use that simulates a traditional typesetting practice effectively. Other uses have been invented or will be invented that will enhance and enlarge traditional typesetting practices. Imitate what others do, keep an open mind, and experiment. But also realize that there is a downside to using frames.

Many uses of frames on the Web are awkward and confusing to Web site visitors. Where this is the case, they do not enhance readability or effective communication. Avoid extravagant and complex uses of frames. Such uses may be functional and logical (and even structurally pleasing to their inventors), but if Web site visitors cannot use such frame schemes efficiently and effectively, what good are they? When in doubt, avoid frames and find a different way to do what you intended to do with frames.

Many Web sites use frames for running heads or foots that feature a navigation control (see Figure 7.4). Such controls as strips down the left or right side of the Web page (running side?) instead of the head or foot are popular too. These often feature indexes which make good navigational devices. In many cases, a running head, foot, or side provides a real asset to navigation if it is simple, easy to understand, and readable. If not, you should think about using a device other than frames to aid navigation. Navigation aids are an important part of Web typography, even if expressed in an image rather than in type. Frames enable new navigational schemes for reading digital text, but they're only valuable if they help rather than hinder reading.

The *<frame>* tag must be used within the *<frameset>* tag to set up frames within a Web page. The relevant attributes for *<frame>* follow:

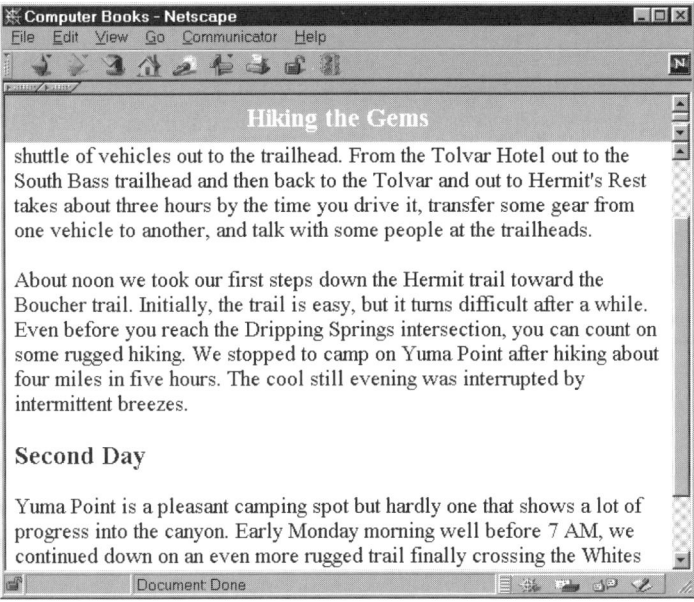

Figure 7.4 *Running head using frames.*

align	Aligns the frame at the top, bottom, left side, right side, or center.
bordercolor	Sets the frame border color.
frameborder	Sets the border to be visible or invisible.
marginheigtht	Sets the frame margin (top and bottom) in pixels.
marginwidth	Sets the frame margin (left and right) in pixels.
scrolling	Sets the frame to scroll or not to scroll.
src	Sets the URL of the frame.

⟨frameset⟩

This tag encloses the frames as defined individually by the ⟨frame⟩ tag. The ⟨frameset⟩ tag defines the Web page while the ⟨frame⟩ tag defines each framed portion of the Web page.

The attributes for the *<frameset>* tag are similar to the *<frame>* tag:

border	Sets the size of frame borders (zero = no border).
bordercolor	Sets frame's border color.
frameborder	Sets the border to be visible or invisible.
cols	Sets width of each vertical frame.
rows	Sets height of each horizontal frame.

You can nest *<frameset>* (have a frame set within a frame set). You can express the value for the columns (cols) and rows in pixels (absolute) or percentages (relative and resizable). This scheme provides unlimited combinations of frames within one Web document.

Keep in mind that the frame set itself and the individual frames are each individual HTML documents.

`<h1>...<h6>`

These tags are for headings. The tags *<h1>*, *<h2>*, and *<h3>* are quite useful for typesetting. The remainder are not very useful, because due to their small size, you're never quite sure how they will work in relation to text blocks. For subheads below *<h3>*, you might feel more in control if you use regular type in bold instead of *h4* and in italics instead of *h5*. Another strategy is to assign *<h4>*, *<h5>*, and *<h6>* your own style using CSS (see Chapter 10).

These headings are pretty plain, right? Plain or not, don't underestimate the usefulness of the headings 1–3. They are simple, elegant, and functional. And you can make them bold where appropriate (i.e., add the *<b>* tag).

`<hr>`

This tag generates a horizontal rule. Although rules may be appropriate in certain situations in general typography, because they have been available in HTML since the beginning, they have been overused. Use rules where they are a rational part of an overall layout and design. Otherwise, don't use them. Likewise, don't feel that they have to be part of every page design just because they are widely used on the Web. Use them sparingly and only in situations where they make sense. You can use the attributes for the *<hr>* tag to control thickness, length, color, and shading. You can also create your own decorator rules as GIFs, but use decorator rules sparingly too.

<i>

This tag encloses italic text. The *<i>* tag is quite useful. Use it for all appropriate purposes, including emphasis within text blocks. The problem with using italics on the Web, however, is that they don't render as well as regular type due to their slanted nature. Therefore, avoid using them for text blocks on the Web, because they are more difficult to read. Nonetheless, keep in mind that new Web typographic technology and greater resolution in monitors will eventually renders italics much better. When this is the case, you can safely use them for text blocks. Assuming high resolution, for many typefaces italics are as readable as normal text (see Chapter 8).

<img>

This tag inserts an image into a Web page. It is important to understand how the image can align with the text. Use the *align* attribute with the following values:

left	Aligns image with left margin.
right	Aligns image with right margin.

The left and right values locate an image to the left or right side of the Web page and enable the text to wrap around it. The remainder of the attributes place the image in relation to the line of text (see Figure 7.5).

top	Aligns top of image with top of tallest item in line.
absmiddle	Aligns middle of image with the middle of the text.
absbottom	Aligns bottom of image with bottom of lowest item in line.
texttop	Aligns top of image with top of tallest text in line.
middle	Aligns middle of image with baseline of text.
baseline	Aligns bottom of image with baseline of text.
bottom	Aligns bottom of image with baseline of text.

Note that the other alignments allow the image's top or bottom, or both, to project above or below the line of text. For instance, an image aligned with the *top* value aligns the top of the image with the top of the tallest item in the line. That makes for a neat and clean placement at the top of the line, but what about the bottom? The image, if large enough, will project well below the bottom of the line, creating an abnormally large space between that line and the succeeding line. In other words, the *align* attribute aligns the image only to the line that the image occupies, not to the preceding or succeeding lines.

Keep in mind that, when you use the <*img*> tag with the <*br*> tag and its *clear* attribute, you can get some confusing combinations regarding the relationship of the image to the

Figure 7.5 *Netscape Composer choices for image placement.*

text. When using these two tags together, you should experiment to see what works with what effects.

The *<img>* tag also has other handy attributes for creating space between an image and the text:

border	Sets width of the border. If you use the image as a hyperlink, the border has a color (unvisited) that changes to another color (visited) when a Web site visitor uses the hyperlink.
hspace	Sets the width of space on the top and bottom of an image.
vspace	Sets the width of space on the left and right of an image.

Allow the default *border* attribute only where it is compellingly necessary to advertise that the image is a hyperlink. Otherwise, make sure that this attribute is set to zero for images that are hyperlinks. Most Web site visitors will suspect when an image is a hyperlink and run their mouse over it to find out. The colored border is unsightly. Use the *hspace* and *vspace* attributes to create appropriate space between an image and the surrounding text.

<kbd>

This tag is not recommended for HTML typesetting. It displays text in a way determined by the browser. It does nothing that you cannot do with the *<i>* tag (italics) or *<code>* tags (monospaced typeface). However, this makes a good structure tag to use with CSS (see Chapter 10), where you can give it any style and layout specifications you desire.

<li>

This tag indicates an item in a list. You can use it with *<dir>*, *<dl>*, *<menu>*, *<ol>*, and *<ul>*. The attributes *type* and *value* used with these tags give some special character to the

<li> tag. The values for the *type* attribute used with the *<li>* tag follow:

disc	Specifies a bullet.
circle	Specifies a hollow bullet.
square	Specifies a square bullet.
A	Specifies uppercase letters.
a	Specifies lowercase letters.
I	Specifies uppercase Roman numerals.
i	Specifies lowercase Roman numerals.
1	Specifies numbers.

The value for the *value* attribute is the starting number for an item in a numbered (ordered) list. Taken together with the other list tags, the *<li>* tag is very handy for typesetting.

`<menu>` Deprecated

This tag is not recommended. It duplicates the *<ul>* tag. However, this makes a good structure tag to use with CSS (see Chapter 10), where you can give it any style and layout specifications you desire.

`<nobr>`

This tag turns off line breaking. It's handy for a line of text that should not be broken. For a large block of text, this enables your Web site visitors to scroll *right* from here to eternity. Thus, it's very handy for situations where you don't want people to read the text. This display technique is difficult to duplicate in print except with a horizontal banner printed by a computer printer.

`<noframes>`

This tag encloses content that displays as an alternative to a frames scheme, and it goes inside the *<frameset>* tag. Only Web site visitors using browsers without frames capability will see the content. Some Web site visitors still use older browsers, so this is a tag that you should consider using. Note that you can include an *entire* alternative Web page using the *<noframes>* tag (i.e., you can include more than just a sentence or two).

`<ol>`

This tag indicates an ordered (numbered) list. Use the *<li>* tag with this. The *type* attribute enables several numbering schemes. The *value* attribute enables a starting number greater than 1.

The values for the *type* attribute follow:

A	Specifies uppercase letters.
a	Specifies lowercase letters.
I	Specifies uppercase Roman numerals.
i	Specifies lowercase Roman numerals.
1	Specifies numbers.

`<p>`

This tag indicates a paragraph. That is, it breaks the text and adds a line of space before the next text block. It does not require an end tag. It is, of course, one of the most well-used markups. It has an *align* attribute that enables you to set a flush left, flush right, or a centered (ragged left and right) paragraph.

You can get away with using the *<p>* tag for HTML without always putting it at the front of paragraphs. But you cannot do so for use with CSS. Make sure you use the *<p>* at the beginning of each paragraph.

This tag is a problem waiting to happen. Everyone has used it without an end tag. That works for HTML. However, it will not work for XML. For XML, you will need to use the *</p>* tag also.

`<plaintext>` *Obsolete*

This tag renders the text after the tag into a plain text monospaced typeface and *turns off* the reading of all HTML tags. The *remainder* of the Web page after the tag will be in plain text with all HTML tags ignored by the browser. This has limited use. This tag is now obsolete. Use *<pre>* instead.

`<pre>`

This tag displays the text that it encloses into a plain text monospaced typeface while preserving the original layout, including the original spacing and line breaking. The reading of HTML tags is not turned off. Consequently, you need to be careful about any HTML tags included in the plain text, because the browser will read them. Use special symbols for characters that have a meaning in HTML (e.g., substitute *&lt* for the *<* symbol). The *<pre>* tag creates a stand-alone paragraph with a line space before and after.

Use the *<pre>* tag to create line spacing. As you know, HTML will read one *<p>* tag or 30 *<p>* tags as one line space. But HTML will faithfully render the space enclosed by the *<pre>* tag.

`<s> Deprecated`

This tag is the same as *<strike>*.

`<samp>`

This tag is not recommended for HTML typesetting. It displays text in a way determined by the browser. It does nothing that you cannot do with the *<i>* tag (italics) or *<code>* tags (monospaced typeface). However, this makes a good structure tag to use with CSS (see Chapter 10), where you can give it any style and layout specifications you desire. Use *<code>* instead.

`<small>`

This tag reduces the text that it encloses to a type size one size smaller than the default size. It's the opposite of the *<big>* tag. The *<small>* tag can be handy in appropriate situations such as reducing the size of the text in a block quote.

`<span>`

This tag designates any piece of text for styling. Use the *style* attribute to apply the styling. This proves handy for use with CSS. You can also use it for modular construction, as outlined in Chapter 9. Keep this tag in mind.

`<strike>` *Deprecated*

This tag enables you to designate some text as being struck out. This tag is now deprecated. Consider using CSS instead.

`<strong>`

This tag is not recommended for HTML typesetting. It displays text in a way determined by the browser. It does nothing that you cannot do with the *<i>* tag (italics) or *<code>* tags (monospaced typeface). However, this makes a good structure tag to use with CSS (see Chapter 10), where you can give it any style and layout specifications you desire.

`<sub>`

The *<sub>* tag displays the enclosed characters or text as a subscript below baseline and in a smaller type size. This is handy and can give your typesetting a professional look where used appropriately, such as for chemical notation.

`<sup>`

The *<sup>* tag displays the enclosed characters or text as a superscript above baseline and in a smaller type size. This is handy and can give your typesetting a professional look where used appropriately, such as for mathematical notation.

`<table>`

This tag, together with the *<td>* and *<tr>* tags, defines a table. The *<table>* is very useful for putting tables into a Web page, a process that, without the *<table>* tag, is very painful. The *<td>* and *<tr>* tags go inside the *<table>* tag. Because

Chapter 9 covers the use of the *<table>* tag extensively for layout, it is not discussed here. Nonetheless, if you need to put a table into a Web page, the straightforward use of this tag does a good job.

`<td>`

The *<td>* tag indicates table data; that is, a table cell (single column entry). For instance, there are likely to be several column entries or more for each table row. The *<td>* tag goes inside the table row *<tr>* tag.

`<th>`

This tag goes inside the *<table>* tag and inside a *<tr>* tag and displays a table cell wherein the text is in bold. Use it for column headings.

`<tr>`

This tag goes inside the *<table>* tag and indicates a table row. The table data cells, as defined by the *<td>* tags, go inside the *<tr>* tag. The *<tr>* tags go inside the <table> tag.

`<tt>`

This tag is not recommended for HTML typesetting. It displays text in a way determined by the browser. It does nothing that you cannot do with the *<i>* tag (italics) or *<code>* tags (monospaced typeface). However, this makes a good structure tag to use with CSS (see Chapter 10), where you can give it any style and layout specifications you desire.

`<u>` *Deprecated*

This tag puts a line under the text that it encloses. Use it for underlining. Remember that underlining is not appropriate for very many uses in polished typesetting. This tag is now deprecated. Use CSS instead for underlining.

Beyond its limited use, however, underlining can cause confusion for Web browser users. Underlining designates hyperlinks in many Web browsers unless users turn off the hyperlink underlining. Consequently, underlining has taken on a new significance in Web publishing that it did not have before in print publishing. For this reason alone, you should avoid its use. It has the potential to cause much confusion.

`<ul>`

Use this tag for unnumbered (unordered) lists. Use the *<li>* tag to designate list entries. The values for the *type* attribute follow:

disc	Specifies a bullet.
circle	Specifies a hollow bullet.
square	Specifies a square bullet.

The default is *disc*. If you want a line space between the list entries, you will have to use the *<p>* tag. There is no provision in the *<ul>* tag for a bulletless list. Use *<dl>* and *<dd>* instead for a bulletless list.

`<wbr>`

This tag used inside the *<nbr>* tag suggests a point at which the line can break if the browser window gets too small. At some point where a browser window is adjusted to a small size by a browser user, the browser will decide to put the *<wbr>* into effect and break the line. Otherwise, the *<wbr>* has no effect. This is the kind of capability that's handy to have, but one that you probably won't use very often.

`<xmp>` `Obsolete`

This tag displays the text that it encloses into a plain text monospaced typeface, while preserving the original layout, including the original spacing and line breaking. The reading of HTML tags is *turned off* as it is for the *<plaintext>* tag. Unlike the *<plaintext>* tag, it doesn't turn off the reading of HTML tags for the remainder of the document after the end tag,

</*xmp*>. The <*xmp*> tag creates a stand-alone paragraph with a line space before and after. This tag is now obsolete. Use <*pre*> instead.

Universal Attributes

The new universal attributes include *class* which specifies a CSS class, *lang* which indicates a language, *id* which can act as an anchor or specify a style, and *style* which specifies a style. You can use *style* to place a mini style sheet right in the text of a Web page (see Chapter 10).

HTML Groups

Certain groups of tags must be considered together to understand their function. This section offers some groupings to assist you in using HTML more adroitly for typesetting.

Plain Text

HTML offers several ways to display plain text; that is, text typeset in a monospaced typeface (see Table 7.1). You can ignore all but two of these.

Table 7.1 *Plain Text in HTML*

	Read HTML?	Format Preserved?	Monospaced?	Use?
<*code*>	Yes	No	Yes	Yes
<*kbd*>	Yes	No	Yes	Ignore
<*plaintext*>	No	No	Yes	Obsolete
<*pre*>	Yes	Yes	Yes	Yes
<*samp*>	Yes	No	Yes	Ignore
<*tt*>	Yes	No	Yes	Ignore
<*xmp*>	No	Yes	Yes	Obsolete

Why do you need all these? You don't. Use *<code>* and ignore *<kdb>*, *<samp>*, and *<tt>*. Use *<code>* to change text within an existing paragraph. The tags that you ignore (don't use), however, may come in handy for use with CSS (see Chapter 10).

Use *<pre>* for long sections of code where you want to preserve the formatting. Use also for vertical spacing.

Lists

You can ignore the deprecated tags:

<dl>	Definition list.
<dt>	Term list item for *<dl>*.
<dd>	Definition list item for *<dl>*.
<dir>	Bulleted list for short list items (20 characters maximum). Deprecated.
<menu>	Bulleted list for one-line list items. Deprecated.
<ol>	Ordered list.
<ul>	Unordered (bulleted) list.
<li>	List item for *<dir>*, *<menu>*, *<ol>*, and *<ul>*.

Ignore the *<dir>* and *<menu>* tags. Use the *<ul>* tag instead. The combination of *<dl>* and *<dd>* will display a definition list item with an indent but without a number or bullet. This can be handy.

Text Treatments

You can ignore several text treatment tags:

<address>	Ignore. Use something else.
<b>	Valuable for typesetting bold.
<big>	Occasionally useful for increasing the type size.

<*blockquote*>	Valuable for typesetting text blocks indented on both sides.
<*cite*>	Ignore. Use <i> instead.
<*em*>	Ignore. Use <i> instead.
<*i*>	Valuable for typesetting italic.
<*s*>	Same as <strike>. Deprecated.
<*small*>	Occasionally useful for decreasing the text size.
<*strike*>	Specialized typesetting (e.g., editing projects). Deprecated.
<*strong*>	Ignore. Use <i> instead.
<*sub*>	Valuable for typesetting superscripts.
<*sup*>	Valuable for typesetting subscripts.
<*u*>	Underlining. Deprecated.

As you can see, there are four tags that you can ignore: <*address*>, <*cite*>, <*em*>, and <*strong*>. Note also that <*s*> and <*strike*> are deprecated.

Global Settings

These tags establish global defaults.

<*basefont*>	Sets the default font. Deprecated.
<*body*>	Sets the default background and text colors.
<*div*>	Sets the alignment for a division of text.
<*font*>	Overrides the <*basefont*> font and overrides the <*body*> text colors. Deprecated.

These are time-savers for typography. Note, however, that <*basefont*> and <*font*> are deprecated. Consider using CSS instead.

More Text Controls

These text controls can be handy:

* *	Breaks line.
<center>	Centers text. Deprecated.
<hr>	Adds horizontal rule.
<nobr>	Prevents line breaks.
<p>	Breaks line and adds line space. Use at beginning of paragraph.
<pre>	Adds line spacing.
<wbr>	Adds "soft" line break within the *<nobr>* tag.
<xmp>	Adds line spacing. Obsolete.

Note that *<center>* is deprecated, and *<xmp>* is obsolete.

Columns

Columns don't work so well for the Web, unless you keep them very short. Otherwise, Web site visitors must scroll down, and then scroll up and down again. However, you may find limited use for them, particularly if you keep them short.

Practical Considerations

The following are some practical considerations sometimes overlooked by Web developers.

Resolution

There are three popular digital screen resolutions (four if you add NetTV).

544 × 378	NetTV.
640 × 480	Old standard.

800×600	Current standard.
1024×768	For large monitors (17+ inches).

Less Than Full Most display size considerations *assume that the browser is opened to its fullest size.* In fact, a browser user often uses his or her browser in a window that's smaller than the browser's full display. This makes it doubly difficult to predict the display sizes that Web site visitors use.

These numbers indicate pixel dimensions (see Figure 7.6). Consequently, a graphic 700×200 that fits nicely inside a 800×600 display will be only partially visible inside a 640×480 display. NetTV shrinks graphics up to 10 percent.

Digital type size is tied to pixel dimensions. For instance, 12-point New Century Schoolbook is visibly larger on the same monitor in a 640×480 display than in a 1024×768 display. This makes it difficult to choose fonts and font sizes that will display identically in all screen resolutions. You will have to experiment to find fonts and font sizes that make an optimal presentation in all resolutions.

Keep in mind that NetTVs resize the fonts, the images, the entire display, or all three. It's difficult to predict how a Web page will display until you experiment and get some experience.

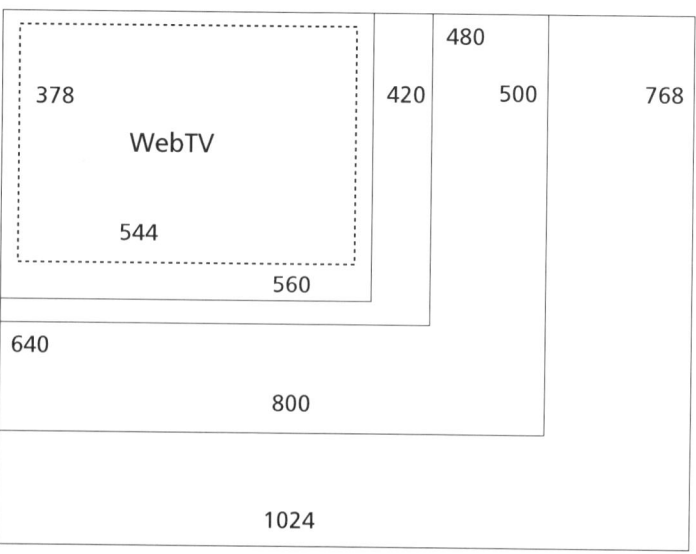

Figure 7.6 *Screen resolutions.*

Text Wrapping

Is text wrapping a bane or benefit for Web typographers? With text wrapping, you never know how the text will display. The wrap depends on the display resolution and whether the browser is opened to a full display or is in a smaller window. This is not a comfortable situation for typographers who like to be precise.

Whether you like it or not, text wrapping is the technology that makes the Web work for a variety of computers and computer monitors. The text wraps neatly at the edge of the browser and will adapt to any size of browser window. Thus, it is a real benefit because it makes the Web work for everyone. The challenge is to minimize the impact of text wrapping on Web typesetting and layout.

Wrapping text around images complicates Web page layout considerably. You need to be very careful when you do this. The text wrapping around images is always an area of the Web page that you will want to check in your testing. The image *<img>* section earlier in this chapter gives you an idea of how text wrapping works with images.

Perhaps a viable approach is to avoid wrapping text around images wherever possible. Use text blocks that are above, below, or adjacent to images but that do not wrap around the images. With the use of the *<table>* tag covered in Chapter 9, you can put text adjacent to images without wrapping them.

Background and Foreground (Text) Colors

Color presents a problem for Web publishers. Black on white may not be the optimal color. The following considerations make color a complex and even emotional issue:

- Some people are more sensitive to light than others. Those who are more sensitive will have a difficult time reading blocks on pure white comfortably.

- People's monitor adjustments vary greatly. Contrast and brightness may be adjusted high or low. Some people may not even know how to adjust their monitors, or may set them once and never change them.

- People have different hardware color capability. Many have only 8-bit (256 colors) color cards. Others have 16-bit (64,000 colors) or 24-bit (16,000,000 colors) color cards.

- White, the most widely used background for Web publishing, may be set as pure white, off white, dirty white, or very light gray, making casual user surveys inconclusive.

- People vary in their ability to use software. Some adjust the color schemes for their operating systems. Others do not know how to do so. Some change the default fonts. Others do not know how to do so. Some set the font size larger or smaller. Others do not change the default.

- Some people accept the default black on white as being desirable because it simulates paper. Others experiment to find more comfortable color settings. Simulating paper may not provide optimal readability.

- Some people never read for more than a short time on a monitor. Others must work all day on a monitor.

- Many people find that reading on a monitor causes eye-strain or fatigue. Others can work endlessly without experiencing discomfort.

- The cultural component of color is a subject covered in countless psychology, anthropology, and other nondigital books.

It is my opinion that Web publishers should not use white as a background. With CRTs blasting out light, white seems too likely to cause eyestrain and discomfort for reading for many people. It seems technically safer to use black type with a culturally neutral light color for the background such as cream, light gray, mint green, light turquoise, or beige. Other light colors such as pastel rose, fuchsia, or mauve may be unsuitable choices for general use but OK for certain specialized uses. Cultural choices are often more difficult to make than technical choices. Some medium and medium-light colors make good background colors for reading, too, particularly for long documents. Microsoft offers a variety of ergonomic color in its operating system selections that Web publishers might consider emulating. (Microsoft Word also offers an ergonomic choice of dark blue with white text as an alternative to the default Windows colors.) But it is best to use browser-safe colors (00, 33, 66, 99, cc, ff—as mentioned in Chapter 10). Try the 6x6x6 Color Cube (http://www.fleetingimage.com/wij/color/index.html) for more information on browser-safe color combinations, including many examples of text/background combinations. Regardless of what colors you choose to use for publishing, the text and background colors must have maximum contrast.

Black backgrounds are popular for NetTV gateway Web sites such as those operated by WebTV and NetChannel where readability needs help on the television screen (see Chapter 17). Black backgrounds seem a little boring and oppressive in large doses, yet they illustrate that even dark backgrounds can work well on a CRT for television viewing.

Perhaps when active matrix LCD flat panel monitors become the norm (less light blasting out), white backgrounds will present less risk of eyestrain and fatigue. But for now, avoid them. Is it possible for white to be an ergonomic background color on a CRT? Sure. With proper hardware and software settings, many people use it comfortably. Unfortunately, as a publisher, you have no control over some of the variables, and light colors seem safer than white.

Almost any background color is better than a background graphic. Avoid graphics or tiled graphics in the background. They inhibit readability tremendously. In most cases, text blocks over a graphic background are illegible. In a few cases where the background graphic is very faint and washed out, readability may prove acceptable.

Type and type sizes also factor into the choice of color combinations. Poorly defined type and small type both require

Experiment You will find bad advice—even from good typographers—and plenty of bad examples on the Web regarding background and text colors. Consequently, you may grow to distrust everyone's advice. Experiment with yourself as the subject by reading long passages of text (e.g., 2,000 words or more) in your word processor where you can control the background and text colors as well as the text typefaces easily. Take your time. Try a lot of things. Eventually, try some very long text passages (10,000 words). Reach your own conclusions. But always remember that it's not solely a matter of taste. It's a matter of readability. Even the renowned typographer Jan Tschichold (1902–1974) in his book *The Form of the Book*, Hartley & Marks, 1991, argued that books should be printed on natural colored paper (an écru color) rather than on stark white paper, because white is hard on the eyes.

greater contrast to be readable. If you're dead set on using your favorite typestyle and it happens to have a weak screen definition, you may have to use black on white to make it readable at all.

Fonts

Keep in mind that Web site visitors cannot use fonts that they do not have. Your only options for fonts are Times New Roman (Times), Arial (Helvetica), and Courier and the Mac fonts. Although these are excellent fonts in every way, they are boring due to overuse.

Imagelike Page Objects

Although they are not covered in this book, page objects such as Java applets and media players should be treated as images. You need to size them, add space around them, and place them properly in the Web page. The HTML for embedding them in Web pages provides you with the capability to do so with attributes similar to the *<img>* tag attributes. You want to be especially careful that text does not butt up against such objects so closely as to be unreadable.

Extended Character Set

An extended character set window such as that found in a typical HTML editor or authoring program will enable you to insert the special characters found in the extended character set. The characters you use in the extended character set appear in their normal form on the screen in a Web browser but in code in the HTML file. HTML has two codes for each standard extended character, the standard code and the numerical code. Outside the standard codes, the only way you can use an extended character is to specify the character's numerical code using the & code, but the numerical code works only for Windows.

Extra characters can make your printed page look more professional. You simply look up the character you need in the extended character set window and click on the character or enter the proper combination of keystrokes (see Figure 7.7).

For the Web, use the & code. For instance, use the HTML extended character code &*copy*; or &*#169*; for the copyright symbol ©. Or, pop up the Web extended character set window in your Web editor and select the character that you want to use.

You will find the extended characters for Windows and Mac in Appendix 1, together with the HTML extended character set.

Printing Web Pages

Did you ever notice that many Web publishers use a white background with small black text? What are they thinking? Small text is difficult to read on the screen. Probably what they

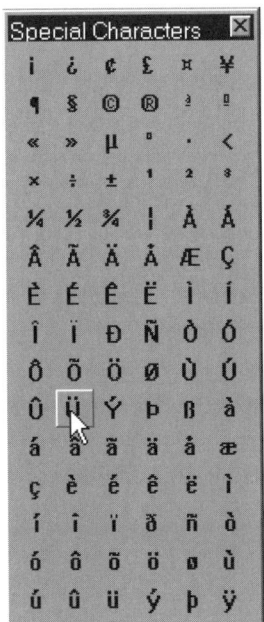

Figure 7.7 *Extended character set window for the Web in HoTMetaL Pro 4.0.*

Common Extended Characters for the Web Take a look at a few of the extended characters you may find useful.

- Use three fractions: one-quarter (&*frac14*; or &*#188*;), one-half (&*frac12*; or &*#189*;), and three-quarters (&*frac34*; or &*#190*;).
- Both the registered trademark sign (&*reg*; or &*#174*;) and the copyright sign (&*copy*; or &*#169*;) are available.
- Use the multiplication (&*times*; or &*#215*;) and division (&*divide*; or &*#247*;) signs.
- How about using the acute accent for the e in cafe: café (&*eacute*; or &*#233*;).
- One useful character missing from the standard code is the em dash: —. Although the em dash is essential for writing and typesetting, you may not be able to use it without writing the numerical code for it: &*#151*; however, the numerical code will not work for the Mac.

think is that Web site visitors will print the Web pages on their laser printers rather than read them on the screen. If so, black on white provides the best contrast for printing, and small type (e.g., 10 points) provides a normal magazinelike reading environment. In fact, the Web, when combined with a high-resolution computer printer, makes a pretty good printing medium. It prints sharp text (assuming high-quality fonts) and even sharp graphics. Printers with a small amount of RAM sometimes have trouble handling the graphics, but on the whole, the Web handles printing surprisingly well.

Yet, Web printing presents several problems. First, the displays that are best for reading on the screen (light color and larger type) may not print well. The displays that print well may not be very readable on the screen. You have to make a choice. Second, you may have a difficult time knowing where the page breaks will be without experimenting. Third, you are relegated to an 8.5 × 11 page. That's what people use in their printers, and that's how they will print Web pages. In the future, more control over printing is promised by the Web Consortium, and CSS 2 delivers on that promise (see Chapter 11). Nonetheless, the Web makes an excellent printing press today, albeit one that can benefit from much improvement.

Experimentation

Is experimentation with our sacred grammar and typography a possibility? Take a look at *Cold Mountain*, by Charles Frazier (Atlantic Monthly Press, 1997), a best-selling novel in print. It has plenty of dialog but uses no quotation marks or commas with quotes.

> —How did you learn to write and read and draw? Inman asked.

> —Same way you did. Somebody taught me.

> —And you've spent your life this way?

> —So far I have. I'm not dead yet. (from page 221)

The book starts each paragraph of dialog with an indent and an em dash. Although *Cold Mountain* forsakes quotation marks and commas for quotes and uses an em dash to start paragraphs of dialog, *I was halfway through the book before I even noticed it*. A compelling book? A viable typography? A senile reader? A little of all three? Who knows? If publishers can experiment in print to this extreme, is it unreasonable to experiment a little on the Web? All things considered, it seems a dangerous business to tamper with our traditions, but it would seem more justified on the Web than in print.

What's New in HTML 4.0 ?

Here's what's new in HTML 4.0. It's not very revolutionary, but keep in mind that CSS came along at the same time. Although HTML 4.0 has provided a few new markups, they have not been universally implemented.

Obsolete

The following tags have become *obsolete*:

    <xmp>
    <plaintext>

Use the *<pre>* tag instead.

Deprecated

The following tags have been classified *deprecated*:

    <basefont>
    <center>
    <dir>
    <font>
    <menu>

\<s\>

\<strike\>

\<u\>

All have been replaced by CSS. In addition, all color attributes for markups have been deprecated and replaced by CSS.

HoTMetaL PRO

SoftQuad's HoTMetaL PRO 4.0 (http://www.sq.com) is a full-featured HTML authoring program and Web site builder as well as an HTML editor. It is especially appropriate for typographic work. It provides three views:

* Source code for direct editing.
* Tagged text like an SGML editor.
* WYSIWYG like a word processor.

Thus, you can author with the WYSIWYG or edit the source code. The tagged text (see Figure 7.8) and HoTMetaL PRO's capability to hold you to the HTML DTD make this program act like an SGML authoring program too, a nice feature that may save you some testing. SoftQuad is considering selling an SGML/XML authoring program, tentatively named XMetal, at a reasonably low price (not yet announced at the time this book went to press), which may someday be merged into HoTMetaL PRO.

HoTMetaL PRO also provides the capability to create CSS, a crucial requirement for up-to-date HTML authoring (covered in Chapters 10 and 11 and see Figure 7.9). SoftQuad has been one of the leaders in the SGML industry and provides excellent HTML software too.

Testing

Later chapters will offer information on testing CSS, TrueDoc, font embedding, and NetTV. The level of complexity for

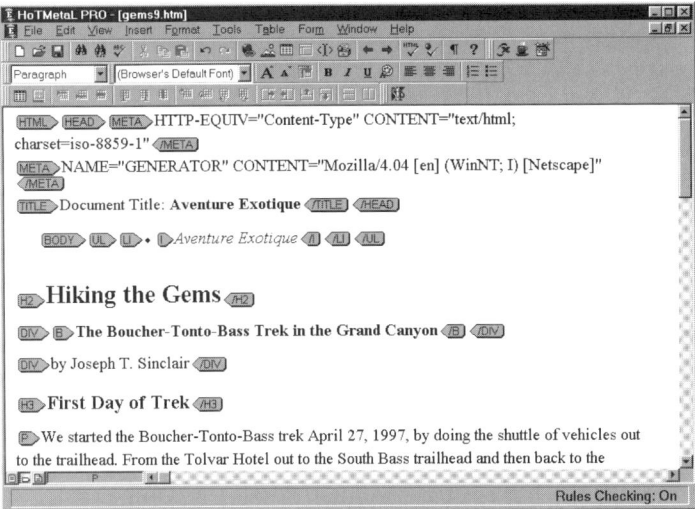

Figure 7.8 *HoTMetaL PRO tagged text view.*

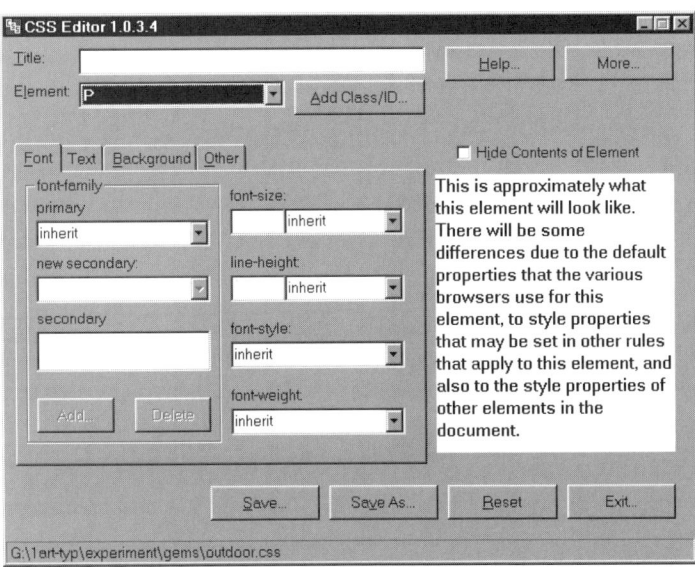

Figure 7.9 *HoTMetaL PRO CSS editor.*

developing and testing your work has quadrupled almost overnight. Don't try to do it all at the same time. Your testing should go in this order:

1. Test your HTML.
2. Test for NetTV.
3. Test your CSS.
4. Test your TrueDoc typesetting,
5. Test your font embedding.

The only way to test your HTML is to test it on all the browsers that you hope to satisfy. That seems to be two these days. Unfortunately, these two have several versions, so you may have to test your Web pages on five or six browsers to cover the market to your satisfaction. On the other hand, some experts have predicted that, by the summer of 1998, 80 percent of the people on the Web will be using 4.0 browsers. That might be true now that they're both free. Subsequent upgrades might receive quick acceptance as well, now that the pace of Web browser development has slowed a little. But predictions are prone to inaccuracy, and a conservative approach will probably maximize your audience.

Good planning will minimize your testing. For instance, if you're going to develop with the purpose of making television viewers happy, you will have to keep WebTV (Sony and Phillips set-tops) and NetChannel (RCA set-tops) in mind. There will be other national TVSPs eventually, too. If you learn about NetTV up front, when it comes time to test, the glitches will be manageable. Otherwise, you may have to start over from scratch. And the only way to test NetTV is with a set-top, although WebTV offers a set-top simulator for a PC.

If you develop for the two PC browsers and NetTV, test using the browsers first. Then test on NetTV using a set-top. Next develop your CSS, presumably modifying your HTML as little as possible. The CSS will work primarily to make your Web pages look better on the 4.0 (and later) browsers. Then apply TrueDoc and font embedding. By this time, you will already have done your Web typesetting and layout on your own PC where the fonts work just fine. So, applying TrueDoc and font embedding should be a mechanical, rather than creative, process. But, to get to the point where it's a mechanical process, you will first have to experiment a lot with generic TrueDoc and font embedding.

Summary

Again, this chapter is not an HTML primer. It simply offers comments on markups that are significant to Web typography and common to both the Netscape and Microsoft browsers. These markups are the basics. The next chapter will cover special techniques for Web typesetting, and the subsequent chapter will cover using the *<table>* markup for Web page layout.

Using Special HTML Techniques

This chapter covers typographical techniques beyond the simple straight-forward use of HTML tags, providing an assortment of techniques, a few I invented, but most collected from other sources and invented by other people. Some have been rendered obsolete by CSS; others will remain useful for a long time.

Using GIFs

Using small transparent spacer GIFs to add space to Web pages and to otherwise exercise some control over layout has proven valuable to many webmasters. And it's easy to do.

Spacer GIFs

A spacer GIF is 1 pixel high and as long as you want it to be. Name your spacer GIFs *s1.gif*, *s5.gif*, *s20.gif*, and so forth, depending on how many pixels wide they are. Spacer GIFs are one color, and you make that color transparent. You can use the same spacer GIF once or several times to create space, or you can use a combination of spacer GIFs. You can even create custom-width spacer GIFs for a Web page. Use a graphics program such as Photoshop to create spacer GIFs.

```
<img src=s20.gif>
```

Horizontal Rules A horizontal rule is not a substitute for a vertical space. Rules are not often used in printing, and there's no reason that they should be used more frequently on the Web. Don't use rules to create space.

Vertical Spacer GIFs

A spacer GIF can be vertical; that is, it can be one or two pixels wide and as many pixels high as you want it to be. Name your vertical spacer GIFs *vs10.gif* and so forth, depending on their height.

```
<img src=vs10.gif>
```

<img> Attributes

You can also use the *hspace* or *vspace* attributes of the *<img>* tag to add space to a spacer GIF. If you choose to operate this way, you need only one spacer GIF, 1 pixel wide and 1 pixel high. Remember that *hspace* will add an equal number of pixels on the right and on the left of the spacer GIF. Thus, *hspace="1"* generates a space 3 pixels wide for a 1 × 1 spacer GIF. Likewise, *vspace* will add an equal number of pixels above and below the spacer GIF. Thus, *vspace="1"* generates a space 3 pixels high for a 1 × 1 spacer GIF.

```
<img src=s1.gif hspace=1>
<img src=s1.gif vspace=1>
```

This is perhaps the best way to handle spacer GIFs, but some people prefer using fixed-length spacer GIFs, as outlined in the prior two sections.

Using Spacer GIFs for Layout

Use spacer GIFs for layout purposes to create space that separates page elements. If you had to lay out everything using spacer GIFs, it might prove tedious. Usually, you resort to spacer GIFs when all else fails. Regardless, you will find spacer GIFs useful in many situations.

Note that every browser has an offset, and it's different for every browser, or even between browsers created by the same software vendor. This is one more reason why it's diffi-cult to do precision layout for a Web page, even with precise spacer GIFs.

Space

Use spacer GIFs to create white space. That means, to use them to move objects away from the left margin, away from the right margin, or away from other objects (see Figure 8.1). Objects might be graphics, Java applets, or text. This works whether you use fixed-length spacer GIFs or spacer GIFs that use the <*img*> tag border space attributes.

```
<center>
<img src="image1.jpg">
<img src="s30.gif">
<img src="image2.jpg">
<img src="s30.gif">
<img src="image3.jpg">
</center>
```

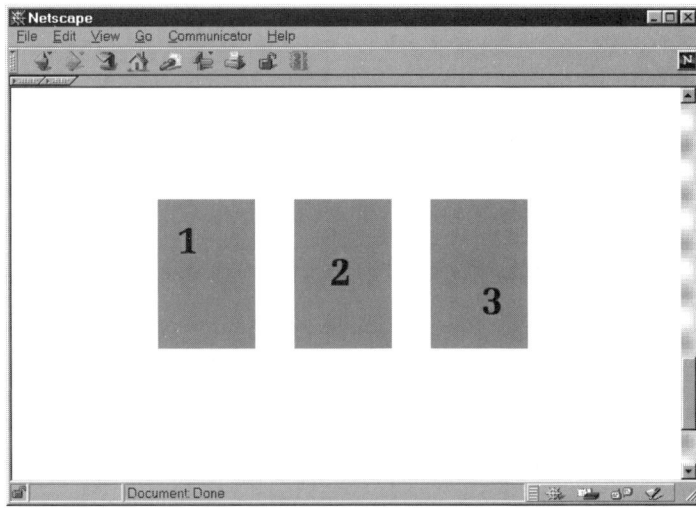

Figure 8.1 *Centered images separated by spacer GIF.*

Spacer GIFs work for creating vertical white space too. Make them tall. If you have a better feeling for normal text lines than for pixels, however, you may find the *<pre>* tag more convenient for creating tall vertical spacing.

Paragraph Indentations

Use a spacer GIF for a paragraph indentation. About 25 pixels suffices, although it is a matter of judgment and the width of the text blocks. Normally, you use an *em* space for a paragraph indent. When you use paragraph indentations, you don't have to use space between paragraphs (see Figure 8.2). David Siegel, in his book *Creating Killer Web Sites* (Hayden, 1996), is adamant about laying out paragraphs this way to improve readability. It works well in print, but I'm not convinced it works as well on a Web page. A line space, or better a half-line space, between paragraphs seems OK for now and will continue to read OK until the Web has higher physical resolution. But use an indent for a page turning system where Web site visitors do not have to scroll.

```
<img src="s15.gif">
```

First Paragraph Don't indent the first paragraph after a heading, subheading, or headline when you use paragraph indenting. Note that in order to illustrate paragraph indenting, the book's examples ignore this important rule.

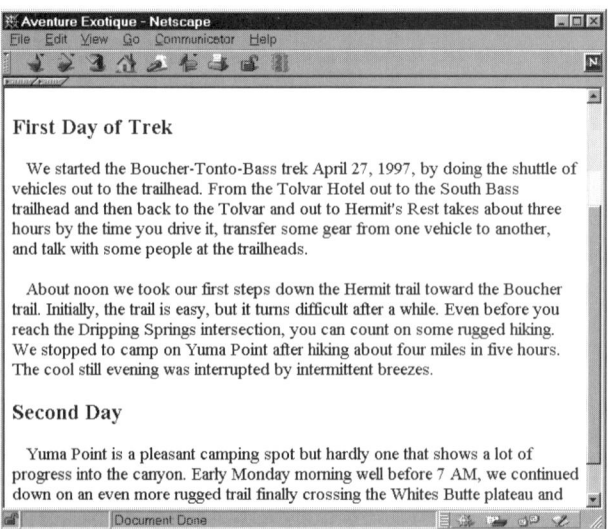

Figure 8.2 *Indent paragraphs with spacer GIFs. Next, remove the line spaces between paragraphs.*

Leading for Text Blocks

You can increase the leading in a text block by sprinkling in vertical spacer GIFs. The trick here is to make sure you have one vertical spacer GIF for each line (see Figure 8.3). This technique doesn't work, of course, to decrease the leading.

```
<img src="vs40.gif">
```

Leading for Headings and Paragraphs

Using the spacer GIF and the *
* tag together, you can create a line space of any height. For instance, you might use a 10-pixel line space above a heading to give the heading a more professional look. Remember, HTML headings have a line space above and below. By adding an additional line space above, you have made the space above bigger than the space below.

If you don't like that approach, you can create your own headings with your own amount of line space above and below

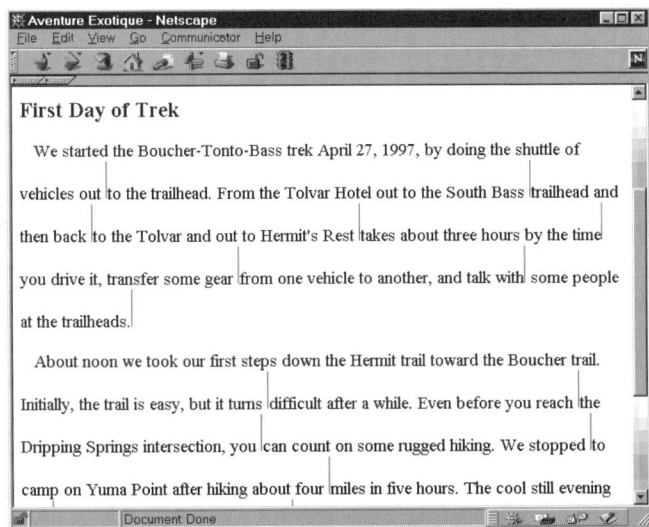

Figure 8.3 *Vertical spacer GIFs used for leading. (GIFs are opaque for display purposes.)*

(see Figure 8.4). It seems like a lot of trouble, but after you've done it once, you can copy and paste to duplicate your work easily for subsequent headings.

```
[preceding paragraph text]<br>
<img src="s1.gif" vspace=10><br>
<b><font size=+1>[heading
text]</font></b><br>
<img src="s1.gif" vspace=4><br>
[following paragraph text]
```

You can use this technique to create paragraphs and provide a line space between paragraphs, but not a whole line height of space. How about a 10-pixel-high line? That will look more professional than a whole line and will not require the use of paragraph indentation (see Figure 8.4).

```
[first paragraph text]<br>
<img src="s1.gif" vspace=3><br>
[next paragraph text]
```

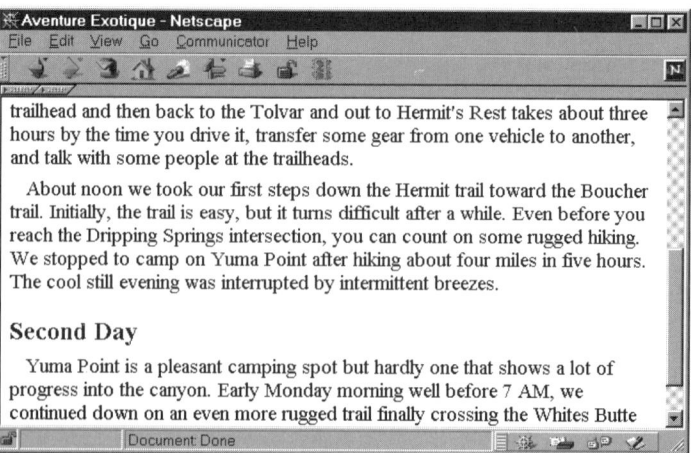

Figure 8.4 *Create special headings and special paragraph spacing using spacer GIFs. Next, remove the paragraph indents.*

LETTER SPACING

It's a no-no to put spacing between lowercase letters in normal text. It significantly impairs readability. Spacing between letters, however, can look attractive for headings and titles. The spacing must be relatively small to be readable; and for a large group of headings, the HTML work will be tedious using spacer GIFs. But it works.

Em Dash

Use a single-pixel GIF about 8 pixels long (experiment) for an em dash. In this case, the GIF must be the color of the type, rather than transparent. Align the GIF to the middle of the line. Note: For NetTV, make it 2 pixels high (see Chapter 17).

Judgment

People use their computers displaying different resolutions with browser windows that are maximized or less than maximized. Spacer GIFs do nothing to overcome this essential fact of Web life. Therefore, when you use spacer GIFs, try to imagine how the Web page will display in different configurations. Use your good judgment rather than seeking an engineer's precision. A Web page full of spacer GIFs can potentially turn into a mess in a small browser window.

Heading GIFs

You don't have to use Web typography for headings. You can use image headings instead. This takes more time, energy, and expertise, but the result can be spectacular. You do your headings in an image manipulation program such as Photoshop. You can start with characters made with fonts and apply all sorts of special effects. You can incorporate creative design elements or make the headings plain on a plain background.

If you use a plain one-color background, you can make the background color transparent, and the characters will appear to be printed in the page. Where you give the characters special treatment like drop shadows on a plain background, making the background color transparent will make the characters appear to float above the page (see Figure 8.5).

Although using GIFs is not an efficient way to make headings, subheadings, headlines, and titles, it can create an aesthetic appeal in many situations that ordinary typography alone cannot achieve. Because so many other books have covered this topic well, however, this book does not dwell on image headings. Keep in mind, though, that all the rules of typography apply to image headings that you want Web site visitors to read. If readability is important, don't ignore typographic principles in order to provide aesthetic frills. Find an aesthetic approach that does not impair readability.

———

Antialiasing Halo When creating a text GIF that you will use on a Web page with the background color of the GIF made transparent, create it over the same color background as the Web page. Then antialias it. For instance, if the Web page is mint green, create your text GIF over a mint green background and antialias it.

Because altialiasing uses interim colors at the edges of the characters, a text GIF antialiased over a white background will have a white–gray halo effect when transferred to a mint green background (or another color background).

Survey of Techniques

This section contains a number of typography techniques that you can use with HTML. Keep in mind that the guidelines in this section apply to text intended to be read.

Scrolling and Page Flipping Controls

Is page turning part of typography? Over the years, many typographers have devoted considerable attention to how people use pages and how people use books. It's not too much of a stretch to think about paging controls for the screen. Such controls should:

- Be in one place.
- Be small enough to stay out of the way.
- Be large enough to use easily.
- Be simple and intuitive.

Hiking the Gems

Figure 8.5 *Heading GIF.*

Although you don't have much to say about what the navigation controls for a browser will look like, you do exercise jurisdiction over your own Web site. When you create controls in Web pages or Java, keep the preceding guidelines in mind.

Readers do not like to be distracted. By placing the controls in only one place, readers do not have to wander all over the screen pursuing navigation controls with their mouse pointers. By making the controls small, the controls can be tucked out of the way so as not to distract. By making the controls reasonably large, your visitors will not have to have the manual dexterity of a cardiovascular surgeon to click on them. By keeping the controls simple, people can spend their time reading rather than navigating. Intuitive? This last guideline is an elusive goal. Everyone knows they need to provide intuitive controls, and everyone claims to do so. Yet many navigation controls on the Web are anything but intuitive. A few are even impossible to figure out. See Figure 8.6 for an example of navigation controls. Think of navigation controls as dynamic typography, an important part of the text.

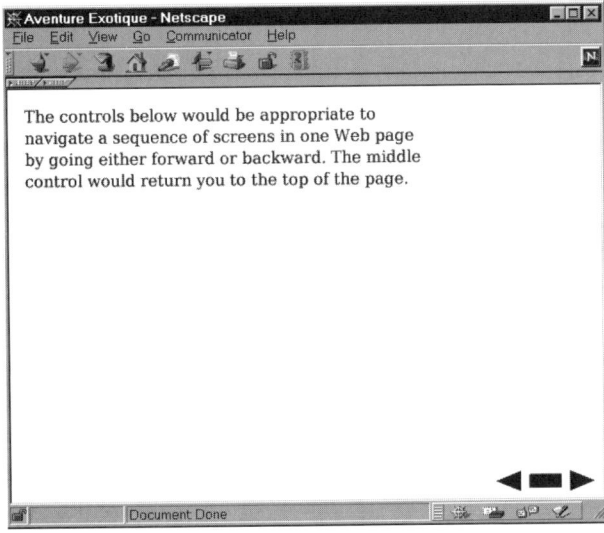

Figure 8.6 *Navigation controls.*

—◦◦◦—

Does Anyone Really Like to Scroll? Scrolling may not be as bad as some Web typographers would lead us to believe. After all, scrolling is not unique to the Web. Web site visitors readily use scrolling in their other programs such as word processors and spreadsheets. They don't necessarily go dumb when they have to scroll down a Web page.

Nonetheless, page flipping is an idea worth some experimentation. The trick is not to make it work. That's easy. The trick is to devise a method that not only works well but is also easy to author. When you have thousands of words to publish and keep up to date, easy authoring is essential.

See the User Interface Engineering Web site (http://www.uie.com) for more information on issues such as scrolling.

In the second century BC, King Ptolemy of Egypt kept the production of papyrus a secret and forbid export in order to enable his library at Alexandria, which housed scrolls, to lead the ancient world. Consequently, Eumenes, ruler of Peramum, sought and found a new material for books: parchment. Although parchment was made into scrolls, most parchment texts were made into codexes; that is, sheets of parchment bound together. By the fourth century AD, codexes had replaced scrolls as the predominate form for books. Codexes were more comfortable to read, easier to notate, and more convenient to store and transport. Not only that, but both sides of a page could be used for text. The codex had other desirable attributes, not the least of which was page flipping for easy and quick navigation.

Can a parallel be made today? Instead of scrolling, is page flipping a more ergonomic navigation device? See the Ion EZ Text Java document in Chapter 19, which features page flipping rather than scrolling. If you have a lengthy document that you desire people to read, you might consider page flipping.

One way to code page flipping with HTML is to keep text inside an imaginary box of a smaller size than the smallest screen that you expect Web site visitors to use for browsing (e.g., 460 × 360). Provide each text block (box) an anchor at the beginning. At the end of each text block, place a hyperlink to the anchor of the next block. Web site visitors can flip pages, in effect, by clicking on the hyperlinks. You might want to include a hyperlink that takes the reader back to prior pages too. This is an awkward way to develop text, but page flipping done properly may be more satisfying to many Web site visitors.

Background Images

Background images interfere with reading, plain and simple. Don't use background images behind text that you expect people to read. The one exception is a faint background image that you can hardly see. If you antialias text over a background image, it reads much better than text without antialiasing. This is one of the benefits of TrueDoc (see Chapter 12).

SMALL CAPS

Use small caps for acronyms and other appropriate uses. Also put them to work by using them for titles or headings, with the first letter of each word a full capital and the subsequent letters small caps. If you don't have a small caps font, use normal caps one size smaller; it's not great, but on a CRT it looks OK.

Type Color

Vary the color of the type in your Web pages to give long text passages some relief. But don't overdo it. For instance, make section headings a unique color and typeface. Although this may look a little amateurish with normal headings, when combined with *creative* headings, it can provide an attractive effect. Try using a special color for sidebars. Use color to indicate certain types of text devices. For instance, make all navigation aids or all indexes a special color. Make sure the color doesn't clash with the normal text color. Whatever you do to make a Web page more attractive, don't impair reading by causing distractions.

The eye races through text, interpreting a long stream of words created by monocolored characters with very subtle nuances of shape. It doesn't take much to catch the eye's attention. Subtle variations in color usually do the trick. You don't have to wave a red flag, nor do you have to use red characters. And certainly you don't have to make words blink!

Treat text hyperlinks with subtlety. The color of previsited and visited hyperlinks should differ only modestly from the text, enough to be seen easily but not enough to slow down reading. Text hyperlinks should not jump off the page. If they do, they will disrupt reading, and people do not like to be disrupted in their reading (see Chapter 18). The more hyperlinks, the more this guideline applies. Don't worry about readers seeing the hyperlinks. They will.

For text in page-head designs, in indexes, and in navigation bars, aesthetic design remains important. Almost anything goes. But for reading, keep color variation from being disruptive. Don't go to extremes.

The <dl> and <dd> Tags

Use the *<dd>* tag with the *<dl>* tag to create a left margin or to walk an HTML element across the screen from left to right: pretty simple and handy. You can also use the *compact* attribute with the *<dl>* tag. This has the effect of putting the definition on the same line as the term defined, as shown by the following markups (see Figure 8.7).

```
<dl compact>
<dt>ink
<dd>Colored liquid used for writing.
<dt>mug
<dd>A cylindrical cup for drinking.
<dt>spa
<dd>A resort featuring mineral
springs.
</dl>
```

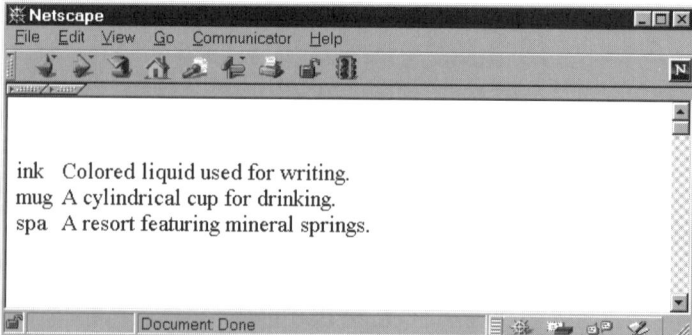

Figure 8.7 *Definition and term defined on same line.*

Vertical Rule

Create a vertical rule with a tall and narrow graphic. For instance, use a graphic 2 pixels wide and 300 pixels high. Because it's a tall graphic, you have to work around it, but it provides a vertical rule for typography where necessary. You can create the same effect employing tables by using a narrow column, rowspan, and the requisite color background (see Chapter 9).

Initial Caps

One oversized letter at the beginning of the first paragraph of a chapter or section draws attention and invites the reader into the page. A raised cap has the same baseline as the first line of text and towers above the text.

The text actually wraps a drop cap which has the same baseline as the second, third, or fourth line of text (see Figure 8.8). One of the problems with drop caps is that you don't know how large a Web site visitor's type will be unless you control the typesetting. Therefore, you may have trouble placing the initial in the text properly. Also, for drop caps, be sure to place adequate spacing *around* them.

Use GIFs or CSS for initial caps (otherwise you will have too much spacing under the first line of text for raised caps).

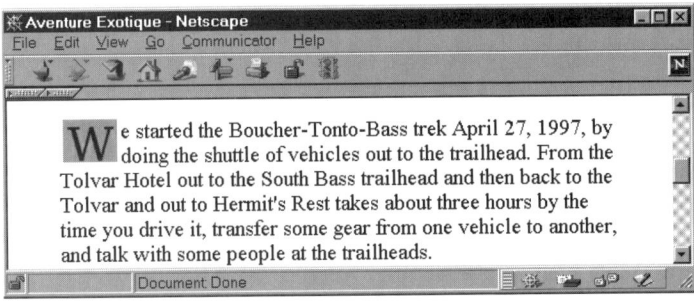

Figure 8.8 *Drop cap.*

Raised caps should be unbounded (transparent background). Drop caps can be bounded (have their own backgrounds).

Offset Text Blocks

If you need to place a block of text in an offset or otherwise awkward alignment (e.g., a pull quote—see Figure 8.9), there are two easy ways to do it. First, use the split image in a table. Place half of the image containing the text in the desired location (cell) on the Web page. Place the other half adjacent to it (adjacent cell) and flush against it, perfectly aligned.

Second, in tables (see Chapter 9), use the *colspan* attribute or the *rowspan* attribute of the *<td>* tag to make a cell span two or more columns, or two or more rows. It is a single cell but it extends across multiple columns, or up/down multiple rows. By using *colspan* and *rowspan*, you can create text blocks that surround a text block or a graphic that is a pull quote like the one in Figure 8.9. Unfortunately, the text does not flow through all the surrounding text blocks. Thus, this second technique is

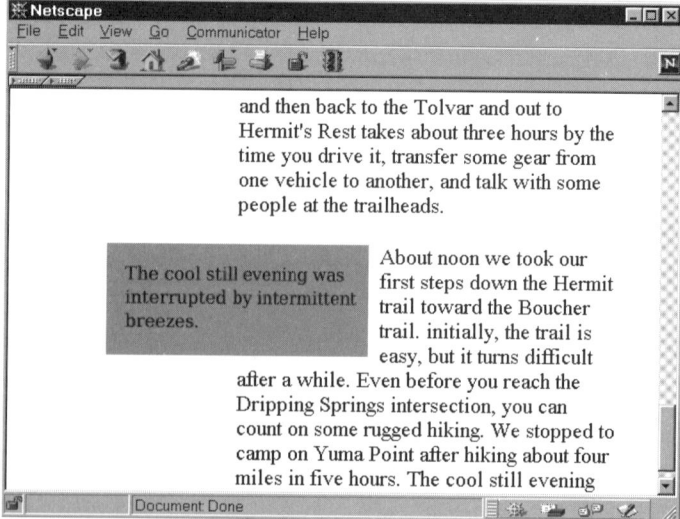

Figure 8.9 *Pull quote made using tables.*

contorted and appropriate only for short, highly tuned advertising pieces but not for normal text documents.

White Space

Good typography requires white space between page objects (text blocks, images, headings, etc.). Sometimes this is difficult to achieve with Web typography. Use spacer GIFs. You can also use the relative positioning capability of CSS to have text objects maintain space, if you have such a problem on one of your Web pages (see Chapters 10 and 11).

Captions

Lack of captions on graphics was a complaint of Wheildon's research subjects in his readability research (see Chapter 18). Does this need for captions hold true on the Web? Should you put captions under graphics that relate to the text? The answer is yes and no. In a Web page, you can easily place a graphic precisely in relation to the text. (For print, it often becomes a significant layout problem, and graphics often end up separated from the text to which they relate; for that reason, they need captions.) Where you place a graphic precisely in a Web page so that it relates directly and immediately to the text that wraps it, captions may not be needed. On the other hand, people are used to captions on graphics and won't find them distracting. Therefore, it's probably better to use captions than not, and captions will certainly give your Web pages a professional look (see Figure 8.10).

You can add the captions to the graphics (i.e., make the caption part of the graphic). Make the caption text a little smaller than normal text, but not as small as a printed caption. Or, you can use a two-cell (two-row, one-column) table for captions, with the graphic in the upper cell and the caption in the lower cell. Set the width of the table by the pixel width of the graphic, and make the borders invisible. The text will wrap

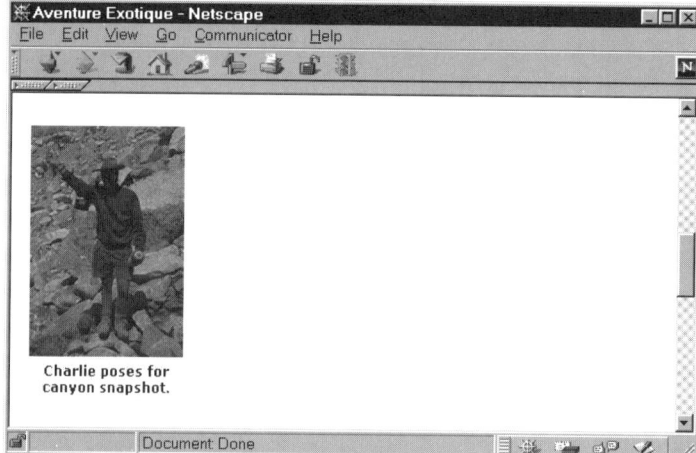

Figure 8.10 *Graphic with caption.*

within this width and will look appropriate. See Chapter 9 for further information on using tables.

Framing Images

Use a one-cell table (one column, one row) to frame an image. You can change the thickness and color of the border. Unfortunately, you can't also put the caption under this framed image in a two-cell table without framing the caption too, a strange look. You can also create frames around an image with CSS (see Chapter 11).

Text Shaping

You can mold text into clever shapes on the page using either the *<pre>* tag or spacer GIFs. Since the *<pre>* tag preserves spacing, you can create whatever shapes with text that you can inside the *<pre>* tag, and they will be preserved. The text will be a monospaced font. Without the *<pre>* tag, you can also use spacer GIFs on either side of the text, or on both sides to shape it. Regardless of how clever the shaped text is, it is not readable.

This is not a sound practice for those who want to have their text read. On the other hand, shaped arrangements of words or creative alignment of words (created by text shaping) can make attractive indexes or navigation bars.

Forms

Forms are beyond the scope of this book. Consult an HTML book for the proper use of forms. The trouble is that forms are ugly on the Web, compared with normal text. Eventually, that will change. Until it does, you may want to keep your forms out of sight as much as possible. Using tables to lay out forms makes using them much easier and more orderly. Or, use CSS to position forms.

Offsets

Each browser has a different offset, a small space at the side edge of the screen that prevents Web page elements from butting up against the edge of the screen. This offset sometimes makes it difficult to align Web page elements properly. Precise adjustments may not work well for certain browsers.

Metainformation

Having the search engines find your Web site is an art as well as a science. There are at least four ways to handle metatext (text through which you want the search engines to search):

- Place it untypeset in the *<head>* using the *<meta>* tag.
- Place it typeset as part of the text of the Web page. In other words, your page presentation is your metatext. There's nothing wrong with this.
- Place it typeset well below the essential portions of the Web page, separated by substantial vertical space. This way, most people won't bother to scroll down through blank space to look at it. Some people will scroll down, however, making this technique a little awkward.

- Place it typeset below the essential portions of the Web page, but make it invisible by using text that is the same color as the background color. This works well but isn't completely secret due to the controls that Web site visitors have over text in their browsers.

HTML Everywhere

Who is to say that a Web site must be on the Web? You can have a Web site (Web pages) on a hard disk, a floppy disk, or a CD. You do not need a Web server to access Web pages locally. You can access Web pages on a hard disk, a floppy, or a CD in *local host mode* just fine without a Web server. In fact, you have undoubtedly tested your Web pages in local host mode.

This capability has significance for publishing. You can publish writings as Web pages and deliver them attached to an e-mail message, via a floppy, or on a CD. Indeed, a floppy will hold as much as two full-length books in HTML (without graphics). With compression, a floppy will hold as many as four books. An ordinary CD will hold a book and hundreds or even thousands of color graphics; an up-to-date CD (DVD) will hold 27 times more. Clearly, HTML offers publishing for all seasons. Readers need only their Web browsers.

When you do an HTML presentation off the Web, treat it like a Web site. It's even a good idea to make *index.htm* the home page. Make it a logical and self-contained system just like a well-functioning Web site should be. It doesn't have to be a Web site in the sense of entertaining or impressing people with a lot of glitz. It can be a tutorial, a report, a pamphlet, a technical manual, or a book. By using the typographic techniques covered in this book, you can make it a first-rate product that is quite useful to recipients.

Xanthus iWrite

To usher you into the future, Xanthus (http://www.xanthus .com) has recently introduced iWrite, an HTML word processor that creates and uses CSS. Although Netscape Composer (covered in Chapter 9) and Microsoft FrontPage Express are HTML word processors, they have only basic features. The iWrite word processor is a full-fledged word processor which enables you to publish on the Web in much the same way that you use a normal word processor (see Figure 8.11) to publish in the office. Instead of proprietary markup languages such as Word or WordPerfect use, iWrite uses standards such as HTML and CSS.

The iWrite word processor features:

- Document authoring environment with rich features.
- Handles sophisticated and long documents.
- Capabilities include spell check, pagination, and running foot/head.
- Word-processor-like interface.
- Global control of style via CSS.
- WYSIWYG, source code, and CSS views.
- FTP uploads via a simple interface.

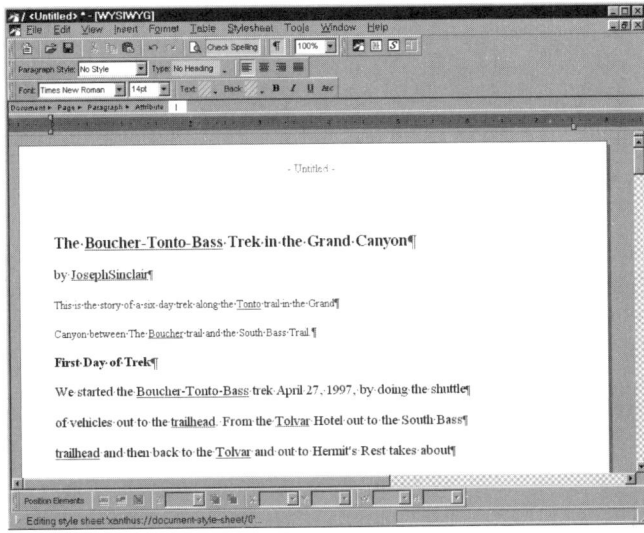

Figure 8.11 *Xanthus iWrite HTML/CSS word processor.*

This software makes it easy to do anything with text on the Web. The initial version is only the beginning, however, as Xanthus indicates that iWrite will evolve into an XML/XSL word processor as those standards emerge. This software is for workhorse publishing on the Web, albeit workhorse publishing with style.

Summary

To make HTML a useful typographical system, you have to resort to techniques like spacer GIFs and other contortions. That's part of the headache, but it's also part of the fun. Tables covered in the next chapter bring considerable additional typographic control to HTML.

Using HTML Layout Techniques

Plenty of information exists to assist you with the layout and design of pages intended to be read; that is, pages with abundant content, particularly text. Proven designs for printed books and periodicals make a good place to start. Such designs intelligently adapted to Web publishing will result in readable text and provide the basis for ongoing innovation in Web publishing. *Book Design & Production for the Small Publisher*, by Malcolm E. Barker, (PO Box 77246, San Francisco 94107-0246: Londonborn Publications, 1990) is one of many books that you may find helpful. Barker's book is full of ideas regarding layout that seem to me easily translatable to the Web. For a more aesthetic yet equally practical approach to book design, read *The Form of the Book*, by Jan Tschicold (Hartley & Marks, 1991). It provides specific classical guidelines for elegant book design, but presents a much more specific point of view than Barker's book.

This chapter presents layout techniques that you can use with the table tags to make your Web pages readable. This chapter also covers modular construction briefly. The next chapter, Chapter 10, provides up-to-date information on Web layout techniques using Cascading Style Sheets (CSS). Unfortunately, CSS requires the 4.0 versions of the leading browsers. Until the use of the prior browsers shrinks to an insignificant portion of the Web audience, which will happen before long, you will have to settle for using tables and other techniques to make your layout as precise as possible. This raises a bothersome question. Can you use tables and CSS to lay out the same Web page? The answer is a qualified yes. The Web Consortium made tables and CSS compatible, with the idea of using tables for structure and CSS for style. But page layout is a different matter.

Traditional Tables You should use the table tags to create normal tables in Web pages. This is a straightforward use of these tags, and the tables that are created will be referred to as *traditional* tables. However, this chapter covers using the table tags for laying out Web pages. The table tags were not intended for this use but nonetheless work well. In this chapter, you need to be aware of which use of the table tags is being discussed: the *traditional* use or the *layout* use. Most of the chapter is devoted to the *layout* use.

When it comes to *traditional* tables, they are compatible with CSS, because you use the table tags simply to structure a specific traditional table, not the entire Web page. In other words, a traditional table is just another element (like an image) in the Web page, and you lay out the entire Web page using CSS, not tables.

Although you can use both tables and CSS to do layout, such an approach is hopelessly complex in many situations. It's probably best to consider tables and CSS mutually incompatible for layout purposes. Thus, you may have to choose one or the other to do your layout. Nonetheless, you can do many things with CSS that will not interfere with tables. For instance, you can indent paragraphs.

One strategy for using tables and CSS together for layout is to establish a master style sheet specifically to be used with tables to do layout. The style sheet would be general and reusable. In other words, it would constitute the basic building block for every new Web page you develop.

Tables

The *<table>* tag and its ancillary tags provide an excellent way to lay out a Web page. In effect, you can set up a grid that furnishes a practical content placement and spacing system. It's not perfect, but it's powerful and it works.

Start with the <table> Tag

You start with the *<table>* tag which encloses the ancillary table tags *<td>* and *<tr>*. The table tag has a number of useful attributes:

align	Aligns entire table.
bgcolor	Sets background color for table.
border	Sets width of border.
cellpadding	Sets space between border and content.
cellspacing	Sets space between cells.
width	Sets width of table in pixels or as percentage of page.

The attributes are for the *<table>* tag, and the ancillary tags have attributes that can modify the *<table>* attributes.

Rows

The <*tr*> tag encloses the columns (cells) of the table, as indicated by the <*td*> tags. It does so for only one row. The <*tr*> tag has the following attributes:

align	Aligns table.
bgcolor	Sets background color for row.
valign	Aligns text vertically.

These attributes can be modified by the <*td*> attributes.

Columns (Cells)

The <*td*> tag encloses the content (e.g., text, images) of the columns (cells). Since no global markup exists that controls columns, you need to set the column entries individually for each row. In that sense, they become cells, and it is into these cells that you put the content. The attributes for the <*td*> tag are an important control for the layout process:

align	Aligns table.
bgcolor	Sets background for cell.
colspan	Sets number of columns that the cell spans.
nowrap	Indicates that lines in cell cannot wrap.
rowspan	Sets the number of rows that the cell spans.
valign	Aligns text vertically.

The cell designated by the <*td*> tag is the smallest unit in a table.

Full Window

If you want to fill the browser window with the table, no matter what size window, use the *width* and *height* attributes of the

<*table*> tag. The following table will fill a browser window, no matter how small or large:

```
<table width=100% height=100%>
```

Keep in mind that, when you specify 100 percent for both the width and the height, the portion of the Web page in the table may get compressed or stretched out in strange ways. Normally, you will set only the *width* attribute to 100 percent to make sure the width of the table fills the browser window, regardless of the window size. Leave the height undefined to allow the document to develop naturally. After all, people find it normal to scroll up and down.

Sample Table

A sample layout table containing three rows and five columns follows. It displays in Netscape Composer, with dashed lines for borders providing a grid (see Figure 9.1).

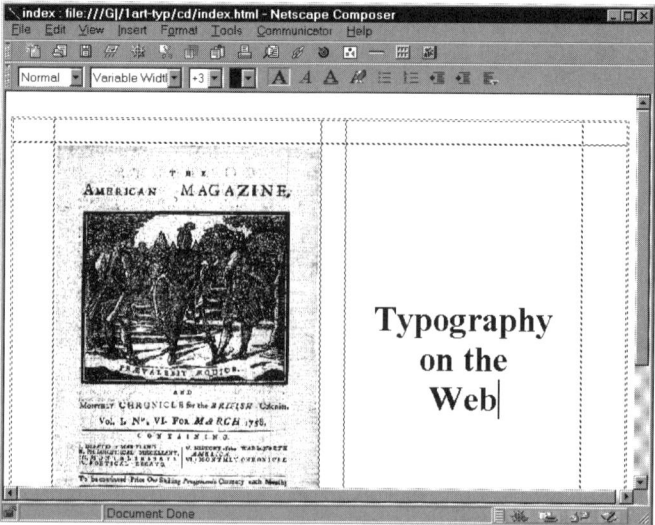

Figure 9.1 *Using a table for a grid to lay out a Web page heading.*

This is the title portion of a prototype Web home page (index.html) for the CD that accompanies this book. The first row contains no content or spacing information. In the second row, notice that the first column is a margin on the left (10 percent of the page width). The second column contains a graphic. The third column serves as a space (5 percent of the page width) between the columns that contain content. The fourth column contains some text. The fifth column is a margin on the right (10 percent of the page width). The third row contains no content or spacing information.

Note that the second row shows a graphic in column 2 and text in column 4. These two columns will take up the remainder of the width of the page after allowing for columns 1, 3, and 5 which combined take up 25 percent of the page width (10 + 5 + 10 = 25). The HTML code for the grid shows as follows:

```
<TABLE WIDTH="100%" >
<!-------------------- First row>
<TR>
<TD></TD>
<TD></TD>
<TD></TD>
<TD></TD>
<TD></TD>
</TR>
<!-------------------- Second row>
<TR>
<TD WIDTH="10%"></TD>
<TD><CENTER><IMG SRC="title1.gif"
HEIGHT=40 WIDTH=40></CENTER></TD>
<TD WIDTH="5%"></TD>
<TD><pre>

</pre><center><b>Typography<br>
on the<br>
Web</b></center></TD>
<TD WIDTH="10%"></TD>
</TR>
<!-------------------- Third row>
```

```
<TR>
<TD></TD>
<TD></TD>
<TD></TD>
<TD></TD>
<TD></TD>
</TR>
<!------------------- >
</TABLE>
```

This grid provides space in the first row which can serve as a space above the content. It can be deleted when fine tuning the page, if desired. The second row contains the content, which consists of one graphic and some text. Columns 1, 3, and 5 provide space. The third row can serve as a space below the graphics which can also be deleted when fine-tuning the page, if desired. This table makes a convenient module that can be moved elsewhere in the page if necessary.

Using Netscape Composer for Tables

Using Netscape Composer for tables is a good example of using tables for creating a grid for layout. The *<table>*, *<td>*, and *<tr>* tags can generate infinite complexity as well as elegant simplicity, but the HTML coding itself is most often complex. It's well beyond the scope of this book to explain and experiment with the HTML coding for tables. It makes more sense to use an HTML authoring program to demonstrate how tables can provide you with considerable layout control. Netscape Composer (bundled with the Netscape browser) is a simple yet powerful HTML authoring program that handles tables conveniently. Microsoft FrontPage Express is comparable. Certainly, there are others that do a good job too. In the following demonstrations of Netscape Composer, keep in mind that Composer uses the *<table>*, *<td>*, and *<tr>* tags, as outlined in the preceding sections.

Grid

Use tables to set up a grid (see Figure 9.1). As Barker's book (mentioned earlier) indicates, a grid is an important concept for doing a layout. What is a basic grid for a Web page? First, you must decide how many columns you need. Then you must add columns for spacing between columns and for left and right margins.

For instance, suppose you need two columns, one for navigation and one for a reasonably wide—but not full-page width—text column. You will need additional columns for the left and right margins and for the space between columns. In other words, you will need five columns.

1. Left margin.
2. Navigation text or images.
3. Space between content columns.
4. Content text or images.
5. Right margin.

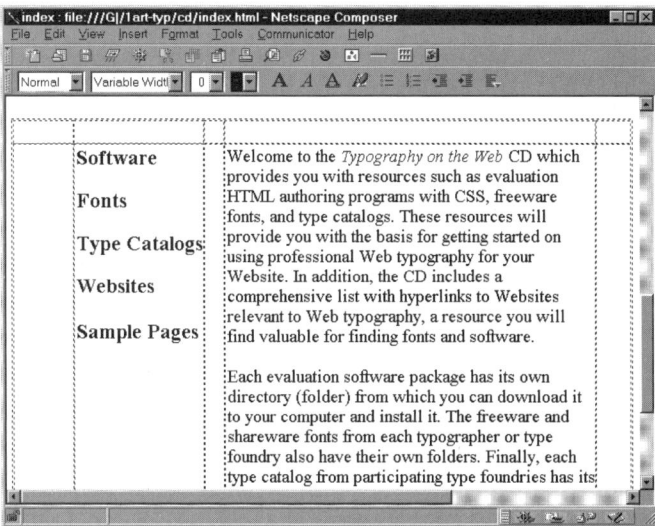

Figure 9.2 *Using a table to lay out text.*

Of course, you can use two columns and use *cellpadding* and *cellspacing* to arrange the requisite space. That seems more complex, however, than just creating extra columns, at least for general layout purposes; and you may not be able to achieve your objectives. When you use the tables tags for layout, the process is always a creative one that might result in an orderly table but is more likely to result in a complex, asymmetrical page arrangement.

Basics

There is enough meat in the table tags to create a table with a degree of complexity that you will regret later. Think in terms of simplicity when creating a table. Don't be afraid to create lots of columns. Sometimes more columns means more simplicity. For instance, a basic rule is that, for each segment of content, you will need a column. For each margin (left and right), you will need a column. For the vertical spaces between content columns, you will need columns. With this basic concept in mind, you can save much time and trouble.

Nonetheless, you may have good reasons to take an approach that leads to more complex tables. That's fine so long as you have the time and energy to see it through. The whole point of using tables for layout is that you can do things more precisely without as much effort, but if you want to do something really intricate, you can use tables for that too.

One Table or More?

Do you use one table for the entire Web page? That depends on the layout. If part of a table becomes unduly complex, you will probably do well to split it off into a separate table. The *colspan* and *rowspan* attributes provide you with the creative capability to make custom cells that span multiple columns or rows and do so with relative simplicity. Sometimes using *colspan* and *rowspan* makes a table overly complex, and you will find that breaking up the table into separate tables is a much easier approach.

For Traditional Tables

The *<table>* tag is great for creating traditional tables. For such tables, you can use cellpadding, cellspacing, and other attributes productively. Everything is nice and orderly because the layout is, in fact, a traditional table with well-ordered rows and columns.

However, breaking up the Web page into two or more tables for layout purposes applies only to successive tables, not nesting tables. Yes, tables will nest. Certainly this provides you with added creative capability for layout. Unfortunately, it comes with a price of additional complexity. For an obscure Web page, it might make good logic to use nested tables at the time you create it, but during a later revision it may be difficult to figure out what you did. On the other hand, for primary Web pages that you revise and tune continuously, using nested tables may work out well, because you stay familiar with the complexity.

Suppose in the heading portion of a Web page that you want to position a title and an image in a precise juxtaposition. A simple five-column table will work well for the layout task, as demonstrated in a previous sample. The remainder of the document is just a text column less than full-page width for easy reading. That portion of the page calls for a three-column table (two margin columns and a text column). Then at the bottom of the Web page you need to provide standard navigation hyperlinks and copyright information. You need a nine-column table for that, with four button columns, three space columns, and two margin columns (see Figure 9.3).

Does this three-table approach make sense? Sure. You may be able to use the heading table for other headings in other

Nesting Modules Where you use a table, usually a small one, as a modular component of Web page layout, nesting tables make sense. You become familiar with the modular component because you use it in multiple Web pages. To place it in a table as a nesting table does not create as much complexity as creating a unique table layout with nesting tables. For instance, a one-column, two-row table (two cells) makes a good module for a graphic and its caption. It's a reusable module that you might use anywhere, including inside another table.

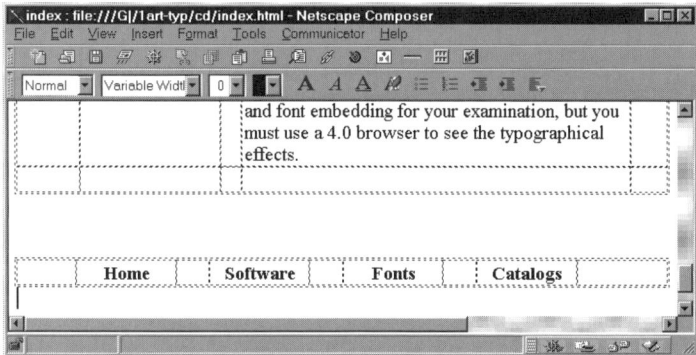

Figure 9.3 *Using a table to lay out a navigation bar.*

Web pages. You will probably be able to use the text table for other text in other Web pages. And certainly, you will be able to use the navigation table in other Web pages. You have inadvertently (or purposely) created a modular system that makes sense.

Now suppose that you want to add a traditional table to the text which is in the middle layout table. Rather than nest it in the middle table, you may find it easier to divide the middle table into two text layout tables and put one before the traditional table and one after the traditional table (see Figure 9.4). Remember, for the traditional table, you use the table tags as they were designed. For the layout tables, you simply create a page layout grid into which you place content.

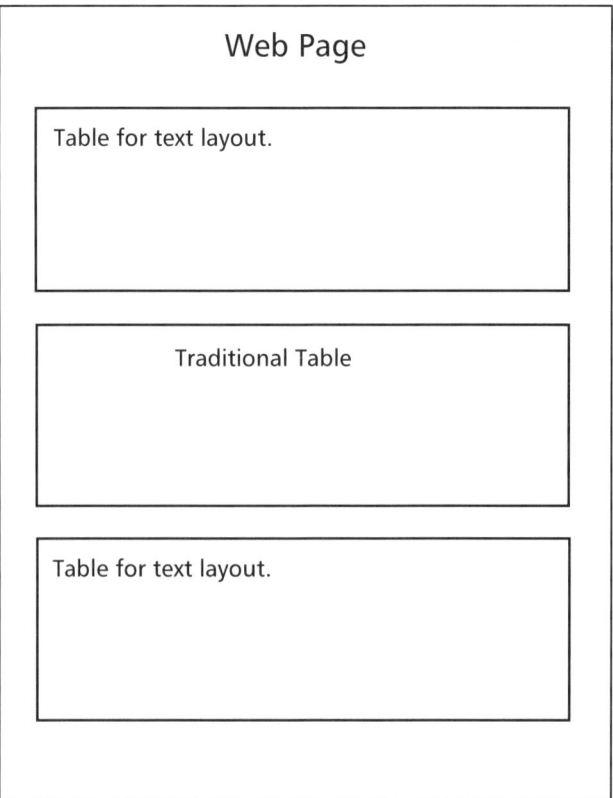

Figure 9.4 *Using tables in a Web Page.*

Rows Too

You must take rows into consideration, too, when setting up your table. Just as you need extra columns for space between columns, you also need extra rows for vertical space between page objects. Always start and end with a blank row. After you finish laying out the page, you can delete these if you don't need them. But they might come in handy in the meanwhile.

Spacer GIFs

Blank rows, columns, and cells don't always act the way they should. Sometimes they collapse. One way to force them to behave is put in some content. Add a spacer GIF (transparent) as a means of adding content without changing the visual content of the Web page. Adding a spacer GIF to the first cell at the top or to the first cell to the left will cure the problem. For instance, if the first row of a table collapses because it's blank, add a spacer GIF to the cell at the top left. The row will remain blank and will not collapse.

Borders

For a traditional table, you can leave the borders turned on for purposes of showing a visible grid. This is not good typesetting practice, however, and you should publish without a visible grid. You can give a professional look to the table through proper column alignment and by using bold column heads and row labels.

In using tables for layout, you never permit the borders to show. For the purpose of doing the layout, the grid needs to show, but it doesn't show in the final product. Netscape Composer conveniently shows the grid with dashed lines that do not appear in the finished Web page.

Width

How do you specify width? With an absolute measurement or a flexible setting? That depends on your objective. If your objective is to have a Web page that adjusts itself to the size of the browser window agilely, use percentages to set table widths. Otherwise, use absolute measurements (i.e., pixels).

For example, suppose you want a flexible Web presentation for a navigation column and a text column (as in the previous example in the Grid section). That will require five columns (see Figure 9.2).

1. Left margin.	20%
2. Navigation text or images.	20%
3. Space between content columns.	5%
4. Content text or images.	45%
5. Right margin.	10%

Notice that this layout is asymmetrical. The margin on the left side is larger (first column is 20 percent of page width) than on the right side (fifth column – 10 percent of page width). The space between the navigation column and the text column is modest but significant (third column is 5 percent of page width). The navigation column is 20 percent of page width, providing enough room for some image hyperlinks. The text column is 45 percent of page width, providing room for a column of text. Since people read text easier in a column than in full-page width, this layout seems reasonable. And its asymmetrical appearance adds interest.

The problem is, what happens to this layout in a very small or very large browser window? Will the text display optimally? Unfortunately, if the text column is too narrow, Web site visitors will find it difficult to read. Likewise, if the text column is too wide, they will also find it difficult to read. About a dozen words wide makes an optimal column width for reading. Clearly, with a percentage scheme, you cannot guarantee that the column width will stay within an optimal width range for all Web site visitors (see Figures 9.5, 9.6, and 9.7).

One way to keep your text column about a dozen words wide is to make it a fixed width. Use a 400-pixel width for

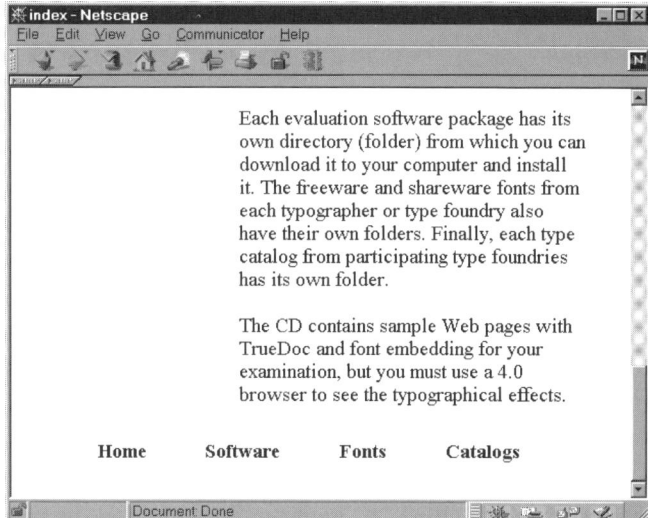

Figure 9.5 *Navigation/text layout table at 800 × 600, less than full window (roughly simulates 640 × 480).*

readable text (for normal type size). A fixed width will keep the text block from getting bigger in a very large browser window,

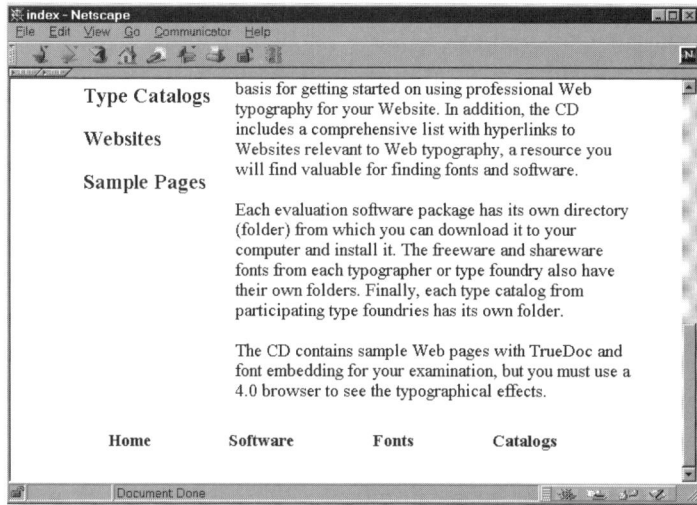

Figure 9.6 *Navigation/text layout table at 800 × 600, full window.*

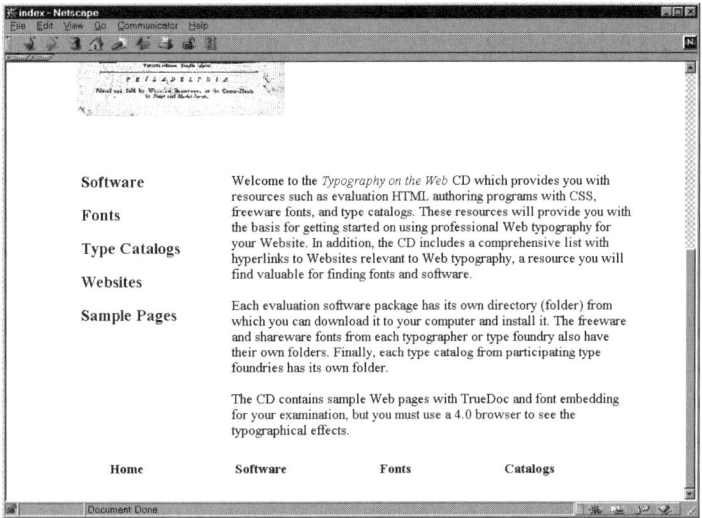

Figure 9.7 *Navigation/text layout table at 1024 × 768, full window.*

Serve Everyone? Do you have to make your Web site work for everyone? This question arose earlier in regard to making your Web site work for all Web browsers. Perhaps you will be satisfied making your Web site work for only Netscape and Microsoft Web browsers. Likewise, perhaps you shouldn't worry about Web site visitors who use very small browser windows or very large browser windows. They probably are only a small segment of the market. Or are they? This is pure speculation, and there are probably no statistics on it.

but a person with an especially small browser window may have to scroll *right* to read all of the text.

The use of tables provides you with much flexibility in meeting your design requirements by adjusting column widths and margins using fixed-width columns, relative-width columns, or both in a variety of combinations.

Alignment

Alignment within cells can prove very handy. You can align both horizontally and vertically. Sometimes this helps you to position objects better than trying more complex techniques. Thus, the *cellpadding* and *cellspacing* attributes may come in handy for moving things a little here and there.

Color

Remember, you can set the colors of tables or table cells. This can be handy to provide a suitable color background for reading text blocks on a Web page that is otherwise a poor color for reading (see Figure 9.8).

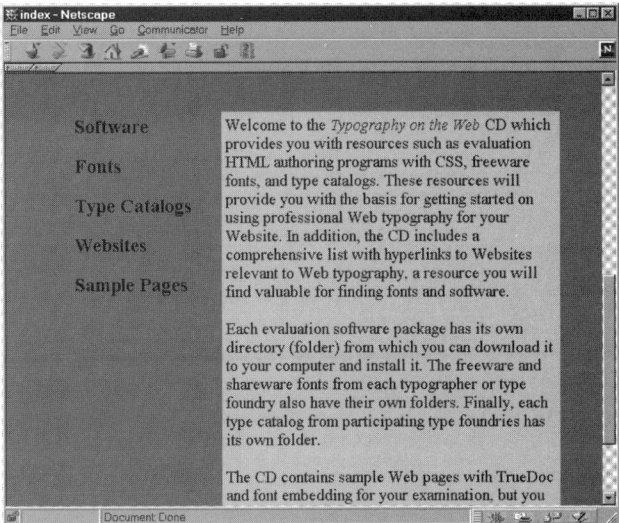

Figure 9.8 *Text layout table with its own background color.*

Beyond a background color for a text block, you can also use tables, the *bgcolor* attribute of the *<td>* tag, and the *<td>* tag itself for creative organization of page elements, each with its own specified background color. Don't overlook this ingenious technique. Of course, to maintain readability, don't get carried away with a complex collage of multiple backgrounds either.

Vertical Rule

With a narrow column, *rowspan*, and a background color, you can create a vertical rule (see Figure 9.9). In this case, the column will be as narrow as 2 pixels. The rule can only be as tall as the table, but you can make it shorter too.

Experimentation

As you can tell from reading this chapter, using tables for layout is as much an art as a craft. You have many variables. You have to experiment to get the hang of it. When in doubt about

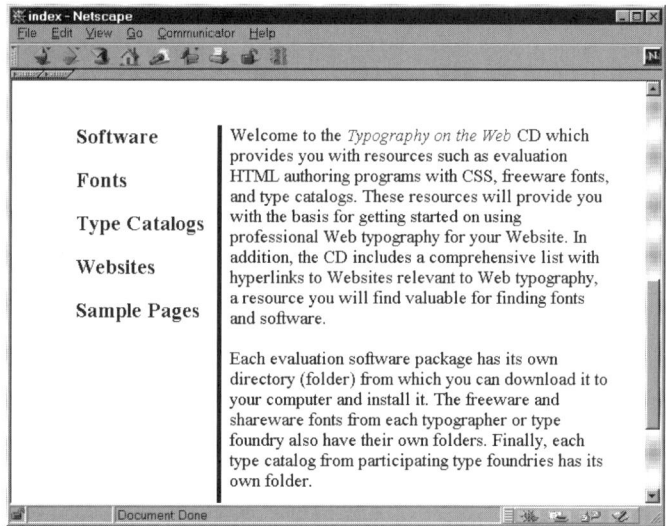

Figure 9.9 *Vertical rule made in a table.*

what you can do, create more columns and rows. With enough columns and rows, you can do almost anything. Of course, with many columns and rows, you must be careful not to create a monster of complexity that you no longer understand at a later date when you need to make adjustments to accommodate changes in content.

Experiment also with your resulting Web pages by viewing them in different size browser windows, from very small to very large. This is the ultimate test. With the proper combination of fixed-width columns (absolute width) and relative-width columns (percentage width), you can create more stable Web pages that enable readability while still adjusting to various browser window sizes.

Boxed Text

Use a single-row, single-column table with the border showing for boxed text, usually called a sidebar. Make sure you use *cell-padding* to make the box look proper; that is, use a margin on all sides inside a box of text. Don't let the text touch the box borders. Headings inside boxed text provide readers with a quick indication of whether it's something they want to read immediately or whether it can wait until they finish the section of text that they are currently reading.

In place of boxed text, the Web provides a unique opportunity to make sidebars into separate Web pages that are quickly accessed via a hyperlink. Using this technique, almost anything on the Internet can be made into a sidebar.

A sidebar is like a detailed footnote, but it's difficult to read through because it's in the middle of the page. If your boxes of text become reading roadblocks and are of marginal importance, you might consider putting them in separate Web pages. Hyperlinks will take Web site visitors to such sidebars. Hyperlinks of a proper color (similar to the text color) are much easier to read through than boxed text and are thus less disruptive to reading.

Modular Structure

Making Web pages in reusable parts can save you time and energy. This is particularly true of common page elements such as navigation bars and copyright information.

Planning

Modular construction requires advanced planning. Modular construction doesn't work if each Web page remains unique in its layout. Thus, you must first identify the common page elements that you want to duplicate or for which templates will save development time.

Templates

Templates are simply page layouts waiting to be filled with content. Templates do not have to be entire Web pages. They can be portions of Web pages. For instance, a section at the bottom of a Web page that contains a navigation bar and copyright information can be made into a template (see Figure 9.10). Call it the *page end* module. Suppose the navigation part of the page end has four hyperlinks. Three are common to every Web page, as is the copyright information. That means that the *page end* is a template that requires only that one blank hyperlink be filled with content (assuming that the URLs for the other buttons do not change). You simply copy and paste the template into a Web page, add the URL for the hyperlink, and you're done.

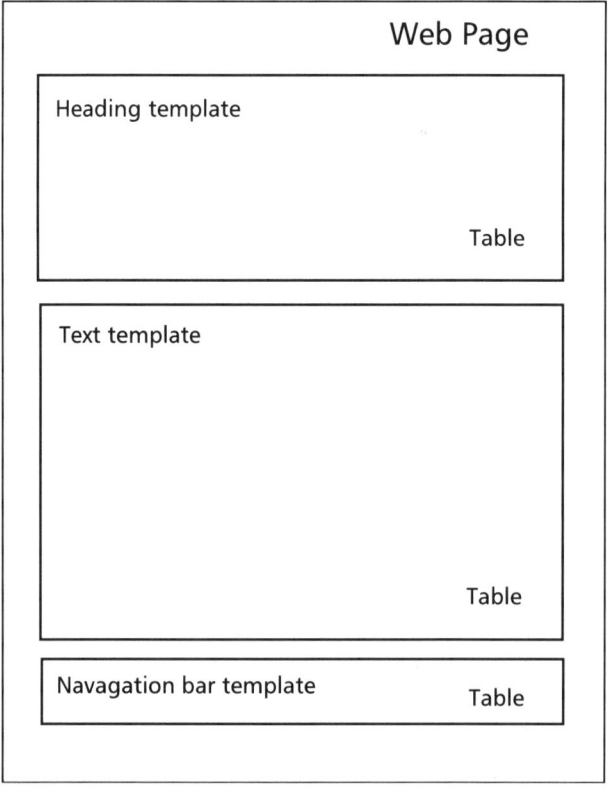

Figure 9.10 *Use modular templates for Web page layout.*

Table Modules

Why talk about modules in the chapter on table layout? Because tables make convenient containers for modules, as well as a convenient means of laying out a Web page. When using tables this way, you must make sure that all your tables are full-page width or of identical width. Otherwise, they may not align properly. Making your modular tables align properly is something you want to establish in the planning process. Remember also that tables with blank rows and columns may align strangely or otherwise misbehave. Use spacer GIFs in strategic cells to remedy this problem.

The use of table modules as nested tables in larger tables also works as a modular technique. In fact, one strategy is to build only table modules and arrange them on a Web page inside the framework of a large master table.

The Division Markup

You can also use the *<div>* tag to create modules. The *<div>* tag gives uniform alignment to everything that it encloses (e.g., flush right). You use the *align* attribute to indicate *left*, *center*, or *right*.

The Span Markup

You can use the *<span>* tag to apply *style* to one word or an unlimited amount of content. For one word, it doesn't make a module. For a large section of content, however, you might use it as the glue (style) that holds the section together as a module.

Netscape Composer

Netscape Composer used for this chapter to lay out Web pages is the WYSIWYG authoring program that comes in Netscape Communicator. It does not attempt to be a full-fledged HTML

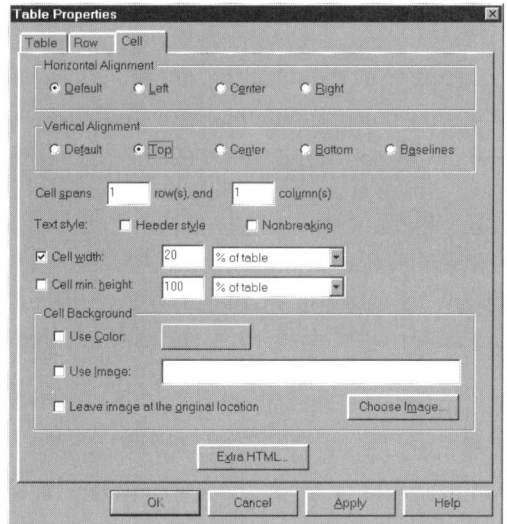

CSS Note that, although Composer makes tables easy by providing a grid and showing the effect of tables in the authoring mode, it does not show the effects of a linked CSS in the authoring mode.

Figure 9.11 *Netscape Composer table formatting.*

Web site builder. Think of it more as an HTML word processor. It enables you to create Web text document agilely and is especially handy for using tables for layout. It also includes an e-mail version for creating HTML e-mail directly, something that everyone will be doing before long. With the TrueDoc plug-in, you can use Composer to typeset your Web document (see Chapters 12 and 13).

Summary

Are tables much ado about nothing? Or are they valuable? The answers are yes and no to both questions. Tables used for layout are obsolete for the 4.0 browsers. You now have CSS to do the layout work. On the other hand, for the 3.0 and 4.0 browsers, tables work great for layout, and it may be a few years before Web developers quit using tables for layout. In any event, even for the 4.0 browsers, use the *<table>* tag to create *traditional* tables.

If you don't want to learn CSS or an authoring program that incorporates CSS, tables will get you by for a while. But the course of the future has been set, and it's CSS. Already some of the tags that you need in order to work with tables effectively, such as the *<font>* tag, have been deprecated. That means they're on the way out. Coming up next: CSS in Chapter 10.

Part Four

Cascading Style Sheets

Using Cascading Style Sheets

Analyze this *declaration* in a Cascading Style Sheet (CSS). It is a map that matches an HTML tag to a style. The map is expressed in the formal format of the CSS scripting language, a simple language for non-programmers.

h1 { font-family: times, serif } declaration

It says simply to set *h1* headings in Times (first choice) or a default serif font for the second choice if the first choice is not available. See the following CSS *property* (the second half of this declaration):

{ font-family: times, serif } property

To map (connect) the property to the requisite HTML markup, simply place the markup in front of it:

h1 { font-family: times, serif } declaration

Now you have a declaration. Hey, that's not so tough. The CSS 1 Recommendation, December, 1996, that set the standard for CSS, states, "We do not expect CSS to evolve into a programming language." That's comforting. Take a peek at the *Outdoor* CSS (which you will see again in the Link It subsection of the Adding a Style Sheet to a Web Page section in this chapter). With what you know already, you can read it:

```
<!-- OUTDOOR style sheet. Use for
outdoor feature articles in third-
quarter and fourth-quarter issues.
Don't use for editorials, columns,
or news. 5/97-->

body { background-color: teal }
b { color: white }
p { margin-left: 20% }
p { margin-right: 10% }
```

What Is a Style Sheet?

HTML provides structure for content. It marks text blocks, headings, block quotes, and the like. These arrange the text into different kinds of communication and establish their relationship to each other. For instance, *h1* indicates the highest-level heading that you might use for a title line.

The browser provides the style; that is, the fonts, font sizes, font styles, and the like. For *h1*, the browser may designate 20-point Times New Roman to be used in the screen display. Layout is generated by a combination of the formatting scheme programmed into the browser and the use of the structural markups to concoct formatting. Unfortunately, you have little control over the style and formatting programmed into the browser.

This combination works for *custom* HTML documents, so long as you are satisfied with the style and formatting programmed into the browser. But many HTML documents do not need to be custom made. For Web sites with a large number of documents, many of which are identical except for content, it makes sense to separate structure and style for the sake of flexibility and efficiency. In addition, most professional designers and typographers want to control the style and formatting completely, rather than relegate control to software vendors or browser users. Consequently, CSS, which provides for the separation of style and layout from structure and gives control over style and layout to designers and typographers, offers a valuable new Web development resource.

Content

The content can come from any source that can export it as ASCII text, or can exist in any form that can be easily converted into ASCII text. You do not need to create or edit content while it is in an HTML document. You can create it and edit it wherever convenient (e.g., in a word processor), and then export it as ASCII text into an HTML document.

Structure

Relatively simple HTML code provides the structure. If you have control over structure and style and can keep style separate, you can keep the markups straightforward, minimizing the amount of work required to convert ASCII content into HTML documents. This is true regardless of whether the content is converted to HTML automatically or manually. Mixing structure and formatting (styling) into one process is more complex and less flexible. Therefore, use HTML to structure the content, keeping in mind that you, not the browser, will control the structure and style.

Style

Style sheets provide aesthetics and formatting (layout and typesetting) to content that has already been structured. For the Web's HTML system, browsers normally provide the style. But you can now use CSS to provide the style. You map the style specifications to the structure; that is, you match up such specifications with the structural elements in an HTML document. For instance, you might create the following table to map specific HTML tags to specific style instructions (see Table 9.1).

Table 9.1 *Mapping Table*

Tag	Layout and Style Specifications
<p>	Left margin 1 inch, right margin 1.5 inches, 12-point Century
<h1>	Left margin 0.5 inch, right margin 2.5 inches, 24-point Century bold
<h2>	Left margin 0.5 inch, right margin 2.5 inches, 18-point Century bold
<h3>	Left margin 0.5 inch, right margin 2.5 inches, 14-point Century bold
<h4>	Left margin 0.5 inch, right margin 2.5 inches, 13-point Arial italic

By changing the specifications in this mapping table, you can give the document a completely different look without changing the structure or content. This is exactly what CSS does.

Browsers

Web browsers, in effect, map the HTML structure to the style schemes programmed into the browsers. In fact, the browsers even enable users to control the style to some degree. That leaves webmasters only partial control over the way their content is presented.

Word Processors

With word processors, users create structure, style, and layout together, not separately. Word processors use proprietary markup languages and make the markup work transparent for users by providing WYSIWYG displays and drag & drop interfaces. While authoring, content authors must create style simultaneously, an extra burden. For example, if an author uses anything except the default style of the word processor, he or she must create it.

Word processor templates provide a preconstructed amalgam of structure and style. They take most of the burden off authors for style and layout tasks. Yet, since the structure and formatting remain together in the document, changing the formatting in the document requires changing the document.

SGML

SGML is the mother of all markup languages, literally (see Chapter 6). SGML provides structure, nothing more. To use SGML, you have to create a Document Type Definition (DTD) that defines the structure of the document you need to use. For instance, HTML is a DTD of SGML.

Once you have a DTD, you create a style sheet to go with it that defines the presentation of the documents that you author. The whole point of SGML is to be able to convert a structured document easily to any media, whether print or electronic. If you want to change the presentation, you create another style sheet or modify the original style sheet. The structure and content stay the same.

How do you create a DTD? You study SGML and then code one manually, or you use an SGML development program that enables you to create a DTD. How do you create a style sheet? You study a style language and then code one manually, or you use an SGML development program that enables you to create a style sheet.

How do you use a DTD? You use an SGML authoring program (widely available and easy to use) with a DTD to structure content. The DTD plugs into the SGML authoring program, in effect. After an author finishes creating the content and structuring the document, he or she (or someone else) applies a style sheet to give the document its presentation qualities.

For HTML, you don't need to use an SGML authoring program, although you can use one if you want to (with the HTML DTD). Because of HTML's popularity, special HTML editors and authoring programs designed just for the HTML DTD have proliferated. Many have incorporated CSS capabilities.

DTDs If you don't want to create a DTD, you may be able to get one suitable for your purposes from an industry association or a software vendor. In the case of HTML, the WWW Consortium provides it to you.

CSS

CSS is a very simple scripting language that enables you to create style sheets for HTML documents. CSS simply maps style and layout to HTML structure and instructs the computer to render the HTML document according to the map. In other words, with CSS, you create style sheets for the HTML DTD (see Figure 10.1).

It is important to note that CSS was not an afterthought developed because HTML was not robust enough. It resulted from the natural evolution of this important and popular DTD, and it provides the means to easily create style sheets for HTML documents without using one of the complex style languages developed for SGML. *CSS was not designed for programmers.* Like HTML, CSS was designed for nonprogrammers who desire to publish something on the Web.

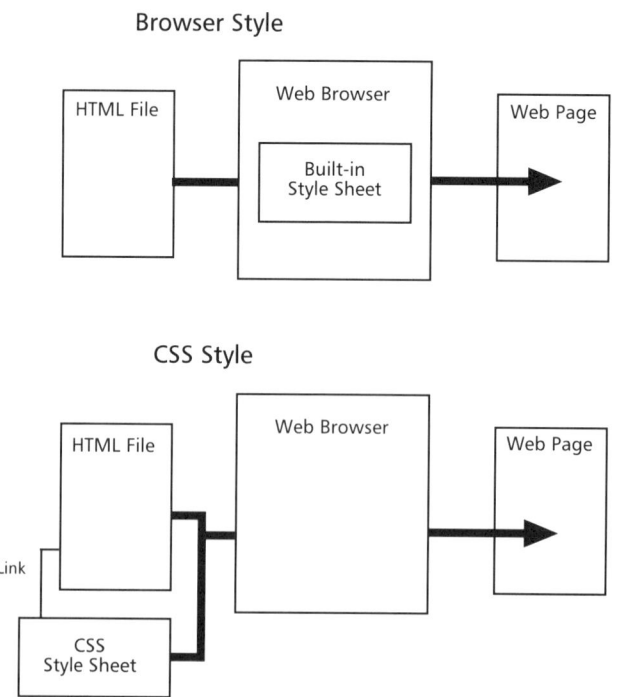

Figure 10.1 *The CSS system.*

Anatomy

A *selector* and a *declaration* make up each CSS *style* or *rule*. This may sound like programming, but you will find it to be pretty easy. A selector is an HTML markup. A declaration applies a property to the selector. The property portion of the declaration has two parts, a *property* and a *value*:

selector = HTML markup

declaration = { property: value }

An actual example of a declaration is:

p { font-family: times }

This example typesets normal paragraphs in Times. Note that you must separate the braces { } from the declaration with spaces. CSS has about 34 properties divided into four groups:

Font	*Color & Background*
font-family	*color*
font-style	*background-color*
font-variant	*background-image*
font-weight	*background-repeat*
font-size	*background-attachment*
font	*background-position*
	background

Text	*Classification*
word-spacing	*display*
letter-spacing	*white-space*
text-decoration	*list-style-type*
vertical-align	*list-style-image*
text-transform	*list-style-position*
text-align	*list-style*

text-indent

line-height

Layout

margin-top, margin-right, margin-bottom, margin-left

margin

padding-top, padding-right, padding-bottom, padding-left

padding

border-top-width, border-right-width, border-bottom-width, border-left-width

border-width

border-color

border-style

border-top, border-right, border-bottom, border-left

border

width

height

float

clear

Chapter 11 organizes the properties into these groups and covers them in individual detail. It seems like a lot, but there's actually not much to it.

Multiple selectors (markups) can share a declaration, and you separate the selectors with commas.

h1, h2, h3 { font-family: times }

You can also group declarations together, separating them with semicolons:

p { font-family: times; font-style: italics; }

or

```
p {
font-family: times;
font-style: italics;
}
```

Note that you must always add a semicolon after the last property for multiple-property declarations.

Controls

Controls provide a basic means of adjusting the visual elements on a page, and Web developers use two types of controls for HTML elements: measurements and color coding.

Measurements (length)

Dimensions that CSS calls *length* provide a means of measuring the horizontal or vertical size of HTML elements, as well as space. CSS uses three types of measurements for dimensions: absolute, percentage, and relative.

Absolute

Absolute length expresses dimensions in commonly used physical measurements such as inches or millimeters.

Unfortunately, these don't work quite as well for some HTML elements, because it's impossible to predict the size of the window with which Web site visitors will view your HTML documents. For instance, if you make your Web page 14 inches wide, even a person with a 1024 × 768 display won't be able to see the your entire Web page on his or her monitor. In an era where displays go from 544 × 378 (WebTV) to 1024 × 768 (commonly used with PCs) and users open their browsers to a full screen or only a partial screen, absolute measurements don't make much sense for designating large spaces. For small spaces, you may find them useful.

Inches, Millimeters, and Centimeters

CSS supports measurements in inches, millimeters, and centimeters. You express them as follows:

in = inches

mm = millimeters

cm = centimeters

Points and Picas

You can also use points and picas, the traditional measurements for typography. Use the following to express these measurements:

pt = point

pc = pica

Although picas have fallen out of use in digital typography, points remain an acceptable measurement for type and for spacing between type. Such spaces are small and do not cause the potential problems that result from using absolute measurements for larger spaces. For example, to designate the size of the type used in a type block, you use the following property:

{ type-size: 12pt }

Percentage

A more useful means of control for many situations is a percentage. You should think of the size of the window that Web site visitors use to view your Web site as being dynamic; that is, each visitor uses a different size browser window. Consequently, expressing some dimensions as percentages makes sense.

{ margin-left: 15% }

This property indicates that the left-hand margin will be 15% of the width of the browser window. The absolute value of the margin expands and contracts for different size browser windows, providing a dynamic adjustment that maintains a desired look for the HTML document. Other percentage measurements are not so straightforward. For instance, you can use a percentage measurement with the *line-height* property:

{ line-height: 125% }

This means that the size of the leading will be 25% of the font size (e.g. 2.5 points for 10-point type).

Relative

Relative sizes provide useful measurements too. The *em* is relative to the font. In CSS an em equals the height of an HTML element's font and thus is different for different font sizes. (The em equals the width of the letter *m*, which is more or less square for normal typefaces. Thus, the height of *m* is the same as the width, and a 10-point font size will have a 10-point em in CSS.) The *ex* is the *x*-height of the font, which is different for different font sizes. The pixel is relative to the number of pixels displayed by the browser window; a larger display displays more pixels. For example, a 800 × 600 display is 160 pixels wider than a 640 × 480 display.

em = height of font
ex = x-height of font
px = pixel

Suppose you want to make an indented paragraph. Using the em makes a functional indent that changes with the size of the font, as it should.

{ font-indent: 1em }

Use the em When used for the *font-size* property, the em is relative to the parent (often the normal size text type, usually about 12 points). For 12-point normal text, 1.5 em would be 18 points, and 0.5 em would be 6 points. Many Web typographers recommend that you use the em for type size. This proves to be a great idea because, if you change the parent text size, all the other size variations (the children) change size with the parent proportionally.

This can be confusing, however, because you must use an absolute size to set the size for the parent in the first instance. If you don't set the type size for the parent, the type size will be either the user-set type size or the browser default type size for normal text.

The pixel does not make a flexible measurement, because the pixel dimensions of browser windows vary widely. For instance, a 640 × 480 display with the browser at full screen displays a useable space about 600 pixels wide (taking into account space for the browser frame). A 1024 × 768 display with the browser at full screen displays a useable space almost 1000 pixels wide. Consequently, a pixel appears smaller in the 1024 × 768 display than it does in the 640 × 480 display. Nonetheless, you should use pixels to define the space in which you display a graphic, because a graphic has fixed pixel dimensions. Thus, if you want to display a vertical bar 120 pixels wide (e.g., an image map for navigation) in the left margin, you can offset the text block by 125 pixels from the left to create a nice effect, which is currently popular in Web publishing (see Figure 10.2).

{ margin-left: 125px }

Keep in mind that video systems define font point sizes in pixels. Thus, 12-point type has a fixed pixel size and is larger

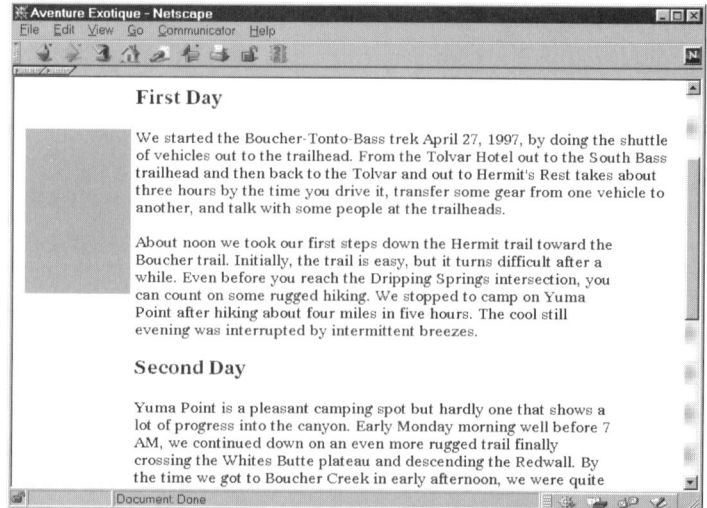

Figure 10.2 *A vertical bar (e.g., image map) used with text.*

on a 640 × 480 display than on a 1024 × 768 display. (The 1024 × 768 display has to cram more pixels into the same screen real estate, making each pixel smaller on the same monitor, in effect.) Thus, you gain nothing by defining type size in pixels using the *font-size* property, and you lose your traditional feeling for type size, which is undoubtedly based on point measurements.

Color Coding

You designate color for CSS just as you do for HTML. You can use the color names listed for browsers, or you can use hex RGB numbers. You can even use RGB values.

```
{ color: lime }
{ color:  #0f0 } or { color: #00ff00 }
{ color: rgb(000,255,000) }
```

Keep in mind that, if you use colors completely made up of the following hex RGB pairs, such colors will be browser-safe:

```
00, 33, 66, 99, cc, ff
```

For example, #00ff00 (lime) is browser-safe. The color #00ff01 is not. You will see the hex number contraction used for browser-safe colors. Thus, #0f0 replaces #00ff00. There's no sense in expressing both of the numbers in a pair when they are the same. On the other hand, you cannot use a contraction for #00ff01.

The browser-safe color palette made up of only the RGB pairs just defined has some very pleasant colors. Get in the habit of using them, and many of your color problems will disappear. Allaire's Home site HTML editor briefly described at the end of this chapter has a browser-safe color palette. Remember also that the colors designated by named colors for browsers are not necessarily browser-safe colors.

Video System Fonts Most video accelerators (color cards, video boards, etc.) offer small-font and large-font options for system fonts. You use small fonts for 640 × 480 displays. But for 1024 × 768 displays, you use large fonts. Without the large fonts, you would have difficulty seeing the system fonts for 1024 × 768. For 800 × 600, you can use either small or large system fonts, depending on your eyesight.

Oddly enough, you can use percentages to define colors. In this system, you use a percentage in the RGB value scheme in place of a number between 1 and 255. Thus, you specify lime as:

{ color: rgb(0%,100%,0%) }

Why not? "Hey, buddy. Your communication interface is about 95% R." Translation: Your face is flush. Better cut back on the booze.

Classes

You can map the standard HTML markups to style using CSS, but you can also do more. CSS provides pseudoclasses and enables you to invent classes.

Classes

A class is a declaration or a set of declarations that defines an HTML element or that independently defines multiple elements. You can make up any name you want to use for a class. You designate an independent class as a selector beginning with a period:

.layoutfun5 { text-indent: 1em }

In this case, you made up the name *layoutfun5* (i.e., layout fun number 5). You can also designate a class associated with an HTML element (selector) as a suffix:

p. layoutfun5 { text-indent: 1em }

Thus, you have associated *.layoutfun5* with the paragraph markup. Suppose you write a style sheet containing the following:

p { color: navy }
. limelight { color: lime }

In the following paragraph, the text is navy, and you apply the *<span>* tag with the *class* attribute to make the statement about the weather stand out. The style sheet turns the spanned sentence lime green (see Figure 10.3).

```
<p>So, we started out of Boucher
Creek in Topaz Canyon and camped up
on the Tonto about a mile along the
Tonto trail. Again, it was a
pleasant campsite. <span
class=limelight>The evening was
warm with intermittent
breezes.</span> Oddly enough on the
Tonto, a seemingly long way from
water, there was a small mosquito
problem.</p>
```

Suppose you want to turn this entire paragraph lime without affecting prior or subsequent paragraphs. You can use the *.limelight* class with the *<p>* tag:

```
<p class=limelight>So, we started
out of Boucher Creek in Topaz
Canyon and camped up on the Tonto
about a mile along the Tonto trail.
Again, it was a pleasant campsite.
The evening was warm with
```

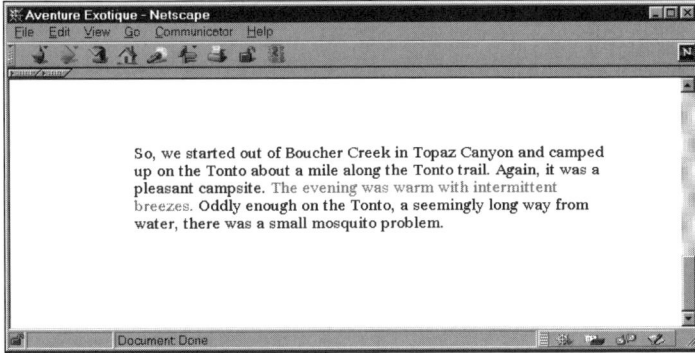

Figure 10.3 *The limelighted sentence.*

```
intermittent breezes. Oddly enough
on the Tonto, a seemingly long way
from water, there was a small
mosquito problem.</p>
```

This turns the whole paragraph lime. The independent *.lime-light* class provides you with more flexibility, because you can use it with any tag. In situations where you want to limit its use, however, you can limit it to one tag by defining it in your style sheet associated with one tag (e.g., *p.limelight*). Therefore, to turn the entire paragraph lime, you could have also used the following declaration in your style sheet:

```
p. limelight { color: lime }
```

When you apply this, it turns the whole paragraph to lime:

```
<p.limelight>So, we started out of
Boucher Creek in Topaz Canyon and
camped up on the Tonto about a mile
along the Tonto trail. Again, it
was a pleasant campsite. The
evening was warm with intermittent
breezes. Oddly enough on the Tonto,
a seemingly long way from water,
there was a small mosquito
problem.</p>
```

But this declaration won't work with the *<span>* tag. Only the independent class declaration (i.e., *.limelight*) will create a class that you can use with multiple tags.

The capability to create classes provides you with a license to create a simple or an elaborate markup system for refining your styling of Web pages as much as you desire. Powerful!

Pseudoclasses

Pseudoclasses differentiate between identical HTML elements. Pseudoelements refer to sections of elements. You designate them with a colon rather than a period. For example, you can set the colors for the <*a*> link using the *link* pseudoclass:

```
a:link { color: gray }
a:visited { color: purple }
a:active { color: red }
```

When a Web site visitor clicks on a gray hyperlink, it will light up red and then change to and remain purple. Likewise, you can use the *first-letter* pseudoelement to make an initial a raised cap (see Figure 10.4):

```
p:first-letter { font-size: 36pt }
```

See the Classifications section of the next chapter for all the pseudoelements you can use. There are only a few. Note that you cannot make up your own pseudoelements.

Inheritance

Inheritance is simply all the characteristics of an element that its successor inherits when you modify that element with a

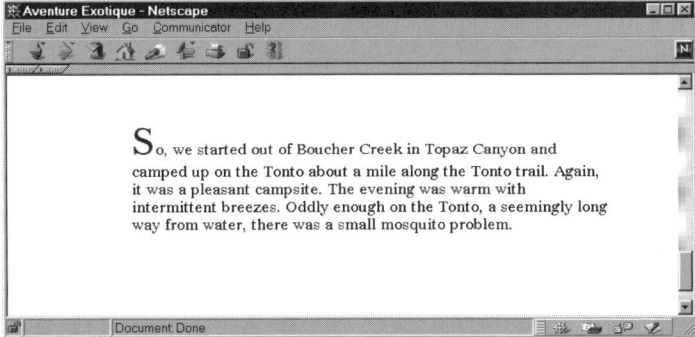

Figure 10.4 *A simulated raised cap. (The 4.0 browsers do not support this particular pseudoelement. Notice that there is too much line space between the first and second lines. Presumably, the first-letter pseudo-element, when enabled by the 5.0 browsers, will correct this.)*

declaration. For instance, when you apply the <*i*> tag to a word of text, it turns that word into italics, but the word still retains (inherits) all the other characteristics of the original word, such as typeface, font size, and color.

If you create a style sheet, do you have to define every tag in HTML? No. You can define as few or as many as you wish with CSS declarations. The document will inherit all the normal characteristics of an HTML document except the ones that you have modified with the style sheet. Hence, a style sheet can have one declaration or a thousand.

In HTML, you use most tags inside the <*body*> tags. Therefore, all the elements you use inside the <*body*> element inherit the formatting of the <*body*> element. The <*body*> element is the parent, and the other elements are the children (e.g., the <*p*> element is a child to the <*body*> element). Inheritance can get tricky if you code carelessly. When using CSS, it is important to pay attention to inheritance. Only trial and error will help you develop a sensitivity to keeping inheritance sorted out.

Adding a Style Sheet to a Web Page

Now you know that one declaration alone can be a style sheet, and you have a feeling for how to write declarations. It's time to create a style sheet. Here's what a simple style sheet looks like:

```
body { background-color: teal }
b { color: white }
p { margin-left: 20% }
p { margin-right: 10% }
```

Analyze this style sheet. The background is teal. Bold type is white. The style sheet declares nothing about normal type, so normal type remains the default (black). The style sheet also sets the margins for the <*p*> elements. Now the question is, how do you install this style sheet? You have four ways: embedding, linking, importing, and inserting inline.

Embed It

You embed your style sheet in the *<head>* using the *<style>* tag. That's simple enough. Just do it (see Figure 10.5):

```
<head><title>Aventure
Exotique</title>
<style type="text/css">
<!--
body { background-color: teal }
b { color: white }
p { margin-left: 20% }
p { margin-right: 10% }
-->
</style>
```

Notice that you put the *<!-- -->* tag around the style sheet so that old browsers won't display it as text. This style sheet will give you a background that's easy on the eyes (teal), black text (default), white bold text wherever the *<b>* tag is used, and a dynamic margin on the left and right.

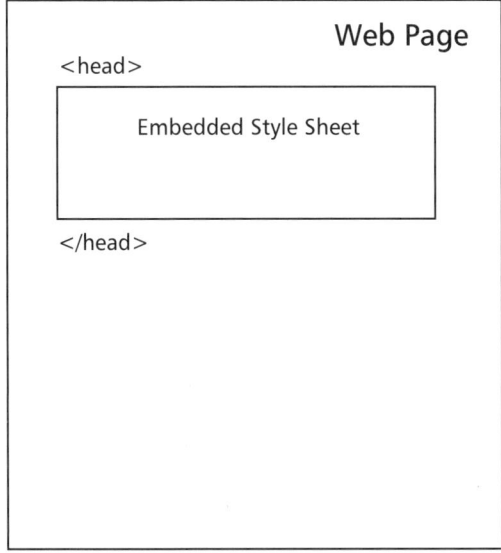

Figure 10.5 *Embedded style sheet.*

Link It

You don't have to put the style sheet in the *<head>*. You can make it a separate ASCII document and link to it via the *<link>* tag which goes in the *<head>*. The style sheet ASCII file needs to have the extension *.css* to function as a style sheet. Suppose you name your style sheet *Outdoor*, because you want to use it to set the format for outdoor stories that you will publish in a Web adventure magazine. Thus, you name the style sheet file *outdoor.css*, and you can upload it anywhere on the Internet and link to it (see Figure 10.6).

```
<link rel=stylesheet
href="outdoor.css" type="text/css"
title="Outdoor">
```

Note that, although the CSS file might be anywhere on the Internet and linked by its URL, in the previous example, the CSS file is in the same directory as the HTML document. The *type* attribute *text/css* is for MIME purposes (beyond the scope of the book). Just include it. The *outdoor.css* document will look like the following. The notation at the top is for administrative purposes, of course.

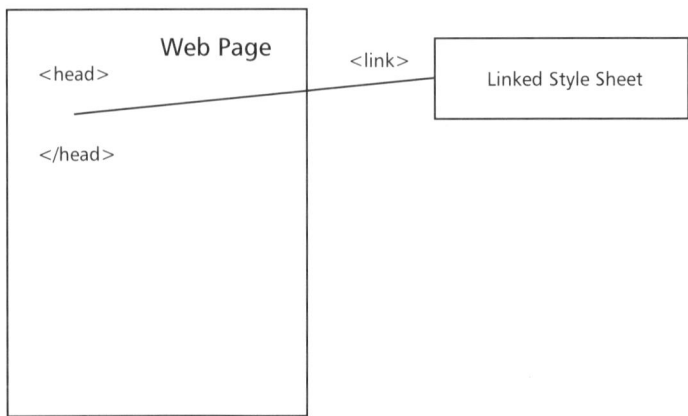

Figure 10.6 *Linked style sheet.*

```
<!-- OUTDOOR style sheet. Use for
outdoor feature articles in third-
quarter and fourth-quarter issues.
Don't use for editorials, columns,
or news. 5/97-->

body { background-color: teal }
b { color: white }
p { margin-left: 20% }
p { margin-right: 10% }
```

This CSS file is an extra file to be downloaded (by Web site visitors), and the download time for both the HTML document and the CSS file will be slightly longer than if the style sheet were incorporated into the HTML document itself. However, by being separate, the CSS file can serve multiple HTML documents. A change in the style sheet will generate that change in every HTML document that the style sheet serves. Slick! Megaslick!

Import It

You can also import *outdoor.css* into an HTML document. But you cannot import it by linking to it. You can only import it into an existing style sheet in the HTML document. Suppose you have the following existing style sheet in an HTML document:

```
<head><title> Aventure
Exotique</title>
<style type="text/css">
<!--
i { color: lime }
-->
</style>
```

You can import *outdoor.css* by using the *@import* command (see Figure 10.7):

```
<head><title> Aventure
Exotique</title>
<style type="text/css">
<!--
i { color: lime }
@import url(outdoor.css)
-->
</style>
```

Now you have effectively combined *outdoor.css* and the style sheet in the HTML document. Again, a change in *outdoor.css* will generate the change in all the HTML documents that it serves. Megaslick again!

Slip It Inline

As you have seen, a style sheet does not have to be lengthy. It can even be a one-liner. Conveniently, you can slip a style sheet right into the HTML document almost anywhere you want to put it.

```
<p>So, we started out of Boucher
Creek in Topaz Canyon and camped up
on the Tonto about a mile along the
```

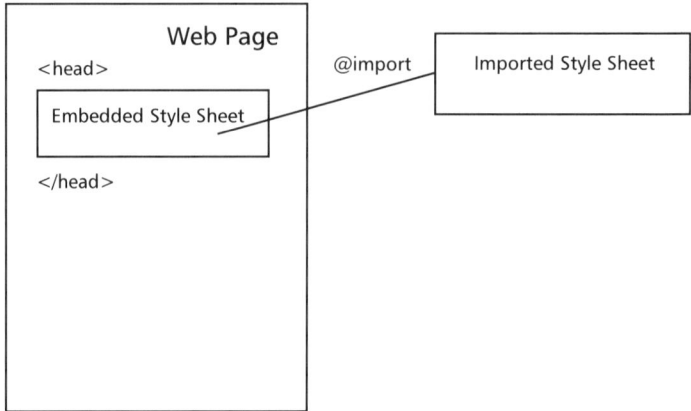

Figure 10.7 *Imported style sheet.*

```
Tonto trail. Again, it was a
pleasant campsite. The evening was
warm with intermittent breezes.
Oddly enough on the Tonto, a
seemingly long way from water, there
was a small <strong style="color:
yellow">mosquito</strong>
problem.</p>
```

The <span> Tag The *<span>* tag works great for inserting style inline. Keep it in mind.

This style sheet for the *<strong>* tag changes the color of the tagged text to yellow. You put the declaration right between the quotation marks as a value for the *style* attribute.

What Do These Four Methods All Mean?

The Cascading Style Sheet provides layout and typesetting capability over and above that found currently in HTML. For that reason alone, it constitutes a valuable addition to your HTML bag of tricks. As you use CSS, you will come to appreciate its capability to create a precise and attractive HTML document.

Inline

By using simple inline style sheets, you can take advantage of the additional formatting capability that CSS brings to HTML and apply it directly. This can be a handy way to use CSS.

Embedded

By using embedded style sheets, you can also take advantage of CSS formatting. This technique provides an option that's much like using a word processor. The formatting from the style sheet and the structuring from the HTML markups work together to define the HTML document. Like a word processor document, however, you have to change the embedded style sheet to change the layout and style. So, although the style sheet provides advantages, it does not provide the ultimate advantage of being a separate file.

Linked or Imported

A style sheet, when used via linking or importing, provides style as it was meant to be provided by SGML: separately. A separate style sheet can serve many documents. When you change the style sheet, the presentation of all the documents changes. This is a primary benefit of SGML and the DTDs of SGML (e.g., HTML). At least, use this technique to put all the basic style for your HTML documents into one CSS file. When you want to change something basic, you simple change the CSS file, and your entire Web site changes.

Cascade

Wait a minute! With these four ways to incorporate style sheets into HTML documents and the capability to use more than one style sheet at once, how do you keep everything sorted out when there are conflicts in the style sheets? That's where the *cascading* part comes in. The dictionary definition of an electronic cascade is: "A series of components or networks, the output of each of which serves as the input for the next." In this case, the components are software components, specifically, the style sheets. A browser that is CSS-enabled uses a set of rules to resolve the conflicts in the style sheets when it cascades them.

Conflicts between Style Sheets

As an overview, the cascading of style sheets works like this:

1. Inline style sheet declarations take top priority. This makes sense, because this type of style sheet usually tweaks one specific element of one HTML document.
2. Embedded style sheets take the next priority. This also makes sense, because this formats one specific HTML document.

3. Linked style sheets take the next priority. These format Web pages at the document system level (multiple HTML documents) and provide a generalized sort of formatting.

4. Likewise, imported style sheets provide formatting for document systems and take the next priority.

5. Don't forget Web site visitors. They have some residual control over how their browsers format HTML documents. They take the next priority.

6. Finally, the browsers have defaults. The browsers will format everything left unformatted. The browsers have the last priority.

It's not quite as simple as all that, but you get the idea. Can you make adjustments? Yes, you can designate any declaration with *! important* to have it go to the top of the priority ranking. The following declaration will take priority over any other declaration regarding the color of italic type.

```
i { color: lime ! important }
```

Conflicts within Style Sheets

Now, get down to the business of resolving conflicts within the same style sheet. In this case, it's not a matter of choosing one style sheet over another. It's a matter of resolving conflicts between declarations within the same style sheet. Here's how CCS makes such a resolution:

1. CSS formats according to specific declarations and then according to inheritance. For instance, a declaration for bold has greater priority than a declaration for paragraph.

2. CSS formats according to importance (i.e., use of the *! importance* property). A declaration that contains the *! important* property takes priority. For instance, if you designate a declaration for paragraph as important, it will take priority over a declaration for bold that does not have the *! importance* property.

3. CSS formats according to the specificity of the selector. Some selectors are intrinsically more specific than others even though they may otherwise be of equal weight. The more specific selectors take priority. You may not want to look under the hood on this one; the rules for determining the comparative intrinsic specificity of selectors get a little complicated.

4. CSS formats according to the order specified in the HTML document. If all else fails to resolve conflicts, a declaration that appears later in the HTML document takes priority over one appearing earlier; that is, the declaration closest to the bottom of the document takes priority.

A Strategy

What can you make of all this conflict resolution? Here are some guidelines that will help you avoid getting a headache over conflicts.

• Be generally aware of the rules governing conflict and plan your style sheets carefully to avoid conflicts. In the alternate, just plan carefully.

• Build style sheets from the general to the specific.

• Take advantage of linked and imported style sheets where they prove useful. They provide you with a powerful tool for building Web site document systems that are efficient to construct and maintain. But don't use them where you can't achieve these efficiencies.

• Use linked or imported style sheets for general formatting and embedded or inline style sheets for more specific formatting.

• Keep style sheets as simple as possible. Remember, you don't have to redefine all of HTML for every style sheet.

• Procure style sheets that provide formatting that you want to use. Authoring programs will contain useful style sheets. You can buy collections of style sheets. And you can obtain the style sheet of any HTML document on the Internet (see sidebar).

- Test and retest your style sheets as you build them. Don't wait until you have finished them to test them.

- Pay attention to degradability (see end of chapter).

Just as for HTML, sometimes CSS-capable authoring programs work well and save lots of time, but sometimes you also have to edit at the code level to make the adjustments you need. Don't try to substitute an authoring program for basic knowledge about CSS.

Keep in mind that the browsers do not implement CSS reliably and uniformly yet. You will have to experiment a lot to get style sheets to work well, not only for one browser, but for two browsers. Nonetheless, as soon as things settle down a little, style sheets will prove a valuable addition to HTML and a welcome time saver for Web developers.

First Example

Now it's time for an example. The following is part of a simple HTML document that composes an outdoor article for a Web adventure magazine. You can see that, by creating a style sheet for the document, you can easily improve the formatting (see Figure 10.8).

```
<html><head><title>Aventure
Exotique</title></head>
<body>
<ul><i>Aventure Exotique</i></ul>
<center><h2>Hiking the Gems</h2>
<b>The Boucher-Tonto-Bass Trek in
the Grand Canyon</b>
<p>
by Joseph T. Sinclair</center>
<h3>First Day of Trek</h3>
We started the Boucher-Tonto-Bass
trek April 27, 1997, by doing the
shuttle of vehicles out to the
trailhead. From the Tolvar Hotel
out to the South Bass trailhead and
then back to the Tolvar and out to
```

Style Sheets from the Web To obtain any style sheet from the Web, look at the source code of the document. If the document uses a linked or imported style sheet, get the CSS file name from the source code. Place the URL of the CSS file in your browser in the *Open Page* input. Access and download the CSS file.

Keep in mind that the copyright laws protect content on the Web (text, graphics, etc.). They do not protect the structure and formatting of Web documents. However, they do protect the code that creates the structure and formatting of documents. Hence, you cannot legally use or resell CSS "as is" without a license from the author. But without a license, you can certainly use such style sheets as a guideline for creating your own similar style sheets.

```
Hermit's Rest takes about three
hours by the time you drive it,
transfer some gear from one vehicle
to another, and talk with some
people at the trailheads.
<p>
About noon we took our first steps
down the Hermit trail toward the
Boucher trail. Initially, the trail
is easy, but it turns difficult
after a while. Even before you
reach the Dripping Springs
intersection, you can count on some
rugged hiking. We stopped to camp
on Yuma Point after hiking about
four miles in five hours. The cool
still evening was interrupted by
intermittent breezes.
<h3>Second Day</h3>
Yuma Point is a pleasant camping
spot but hardly one that shows a
lot of progress into the canyon.
Early Monday morning well before 7
AM, we continued down on an even
more rugged trail finally crossing
the Whites Butte plateau and
descending the Redwall. By the time
we got to Boucher Creek in early
afternoon, we were quite tired.
<p>
```

Take the simple style sheet from earlier in this chapter (*out-door.css*) and incorporate it into this HTML document (see Figure 10.9):

```
<html><head><title>Aventure
Exotique</title>
<style type="text/css">
<!--
body { background-color: teal }
b { color: white }
```

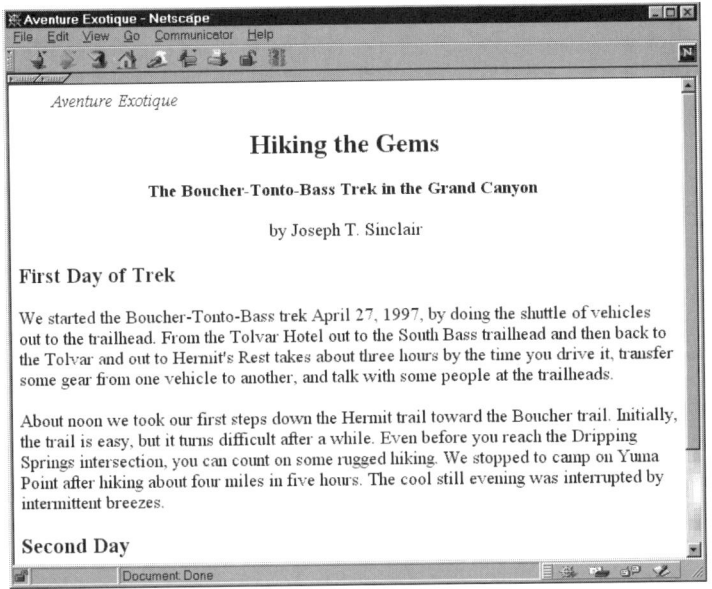

Figure 10.8 *Web adventure magazine article in simple HTML.*

Paragraph Tag We have to start thinking of paragraph tags as being containers. Use the </p> tag as well as the <p> tag. Apply the <p></p> tags to every paragraph in the document. This will ensure that your documents are ready for XML. Actually, you don't have to do this for HTML because the browsers will imply the second tag, the </p> tag. But you do have to put the <p> tag at the *beginning* of every paragraph for CSS to work.

```
p { margin-left: 20% }
p { margin-right: 10% }
-->
</style>
</head>
```

Notice in Figure 10.9 that the first paragraph has not conformed to the paragraph formatting.

Apply the <p> tag to the beginning of each paragraph, and the magazine article looks as it should (see Figure 10.10).

This is now a readable document. But it needs a final touch. The section headings are flush left and might look better with a left margin. Add the following declaration to the style sheet:

```
h3 { margin-left: 15% }
```

Figure 10.11 shows the result.

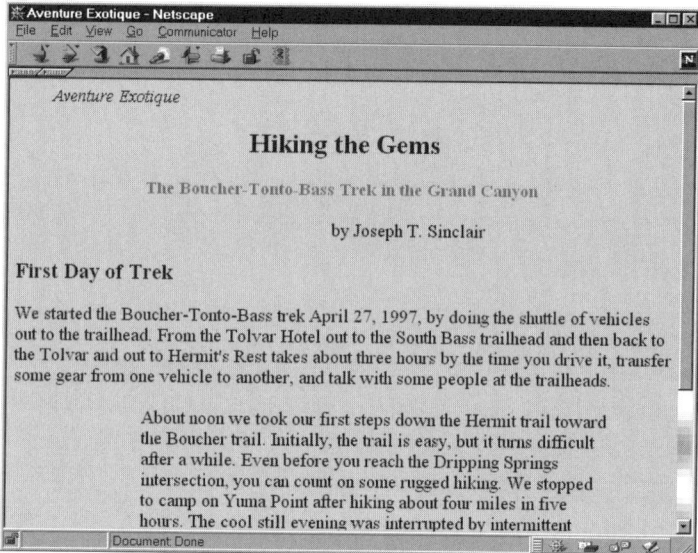

Figure 10.9 *Magazine article with style sheet.*

The title, subtitle, and byline don't seem to be centered properly. Take out the </center> tag after *Sinclair*, and reposition it

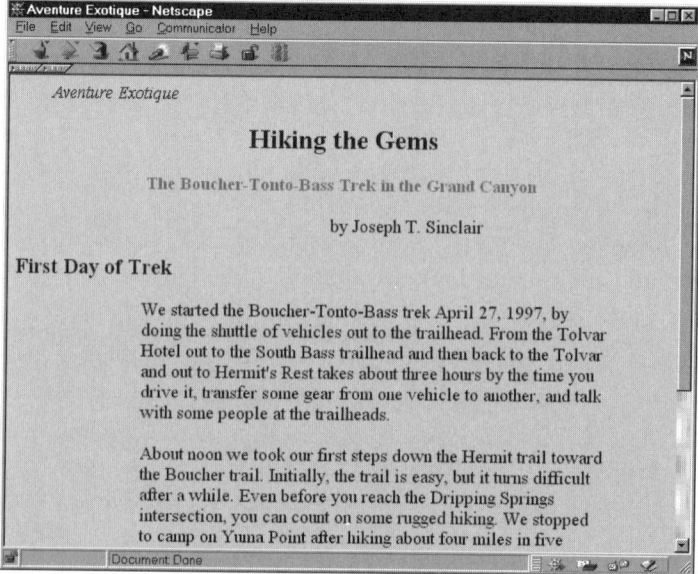

Figure 10.10 *Magazine article with correct <p> tags.*

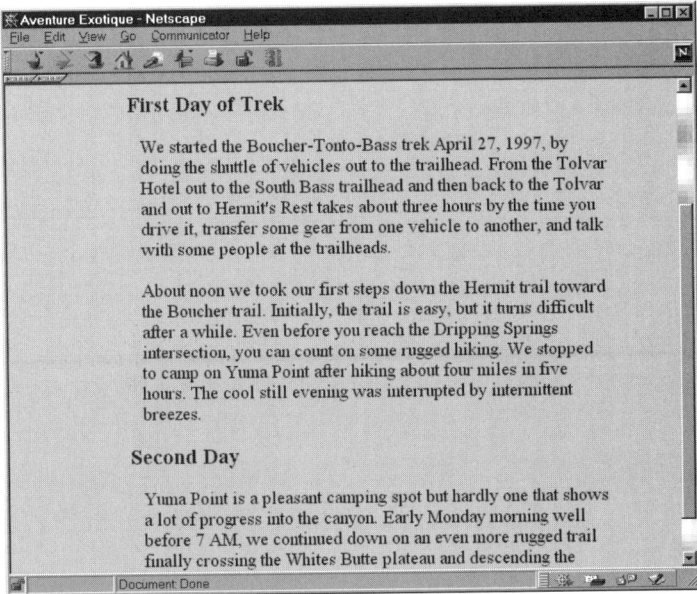

Figure 10.11 *Magazine article with section headings positioned.*

after *Gems</h2>*. You can center the subtitle and byline simply by applying the *<p align=center>* tag to each line. You have to break the line with the *
* tag for each line of the subtitle and byline, or the centering won't work. For the title, you must make a special class *.mar21* as follows:

```
.mar21 { margin-left: 20% }
.mar21 { margin-right: 10% }
```

This matches the paragraph margins. Use the following for the *<center>* tag to center the title:

```
<center class=mar21>
```

Figure 10.12 shows the finished document. Not too fancy, but it's readable online (800 × 600, less than full window). Figures

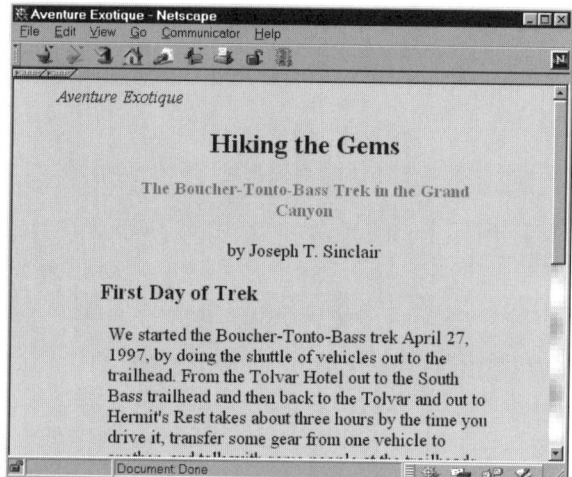

Figure 10.12 *Magazine article with a format that's readable online (800 × 600, less than full window, roughly simulates 640 × 480).*

10.13 and 10.14 show the document at 800 × 600 (full window) and 1024 × 768 (full window) resolutions respectively.

And by the way, it's time to learn that you can compress the style sheets by using commas and semicolons. The style sheet looks like this:

```
body { background-color: teal }
b { color: white }
p { margin-left: 20% }
p { margin-right: 10% }
h3 { margin-left: 15% }
.mar21 { margin-left: 20% }
.mar21 { margin-right: 10% }
```

After compression, the style sheet looks like this:

```
body { background-color: teal }
b { color: white }
p, .mar21 { margin-left: 20%;
margin-right: 10%; }
h3 { margin-left: 15% }
```

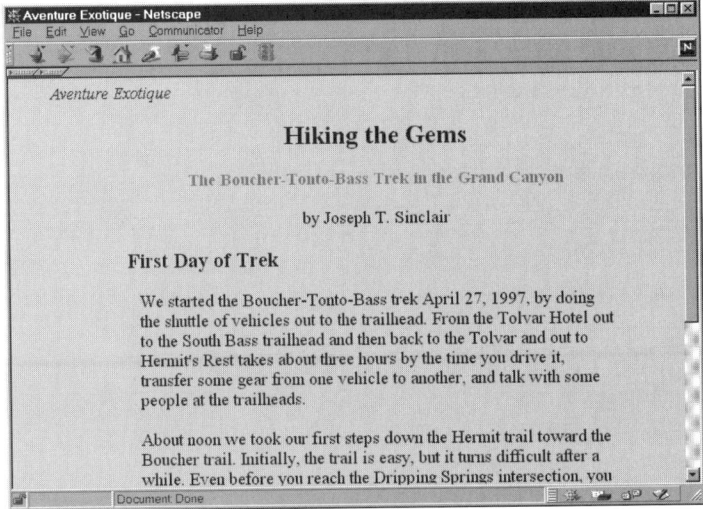

Figure 10.13 *Magazine article with a format that's readable online (800 × 600, full window).*

Use a comma to separate selectors or classes (e.g., *p* and *.mar21*). Likewise, use a semicolon to separate properties such

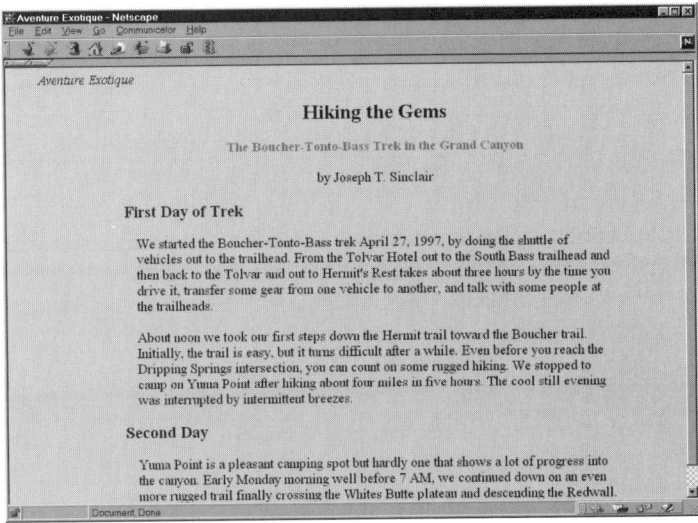

Figure 10.14 *Magazine article with a format that's readable online (1024 × 768, full window).*

as *margin-left* and *margin-right*. In addition, a semicolon must follow the last property. The code for the finished HTML document follows. Notice that each paragraph has a *<p>* tag now.

```
<html><head><title>Aventure
Exotique</title>
<style type="text/css">
<!--
body { background-color: teal }
b { color: white }
p, .mar21 { margin-left: 20%;
margin-right: 10%; }
h3 { margin-left: 15% }
-->
</style>
</head><body>
<ul><i>Aventure Exotique</i></ul>
<center class=mar21><h2>Hiking the
Gems</h2></center>
<p align=center><b>The Boucher-
Tonto-Bass Trek in the Grand
Canyon</b><br>
<p align=center>by Joseph T.
Sinclair<br>
<h3>First Day of Trek</h3>
<p>We started the Boucher-Tonto-
Bass trek April 27, 1997, by doing
the shuttle of vehicles out to the
trailhead. From the Tolvar Hotel
out to the South Bass trailhead and
then back to the Tolvar and out to
Hermit's Rest takes about three
hours by the time you drive it,
transfer some gear from one vehicle
to another, and talk with some
people at the trailheads.
<p>About noon we took our first
steps down the Hermit trail toward
the Boucher trail. Initially, the
trail is easy, but it turns
difficult after a while. Even
before you reach the Dripping
```

```
Springs intersection, you can count
on some rugged hiking. We stopped
to camp on Yuma Point after hiking
about four miles in five hours. The
cool still evening was interrupted
by intermittent breezes.
<h3>Second Day</h3>
<p>Yuma Point is a pleasant camping
spot but hardly one that shows a
lot of progress into the canyon.
Early Monday morning well before 7
AM, we continued down on an even
more rugged trail finally crossing
the Whites Butte plateau and
descending the Redwall. By the time
we got to Boucher Creek in early
afternoon, we were quite tired.
```

This wasn't too much work. And the good news is that you can use this same style sheet for multiple outdoor articles without any further toil except the rudimentary HTML tagging of the document. Of course, you will have to extract the style sheet and put it in its own CSS file. See the following updated *outdoor.css* file:

```
<!-- OUTDOOR style sheet. Use for
outdoor feature articles in third-
quarter and fourth-quarter issues.
Don't use for editorials, columns,
or news. 5/97-->

body { background-color: teal }
b { color: white }
p, .mar21 { margin-left: 20%;
margin-right: 10%; }
h3 { margin-left: 15% }
```

Remember, after putting this style sheet in its own CSS file *outdoor.css*, you link it to the HTML document that you want to style by using the *<link>* tag in the *<head>* of the HTML document.

Second Example

Style sheets also handle typesetting well. This example will continue with the outdoor magazine article from the preceding section. First, you will need to typeset the text of the article:

```
body { font-family: imperial bt }
body { font-size: 10pt }
```

This will render all text, including headings, in 10-point Imperial BT, a typeface that you will find easy to read online. This typeface runs large, so you will want to designate a smaller size than you might use for other typefaces. You need a larger type size for the headings in the article, say 16 points. It would be nice to give special treatment to the title, subtitle, and byline. The title will look good at 24 points, and the subtitle and byline will look good at 12 points. Create two classes to designate these sizes:

```
h3 {font-size: 16pt }
.type12 { font-size: 12pt }
.mar21 { margin-left: 20%; margin-right: 10%;
font-size: 24pt; }
```

Incorporate these in the style sheet after condensing them:

```
body { background-color: teal;
font-family: imperial bt; font-
size: 10pt; }
b { color: white }
p { margin-left: 20%; margin-right:
10%; }
h3 { margin-left: 15%; font-size:
16pt; }
.type12 { font-size: 12pt }
.mar21 { margin-left: 20%; margin-
right: 10%; font-size: 24pt; }
```

Next, apply the classes to the subtitle and byline:

```
<p align=center class=type12><b>The
Boucher-Tonto-Bass Trek in the
Grand Canyon </b><br>
<p align=center class=type12>by
Joseph T. Sinclair<br>
```

Make the Outdoor style sheet a separate file *outdoor.css*, and put the following *<link>* tag in the head of the HTML document. This HTML document links to *outdoor.css*.

```
<link rel=stylesheet
href="outdoor.css" type="text/css"
title="Outdoor">
```

Figure 10.15 shows how this changes the typesetting.

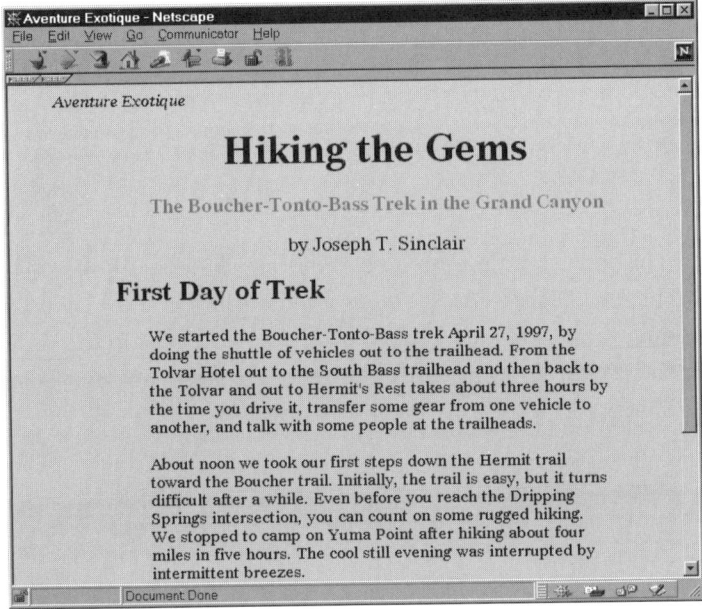

Figure 10.15 *Magazine article with new typesetting.*

Next, change the logo to its proper typeface which is Century Gothic bold italic. This will require another class designating the typeface, the weight, and the size,

```
.logo { font-family: century gothic; font-weight:
bold; font-size: 12pt; }
```

and another modification of the HTML document:

```
<ul><i class=logo>Aventure
Exotique</i></ul>
```

To tweak the article a little, move the title, subtitle, and byline to the left margin (left justified) by removing the *<center>* tag from the title and the *<p align=center>* tags from the subtitle and byline and then replacing them with the following:

```
<h2 class=mar21>Hiking the
Gems</h2>
<p class=type12><b>The Boucher-
Tonto-Bass Trek in the Grand Canyon
</b><br>
<p class=type12>by Joseph T.
Sinclair<br>
```

This looks a little more contemporary. And finally, it would be nice to decrease the leading for the subtitle and byline by adding the *line-height* property to the *.type12* class in the style sheet. Might as well justify the text, too, with the *text-align* property for potentially greater readability:

```
.type12 { font-size: 12pt; line-height: 70%; }
p { margin-left: 20%; margin-right: 10%; text-
align: justify }
```

Modify these in the style sheet. Now Figure 10.16 shows a more sophisticated typeset look.

Probably Not a Good Idea Notice that the *<i>* tag has been modified by the *.logo* style, which includes bold. This is the kind of innocent modification that may backfire later. It's probably not a good idea to modify a style tag with style treatment. Chapter 13 reconsiders this treatment as Netscape Composer applies TrueDoc. But for now, move ahead with the *.logo* modification the way it is set here.

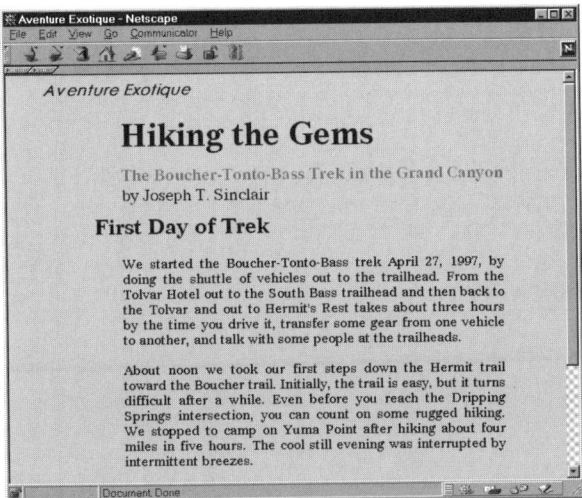

Figure 10.16 *Magazine article with more sophisticated typesetting.*

Spacing needs to be added between the byline and the first section heading in Figure 10.16 and also below the logo. Because the *line-height* (leading) property adds or subtracts *both* above and below the line, that will not provide the additional leading needed. Consequently, use the *margin-bottom* property inside the HTML tags for the logo and the byline to add the line spacing.

```
style="margin-bottom: 20pt"
```

```
<ul><i class=logo style="margin-
bottom: 20pt">Aventure
Exotique</i></ul>
```

```
<p class=type12 style="margin-
bottom: 20pt">by Joseph T.
Sinclair<br>
```

The finished typesetting in Figure 10.17 looks better than the original in Figure 10.8, which is plain old HTML.

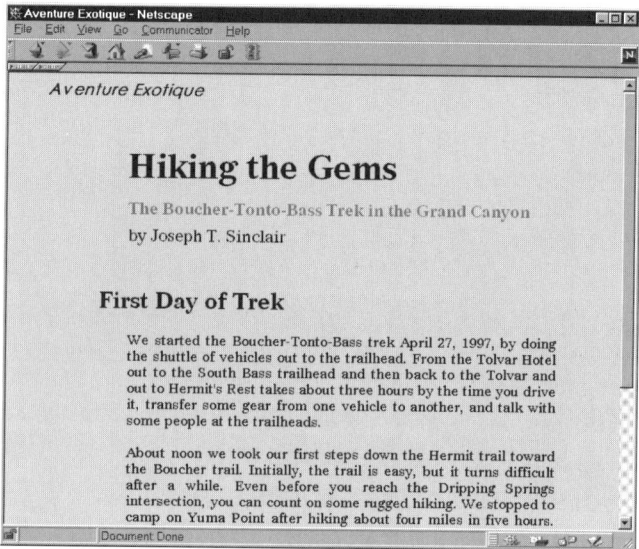

Figure 10.17 *Magazine article with finished typesetting.*

The Outdoor style sheet *outdoor.css* now looks like this:

```
<!-- OUTDOOR style sheet. Use for
outdoor feature articles in third-
quarter and fourth-quarter issues.
Don't use for editorials, columns,
or news. 5/97-->
body { background-color: teal;
font-family: imperial bt; font-
size: 10pt; }
b { color: white }
p { margin-left: 20%; margin-right:
10%; text-align: justify; }
h3 { margin-left: 15%; font-size:
16pt; }
.type12 { font-size: 12pt; line-
height: 70%; }
.mar21 { margin-left: 20%; margin-
right: 10%; font-size: 24pt; }
.logo { font-family: century
gothic; font-weight: bold; font-
size: 12pt; }
```

Where do the fonts come from? Funny you should ask. The fonts come from the Web site visitor's computer, either a TrueDoc file (.pfr) that accompanies the Web page, or a font embedding file (.eot) that accompanies the Web page, or both. See Chapters 12 to 15.

Degradability

The degradability issue has been around since day two. How do you use the latest HTML technology but still have your HTML documents look good to those who are still using the old technology? And where do you draw the line?

For example, should you make your HTML documents look good for those who have text-only browsers and for those who surf the Web with graphics turned off? One approach is purely statistical. How many people still use text-only browsers? Probably not very many. How many surf the Web with graphics turned off? Probably not too many. After all, inline graphics made the Web popular. What percentage of the entire market will you lose by ignoring the text-only segment of the Web population? Probably a small percentage. Therefore, you can reasonably conclude that it is not worth your time and effort to worry about degradability to text-only browsing. On the other hand, if 75 percent of your specific Web audience still uses text-only browsers, you had better make sure your Web site looks good for the text-only crowd.

At each incremental advance in HTML technology, you have to make decisions regarding degradability. Fortunately, CSS is readily degradable. Unfortunately, fostering degradability takes a lot of planning, experimentation, and testing. Here are two basic guidelines for fostering degradability with CSS.

- Use HTML tags for the purpose intended. Don't try to reinvent HTML by contorted use of CSS properties. For instance, use the *<b>* tag to format bold as much as possible.
- Back up CSS with HTML where sensible. Sure you can use CSS to center an element. Use the *<center>* tag, too.

Universal Style Sheet?
Can this style sheet be used for other outdoor articles? Is it universal? You have to ask yourself if everything you need for formatting is in the style sheet (inside the *.css* file). In this case, the answer is yes, except for the last adjustment made. When the *margin-bottom* property was applied to the logo and the byline, it was placed inside the HTML tags for those lines using the *style* attribute, not inside the style sheet. Consequently, the style sheet is almost, but not completely, universal.

Remove the *style* attributes from the logo and byline HTML tags. Add the *margin-bottom* property to the *logo* class. Create a new class for *<p>* that includes the *margin-bottom* property and the *type12* properties together, put the new class in the style sheet, and replace *type12* with the new class as the value for the *class* attribute inside the HTML markup for the byline. Then the style sheet will be universal.

Many factors, such as the cascading order of rules to resolve conflicts or the compatibility of current versions of competing browsers, have an effect on degradability. No easily remembered rules or guidelines are up to the task of making sense of it all. Your best technique is still trial and error.

Allaire's HomeSite

Allaire's HomeSite is a very sophisticated HTML editor that provides some nice features for Web typography. It offers a browser-safe color palette (or any palette you want to use) in plain view and a Quick Font font tagging capability (see Figure 10.18). Perhaps its most outstanding feature is its elegant CSS maker (Wizard) which enables you to create style sheets easily and quickly (see Figure 10.19). Macromedia's Dreamweaver HTML/DHTML authoring program includes a bundled version of HomeSite.

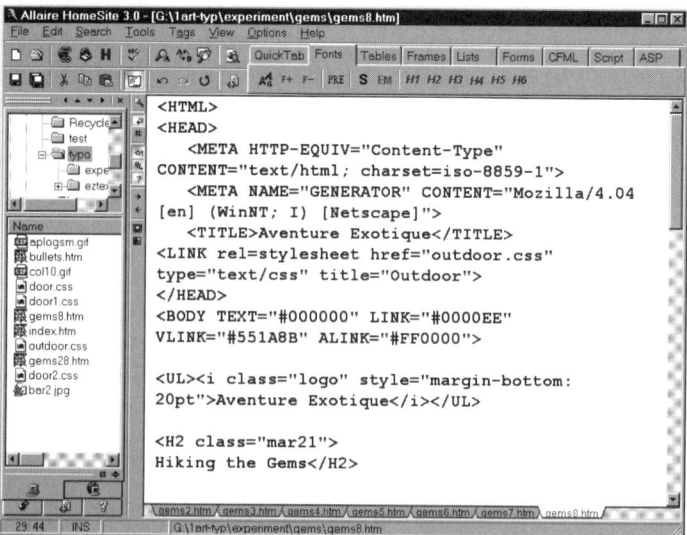

Figure 10.18 *Allaire's HomeSite HTML editor.*

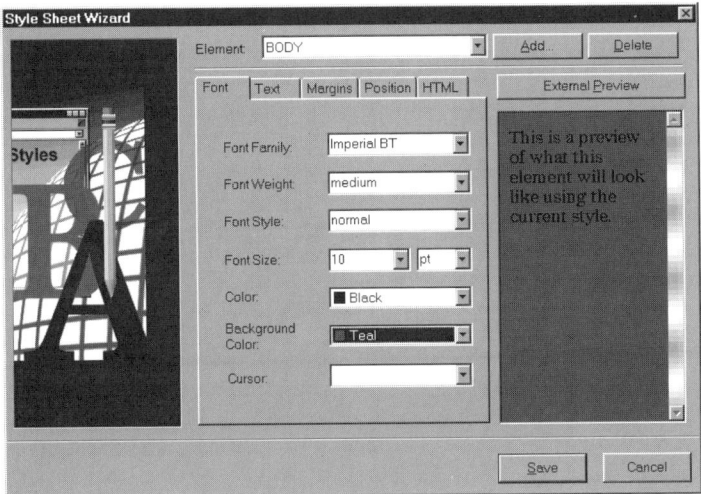

Figure 10.19 *Allaire's HomeSite Style Sheet Wizard.*

Summary

CSS isn't perfect yet, but it gives you a lot of additional control over your Web pages. You can learn it easily, and many HTML editors and authoring programs have already incorporated it. It degrades well, so you can start experimenting with it and using it now. Perhaps best of all, you can start making style sheets to serve multiple documents. That should be a real time-saver when it's time to make formatting changes. The next chapter covers the CSS properties individually in a way that you can use as a reference. But learn more. Buy a book devoted to CSS, and use it as a reference. Cascading Style Sheets are the future.

CSS Reference

SS is the new standard for HTML style sheets now in effect and implemented in the Netscape 4.0 and Microsoft 4.0 browsers. Use this chapter as a reference for the properties, which are presented in six groups:

Fonts

Color and Background

Text

Layout

Classification

Next-Generation Layout

Use this chapter to construct your own style sheets. Keep in mind, however, that this chapter makes no attempt to document which browsers support which CSS properties. That is beyond the scope of the book and will change as vendors release new browser versions. Presumably, someday soon each browser will fully support CSS. Books like *Guide to Web Style Sheets*, by Mulder (Hayden, 1997), go to great lengths to explain CSS fully and to document which browsers support what. Look for Mulder's CSS updates in the Hayden Web site at the Macmillan Web site http://www.mcp.com. Also consult the Style Sheets Compatibility Chart sponsored by *Web Review* at http://style.webreview.com which publishes a current version. This chapter presents CSS properties generally the way they are supposed to work and shows their inherent capability to generate professional-looking and precise HTML documents. Chapter 10 thoroughly acquaints you with CSS, and this chapter provides specific information on each property in an easy-to-use reference format. You can also obtain up-to-date information on CSS at the WWW Consortium's Web site at http://www.w3.org.

Be forewarned that a reading of Chapter 10 may be necessary for you to understand this chapter. For instance, where *length* is an appropriate value for a property, you need to know:

- What is a property?
- What is a value?
- What measurements does *length* include?

Chapter 10 answers these questions and many more. Also note that, for many of the numerical values for the properties, you can use negative numbers.

Although easy to learn, CSS provides the basis for an infinite number of combinations, of which only an infinitesimally small number are covered in this book or in any book. The best way to learn CSS is to experiment.

CSS 1

The properties that follow compose CSS 1. You will find most properties straightforward and easy to understand.

Fonts

Setting font properties, of course, is the most important for typesetting. CSS provides you with five properties for fonts. Note that the sixth font property *font* combines the other five into one property that does it all.

font-family

Specifies the typeface by providing a prioritized list of font names:

```
{ font-family:                }
<family-name>    cursive
serif            fantasy
sans serif       monospace
```

Default: Browser's default
Applies to: All
Inherited: Yes
Value % :   NA

Example:

```
P { font-family: "baskerville mt", times, serif }
```

This property prioritizes fonts according to order. The first font has the greatest priority (i.e., Baskerville MT), followed by the subsequent fonts, if any, in sequence. You designate fonts by their names, and you can also use the generic names listed above. Because Windows and Mac do not necessarily have cursive and fantasy fonts installed, the browser defaults used for those fonts will be one of the other standard fonts, such as Times New Roman or Arial. Put font names containing more than one word in quotes (e.g., Gill Sans becomes "gill sans"). Make sure that the font name you use is the actual name of the font file that the Windows and Mac systems use (e.g., Garamond MT), which may not be the same as the name displayed on the menu.

How does the browser handle font names? The steps in the process follow:

1. The browser creates a database of fonts available. If it finds two fonts with exactly the same name, it ignores one of them.

2. The browser takes the *font-family* one at a time and tries to match them to the declaration or declarations

Font Names The mostly unregulated practice of naming fonts mentioned in Chapter 2 has caused much confusion for typography and has established a shaky basis on which to build digital typography systems. Be careful with font names for CSS, as well as for other Web publishing uses.

regarding the font. It goes through *font-style*, *font-variant*, *font-weight*, and *font-size*.

3. If the browser can't find a match to the *font-family* with the highest priority, it goes to the second *font-family*, or eventually the browser default font.

4. If the character sought is not in the requisite *font-family*, that family will be bypassed.

This process can get complicated, and trial and error may be the best strategy to handle it. Keep in mind that you can even specify type style using this property (e.g., "baskerville mt bold" is a valid font name). The best practice, however, is to specify type style separately with the *font-style* property.

font-style

Specifies the style of the typeface.

{ font-style: }

normal
italic
oblique

Default:	Normal
Applies to:	All
Inherited:	Yes
Value % :	NA

Example:

h4 { font-style: italic }

Lacking an *italic*, a same-family font with a name like *cursive* will be used as the italic. Likewise, lacking an *oblique*, a same-family font with a name like *slanted*, or *incline* will be used as t falls under the

Default:	Normal
Applies to:	All
Inherited:	Yes
Value % :	NA

Example:

em { font-variant: small-caps }

Use this property to specify small caps. Because the *<em>* and the *<strong>* tags do not conform to normal typographical practices, you might use one of them routinely to specify small caps.

font-weight
Specifies the weight of the typeface.

{ font-weight: }

normal	400
bold	500
bolder	600
lighter	700
100	800
200	900
300	

Numerical Values Using the numericals for OpenType, you will be able to set a weight that optimizes a font for reading on the screen.

Default:	Normal
Applies to:	All
Inherited:	Yes
Value % :	NA

Example:

```
p { font-weight: 300 }
```

The number 100 is at the light end, with 900 being at the heavy end. Normal is 400 and bold 700. The browser attempts to sort out and match the numbers to names like *medium*, *book*, *roman*, *light*, *heavy*, *semi bold*, *ultra bold*, and *black*. OpenType fonts will contain the nine numerical values.

font-size

Designates the font size.

```
{ font-size:                    }

<absolute size>
<relative size>
<length>
<percentage>
```

Default:	Defined by browser
Applies to:	All
Inherited:	Yes
Value % :	Relative to parent

Examples:

```
p { font-size: larger }
blockquote { font-size: smaller }
code { font-size: 10pt }
code { font-size: 80% }
```

For *absolute size* use keywords:

xx-small
x-small
small
medium
large
x-large
xx-large

The absolute keywords correspond to the numerical values for browsers (1–7). The relative sizes relate to the parent HTML element. The em (a relative measurement) is popular with Web typographers. For *length*, use normal measurements such as points. For *percentage*, use a percentage of the default font size. Review the Measurements section of Chapter 10 to better understand setting font sizes.

font

Specifies multiple font properties in one declaration.

{ font: }

<font-style>
<font-variant>
<font-weight>
<font-size> / <line-height>
<font-family>

Default:	NA
Applies to:	All
Inherited:	Yes
Value % :	Allowed on *font-size* and *line-height*

Example:

p { font: 12pt/14pt "garamond mt" }

Using the em When used for the *font-size* property, the em is relative to the parent type size (often the normal text type). For 12-point normal text, 1.5 em is 18 points, and 0.5 em is 6 points. This proves to be a good way to size type, because if you change the parent type size, all the other sizes (the children) change with the parent proportionally.

This is confusing, however, because you must use an absolute size or length to set the size for the parent. If you don't set the type size for the parent (i.e., most often, normal text), the type size will be the browser default type size for normal text.

One declaration does all. Use as shorthand for specifying font properties. You do not have to list all the values, but the values you do list must appear with a space between each value in the order listed above, with the *font-family* appearing last.

Color and Background

Use color and background properties to set the foreground (text) color and the background color or images.

color

Specifies text color.

```
{ color:                    }
<color>
```

Default:	Determined by browser
Applies to:	All
Inherited:	Yes
Value % :	NA

Example:

```
i { color: lime }
```

Use to specify text color. See Chapter 10 for the different ways to specify color.

background-color

Specifies background color.

```
{ background-color:                }
<color>
transparent
```

Default:	Transparent
Applies to:	All
Inherited:	Yes
Value % :	NA

Example:

```
body { background-color: teal }
p { background-color: lime }
```

Use to specify background color. See Chapter 10 for different ways to specify color. If you do not specify a color, the Web element is transparent, and the browser or operating system will determine the background color. You can use *background-color* property for any element.

background-image

Specifies an image to be used as the background.

```
{ background-image:                    }
<URL>
none
```

Default:	None
Applies to:	All
Inherited:	No
Value % :	NA

Example:

```
body { background-image: url(pighead.gif) }
p { background-image: url(sand.gif) }
```

Use this property to place a background image for the Web page. Will the image tile? See the *background-repeat* declaration.

Background Use *background-color:* for creating a readable background in an otherwise unsuitable page for reading. You can use it with any page element. For instance, on a dark purple page you might want to use light mauve as a background for <p> so that people so that people can read the black text.

You can use the *background-image* property for any element making it a potentially creative property.

background-repeat

Defines how a background image will tile or not tile.

{ background-repeat: }

repeat
repeat-x
repeat-y
no-repeat

Default:	Repeat
Applies to:	All
Inherited:	No
Value % :	NA

Example:

body { background: url(pighead.gif); background-repeat: repeat-x; }

Once you have specified a background image, it will tile to fill up the HTML document. This property enables you to control the tiling.

repeat	Tiles horizontally and vertically to fill page
repeat-x	Tiles horizontally in one row
repeat-y	Tiles vertically in one column
no-repeat	One image only—does not tile

background-attachment

Specifies how an image will display in relation to the browser window.

{ background-attachment: }
fixed
scroll

Default:	Scroll
Applies to:	All
Inherited:	No
Value % :	NA

Example:

body { background: url(pighead.gif); background-attachment: fixed; }

This property works only when you use a background image property with the *<body>* tag. Normally, the image scrolls with the text. Use *fixed* to have the image stay in place and the text scroll over it.

background-position

Positions a background image.

{ background-position: }
<percentage>
<top, center, or bottom   and   left, center, or right>

Default:	0% 0% or top left
Applies to:	Block-level and replaced elements
Inherited:	No
Value % :	Refer to size of the element

Example:

```
body {

background-image: url(pighead.gif);
background-repeat: no-repeat;
background-position: 50% 50%;
}
```

Use this property to position the center of the background image. The property requires two values (coordinates). You can use percentage indicators (percentage of element):

0%	Top
0%	Left
100%	Bottom
100%	Right
50%	Center

The first value specifies the horizontal and the second the vertical. For instance, *50% 50%* or *center center* puts the center of the image in the center of the browser window. When both values are the same, you can state the value only once (e.g., *50%* instead of *50% 50%* or *center* instead of *center center*). You can also use length measurements for positioning.

background

Specifies multiple background properties.

```
{ background:                    }

<background-color>
<background-image>
<background-repeat>
<background-attachment>
<background-position>
```

Default:	Repeat
Applies to:	All
Inherited:	No
Value % :	NA

Example:

body { background: url(pighead.gif) 50% fixed }

One declaration does all. Use as shorthand for specifying background properties. You do not have to list all the values, but the values you do list must appear with a space between each value, in the order listed above.

Text

Use these CSS properties to format the display of text blocks. You can adjust spacing and orient the text.

word-spacing

Specifies the space between words.

{ word-spacing: }
normal

Default:	Normal
Applies to:	All
Inherited:	Yes
Value % :	NA

Example:

h2 { word-spacing: 0.1em }

This property *adds* spacing to the existing spacing between each word. Use it for special situations. For instance, you might use it for fine-tuning a headline.

letter-spacing

Specifies the space between characters.

{ letter-spacing: }

normal

Default:	Normal
Applies to:	All
Inherited:	Yes
Value % :	NA

Example:

h2 { letter-spacing: 0.2em }

Use *em* to set the space between characters if normal spacing is not desired. For instance, use this property to expand the text (e.g., in a heading). This is what you use to kern characters if you are not satisfied with the automatic kerning.

text-decoration

Specifies certain text treatments.

{ text-decoration: }

none
underline
overline
line-through
blink

Default:	None
Applies to:	All
Inherited:	No
Value % :	NA

Examples:

```
a:link, a:visited { text-decoration: none }
strong { text-decoration: underline }
```

This property is handy for eliminating the underlining for hyperlinks by specifying the *none* value for the *<a>* pseudo-classes. To use underlining, you can specify the *underline* value for one of the little-used tags like *strong* and use that to create underlined text.

vertical-align

Specifies the inline position of an element.

```
{ vertical-align:                    }
```

baseline	middle
sub	bottom
super	text-bottom
top	<percentage>
text-top	

Default:	Baseline
Applies to:	Inline elements
Inherited:	No
Value % :	Refer to the *<line-height>* of the element

Examples:

```
.sub { vertical-align: sub }
<img style="vertical-align: bottom">
```

Use this to align an element vertically relative to its parent. This corresponds to the *align* attribute in HTML and to the *<sup>* and *<sub>* tags.

text-transform

Specifies capitalization treatment of text.

{ text-transform: }

capitalize
uppercase
lowercase
none

Default:	None
Applies to:	All
Inherited:	Yes
Value % :	NA

Example:

h3 { text-transform: capitalize }

Use the value *capitalize* to capitalize the first letter of each word. The values *uppercase* and *lowercase,* making all caps or all lowercase, will come in handy in many situations too.

text-align

Specifies the formatting of text blocks.

{ text-align: }

left
right
center
justify

Default:	Usually left
Applies to:	Block level elements
Inherited:	Yes
Value % :	NA

Example:

```
p { text-align: justify }
```

You are familiar with the values *left*, *right*, and *center* in HTML. CSS adds the value *justify*. Be aware that the justification is dynamic. It changes when Web site visitors resize their browser windows, and it is different for each browser and each size of browser window.

text-indent

Specifies the indentation for the first word in a paragraph and for other elements.

```
{ text-indent:              }
<percentage>
<length>
```

Default:	0
Applies to:	Block-level elements
Inherited:	Yes
Value % :	Refer to parent

Example:

```
p { text-indent: 1em }
```

Use this property to indent the first word only. Use one *em* for normal paragraph indenting. The *percentage* value refers to the width of the element being indented.

line-height

Specifies leading.

{ line-height: }

normal
<number>
<percentage>

Default:	Normal
Applies to:	All
Inherited:	Yes
Value % :	Relative to the font size of element

Examples:

p { line-height: 1.25 }
p { line-height: 125% }
p { font-size: 12pt; line-height: 15pt; }

This property provides you with a number of ways to specify leading. For instance, you can use the value *number* to specify double spacing (i.e., 2). Remember that the real leading is the excess space over and above the height of the font, half of which is added above the line, with the other half added below the line. Thus, the value *15pt* for 12-point type adds 1.5 points above the line and 1.5 points below the line. The *line-height* property does not enable adding leading solely above a line of text or solely below. Use the *margin-top* or *margin-bottom* property to do that.

Layout

You use the layout properties to organize the presentation of text on the page. HTML formats *text between opening and closing tags.* The layout properties define the *space around and inside such tags.* You can think of that space as a box defined by the open and close tags. The box has all the familiar properties of a box, such as margins (outside), borders, and padding (inside) (see Figure 11.1). Layout encompasses complex features. As you might suspect, the layout properties are more numerous than the properties for handling other formatting.

If you think in terms of HTML elements as being boxes, you will find it much easier to understand CSS layout.

margin-top, margin-right, margin-bottom, margin-left

Specifies the margin of space outside an element's border.

```
{ margin-top:              }

{ margin-right:            }
{ margin-bottom:           }
{ margin-left:             }

<length>
<percentage>
auto
```

Default: 0
Applies to: All

HTML Boxes This is a partial list of the various HTML markups that require open and close tags and thereby form boxes:

- *<body>*
- *<h1-6>*
- *<p>* The *</p>* tag is currently implied by most browsers.
- *<blockquote>*
- *<code>*

Style Element Box

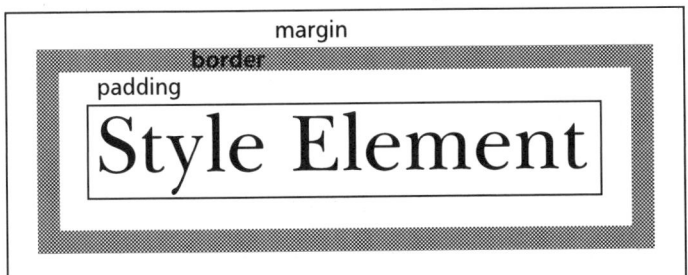

Figure 11.1 *HTML element box for style sheets.*

Inherited:	No
Value % :	Refer to parent element width

Examples:

```
code { margin-bottom: 10pt }
code { margin-left: 10% }
```

Use to create empty space around an element. For instance, you might want to use *h2 { margin-top: 6pt }* for headings to create more space between the heading and the preceding paragraph than between the heading and the succeeding paragraph.

margin

Specifies multiple margin properties.

```
{ margin:                    }
<length>
<percentage>
auto
```

Default:	Not defined
Applies to:	All
Inherited:	No
Value % :	Refer to parent element width

Example:

```
body { margin: 25px 100px 5px 100px }
```

Use as shorthand for setting margins for an element. The example specifies a 25-pixel top margin, a 100-pixel right margin, a 5-pixel bottom margin, and a 100-pixel left margin for the Web page.

padding-top, padding-right, padding-bottom, padding-left

Specifies the margin of space inside an element's border.

```
{ padding-top:              }
{ padding-right:            }
{ padding-bottom:           }
{ padding-left:             }

<length>
<percentage>
```

Default:	0
Applies to:	All
Inherited:	No
Value % :	Refer to parent element width

Example:

```
blockquote { padding-right: 5% }
blockquote { padding-left: 5% }
```

Use to create empty space around an element inside its box. For instance, this is important when you want the border of the box to show (i.e., boxed text), such as for a sidebar. These properties will indent the *blockquote* paragraph on both sides. The percentage is of the parent element such as <*p*>.

padding

Specifies multiple padding properties.

```
{ padding:                  }

<length>
<percentage>
auto
```

Default:	Not defined
Applies to:	All
Inherited:	No
Value % :	Refer to parent element width

Example:

```
blockquote { padding: 2% 5% 2% 5% }
```

Use as shorthand for setting padding for an element. The example specifies a 2-percent top padding, a 5-percent right padding, a 2-percent bottom padding, and a 5-percent left padding. The percentage is of the parent element such as *<p>*.

border-top-width, border-right-width, border-bottom-width, border-left-width

Specifies the thickness of a border.

```
{ border-top-width:               }
{ border-right-width:             }
{ border-bottom-width:            }
{ border-left-width:              }

thin
medium
thick
<length>
```

Default:	Medium
Applies to:	All
Inherited:	No
Value % :	NA

Example:

```
p { border-top-width: 2pt }
```

Use to set the thickness of borders around an element. The width should be minimal for most purposes, unless you desire to color the borders and make them part of a special design. By using all four *border* properties and a border color, you create a box. However, the borders will remain the same color as the element (thus invisible) unless you set a border color.

border-width

Specifies multiple *border-width* properties.

```
{ border-width:                    }
thin
medium
thick
<length>
```

Default:	Not defined
Applies to:	All
Inherited:	No
Value % :	Refer to parent element width

Example:

```
p { border-width: thin thin thin thin }
p { border-width: thin }
```

Use as shorthand for setting border thickness for an element. The two preceding declarations are the same.

border-color

Specifies the color of a border.

```
{ border-color:              }
<color>
```

Default:	<color>
Applies to:	All
Inherited:	No
Value % :	NA

Example:

```
code { border-width: thin; border-color: red; }
```

Use to set the color of an element's borders. Use with the *border-width* property. If you do not set the border color, the border will be the same color of the element it borders; that is, it will be invisible, in effect.

border-style

Specifies the type of line that makes a border.

```
{ border-style:                    }
```

none	groove
dotted	ridge
dashed	inset
solid	outset
double	

Default:	None
Applies to:	All
Inherited:	No
Value % :	NA

Example:

```
code { border-style: ridge }
```

Use to set the line that makes up the border. Some of the choices are:

double	The two lines and the space between equal the *border-width*.
groove	A groove with colors based on the *border-color*.
ridge	A ridge with colors based on the *border-color*.
inset	An inverted bevel with colors based on the *border-color*.
outset	A bevel with colors based on the *border-color*.

border-top, border-right, border-bottom, border-left

Specifies multiple border properties for one edge of border.

```
{ border-top:            }
{ border-right:          }
{ border-bottom:         }
{ border-left:           }

<border-width>
<border style>
<color>
```

Default:	Not defined
Applies to:	All
Inherited:	No
Value % :	NA

Example:

```
code { border-bottom: thin ridge red }
```

Use as shorthand to declare multiple properties for one edge of a border.

border

Specifies multiple border properties for all four edges of border.

{ border: }

<border-width>
<border-style>
<color>

Default:	Not defined
Applies to:	All
Inherited:	No
Value % :	NA

Example:

code { border: thin ridge red }

Use to set multiple characteristics of a border that's the same on each edge.

width

Specifies the width of an image.

{ width: }

<percentage>
auto

Default:	Auto
Applies to:	To block-level and replaced elements

Inherited: No

Value % :   Refer to parent width

Example:

.image04 { width: 116px }

Use to set the width of an image as you do in HTML. You can use this for text blocks too!

height

Specifies the height of an image. Can be used for text blocks too.

{ height: }
<height>
<percentage>
auto

Default: Auto

Applies to: Block-level and replaced elements

Inherited: No

Value % :   Refer to parent element width

Example:

.image04 { height: 152px }

Use to set the height of an image, as you do in HTML. You can use this for text blocks too!

float

Specifies where an image or text block locates.

```
{ float:                  }
left
right
none
```

Default:	None
Applies to:	All
Inherited:	No
Value % :	NA

Example:

```
.image04 { float: left; margin-right: 20px; }
```

Use like the *align* attribute of the $<img>$ tag. Use to position a graphic to the left or right and have the text of the Web page flow around it. This works for text blocks too!

clear

Specifies how text will wrap.

```
{ clear:                  }
none
left
right
both
```

Default:	None
Applies to:	All
Inherited:	No
Value % :	NA

Example:

p { clear: left }

Use this to *prevent* the text from wrapping around a graphic or text block. If you specify *left*, the paragraph text will drop below any left-floating image or text block but not right-floating elements. If you specify *right*, the paragraph will drop below any right-floating elements but not left-floating elements. If you specify *both*, the text will not wrap around any elements. If set to *none* (default), the text element will wrap around other elements either to the left or right of the text element.

Classification

Use these properties to format HTML elements by category rather than by adjusting layout or visual effects.

display

Specifies how elements are displayed in the HTML document.

{ display: }

block
inline
list-item
none

Default:	Block
Applies to:	All
Inherited:	No
Value % :	NA

Example:

h2 { display: block }
i { display: inline }

```
li { display: list-item }
strong { display: list-item }
```

Use this property to change the way that an element displays in a Web page; that is, to change the way the browser normally displays it. For instance, you might want to use the *<strong>* tag for special list items. The *display* property enables you to use it in this special way. Use the value *none* if you want an element not to display at all.

white-space

Specifies how the browser will use empty spaces.

```
{ white-space:                }
normal
pre
nowrap
```

Default:	Normal
Applies to:	Block-level elements
Inherited:	Yes
Value % :	NA

Examples:

```
p { white-space: pre }
address { white-space: nowrap }
```

Normally, browsers reduce all spaces to one space. Use the *pre* value to keep the spaces from being reduced. Note, however, that other characteristics of the *<pre>* tag accompany the value. This is something you will have to experiment with in order to figure out how to use it for the purpose you have in mind. Use *nowrap* to keep lines from breaking, except with the use of *
*.

list-style-type

Specifies how list items should be designated (e.g., with lower-case Roman numerals).

{ list-style-type: }

disc	upper-roman
circle	lower-alpha
square	upper-alpha
decimal	none
lower-roman	

Default:	Disc
Applies to:	Elements with the display list-item
Inherited:	Yes
Value % :	NA

Example:

```
ol { list-style-type: lower-roman }
ul { list-style-type: circle }
```

Use this to change the way list items are designated. Use the *disc*, *circle*, and *square* for unordered lists (bullets) and the remainder for ordered lists (numbers or letters).

list-style-image

Specifies an image to be used to designate the items on a list (e.g., a red roster to substitute for a bullet).

{ list-style-image: }

<URL>
none

Default:	None
Applies to:	Elements with display value list item
Inherited:	Yes
Value % :	NA

Example:

ul { list-style-image: url(redroster.gif) }

Use this to substitute an image for the designators (bullets) in the *list-style-type* property.

list-style-position
Specifies the position of the text in relation to the list item designator.

{ list-style-position: }
inside
outside

Default:	Inside
Applies to:	Elements with the display value list-item
Inherited:	Yes
Value % :	NA

Example:

ol { list-style-position: inside }

Use *inside* to format the text around the list item designator and *outside* to position the list item designator separate from the text block (see Figure 11.2).

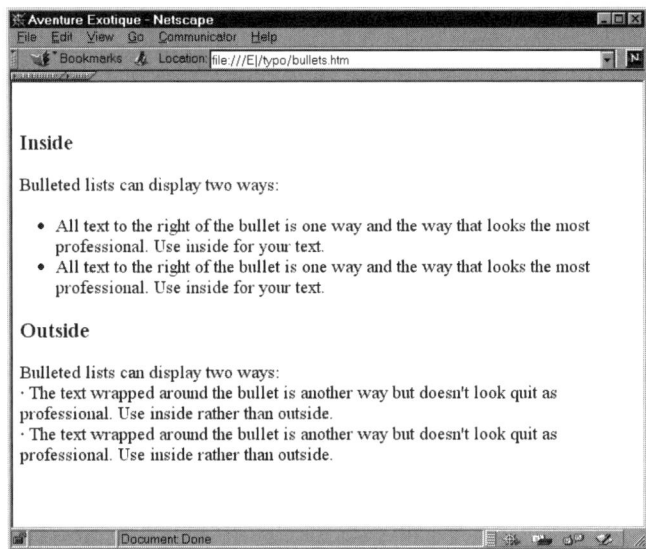

Figure 11.2 *Two ways to show lists.*

list-style

Specifies multiple classification properties in one declaration.

{ list-style: }

<keyword>
<position>
<URL>

Default:	Not defined
Applies to:	Elements with the display value list item
Inherited:	Yes
Value % :	NA

Example:

ol { list-style: outside url(redroster.gif) }

Use as a shorthand expression for classification properties.

Sample CSS 1 Style Sheet

The embedded style sheet for the Web page shown in Figure 11.3 is as follows.

```
<style type="text/css">
<!--
body { background-color:
rgb(0,165,75); font-family:
"imperial bt"; font-size: 10pt; }
p, h1, address { margin-left: 20%;
margin-right: 10%; }
p { text-align: justify }
h1 { text-align: center; font-
family: "arial narrow"; font-size:
17pt; font-weight: bold; }
h2 { margin-left: 15%; font-size:
15pt; font-weight: bold; }
address { font-family: "arial
narrow"; font-size: 8pt; font-
style: normal; text-align: center;
}
-->
</style>
```

CSS 2

This reflects the CSS 2 second working Draft, January, 1998, expected to become a Recommendation by summer 1998. CSS 1 makes an easy step to take. Do it. CSS 2 is just around the corner (but beyond the scope of this book), and is sufficiently enriched that you will want to have some experience with CSS 1 before you tackle its successor. And the further enrichment of Extensible Style Language (XSL) is just beyond CSS 2. Fortunately, XSL will presumably provide some backward compatibility to CSS; and CSS 2 provides backward

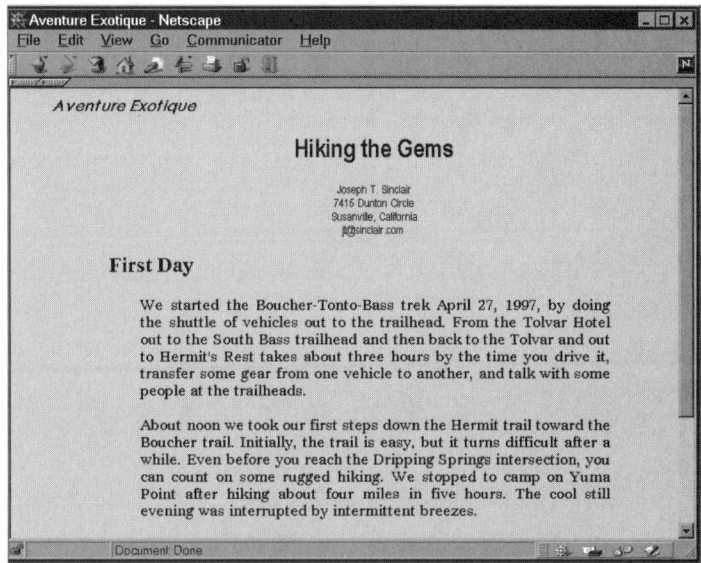

Figure 11.3 *Web page formatted by sample CSS 1 style sheet.*

compatibility to CSS 1. Until XSL is ready, presumably XML will use CSS 2 for style.

Because CSS 2 provides backward compatibility to CSS 1, you need pay attention only to the new capability that CSS 2 adds.

Media Types

The new *@media* rules enable you to specify the media of the style sheet:

all
aural
braille
embossed
handheld
print
projection

screen

tty

tv

Paged Media

The new *@page* rule enables you to engineer pages to be printed from the Web. The Web is a pretty good printing press already but needs a lot of refinement. CSS 2 provides much of that refinement with the *@page* rule.

Although there's not a lot to talk about today in regard to printing Web documents, the *@page* rule will change that as soon as it becomes a standard and is implemented by software vendors in browsers and authoring programs. In a future edition of this book, it has the potential to fill a chapter. See Chapter 20 for further comments on CSS 2 pagination.

Aural Style Sheet

Provides style for aural renderings of text.

Extended Font Selection

Provides for a more extensive font selection process for the substitution of specified fonts not present on the Web site visitor's computer. Adds the following property:

font-size-adjust

Preserves the x-height of the first-choice font in substituted fonts.

```
{ font-size-adjust:              }
z
none
inherit
```

Default:	None
Applies to:	All elements
Inherited:	Yes (but not adjusted values)
Value % :	Relative to parent font size

Example:

```
p { font-size-adjust: 1.72 }
```

Use this to preserve the size characteristics of your first-choice font in substituted fonts.

z = ratio of em- to x-heights of the first-choice font

This keeps a Web document as much the same as possible, regardless of whether a font has been substituted. One can almost fantasize that the *font-size-adjust* property might be a substitute for TrueDoc or font embedding. After all, if a Web site visitor doesn't have the font you specify, she might have something pretty close installed on her computer. Alas, it's not that simple, as you will see when you read the chapters on TrueDoc and font embedding.

In addition, CSS 2 considerably enriches and extends the capability of style sheets to process typography to the point where you have to be a technical expert to take advantage of all it has to offer. Nonetheless, you don't have to use all that capability. You can use CSS 2 much the same as you use CSS 1, and simply specify the fonts you want to use. TrueDoc and font embedding will provide those fonts so that substitutions will not be needed.

Tables

CSS 2 provides extended capability to style tables, a problem not addressed directly in CSS 1. This makes it more possible (but also complex) to use both tables and CSS to style a Web page. By the time CSS 2 is widely implemented in 1999, however, the use of tables for general layout may be a moot point. Will Web masters still worry about compatibility with 3.0 browsers, and will they still use tables to provide style instead of using CSS?

Extended Selector Mechanism

Extends the selector mechanism to accommodate XML as well as HTML.

Relative and Absolute Positioning

Enables more precise positioning of page elements. See Chapter 16 for details on this expanded capability.

Generated Content and Automatic Numbering

Enables the automatic handling of certain style elements. For instance, you can make consecutive numbering for a numbered list automatic.

Text Shadows

Enables you to create drop shadows for text via the *text-shadow* property. This is a somewhat complicated property. If you have created drop shadows with a sophisticated image manipulation program such as Photoshop, however, you will not have trouble using this.

Anchor Pseudoclass

Adds a *hover* pseudoclass to the *<a>* selector (tag). That is, when the cursor hovers over a hyperlink, the hyperlink will turn a designated color.

System Colors

Enables you to takes into account the designated colors of Web site visitors' color schemes and make your color scheme mesh well. This is particularly relevant to Web site visitors who have a visual disability and thus have special color settings.

Conclusion

Is it worth your time to learn CSS 1 and 2? After all, XSL is right around the corner. Indeed, XSL will be somewhat backward compatible with CSS. Actually, this provides you with a wonderfully painless way of easing yourself into XSL via CSS 1 and CSS 2. But if you wait, you'll have to learn everything at once, a more daunting prospect.

Summary

CSS 1 set in the December, 1996, Recommendation was the first style sheet standard. The second working draft of CSS 2 was released in January, 1998. It went to a Proposed Recommendation in March and is expected to be approved as a Recommendation by summer 1998, at which time it will become a standard. The CSS 2 section of this chapter was based on the CSS 2 second working draft.

Dynamic HTML takes CSS and manipulates style sheets with scripts to create an animated effect. Consequently, understanding CSS is the key to understanding DHTML. See Chapter 16 for an overview of how you can use DHTML for dynamic typesetting. Scripting (programming) is beyond the scope of this book, and no attempt is made in Chapter 16 to teach scripting. Yet you will benefit from understanding how scripting works with CSS in order to use the various authoring programs that will incorporate DHTML.

CSS gives you extensive control over the appearance (style: typography and layout) of Web pages. It provides you with professional typographic capabilities for the first time on the Web. Its major drawback is that it works only in the 4.0 browsers, but that won't be a problem for long.

CSS cannot control what is not available. TrueDoc and font embedding, covered in Chapters 12 to 15, provide the fonts for Web pages needed to do professional typesetting.

Part Five

TrueDoc

Introduction to TrueDoc

Bitstream's TrueDoc Web typography technology brings true typesetting to the Web. It enables you to typeset Web pages without interfering with the operation of HTML. It is simple and reasonably lightweight. Indeed, together with CSS, it will enable you to create precise and professional Web pages over which you have considerably more design control than in the past. Originally, TrueDoc worked only in the Netscape 4.0 browser. However, Bitstream has created an ActiveX control that enables TrueDoc to run in the Microsoft 4.0 browser as well.

The TrueDoc System

In creating TrueDoc, Bitstream wanted it to:

- Record any character, whether it be a symbol, a Latin character, or a non-Latin character.
- Have a small and compact PFR (font file).
- Record and play back characters quickly.
- Scale fonts on the fly.
- Provide a resolution-independent final output.
- Retain typographic quality of the original for the final output.
- Port to any platform.
- Provide protection for the intellectual property of font designers and foundries.

Bitstream claims that TrueDoc has achieved its design goals. How does TrueDoc do it? TrueDoc includes three components which together provide typography for the Web.

Character Shape Recorder (CSR)

The Character Shape Recorder (CSR) licensed by Bitstream resides in an HTML editor or authoring program. It is not a retail product. When you use the CSR capability, it records the shapes of the characters used to typeset the Web page. The characters can be TrueType, PostScript, or almost anything. TrueDoc will support OpenType soon too. The CSR records all. In fact, it provides wonderful capability to record non-English characters such as Kanji (the 7,000+ Japanese characters). It records them, but only the ones in the document, not the entire character set.

The CSR records only the shapes and nothing more. A software vendor can implement it two ways. Its software can record all the characters in a character set, or the software can record just the characters in the Web page. The CSR puts the recordings into a file called a Portable Font Resource (PFR) which you upload to your Web site to accompany your Web page (see Figure 12.1). The CSR uses *efficient data descriptions and structures* in creating the PFR which sidesteps the need to use compression. Naturally, the full character set for a specified font requires a larger PFR file than a partial character set. A PFR file can contain multiple fonts and therefore can accommodate a variety of fonts used in one Web page.

Portable Font Resource (PFR)

The CSR generates the PFR as a function of an HTML editor or authoring program. The Web page itself contains a reference to the PFR, and normally you will upload your Web page and the PFR together to the same folder (directory) on the Web server computer. You use the *<link>* tag to reference the PFR (see Figure 12.2).

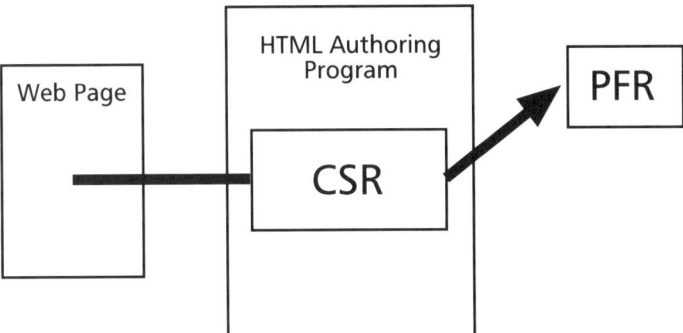

Figure 12.1 *The CSR records the characters from a Web page into a PFR.*

The PFRs are the Dynamic Fonts of the TrueDoc system. To be able to use Dynamic Fonts, a Web site visitor must have *Preferences, Fonts, Use document-specified fonts, including Dynamic Fonts* selected in the Netscape 4.0 browser (default selection). There is an ActiveX control for the Microsoft 4.0 browser.

Character Shape Player (CSP)

The CSP is in the Web browser. Netscape 4.0 was the first browser to include the TrueDoc CSP. The CSP uses the PFR to play back the characters in the Web page (see Figure 12.3). Only Web browsers that have licensed the CSP from Bitstream can use the TrueDoc system (although a free ActiveX control works for the Microsoft 4.0 browser). Via the *<link>* tag in

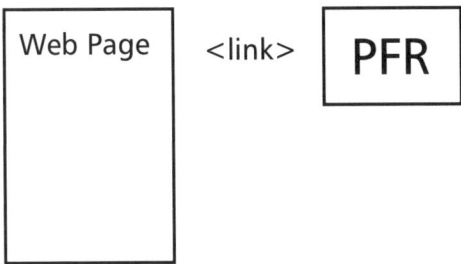

Figure 12.2 *The Web page and the PFR are linked.*

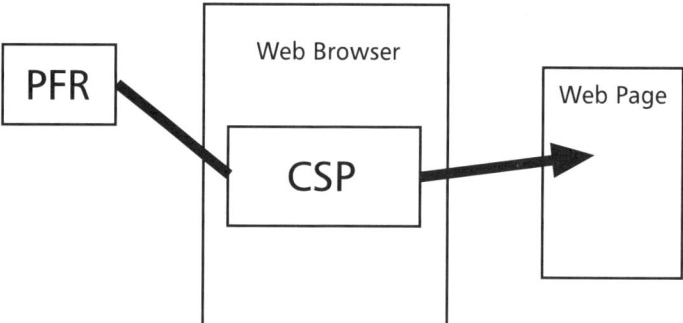

Figure 12.3 *The CSP plays the characters from the PFR into the Web page in a Web site visitor's browser.*

the *<head>* of the Web page, the CSP finds the requisite PFR to use for playback.

Strategies for Using TrueDoc

As you can see, the TrueDoc system is straightforward, and the names for the three components make sense even if they are a little difficult to remember. Like other digital situations, the use of TrueDoc consists of a number of tradeoffs. Suppose, for instance, you have a long document that uses a wide variety of fonts. You will need a substantial PFR document. Because the document is long, each font may require a complete, or nearly complete, character set. Because there may be a variety of fonts used, each font with its nearly complete character set will add to the size of the PFR file required for playback.

How big are PFRs? Suppose you publish a 30-page report as a Web document. You use Century Schoolbook as the normal font, with Lucida Sans for the title and headings. The character set for Century Schoolbook will be nearly complete. Presumably, the character set for Lucida Sans will be sparse. The combination might require a PFR of between 10 and 15 K, a practical size. On the other hand, suppose in addition you use Lucida Bright for the introductory paragraph of each section and Arial Narrow for each of the numerous sidebars. You use Prima Sans for a long paragraph at the end of the report to give credits to those who provided information for the report. The PFR for such a report will be significantly larger and may prove burdensome to download. The tradeoff is providing a report with simpler typesetting in return for having a smaller downloadable PFR file.

Actually, this seems to force more simple Web pages, a trend that will promote more professional typesetting. The first report described in the preceding paragraph has a calm elegance. The second report described is busy with font garnishments and is something of a mishmash. Consequently, the goal of professional typography goes hand in hand with the quest to keep PFR files small. Nonetheless, there are times when including a wide variety of fonts in one Web page does not necessarily means poor typesetting, and for such documents you will need to make a tradeoff between the PFR size and the number of fonts you will use.

For numerous documents with identical or similar typesetting, you may find it expedient to post only one PFR file. For instance, suppose your 30-page report (the one using only Century Schoolbook and Lucida Sans) is one of many similar reports published on your Web site, and each report is a separate Web document with identical typesetting. It might make sense to provide only one PFR file that includes the full character set for both Century Schoolbook and Lucida Sans (see Figure 12.4). After the PFR has been downloaded for the first Web document (report), it need not be downloaded again for subsequent Web documents (i.e., it will be in the browser cache).

In addition, you can use more than one *<link>* in one Web page referring to PFRs (see Figure 12.5). Remember also that one PFR can include multiple fonts. This gives you additional capability and flexibility to build a custom font system that serves your needs. As you can see, you need to make the same kind of tradeoffs for PFR files as you make for graphic files or

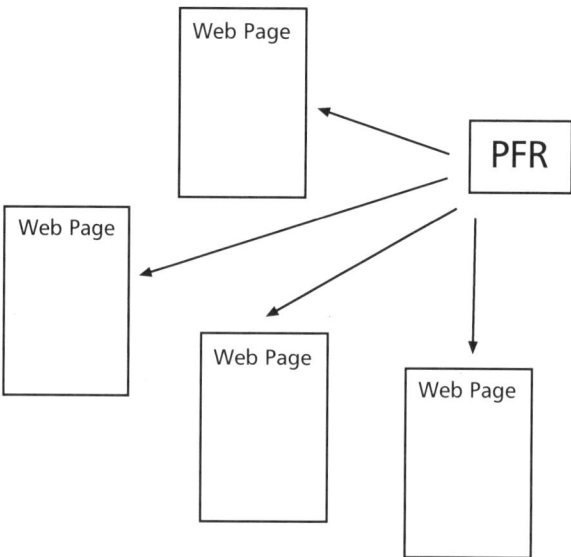

Figure 12.4 *One PFR can serve many Web documents.*

other media. It's nice to have a lot of stuff, but it's nice to have small downloads too.

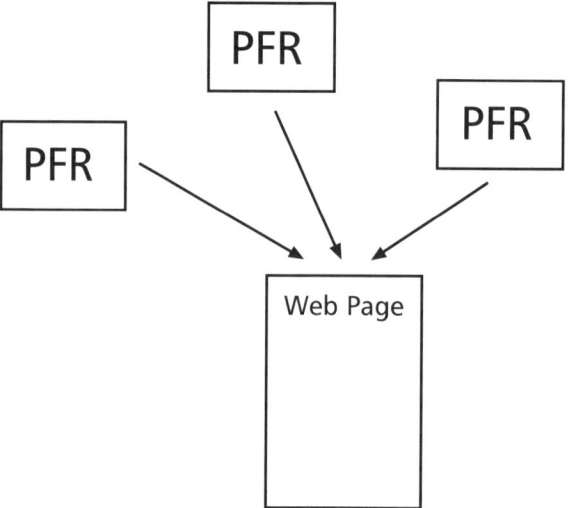

Figure 12.5 *One Web document can have links to multiple PFRs.*

One trick is to use prefetching for the PFRs; that is, reference them in Web pages that don't use them. The PFRs will then be in the browser cache for subsequent Web pages that use them. This does not reduce download times but can redistribute the download burdens according to your purposes. Try downloading a progressively larger font collection with a sequence of Web pages. For instance, if you download a PFR with Goudy regular and italic with Web page A and a PFR with Gill Sans with Web page B, Web page C can use both Goudy and Gill Sans without downloading a PFR by linking to the two PFRs already in the browser cache.

What Fonts?

When the CSR in your HTML editor or authoring program records the character shapes, what does it do? It records the characters made by the fonts in your computer. Hence, you must purchase and install the fonts in your computer first before you can use the fonts on the Web via TrueDoc.

On the other end, the Web site visitor's Netscape 4.0 browser with its CSP (or Microsoft 4.0 browser with the ActiveX control) will use the PFR to play the characters. However, if the font is present and installed in the visitor's computer, TrueDoc will default to the visitor's computer and forego playing back the characters defined by the PFR. Suppose you have used ITC Isbell to typeset a Web page. You process the Web page to create a PFR which you upload to your Web site, along with the Web page. A Web site visitor downloads the Web page (and the PFR automatically). If ITC Isbell is not installed on the visitor's computer, the TrueDoc system will go into action, and the CSP will play back the characters. If ITC Isbell is installed on the visitor's computer, TrueDoc will forego playing back the characters and will allow the visitor's computer to use its ITC Isbell font to form the characters in the Web document.

It Works Differently The text describes the way TrueDoc is supposed to work and originally did work in the Netscape 4.0 browser beta. However, Netscape has programmed the released version of its 4.0 browser to render everything in TrueDoc. See Chapter 13 for additional information. Whether this will be a permanent configuration remains to be seen.

Hinting and Kerning

TrueDoc hints fonts under 15 points with its own hinting. However, as this book went to press, TrueDoc did not do any kerning. By the time you read this, TrueDoc will include automatic kerning, and presumably such kerning will be implemented by the software vendors soon.

TrueDoc: Boon or Threat?

Unfortunately, there was some controversy regarding TrueDoc which seems to have ebbed but is still taken seriously by font vendors and designers. Although it does not concern you, it may be something you need to understand.

Security Objection

At one time, there was an objection that the PFR files you used with your Web documents could be used by others. In other words, people (pirates) who had not purchased the fonts replicated in the PFR file could use those fonts once you uploaded the PFR file to your Web site. A pirate could do this two ways:

- A pirate could reference your PFR file in the *link* value in the *<meta>* tag of his or her own HTML document. The reference would work just as well across the Internet as it would across a hard drive.

- A pirate could enter the URL of the PFR file into his browser's *Open Page* input which would enable him to download the file (*Save As*) into his own computer for further use.

- Note, however, that a pirate cannot install PFRs in a computer or change them with common font tools.

Both of these possibilities seem farfetched. In the first instance, the pirate was at the mercy of what you did at your Web site. If you decided to change or eliminate a Web page and its PFR file to which the pirate had referred, the pirate was out of luck. In the second instance, the pirate procured a file with an incomplete character set (assuming that you had used a PFR file containing only the characters in the document). Few webmasters would use PFRs with full character sets due to the larger size and longer download times for Web site visitors. An incomplete character set isn't much use to anyone. Thus, as a practical matter, this type of piracy seemed unlikely.

Consider, however, two uncommon uses that provided an opportunity for a pirate to procure something useful. First, as mentioned earlier in the chapter, you could use one PFR file on your Web site and have numerous documents refer to it. Presumably, this PFR file would contain the complete character set for a font, the very reason for using it this way. Second, the longer an HTML document, the more likely it would be to contain more characters of the character set. Consequently, a pirate procuring the PFR file for a long document had a good chance of getting a nearly complete character set. Because both of these uses were significant probabilities, it provided realistic opportunities for pirates to procure useable fonts illicitly, if they took the time to find Web sites that used PFRs with complete character sets.

DocLock

Bitstream has provided a remedy for the pirate problem. It has built into the TrueDoc SDK a locking mechanism that locks the PFR file to the URL where it is used. DocLock is the remedy to the security objection, and it makes the TrueDoc system secure against pirates. The PFR can be used only at the URL for which it is generated.

Some webmasters need to use a PFR at more than one Web site (e.g., mirrored sites). DocLock allows the PFR to serve multiple specified sites. Most software vendors have already implemented this feature of TrueDoc, thereby enabling webmasters to use one PFR to serve multiple Web sites, but only Web sites that are specified.

Security is an essential feature for any Web typography system. Obviously, pirating sucks the lifeblood out of the honorable and age-old craft of typography. With the proliferation of small digital type foundries—often one-man or one-woman operations—the theft of fonts gets right down to the personal level.

Your Use

The DocLock feature is a benefit to you. With the locking feature, you don't have to be concerned about illicit use of your PFR files. Moreover, you can upload PFR files that contain the full character sets of specified fonts and serve numerous Web pages at your Web site. In any event, you don't have to do anything to implement DocLock. It's implemented by the software vendor.

Other Objections

Some font vendors have other objections just as important as the security objection. Because the security objection is remediable with the use of the DocLock feature, the objections outlined in this section are perhaps more important. Some font vendors simply don't like the way that TrueDoc treats their fonts. TrueDoc redraws, hints, and antialiases the characters. Bitstream claims that the characters come out looking the same as the original. Some font vendors claim otherwise. Some font vendors argue that their fonts are highly tuned designs that should not be processed at all by someone else's technology; they object to the antialiasing, and they complain that the embedding scheme of TrueType fonts is not preserved by TrueDoc. They have some good points.

Faithful Rendering?

What is to be made of the argument that TrueDoc does not faithfully reproduce fonts? Who knows? Bitstream claims that TrueDoc renders characters more faithfully in Web documents than font embedding. Some font vendors claim otherwise. Can anyone tell the difference on the low-resolution display provided by a CRT monitor?

Font Embedding Microsoft's font embedding competes with TrueDoc by compressing and embedding fonts in a Web page using a different technology which is based on TrueType. Font embedding is covered in Chapters 14 and 15.

By the time you read this chapter, TrueDoc may include additional capability. Bitstream continues to improve TrueDoc. Most additional capability will undoubtedly result in a larger PFR and will have to be implemented by the software vendors, but presumably the resulting type will be a little more readable. Thus, future software products may include advanced capability and may calm the fears of concerned font vendors.

Antialiasing?

The font vendors don't like their fonts being automatically antialiased. Read Chapter 5 for a short discussion on the merits of antialiasing. Sometimes it improves readability. Sometimes it impairs readability. Keep in mind, however, that many people have antialiasing capability built into their version of Windows. If they have antialiasing turned on, the font vendors can't do anything to prevent it. TrueDoc overrides Windows antialiasing, and you don't have to worry about double antialiasing. A software developer can actually turn off the antialiasing in TrueDoc, but few software vendors elect to implement TrueDoc without antialiasing because TrueDoc antialiasing works well.

TrueType Embedding Scheme

This objection is a sticky one. TrueType fonts have a four-way embedding scheme built in (see Chapter 5 for an explanation). The font vendors would like to preserve that scheme. TrueDoc does not preserve it. Many computer users have accumulated a wardrobe of TrueType fonts without any thought of embedding them and without consciousness of the four-way embedding scheme. Now with the capability to embed fonts in Word documents and other word processor documents, people have started to use the embedding capability. With Microsoft font embedding for the Web now available (see Chapter 14), font embedding seems likely to become very popular for the Web. If people find out that their TrueType fonts are not enabled for

Web Page Printing When you print a TrueDoc Web page, TrueDoc provides its own hinting and rendering. This, indeed, is an affront to the font vendors that have produced high-quality fonts for precise printing. Perhaps Bitstream would argue that pages that are readable on the screen do not have to be printed.

It's interesting to note that some laser printers use PFRs (containing fonts licensed from Bitstream) as their native fonts. This shows that TrueDoc provides high quality, even for print.

Windows Antialiasing

TrueDoc antialiasing works reasonably well even below 8-bit color (256 colors). Windows antialiasing requires 16-bit color (64,000 colors).

font embedding, the font vendors are going to feel their wrath. Consumers will have to upgrade or repurchase TrueType fonts that are not enabled with font embedding.

It appears, however, that this will not be a huge problem, as most of the popular TrueType fonts sold have had embedding enabled. If so, why do the font vendors object to the TrueDoc system? Apparently, they want to preserve the *right* to sell TrueDoc fonts with limited functionality. As a matter of practice, however, the font vendors sell fonts with embedding enabled. Therefore, *as a practical matter*, TrueDoc is much the same as the Microsoft font embedding system. The TrueDoc system simply achieves what font embedding achieves, but by a different means. The TrueDoc system allows a Web site visitor to use the PFR only for the Web site in which it is installed. In other words, a Web site visitor does not gain general use of the fonts being rendered by TrueDoc.

Font vendors, of course, can't change the embedding status on fonts already sold. Some font vendors have claimed that they weren't aware of the four-way embedding scheme for TrueType. This stretches their credibility considerably. The scheme was widely discussed at the time Microsoft adopted TrueType for Windows. Perhaps some font vendors will now attempt to charge extra to enable embedding or will disable embedding altogether. If so, it remains to be seen whether such an approach will be competitive. Ironically, as this book went to press, the Microsoft font embedding scheme for the Web had serious security flaws, making TrueDoc the only secure font system for the Web. Fortunately, Bitstream has created an ActiveX control to enable TrueDoc for the Microsoft 4.0 browser.

Sharpness

Another aspect of the font embedding–TrueDoc comparison is that most fonts, even high-quality screen-tuned fonts, look lousy on a CRT. TrueDoc can't make them look much worse, but it does make some of them more readable (see Chapter 13).

The high-quality font vendors have done a superb job of creating type that looks terrific in print. Unfortunately, the low resolution of a CRT does not provide enough substance to create sharp fonts on a screen. The problem is not with the font software. It's with the hardware (CRT monitors). But if high-quality fonts do not look good on the screen, no one is going to use them (purchase them) for the Web. If TrueDoc makes some of them look better, then so much the better for everyone, font vendors included.

Conclusion

Chapter 14 covers Microsoft's font embedding. Is font embedding the answer? (Font embedding seemed to be palatable to the font vendors until the security flaws were discovered.) Font embedding purports to render the fonts faithfully. However, it does nothing to improve the readability of fonts on the screen. Consequently, both TrueDoc and font embedding fall short one way or another in the eyes of consumers or font vendors. Software alone cannot remedy the low physical resolution of computer monitors for all fonts (see Table 12.1). Nonetheless, a few fonts work well for each system.

Whatever the pros and cons of TrueDoc or Microsoft font embedding, you don't need to concern yourself with these wars behind the scenes. Use whatever technology is available to you to make your Web site more readable. As the resolution of computer monitors increases, embedded high-quality fonts will look better than ever on the screen, and font vendors will start to sell a lot of them. By that time, Bitstream will have answered the objections to TrueDoc and improved it. In the meanwhile, font vendors can probably live with the TrueDoc system until something better comes along.

Most fonts below reading size (below 10 points) do not display faithfully on the screen, and all tend to look similar (like a generic serif font), even if readable.

Table 12.1 *Comparison of TrueDoc and Font Embedding*

Qualities	TrueDoc	Font Embedding
Render fonts faithfully on monitor?	Bitstream claims yes; some font vendors claim no	Bitstream claims not as well as TrueDoc; some font vendors claim yes
Security for font vendors?	Via DocLock	No
Render long passages of text readable?	Some fonts (font quality not a factor)	A few high-quality screen-tuned fonts (low-quality fonts look terrible)
Antialias?	Yes	No
Preserve TrueType four-way embedding?	No	Yes
Overall readability	Superior for fonts that work	Average for fonts that work

Network Computers and NetTVs

Sun has licensed TrueDoc for the Java OS (appropriate for NCs). Spyglass and NCI have licensed TrueDoc for use with NCs and NetTVs. At the time this book went to press, these software vendors had not implemented TrueDoc yet. TrueDoc is particularly appropriate for NetTV where fonts must be antialiased to be readable on a television. PFRs are lightweight downloads, an important feature for NCs and NetTVs.

Summary

The TrueDoc system is simple and automated: An authoring program that contains the CSR records the shape of the characters in a document and places them in a PFR file. You upload the Web page and the PFR file to your Web site. A Web site visitor's Netscape 4.0 browser (or Microsoft 4.0 browser with Bitstream ActiveX control) containing a CSP downloads and plays back the characters in the Web page. The result is professional typesetting. That's the outline of the process. The next chapter covers the practical details.

Using TrueDoc in Web Pages

The first step to using TrueDoc is to typeset your Web pages using the *\<font\>* tag. As mentioned in Chapter 7, however, the *\<font\>* tag has been deprecated by HTML 4.0 because CSS implemented in the 4.0 browsers can now do the job better. So, think about using the font properties in CSS and phasing out the *\<font\>* tag eventually. Nonetheless, some authoring programs implementing TrueDoc may not implement CSS yet. So, you'll have to do CSS separately and use the *\<font\>* tag too.

When you create a Web page, specify the fonts for all the headings and text used in the page. Also specify the type sizes; for text, the range of 10–13 points is about right, depending on the particular typeface. If you code by hand, this can be tedious; be sure to take advantage of the *\<basefont\>* tag. It's easier, however, to use an HTML authoring program or CSS.

Remember, once you have set the base font (the parent), it is advisable to use the *em* to specify other font sizes (see Chapters 10 and 11). Also remember that, if the font has two or more words in its name, you must put quotes around it when using the *\<font\>* tag or the font properties in CSS. Having typeset your text, you are ready to create the Portable Font Resource (PFR).

Using HexWeb Typograph

To create the PFR, you need an HTML authoring program that has licensed Bitstream's TrueDoc system and has the capability built in. In other words, the authoring system must have the Character Shape Recorder (CSR). Follow the

More Information The Bitstream Web site (http://www.bitstream.com) provides information about TrueDoc. Bitstream also provides a special Web site for TrueDoc (http://www.truedoc.com) where you can find information and test some Dynamic Fonts. Although this book will suffice to get your Web pages typeset with TrueDoc, when you have technical questions, a visit to the TrueDoc Web site may provide answers.

software documentation. Otherwise, you can use a stand-alone program like HexMac (http://www.hexmac.com) HexWeb Typography 2.0 (HWT). You simply load the Web page into HWT (see Figure 13.1).

Next you click on the *Preferences* button which brings up the *Preferences* window (see Figure 13.2). You enter the requisite URL and your preferences and click on the *OK* button. HWT creates the PFR file with the extension *.pfr* for easy identification and places a link in the Web page as well. HWT also locks the PFR file to your URL. Last, you *Save* the Web page. It's that easy.

When you use dual URLs for your Web site, make sure that you use both URLs for your PFRs (e.g., *www.mountainlass.com* and *mountainlass.com*). TrueDoc may not work properly otherwise.

Using another function of HWT (*Burn PFR fonts*), you can convert entire fonts (or subsets) into PFR files for use on your Web site. Again, HWT locks such PFRs to the Web site. Another HWT software function (*Alternate Fonts*) enables you to insert alternative fonts into HTML font tags (in an HTML document) in bulk.

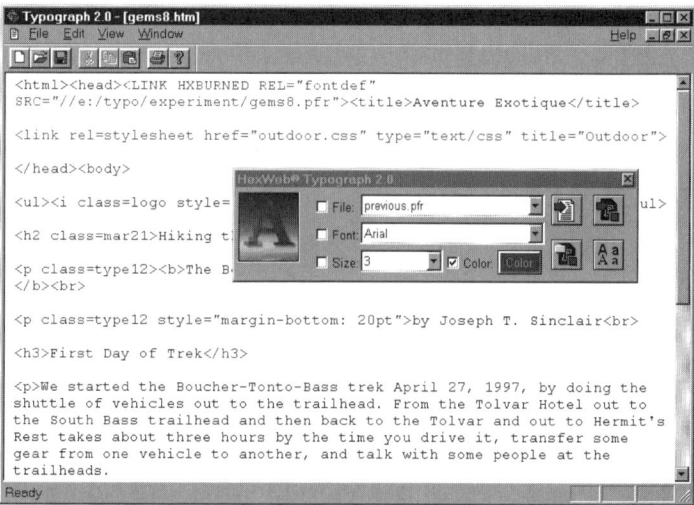

Figure 13.1 *HexWeb Typograph.*

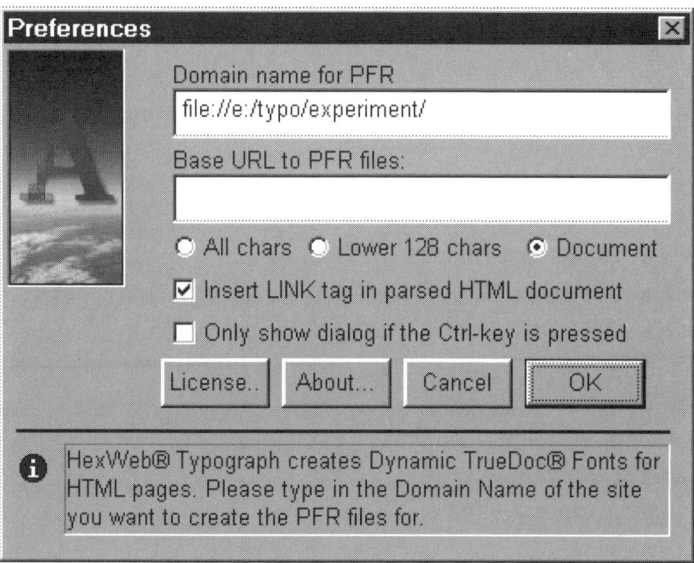

Figure 13.2 *HexWeb Typograph* Preferences *window.*

HWT 2.0 doesn't work with CSS. You have to use the *<font>* tag to do your typesetting.

File Names

The PFR requires a file name. It seems most rational to give it the same name as the Web page file. It will have the *.pfr* file extension to distinguish it. When you use one PFR file for multiple documents, you need to give it an appropriate name that makes sense for your Web site. Note that the names of PFR files are case sensitive.

Placing the Link

Use the *<link>* tag together with the *rel* and *src* attributes inside the *<head>* tags to reference the PFR (see Figure 13.3). Assume that you make a PFR for each Web page and give it the same name as the Web page to avoid confusion. For the Web page *catalog3.html*, you will use the name *catalog3.pfr* for the PFR file and link it to the Web page as follows:

```
<link rel=fontdef
src="catalog3.pfr">
```

HWT places the link in the Web page when you click on the *OK* button to create the PFR. Thus, it saves you the trouble. It uses the Web page name to name the PFR file.

Like using *src* attribute for any tag, the PFR file theoretically can be anywhere on the Internet. Just plug in the full URL. Suppose that you have your Web documents created by a service bureau that provides the font assets at its Web site, not yours. The *src* in the Web page at your Web site might look like this:

```
<link rel=fontdef
src="http://servicebureau.com/pfr/ca
talog3.pfr">
```

Thus, the Web page knows where to find the PFRs. Of course, the service bureau will have to program the PFRs (via DocLock) to enable your Web site documents to use the PFRs for Web site visitors.

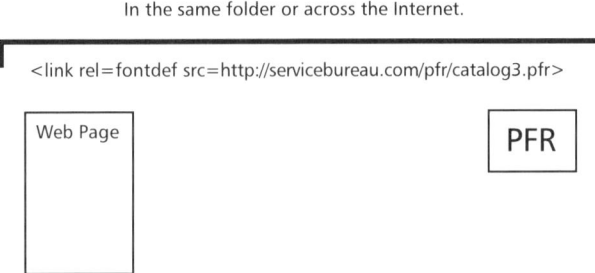

Figure 13.3 *The link ties the Web page to the PFR.*

Uploading

Once you have finished both the Web page and the PFR, upload them to your Web site. Some authoring programs will do this for you automatically. However, it might be less trouble to do it yourself with an FTP program like WS_FTP (http://www.ipswitch.com) than to set up your authoring program to do it for you. Once you upload the files, Web site visitors can use them, and you can test them via the Internet.

Efficiency

HWT loads only characters used in the Web page into the PFR. It does not necessarily load all of the characters in the character set for such a font into the PFR. However, HWT will load the entire character set into a PFR, if you desire. This creates a larger PFR file than simply loading the characters used in a document. That means a longer download for Web site visitors. Nonetheless, it can mean greater efficiency for you. You can use one PFR file to service multiple Web pages that use the same fonts. Once the PFR downloads for the first Web page, it should not have to download for subsequent Web pages during a Web site visitor's surfing session. But the first download might be significantly long. Whether you want to risk longer downloads by creating efficiencies for yourself is a question you should consider carefully.

Using Netscape Composer

Netscape Composer provides another way to use TrueDoc. First, though, you must download the TrueDoc plug-in for Composer from the Netscape Web site and install it in Composer. Use the search engine at the Netscape Web site to find the TrueDoc plug-in.

To typeset in Netscape Composer, simply highlight a word or words and designate the typeface (see Figure 13.4).

Composer Plug-in This is not a browser plug-in. Web site visitors do not need a TrueDoc plug-in, or any kind of plug-in, to see TrueDoc-rendered type in the Netscape 4.0 browser. This plug-in is for authoring Web pages in Netscape Composer 4.0. The plug-in essentially adds the CSR to Composer. Thus, you can create the requisite PFRs for your Web pages without leaving Composer.

First Time The first time that
you run the TrueDoc plug-in,
Java Security will ask you to
grant permission to use system
capabilities. Grant permission
and check the *Remember this decision* box. You will not get the
security window again.

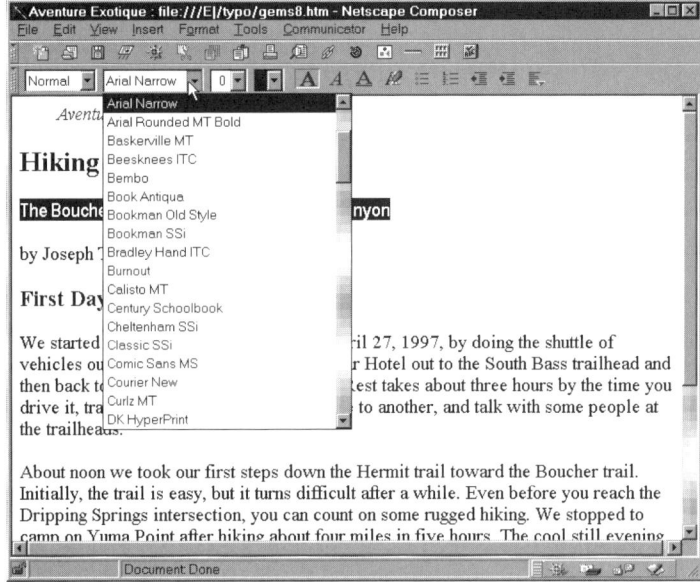

Figure 13.4 *The typography selector in Netscape Composer.*

Once you have finished your typesetting, save the Web page.
Then go *Tools*, *Fonts*, *Font Recorder*. This will bring up the *Record
Fonts* window (see Figure 13.5).

All the fonts are selected, but you can deselect any that you
do not want to include. Enter the Web site URL to which you
will upload this Web page (leave blank for local host mode).
This locks the PFR to the Web site so that no one can use it at
another Web site. To have the CSR record the characters in
your Web page, click on *Record Fonts*. The CSR records only the
characters present in your Web page. When finished, a small
window pops up reminding you that you have to upload the
Web page and the PFRs via the publishing function of
Composer (see Figure 13.6).

Now you are ready to publish your Web page on your Web
site. You must do it through the publishing function of
Composer. When you use dual URLs for your Web site, as
many people do, you need to use both URLs for your PFRs

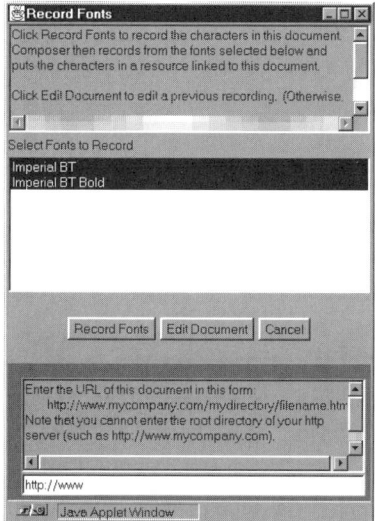

Figure 13.5 *The* Record Fonts *window.*

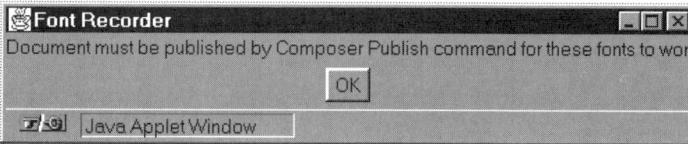

Figure 13.6 *The* Font Recorder *warning window.*

(e.g., *www.bestchance.com* and *bestchance.com*). Otherwise, TrueDoc may not work the way you expect it to.

Extra Font?

In the CSS typesetting example in Chapter 10, originally the *<i>* tag was modified by the *.logo* style in the CSS style. This is the HTML:

```
<ul><i class=logo>Aventure
Exotique</i></ul>
```

This is the *.logo* style (class) in the CSS:

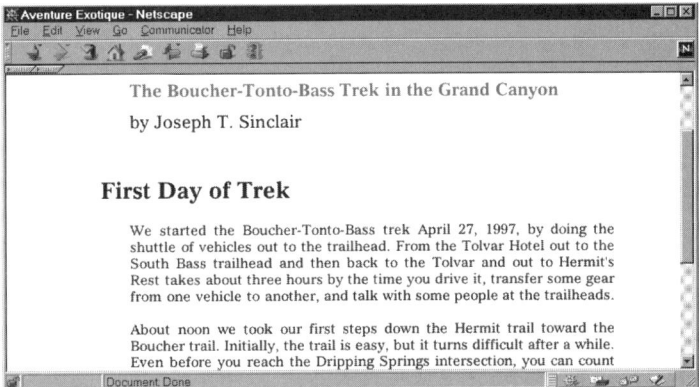

Figure 13.7 *The Web page typeset with TrueDoc.*

.logo { font-family: century gothic; font-weight: bold; font-size: 12pt; }

It's probably not a good idea to modify a style tag with a style treatment (class). It may result in an extra font being created by TrueDoc (i.e., italic for base font plus Century Gothic).

Composer and CSS

Composer doesn't work well with Web pages coded for CSS. It recodes some HTML tags and goofs up your carefully constructed Web page typography. This problem is not unique to Composer. Most authoring programs will take a hand-coded Web page and recode it their way. It may be best to use an HTML editor and code by hand, at least until you get a good grasp of how Composer, CSS, TrueDoc, and font embedding can work together with HTML. Or, use an authoring program like DreamWeaver that will not change your code.

In addition, the beta version of the Composer TrueDoc plug-in does not work with CSS. You have to use the *<font>* tag to make the TrueDoc plug-in work with Composer.

Suitable Fonts

Antialiasing is generally controversial when it comes to reading text on a computer monitor. Sometimes it makes type sharper and easier to read. Sometimes it makes type fuzzier and more difficult to read. Without testing a lot of fonts with different software, it's difficult to predict how it will read.

It's no different for Web pages and TrueDoc. Since TrueDoc antialiases everything, you're stuck with antialiasing, and you have to experiment to see what works. However, you can turn off antialiasing in TrueDoc if the software vendor has implemented such a function in the authoring software you use.

TrueDoc makes all large type look great in a Web page. Small type such as text-size type (under 15 points) doesn't fare so well. Generally, TrueDoc makes type look better, even text-size type. In doing so, however, it makes most text-size type look fuzzy. TrueDoc text-size type has a certain undefined quality that tends to irritate the eye. Nonetheless, you can find some fonts that work very well with TrueDoc and are exceptionally readable for long passages of text. You have to experiment to find them (see Chapter 21).

What makes a font good to use with TrueDoc? It's difficult to say. Some high-quality fonts work well. Many don't. Some low-quality fonts work well. Most don't. It seems to get down to *blackness*. The blacker a font is *after* being rendered by TrueDoc, the sharper and easier to read it is. Unfortunately, before TrueDoc renders a font, you have no idea how much blackness it will have after being rendered. Therefore, in your experimentation, you will need to create the PFRs and render the text in TrueDoc to look for blackness (i.e., the fonts with the greatest blackness). The blackest will prove to be the most readable. Indeed, they will look very good and will provide you with the best Web typography—better than using the best screen-tuned fonts via Microsoft font embedding.

As discussed in the preceding chapter, TrueDoc is not popular with the font vendors specifically because it hints and renders

Experiment I have not found a way to predict accurately whether a font will look good rendered by TrueDoc. You will have to experiment to determine which fonts work and which do not. The capability of Type 1 Multiple Masters and OpenType to provide a variety of weights for a typeface may prove to be very useful in finding fonts that look great in TrueDoc as well as on the screen. See Chapter 21 for font information.

a font with Bitstream processing. Regardless, TrueDoc seems to do a good job of preserving the unique character of a font. Thus, fonts are recognizable on the screen as Bembo or Sabon or whatever after being rendered by TrueDoc.

TrueDoc presents you with a singular opportunity to use low-quality (cheap) fonts and make them look good, right? Unfortunately, it doesn't work out that way. Low-quality fonts sometimes look reasonable in print, but they still don't look nearly as good in print as high-quality fonts. On the screen, they usually look much worse than high-quality fonts. Suppose you use a cheap font named Riverbottom (assumed to be fictitious) that looks great when rendered by TrueDoc. If a Web site visitor has Riverbottom installed on his computer, he will never see the TrueDoc rendering of Riverbottom. The installed font Riverbottom will show instead. And it will probably look awful. In addition, many Web developers will use both TrueDoc and Microsoft font embedding for their Web typography to satisfy both 4.0 browsers. In such a case, you will embed the Riverbottom font in the Web document, and the Web page will look awful to all Web site visitors using Microsoft's 4.0 browser. Consequently, you should use only those low-quality fonts that display well with TrueDoc *and without TrueDoc.*

Ideally, you should use a high-quality screen-tuned font that looks good with font embedding and with TrueDoc too. As a practical matter, if you don't seek and find an ideal solution, your Web site may not look so good to half of the audience.

Keep in mind that, with the Bitstream ActiveX control which enables you to use TrueDoc with the Microsoft 4.0 browser, many of these considerations fade away because you can use TrueDoc exclusively to publish for both of the 4.0 browsers.

Testing

Originally in the Netscape 4.0 browser beta, if a Web site visitor had the same font in her computer that you used via

TrueDoc in a Web page, the CSP in her browser did not play back the font. Instead, it used the font already installed in her computer. This feature of the TrueDoc system made testing difficult and apparently drove the Netscape programmers nuts. Consequently, the released version of the Netscape 4.0 browser *always* plays back the PFR. If it doesn't, you probably don't have things set up correctly. Whether this will be a permanent configuration, or whether a switch will eventually be added to the browser, is not known.

TrueDoc is new technology implemented by a variety of software vendors. It will be a while before all the bugs and glitches are eliminated and the processes are refined to the point where it works faultlessly during the authoring process. You may find yourself experimenting and testing a lot. But it works. And most importantly, it works faultlessly for Web site visitors who have 4.0 browsers.

The Fallback

Keep in mind that not everyone uses the 4.0 browsers. Pre-4.0 browsers will display your Web site with normal HTML typesetting and without the benefits of CSS, TrueDoc, or font embedding. Hence, your Web pages must fall back to looking good when they appear as normal Web pages. This will happen only if you plan it and test it. To test your Web pages as normal Web pages, simply look at them with a pre-4.0 browser.

The Playback

When the Character Shape Player (CSP) plays back the characters on the Web page, it paints them down the page. On a 120-Mhz Pentium, this goes pretty fast but is nonetheless slow enough to be annoying occasionally. On a slower computer, it can be a real irritant. On faster computers, it's not so much of a problem. When you scroll down a Web page, the CSP repaints your every scroll and often interferes with your scrolling, although you get used to it eventually. One assumes that Bitstream will be able to do something in the future to speed up the painting. (Oddly enough, it paints the fastest in the Microsoft 4.0 browser with the Bitstream ActiveX control.) And the speed of the computers used by Web site visitors will increase over time and remedy the problem. In the meanwhile, this aspect of the TrueDoc system—similar to the Adobe Acrobat system—is distracting.

With the Microsoft Browser

Just as this book went to print, Bitstream made public its beta ActiveX control that enables the Microsoft 4.0 browser with TrueDoc. Now TrueDoc works for both 4.0 browsers. Here's how:

1. You put a script in the head of your Web page that instructs a Microsoft 4.0 browser to download the ActiveX control *from Bitstream's Web site*. It gives the browser user the choice to do so. Thus, you do not force it on anyone. The ActiveX file is under 200 K.

2. When downloaded, the ActiveX control installs itself permanently and does not have to be downloaded again.

Now your Web site visitor's Microsoft 4.0 browser is enabled for TrueDoc and can view Web pages nicely typeset with TrueDoc. Eventually, Bitstream intends to authorize other Web sites to distribute the ActiveX control, but it makes no difference to the Web site visitor where his browser gets the ActiveX control. Visit the TrueDoc Web site (http://www.truedoc.com) for the requisite script and for more information on this interesting facilitation.

It appears that your biggest job is to inform your Web site visitors that they will need the ActiveX control to see your typesetting and that the ActiveX control will do them no harm.

Through the ActiveX control, you now have a complete solution for Web typesetting. You may not need to use Microsoft font embedding. Indeed, if the font vendors refuse to sell TrueType fonts with font embedding enabled (for fear of inadequate security) or charge a higher price for such fonts, TrueDoc may become the most reasonable Web font system.

HTML Development

Keep in mind that TrueDoc does not interfere with developing Web pages. You develop as you normally do, using hyperlinks, graphics, streaming media, and other HTML techniques and devices.

Summary

Choose your fonts carefully after adequate experimentation and conscientious selection. If you don't take care to use fonts that work well, TrueDoc has the potential to make your text less readable. This is not a trivial consideration.

Once you have typeset your Web page, TrueDoc requires you to take two additional steps. First, the CSR must create a PFR. This takes place in an HTML authoring program or in a special program. Second, you must upload the PFR file to your Web site. This is not a complicated process. It's straightforward and works well. Use TrueDoc carefully, and you can bring professional typography to your Web site. But unless you facilitate the ActiveX control for Microsoft 4.0 browsers, only Web site visitors who use the Netscape 4.0 browser will see your typesetting. You will have to use Microsoft font embedding to reach the rest of your audience.

Part Six

Font Embedding

Introduction to Font Embedding

Microsoft font embedding is the new typography system for the Microsoft 4.0 browser. It embeds compressed TrueType fonts in Web pages to enable Web site visitors to see typeset Web pages. It is comparable with the TrueDoc system used by the Netscape 4.0 browser but works much differently. Font embedding requires you to use the Web Embedding Font Tool (WEFT), downloadable from the Microsoft Web site. WEFT uses a Wizard to take you through the embedding process.

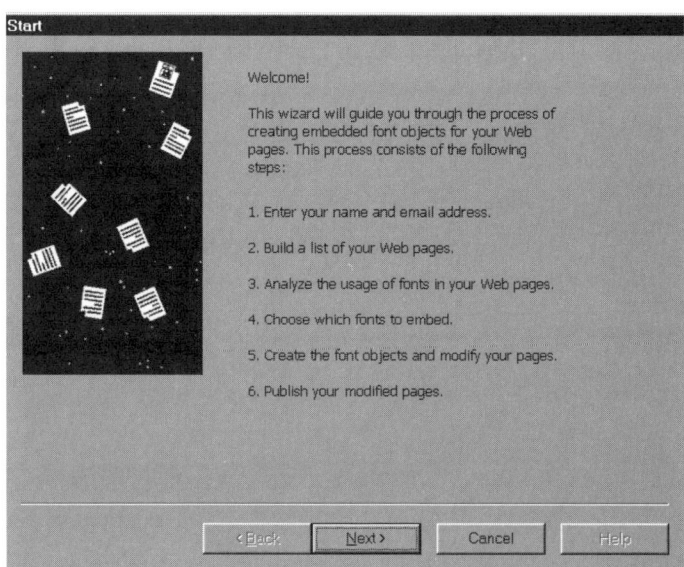

Figure 14.1 *The WEFT Wizard.*

Compression Technology

Font embedding is a feature of the TrueType font system and has been available for a long time. Word for Windows 95 was one of the first programs to enable it. Using Word, you can typeset a document and embed the TrueType fonts. This makes a great feature for reports and proposals that you typeset with typefaces other than Times New Roman and Arial and that you want to preserve for your readers. Unfortunately, a normal font is from 40 to 80 K, and you can considerably increase the size of a Word document by embedding the fonts. Nonetheless, many people now routinely send Word documents (with fonts embedded) over 200 K, some much larger, attached to e-mail messages. As well as this works for business and e-mail, it will not work for the Web. The file sizes are simply too large. That's why Microsoft has started to use compression technology for transporting fonts.

Microsoft uses font compression technology *Font Express* licensed from Agfa. You can use Font Express in Word 8.0. Font Express will embed fonts, compressed, using the entire character set or only the characters used in the document. The following is an experiment that Microsoft ran on an 18-K Word document. The document was short, with some text and a heading.

Word document	18 K
With 7 embedded fonts	464 K (Word 7.0)
With 7 embedded fonts compressed (entire character set)	181 K (Word 8.0)
With 7 embedded fonts compressed (characters in document only)	45 K

Microsoft's font embedding for Web pages naturally includes this compression for TrueType fonts. Moreover, font embedding will handle OpenType, which will enable both the compression for TrueType fonts and the compression for Adobe Type 1 fonts. Consequently, font compression has come to the Web. With compression technology, font embedding for Web documents makes sense, and Microsoft has made WEFT available to do the job.

WEFT

Before you use WEFT, you must do your typesetting using the *<font>* tag or CSS. Make sure that you typeset everything. Anything you leave untypeset will use the default typesetting of Windows.

You start using WEFT by accessing a Web site into which you desire to embed fonts. WEFT builds a list of Web pages that will be analyzed. You can eliminate specific pages, if you desire. Then WEFT proceeds to analyze each Web page. Next, WEFT reports on each font used in the Web pages and indicates whether they are embeddable. This is your chance to edit what WEFT will do. That is, you can decide to embed some fonts but not others. The embedded fonts will be files separate from the Web pages. The embedded fonts use the *.eot* file extension.

Once you have decided on the fonts that you want to embed (or not embed), you decide where the compressed font files will reside and where the Web pages will reside. The fonts can be used only in a designated location. Usually, the font files will be in the same folder (directory) and at the same Web site as the Web pages, but you have some flexibility in the way you set up your Web site file system. Then WEFT creates the compressed font files (*.eot*) and links them via embedded CSS to the Web pages. Note that the Web pages are altered by the linking via the style sheets. The final step is simply publishing the Web pages and fonts; that is, WEFT uploads them where they are supposed to go. As with DocLock, the fonts are locked to a specific directory (folder).

This process goes through some simple steps and is not difficult. Nevertheless, it is more complex than using TrueDoc.

What about TrueDoc? As mentioned in Chapter 12, TrueDoc does not use font compression. TrueDoc uses efficient data descriptions and structures in its PFR files which do not require compression and are, in fact, more compact (smaller) than compressed TrueType fonts.

Download Go to the Microsoft Web site to download WEFT. Start at http://www.microsoft.com/typography.

Embeddable?

The WEFT beta did not do a good job of determining whether fonts are embeddable (Microsoft is aware of this problem). You need to check them yourself prior to any attempt to embed. Use the OpenType Font Properties Shell Extension. You download this utility from the Microsoft Web site (http://www.microsoft.com) and install it. It works automatically every time you look at font characteristics. To look at font properties, select *Control Panel*, *Fonts*, right click on a font, and then select *Properties*. You will get a lot more information doing this after you have installed the OpenType Font Properties Shell Extension than before.

To determine embedability, select *Embedding* in the Shell Extension. It will indicate which of the four embedding functions are available for the font under the TrueType four-way embedding scheme. If embedding is not permitted, the Shell Extension will indicate *Restricted license embedding*. In such a case, contact your font vendor. Otherwise, embedding should work just fine for fonts that do not have restricted licenses. If you have problems with this, make sure that the fonts in question are properly installed in Windows.

Subsets

If a WEFT compressed font (called a font object) contains less than the entire character set, it contains a *subset*. WEFT provides seven ways to do the subsetting.

- **Per page.** WEFT analyzes the Web pages in a folder (directory) or at a Web site and creates font objects page by page for each font present in each page. For instance, if you have 10 Web pages that each use Baskerville, WEFT will create 10 Baskerville font objects. When you expect each of your Web site visitors to access no more than one Web page each, use this selection.
- **Per site.** WEFT analyzes the Web pages and creates font objects font by font, with each font object serving all

---

Beta WEFT was in beta at the time that I experimented with it, and at times did not work the way it was supposed to. Nonetheless, this chapter and the next show WEFT as it is supposed to work.

the pages. For instance, if you have 10 Web pages that each use Century Schoolbook, WEFT will create only one Century Schoolbook font object.

- **Family.** WEFT analyzes the Web pages and creates font objects for the different fonts of a typeface, with each font object having the same character set. For instance, if your Web pages use only the characters a, b, and c for Bodoni regular and *x*, *y*, and *z* for Bodoni italic, WEFT will create a font object for Bodoni regular that contains the characters a, b, c, x, y, and z. It will do likewise for Bodoni italic. This is the WEFT *default* setting.

- **Union.** WEFT analyzes the Web pages and creates font objects for all fonts, with each font having the same character set (not including metacharacters). This works just like the *Family* selection except that the family is extended to include all fonts in all the Web pages. Note that only the typeset characters are included. The unseen metacharacters in the head are not included.

- **Raw.** WEFT analyzes the Web pages and creates font objects for all fonts, with each font having the same character set. This includes metacharacters. Note that the unseen metacharacters in the head are included in the analysis.

- **Language.** WEFT creates font objects based on language parameters. For the normal character set (e.g., Latin 1), this works fine. Using this for a character set like Japanese Kanji (7,000+ characters) will result in a huge font object file.

- **None.** WEFT compresses the entire character set into the font objects. For the normal character set, this works fine, but using this for a character set like Kanji will result in a huge font object file.

This elaborate subsetting system reflects the fact that it's more efficient to use subsets to reduce font object file size which results in shorter download times for Web site visitors. WEFT even enables editing the subsets. Although more flexible than TrueDoc, it is also more complicated.

Don't Embed Naturally, you do not have to embed Times New Roman (Times), Arial (Helvetica), or Courier (and the Mac standard fonts). You can expect these fonts to be on everyone's computer. The WEFT beta embeds these fonts if you specify them to be embedded. Presumably, later versions of WEFT will defer to an installed system font and not embed such a font.

Two Ways to Use WEFT

Many webmasters keep a Web site on their hard disk which parallels their Web site on the Web. After they make a change locally, they upload the requisite files to their Web site on the Web. To analyze Web pages, WEFT obtains copies from the source and stores them inside a temporary folder. Therefore, when you use WEFT, you can use it two ways:

- You can have WEFT obtain the copies of Web pages from your Web site on your hard disk and then publish the modified copies to your Web site on the Web.
- Or, you can have WEFT obtain copies of Web pages from your Web site on the Web and then publish the modified copies back to your Web site on the Web. If you use this latter means of modification, keep in mind that, when you publish the modified Web pages to the Web, you overwrite the originals.

Whatever you do, you will need to coordinate the way you handle font embedding with the way you handle TrueDoc.

Speed

Using WEFT is not a fast process. It's more like backing up a hard disk than it is like using TrueDoc. To use WEFT efficiently, you will have to develop a strategy, including how you will do routine maintenance.

Security

Microsoft font embedding is ostensibly secure. It goes through the same gyrations of locking the fonts to the Web site that TrueDoc goes through. Apparently, though, it is easy for a knowledgeable Web site visitor to crack the Microsoft security and grab the font for his own use. For that reason, font designers and font vendors are up in arms. Whether or when Microsoft will remedy this problem was not known at the time this book went to press.

OpenType enables a digital signature that a user with the appropriate software can use to ascertain whether the OpenType font is original or illicit. This security depends on the user knowing and caring enough to test and knowing *how* to test the font. Do users care? Probably not. Thus, this does not provide much security. However, if the operating system (i.e., Windows NT 5.0) will not accept an OpenType font without a valid digital signature, that provides considerable additional security. When *all* operating systems handle OpenType and digital signatures this way, font designers and font vendors will have meaningful protection, at least against counterfeit fonts or fonts that have been pirated via some sort of alteration, however minor. But that day may be a long way off (a decade?).

In the meanwhile, what about fonts that are not OpenType fonts or what about OpenType fonts used in operating systems other than Windows NT 5.0? If Microsoft font embedding for the Web does not provide adequate protection for fonts (past, present, and future), pirating is likely to become common-place on the Web. This could materialize into a substantial set-back for font designers and font vendors.

Digital Signature A digital signature is an encryption device used to authenticate a document or computer program. If the document or program (font) has been altered one bit (literally), the digital signature be-comes invalid.

Other Considerations

Remember, you cannot embed fonts that you do not have installed in your operating system. If you specify Bodoni in your Web page or CSS coding, forgetting that you removed it from your system a month ago, you will end up with a second choice or perhaps nothing.

Interestingly, WEFT uses the Microsoft 4.0 browser to ana-lyze your Web pages. If you don't have the browser installed, WEFT won't work. In addition, you will need the Microsoft 4.0 browser to see the results. The Netscape browser does not support font embedding.

The beta version of WEFT does not embed Adobe Type 1 fonts. Microsoft has promised, however, that future versions will do so. Although no version of WEFT is planned for Mac, Apple software developers will be able to incorporate WEFT into Mac software. Microsoft has made WEFT technology available to software vendors (Windows or Mac) interested in incorporating it into their authoring software products.

An embedded font acts much the same as a normal font. It has hinting and kerning. For all practical purposes, it's simply a compressed substitute for a font installed on a Web site visitor's operating system. Thus, it's routine TrueType typography.

OpenType is a more robust system than TrueType. Most of the additional robustness focuses on print. Nonetheless, OpenType contains the requisite compression capability for both TrueType and Type 1 fonts and otherwise accommodates font embedding. So, look for font embedding to embrace OpenType and vice versa, and look for OpenType to bring additional capability to font embedding (see Chapter 5 for more on OpenType).

Summary

Microsoft's font embedding for the Web is an extension of the TrueType font embedding capability combined with font compression technology. It provides a reasonable system for bringing professional typography to the Web. Nonetheless, you must choose your fonts carefully to make font embedding work well in providing readable text in Web pages. Chapter 15 gets into the specifics of using WEFT and choosing fonts.

Using Font Embedding in Web Pages

The only way to embed fonts in Web pages is to use Microsoft's Web Embedding Font Tool (WEFT) or an HTML editor or authoring program that includes WEFT. This chapter will provide a step-by-step guide to embedding fonts in a Web page using WEFT. It is assumed that all the Web pages discussed in this chapter have been typeset and that using WEFT will be postproduction work.

Using WEFT

Font embedding with WEFT requires five steps:

1. Create a list of Web page(s) to embed.
2. Analyze the use of fonts in those Web page(s).
3. Choose which fonts to embed or not embed.
4. Create the font objects.
5. Publish the modified Web pages.

Start with the Wizard in WEFT. The first task is deciding what the scope of your work will be. You need to list the Web page that you will process (see Figure 15.1). If the Web pages are on a Web site on the Web, you will have to be online to create the list. WEFT will follow the hyperlinks in the specified Web page and in hyperlinked Web pages to create a tree list of all the pages below the initial page. WEFT downloads such Web pages into a temporary folder. For Web pages on your hard disk, you need to use a URL with three forward slashes:

```
file:///e:/root/folder/webpage.htm
```

Font Embedding? TrueDoc is also a type of font embedding, although it's done with a different process than Microsoft font embedding. However, the term *font embedding* is associated with Microsoft font embedding.

If you use only two slashes, WEFT will only list the Web page specified and will not follow the hyperlinks to list all the Web pages below it. You can add any Web pages you desire that are not in the tree (because they are not hyperlinked) by entering a specific URL. If your purpose is to process only one Web page on your hard disk, use only two slashes in the URL instead of three.

At this point you can choose to exclude Web pages on the list. When you are finished with the list, you click the *Next* button. That takes you to the next page where you click on the *Analyze pages!* button (see Figure 15.2). WEFT next analyzes the Web pages. The analysis takes a long time; for a lot of pages, a very long time. It uses the Microsoft 4.0 browser to do the analysis. Oddly enough, the browser doesn't have to be open, but it must be installed.

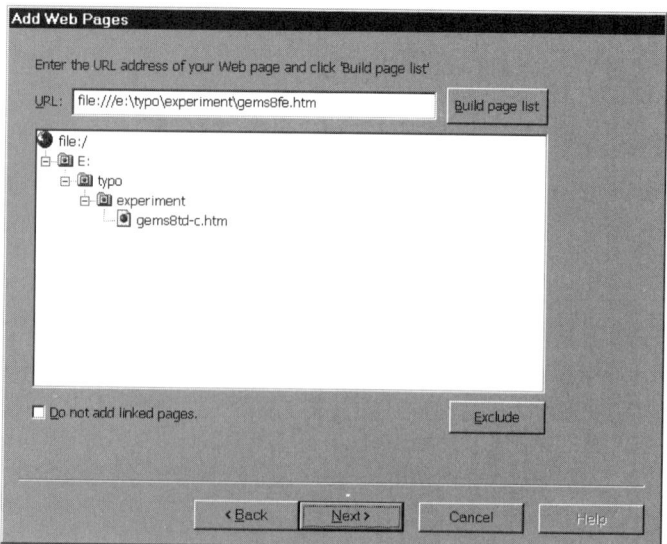

Figure 15.1 *The Wizard:* Add Web Pages.

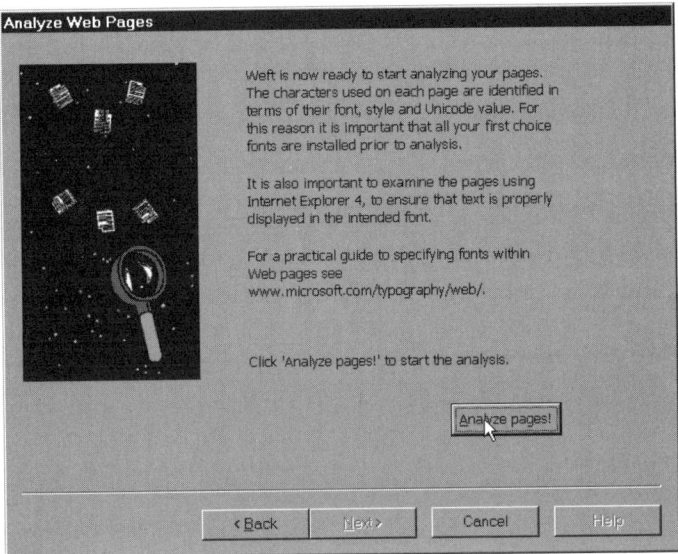

Figure 15.2 *The Wizard:* Analyze Web Pages.

WEFT displays the results in a tabulation of the fonts that it found in the analysis (see Figure 15.3). The tabulation has four columns:

font	Name of font.
info	Information on embedding status.
subset	Number of characters in subset.
embed	Yes (default) or no.

You can choose to edit. For instance, if one of the standard fonts (Times New Roman, Arial, Courier) appears on the list, you may want to change *embed* to *No*.

- Under *info*, you may find *unknown status* or another message that will prevent you from embedding the font. You may have to check the font with the Shell Extension. If you can't find a problem, you may have to replace the font.

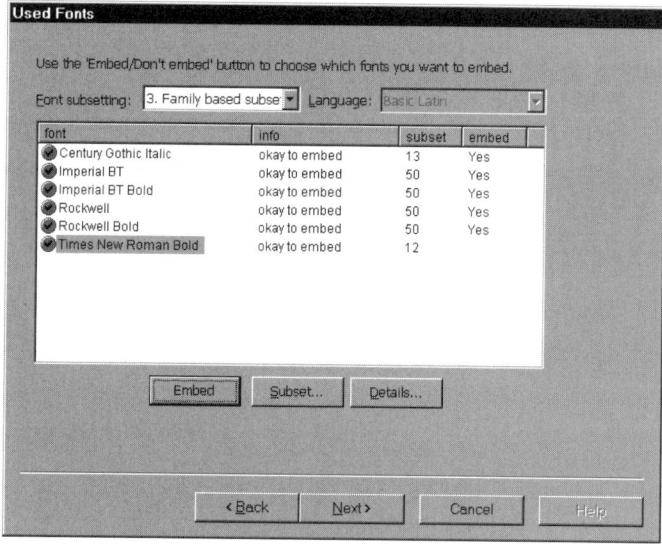

Figure 15.3 *The Wizard:* Used Fonts.

- Click on the *Subset* button and you will see the subset characters in black. You can actually edit the subset, adding or deleting characters. Characters not chosen for the subset appear in gray. When you edit a subset, a star appears next to it on the tabulation.

- Click on the *Details* button, and you will get all the information on the font, just as if you were in the *Font* directory in the *Control* panel.

- Click on *Don't embed*, and you'll change column 4 to *No*. Click again, and it will change back to *Yes*.

- Under *Font subsetting*, you make one of seven choices, as discussed in Chapter 14. The default is number 3: *Family based subsetting*. Make your choices.

Next, click *Next*. Now you are ready to create the embedded fonts, the *font objects*. First, you have to decide where the Web pages will go and where the font objects will go. Normally, they will both go to the same folder (directory) at the same Web site. Enter the URLs (see Figure 15.4). Don't forget the three forward slashes for Web sites on your hard disk (e.g., *file:///e:/root/folder/webpage.htm*). For some situations, you may put the font objects at one address and the Web pages at another. If your Web pages contain server scripts, you will have to specify a download method by clicking on *Advanced*. Normally, however, you will click on *Create fonts* to have WEFT create the font objects.

Now you come to the last step where you publish the Web pages with the fonts embedded to the Web site (see Figure 15.5). Again, if you are publishing to a Web site on the Web, you will have to be online to complete this step. Again, don't forget the three forward slashes for URLs on your hard disk (e.g., *file:///e:/root/folder/webpage.htm*). Again, if you have server scripts in your Web pages, you will have to specify an upload method by clicking on *Advanced*. To upload your Web pages and font objects, click on the *Publish* button. You're done.

When you use dual URLs for your Web site, you need to use both URLs for your *.eot* files (e.g., *www.houselife.com* and *house-life.com*). Otherwise, font embedding may not work properly.

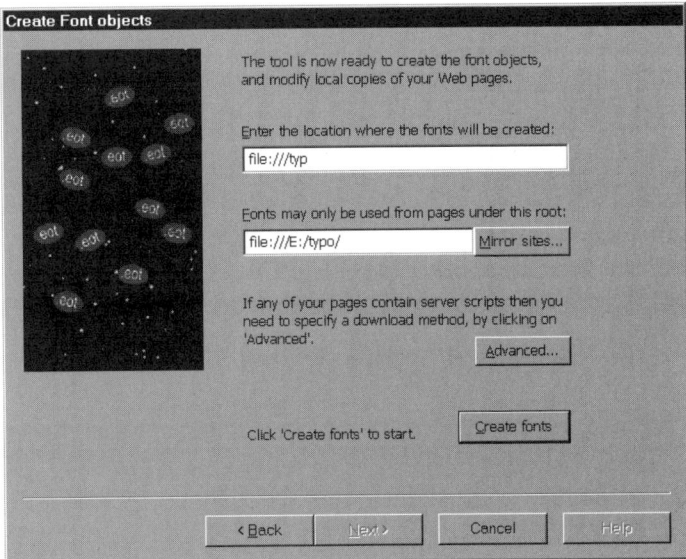

Figure 15.4 *The Wizard:* Create Font Objects.

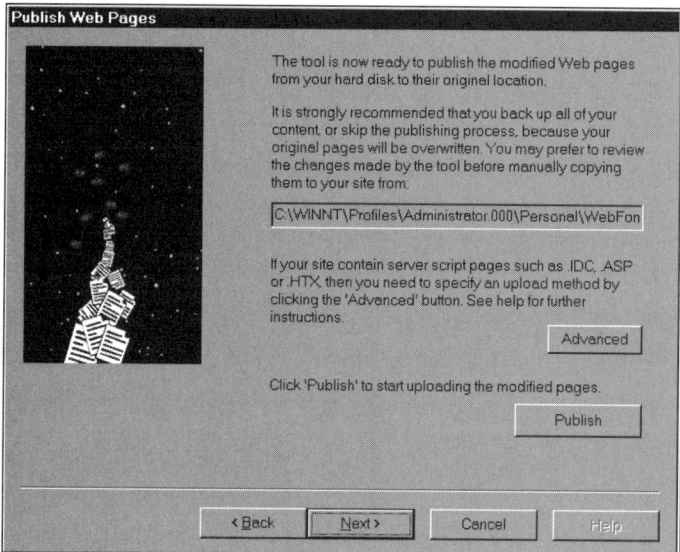

Figure 15.5 *The Wizard:* Publish Web Pages.

As you can see, this process seems a little more complex than using TrueDoc, although similar. It is also seems slower. Fortunately, once you learn how to do it, it becomes just a routine postproduction task.

Next, you need to check the Web site with your Microsoft 4.0 browser to make sure that the font-embedded Web pages work. The presence of *.eot* files shows that the font objects are present. If you click *View*, *Source* for a Web page, you will see that WEFT adds CSS code to the Web page (see the following example of an embedded CSS).

```
<style type="text/css">
<!--
@font-face {
font-family: Baskerville;
font-style: normal;
font-weight: normal;
src: url(baskerv7.eot); }
-->
</style>
```

This is an embedded style sheet that imports a font object. Notice that WEFT uses the CSS import (@) command to import the font object (*baskerv7.eot*) as if it were an external style sheet (see Chapter 10). As you can see, using WEFT is a little more complicated than using TrueDoc. However, for many situations, WEFT provides efficient, albeit slow, bulk treatment for the Web pages at Web sites.

Bulk Treatment

Microsoft designed WEFT for detailed bulk treatment of Web pages at Web sites. That's one reason that it's a little more complicated than using HexWeb Typograph or a similar program for TrueDoc.

Such bulk treatment is not necessarily available for TrueDoc using only the CSR in an authoring program that handles TrueDoc. However, if you create PFR files containing entire character sets and then reference such PFRs with the *<link>* tag in Web pages, you can create a bulk system for TrueDoc. You create the PFRs by processing fonts directly with HexWeb Typograph (or equivalent), electing to create the entire character set for each font. Then, in the Web pages, you simply add the requisite *<link>* tag using copy & paste.

You can use WEFT the same way. Process only a few Web pages with WEFT, electing to create the entire character set for each font. In the unprocessed Web pages, you simply embed the requisite CSS style sheet (copy & paste), which references the font. Why would you do it this way? It might save time. Even if it doesn't save time for existing Web pages, it may save time when you create Web pages from scratch and can include the embedded CSS style sheet in your page templates.

Efficient bulk treatment requires advanced planning. Efficiencies may be difficult to achieve for legacy Web pages. But when you design your typographic system to take advantage of the new Web typography, don't neglect to plan how you will efficiently implement and maintain the system.

Dynamic Content

Dynamic content includes server scripts, client scripts, DHTML, CSS, and the like. How does WEFT work with dynamic content that affects typography? That can get complicated and is beyond the scope of this book. Look for information regarding WEFT and dynamic content at the Microsoft Web site. As WEFT is released and people get experience using it, more information on using WEFT with dynamic content will become available.

When you use CSS, keep in mind that WEFT uses CSS to reference the font objects by embedding a style sheet in each Web page. You will want to plan your use of CSS—keeping in mind the cascading rules of CSS—to coordinate with WEFT's use of CSS. This is not particularly difficult, but you will want to stay conscious of the embedded style sheets that WEFT adds.

Size Comparison

When a short version of the *Hiking the Gems* article was typeset by both TrueDoc and Microsoft font embedding, it required three fonts. The TrueDoc PFR was 9 K, and the font embedding *.eot* files totaled 29 K. TrueDoc was designed to be very compact and does not require compression. Its PFRs are not compressed. Font embedding compresses its *.eot* files, although the compression is transparent to users. Generally, you can expect smaller files (for fonts) for TrueDoc than for font embedding, but this is something you'll want to experiment with yourself.

Screen Tuning

Remember, it's readability that counts. Most fonts are not very readable on a CRT. In fact, looking at printed fonts, it's almost impossible to predict which ones will look good on the screen. Fortunately, one of the best is Times New Roman—and everyone has it. It makes life in front of the monitor a little easier for everyone. But when you see it all day, every day, it gets a little boring. The question is, what can you use in its place? To determine that, you have to experiment.

High-Quality Fonts

Generally, you will find that the fonts from high-quality font vendors look much better in print than do cheap fonts. The screen is no different. The high-quality fonts seem to look even better in comparison on the screen than in print. Therefore, you will want to pick and choose your fonts carefully for use on the Web. The cheap fonts may not suffice.

So, let's turn our attention to high-quality fonts. Only a few of them are acceptable quality for screen display, regardless of how great they may look in print. Is there anything to be done to make them look better? It turns out there is. The font vendors can tune fonts to the screen. Of course, all high-quality fonts are tuned to print. Tuning them to the screen is a new practice inspired by the Web. Does it work?

In general, screen tuning does not work. If a font does not look good on the screen (is not readable), screen tuning probably isn't going to change that. On the other hand, if a font does look good on the screen, screen tuning will make it look sharper. In this sense, screen tuning is a success, and it's worth buying fonts that have been screen tuned.

Naturally, when it comes to the Web, you will want to use the fonts that are the most readable. Those are the fonts where screen tuning really counts. So, make sure you use screen-tuned fonts for your Web pages. Before you buy screen-tuned fonts, however, make sure the normal versions of the fonts that you intend to use look good on the screen and are readable. To summarize, high-quality fonts plus screen tuning do not necessarily yield readable text on the screen. High-quality fonts that yield readable text on the screen, plus screen tuning, yield even greater readability. See Chapter 21 for more information on choosing fonts.

Cheap Fonts

And what about cheap fonts? Most cheap fonts are just poor quality, both for printing and the screen. Some large software vendors, however, have licensed large font collections of considerable quality which they provide, together with their software, to their customers. Such collections have merit but are the exception rather than the rule. For fonts, price is a good indicator of quality. Don't forget that the physical resolution of a CRT is so low that you need all the help you can get to make text readable on the screen. Don't skimp on the fonts.

Font Embedding and TrueDoc

The conclusion of this chapter is that high-quality screen-tuned fonts will provide you with the most readable text for Microsoft font embedding. But how will such fonts look with TrueDoc? That's difficult to predict. Chapter 13 mentions that most fonts look good in TrueDoc, but only some are readable for long text blocks. That gets us down to the bottom line. Use screen-tuned fonts that read well on the screen for both Microsoft font embedding and TrueDoc. Since only some fonts read well in TrueDoc and since only a few screen-tuned fonts read well for Microsoft font embedding, you may find it a considerable task to identify the few fonts that satisfy both Web font systems. See Chapter 21 for more information on this topic.

Summary

You use the WEFT program provided by Microsoft, together with the Microsoft 4.0 browser, to embed fonts in Web pages. It's a simple but slow process, a little more complicated than using TrueDoc. Web pages use the compressed and embedded fonts just as they use operating system fonts, and the result is typesetting as usual.

However, WEFT does nothing to improve the way that fonts look on the screen (nothing to improve readability). You must

TrueDoc and Cheap Fonts In comparison with font embedding, TrueDoc makes all cheap fonts look good. But TrueDoc antialiases. The effect on readability is mixed. Ironically, the fonts that TrueDoc renders well are just as likely to be cheap fonts as high-quality fonts. And the fonts that TrueDoc renders well are quite readable.

identify screen-tuned fonts that are readable and use only those in your Web pages. At the same time, such fonts must work well in the TrueDoc system also. The alternative is to use the TrueDoc system exclusively for both 4.0 browsers and ignore Microsoft font embedding.

Part Seven

Advanced Topics in Web Typography

Sixteen

Using Dynamic HTML for Web Typography

Is Dynamic HTML (DHTML) ready for prime time? Yes and no. Yes, if you program and can write scripts that will work with both Netscape's and Microsoft's DHTML (or if you will seek out scripts to use that work for both browsers). No, if you don't want the hassle of trying to accommodate two different programming systems. The differences are more complex perhaps than the differences between Netscape and Microsoft HTML. Although both Netscape and Microsoft have committed to work out their DHTML differences, you will have to wait until the 5.0 browsers, at least, to enjoy a unified DHTML system. Nonetheless, authoring programs such as Dreamweaver and Fusion 3 will enable you to author DHTML that complies with both Netscape and Microsoft.

DHTML is a programmer's game. Thus, this chapter is only an overview, not a tutorial. Can webmasters use DHTML? Sure. You have three ways:

- Have a programmer do the project for you.
- Work with a programmer and have the programmer do the programming code while you do the HTML, CSS, and creative work.
- Use a DHTML authoring program such as Macromedia Dreamweaver or NetObjects Fusion 3.

DHTML requires a different kind of thinking than normal HTML, regardless of which of the three techniques you use. You must think in motion, and you must think in 3D. First, consider motion. DHTML was invented to move HTML elements around the page. For instance, you might move an image or a paragraph to a different place on the Web page triggered by an *event*. Second, consider 3D. When you start moving elements around, you must decide which one is going to be on top should two elements (or three or four) be in the same place at the same time. This is a kind of 3D animation, a big step away from a normal static two-dimensional Web page.

Can you use DHTML for typographic effects? Sure. Movement brings a new dimension to typography that, although used in films and television, has never before been available to everyone for use in ordinary documents (digital documents).

The basis of DHTML is the *Positioning HTML Elements with Cascading Style Sheets* Working Draft, August 19, 1997, of the Web Consortium. This chapter provides some of the properties (see following section, CSS Positioning Properties) that the Working Draft adds to CSS. These have been incorporated into CSS 2. The CSS positioning properties enable you to place HTML elements *precisely* where you want them in a Web page.

CSS Positioning Properties

The properties that follow are not part of CSS 1. They represent an addition to CSS 1 (now incorporated into CSS 2), and you will want to update the book in regard to these properties by referring to CSS 2 before you put them to use. Presumably, these properties will reach their final definitions as soon as Netscape, Microsoft, and the Web Consortium can agree on the definitions. They add interesting new capability to CSS and are worth your time to review as the basis for understanding DHTML. However, you can also use them for layout without DHTML.

position

Specifies the position of an element in a Web page.

```
{ position:            }
normal
absolute
relative
fixed
inherit
```

Default: Normal

Applies to: All elements

Inherited: No

Value % :   Refers to width of containing block

Media groups: Visual

Example:

```
.firstimage { position: absolute; left: 40px;
top: 25px; }
```

Use to position an element precisely or relative to end position of its parent. For absolute positioning, use the *left* and *top* properties, which provide the coordinates. Elements positioned with absolute positioning can overlap other elements or be overlapped. A child layer overlaps a parent layer. Children can have their own absolute positioning, but it's relative to the absolute positioning of the parent. For example, *<body>* can have an absolute position, and *<p>* can have its own absolute position, but the absolute position of *<p>* will be determined in relation to the beginning (left, top) of *<body>*. The *<p>* layer will overlap the *<body>* layer. That's what you expect (i.e., that text will overlap the body background). But you can absolutely position any text element to overlap another text element (see Figure 16.1).

Relative positioning positions an element relative to its parent (left, top) which is the normal way for a browser to render HTML. But you can use the *left* and *top* properties to position the element relative to the end position (right, bottom) of the parent, not the beginning position of the parent (left, top).

Fixed indicates a fixed position with respect to some reference.

left
Specifies horizontal position.

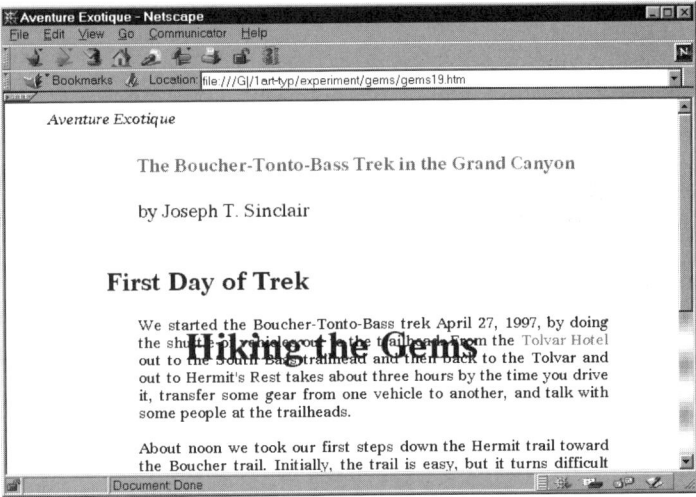

Figure 16.1 *Heading overlap shows that one text element can lay over another with absolute positioning.*

{ left: }

<percentage>
auto
inherit

Default: Auto
Applies to: Elements with position property
Inherited: No
Value % :   Refers to width of containing block
Media groups: Visual

Example:

.image04 { left: 300px }

Use to set the horizontal coordinate (from the left).

top

Specifies vertical position.

```
{ top:               }
<length>
<percentage>
auto
inherit
```

Default:	Normal
Applies to:	All elements
Inherited:	No
Value % :	Refers to width of containing block
Media groups:	Visual

Example:

.image04 { top: 420px }

Use to set the vertical coordinate (from the top).

width

Specifies the width of an element with an absolute position.

```
{ width:             }
<length>
<percentage>
auto
inherit
```

Default:	Normal
Applies to:	All elements
Inherited:	No

Value % :   Refers to width of containing block

Media groups: Visual

Example:

blockquote { position: absolute; width: 220px; }

Use to fix the width of an element that has an absolute position.

height

Specifies the height of an element with an absolute position.

{ height: }

<percentage>
auto
inherit

Default:	Normal
Applies to:	All elements
Inherited:	No
Value % :	Refers to width of containing block
Media groups:	Visual

Example:

h3 { position: absolute; height: 30px; }

Use to fix the height of an element that has an absolute position.

z-index

Controls the order of layers.

```
{ z-index:              }
auto
<integer>
inherit
```

Default:	Normal
Applies to:	Absolutely and relatively positioned elements
Inherited:	No
Value % :	NA
Media groups:	Visual

Example:

```
h2 { z-index: 3 }
```

Use to control the layering of elements with the *position* properties. The lowest number is the top layer. Succeeding numbers are lower layers that may be overlapped by a higher layer.

The complete set of positioning properties found in the Visual rendering model chapter of CSS 2 are more complex than the few summarized here, but these give you a taste of what CSS positioning does.

After Positioning What?

The positioning properties enable you to position any HTML element absolutely, or relative to its normal position. By changing the properties in a style sheet, you create a new style sheet or a series of new style sheets, in effect. With multiple style sheets—like animation cells—you can make HTML elements move gradually or quickly around a Web page. To do this, you use scripts (e.g., JavaScript for Netscape). The scripts express the changes for properties in the initial style sheet.

Naturally, if you do not program, you will not write the scripts. Nonetheless, you still have to develop the concept of what you want to do and conceptually work out both the movement and overlap of the various HTML elements. In other words, you have to understand the capabilities and limitations of the CSS positioning properties.

What HTML Elements?

What HTML elements can you manipulate using CSS and scripts? For Microsoft, everything is fair game. You can manipulate any HTML element (e.g., a heading). Microsoft uses the document object model which dictates that every HTML element is an object. You can manipulate objects using CSS and scripts. If two objects conflict—if they are in the same place at the same time—you determine which object has priority over the other; that is, you decide which one overlaps the other. The one on top, of course, presumably displays the best. As you can envision, the Microsoft system focuses on objects, on moving or changing objects, and on giving some objects priority over others.

How can one object gain priority over another in a two-dimensional system? If two objects are in the same place at the same time, you have to think of one overlapping another; that is, you have to think in layers (see Figure 16.2).

What Layers?

The Netscape DHTML system doesn't use the document object model. It focuses on layers. Using Netscape's new *<layer>* tag for the 4.0 browser, you arrange HTML elements into layers. You can use the *<layer>* tag for one HTML element or for a group of elements. The scripting controls the layers. It changes the properties of the HTML elements in the layers. Unlike Microsoft's system where you must control each object independently, Netscape's system enables you to control the behavior of groups of HTML elements. Just as with Microsoft

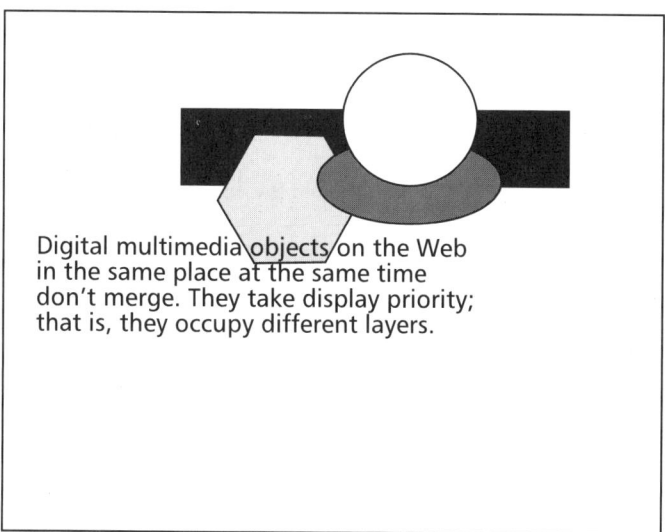

Figure 16.2 *If a graphic moves around a Web page so that it always shows, it appears to be in a higher layer than the text over which it passes.*

DHTML, Netscape DHTML must give priority to layers. The layer with the highest priority overlaps layers with less priority.

Where's the Beef?

As you can imagine, sometimes it's more efficient and provides more flexibility to deal in objects. For other situations, it's better to deal in layers. Keep in mind that the CSS positioning properties support both systems. It is the hope of webmasters everywhere, no doubt, that Netscape and Microsoft will reach an agreement on one system. In the meanwhile, using both systems is something programmers must face. That doesn't mean that you as a webmaster have to deal with the differences. On the contrary, it's your job to conceptualize what you want to do and then direct a programmer to do it. But you can help the programmer by knowing and working with CSS and positioning properties.

What's an Event?

If there is to be movement or interactivity, there has to be a beginning and an end. An *event* triggers the movement or interactivity. In other words, it's the beginning point. What are some events? The following is a partial list.

OnChange	Changing of the content of an object such as text and text area inputs
onClick	Clicking of an object by the mouse such as hyperlinks and images
onLoad	Completion of loading such things as documents or images
onMouseOut	Mouse pointer moving away from an object that it was just over such as a hyperlink or image map area
onMouseOver	Mouse pointer moving over an object such as a link or image map area
onReset	Resetting a form with the reset button
onSubmit	Submitting a form with the *submit* button

Events occur sometimes randomly, sometimes inadvertently. For the most part, however, your job is to induce events. You do that through your content. For instance, when you designate a hyperlink, the hyperlink induces a Web site visitor to execute it. The execution of the hyperlink can be the event that starts something.

Note that the scripts designate the events for DHTML. HTML has events too. But the events reside in markup *attributes* for HTML. In other words, the only way to create an event is inside a markup. Creating the events with scripts provides you with much more flexibility.

Dynamic Text Ideas

You can use DHTML to enable the following ideas. This list just provides a creative spark. You can use DHTML in an infinite number of ways to make your text communicate better.

- A title takes two seconds to move into its permanent resting place (from somewhere else on the Web page), starting the movement one second after the Web page finishes loading (see Figure 16.3)—a nice opening touch.

- A footnote exists in small print in the body of the text. Upon mouse-*over*, the text in the footnote grows larger (i.e., the entire footnote grows larger) for easier reading. Upon mouse-*click*, the footnote expands its text (i.e., expands its content) and displays in a floating box.

- Upon a mouse-click, the color scheme (background and text colors) of the Web page changes to another color combination. Upon a second mouse-click, the Web page changes to yet another color combination, etc. Presumably, these alternative color combinations will enable easy reading and suit a variety of tastes.

- Upon a mouse-click, a paragraph (or sentence or word) permanently highlights for future review. A second mouse-click returns the paragraph to being unhighlighted.

- The text asks a question. A mouse-click on the question reveals an answer that shows as text immediately after the question (a programmed learning system).

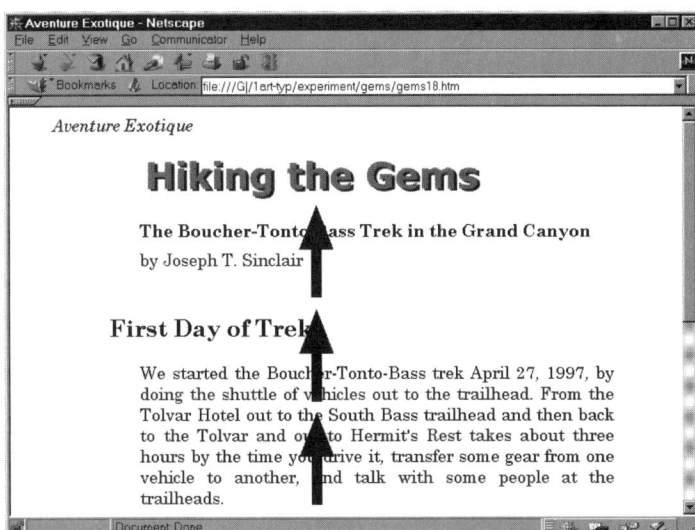

Figure 16.3 *The title moves into place 2 seconds after the Web page finishes loading.*

You can use hyperlinks to create a few of the effects mentioned. DHTML, however, can potentially do it much more elegantly while causing less disruption of reading. As always, for text, a treatment doesn't add much of value unless it acts to enhance readability. DHTML is no different. If it doesn't enhance readability, no matter how clever, it doesn't offer much of value. You will find that DHTML has a tremendous potential to enhance readability, depending on how you use it for your text publishing.

From Here to There

How do you get there from here? To publish an effective DHTML Web page, follow the six easy steps below.

1. Learn CSS and CSS positioning properties.
2. Start thinking of Web pages in 3D and movement.
3. Try a simple project.
4. Always keep readability in mind.
5. Develop your project.
    a. Find a friendly programmer with whom you can experiment on a collaborative basis. This will keep your costs low or nonexistent, at least for an initial project. Or,
    b. Look for scripts published on the Internet that will enable you to do what you want to do (e.g., like looking for CGI scripts). This will allow you to do a project without a programmer. You can probably find scripts that you can use to make an initial project work. Or,
    c. Use an authoring program like Macromedia Dreamweaver or NetObjects Fusion 3. They will enable you to do a robust DHTML project without a programmer. They're like multimedia authoring programs (e.g., Macromedia's Director) but easier to use.
6. Publish your project on your intranet or on the Web. There's no substitute for making it actually work and for

getting comments from visitors on whether your
DHTML typography really enhances readability and
communication.

DHTML is not an end itself. It provides you with the added
capability to introduce movement into published documents
and to provide more subtle interactivity than is possible with
hyperlinks. It is not something to be avoided or feared or
depicted as glitzy technology. It can make a solid contribution
to improving online documents.

One source of ideas for enhancing Web documents is multimedia CDs. These CD productions have used advanced techniques that before now have not been possible to use on the
Web except via Shockwave. DHTML brings the Web much
closer to being the fully robust development environment that
characterizes many CD productions. Consequently, you may
find that a review of your favorite CDs provides you with ideas
you can now use on the Web. Keep in mind that DHTML will
carry over into XML. DHTML is not an offshoot. It is in the
mainstream of the evolution toward richer functionality for
the Web.

Readability

You will see many glitzy uses of DHTML. Gratuitous glitz is of
questionable value. But an animation that makes a Web page
aesthetically more attractive can enhance an otherwise dull
Web document. Moreover, DHTML that provides functions
that enhance readability and communication adds value to Web
publishing. In fact, as discussed in Chapter 18, movement and
interactivity add a fourth dimension to typography, which is
now in the hands of the masses for the first time.

Unquestionably, movement and interactivity—interactivity
beyond hyperlinking—can carry written communication to
heights of effectiveness never before achievable with common
and inexpensive means. Rather than witnessing the decline of
text as a medium, you are about to witness a new golden age

of typography and text, a typography enhanced by a new dimension and integrated comfortably with other media in the same place at the same time.

Don't get caught up in the controversy about which is better, the document object model or layering. That is a programmer's theological debate. Turn your attention instead to making text more effective with DHTML, and perhaps you will take a place in history with Claude Garamond.

Dreamweaver

Macromedia Dreamweaver (http://www.macromedia.com) is an HTML authoring program which is also a DHTML authoring program, quite a combination. Macromedia draws on its experience with Director (a popular multimedia authoring program) and Shockwave to provide you with the capability to create DHTML without coding easily (see Figure 16.4). Gutenberg may have invented movable *type*, but movable *text* online starts with Dreamweaver.

A nice feature of the Dreamweaver HTML authoring program is that it will not change your code like other HTML authoring programs. It even bundles Allaire's HomeSite, a leading HTML editor, for you to create code directly. This is a nice software package for the new golden age of typography.

Fusion 3

NetObjects Fusion 3 (http://www.netobjects.com) can create and manage entire Web sites, but it nicely and precisely lays out individual Web pages too. Web sites are *systems* of Web pages, and Fusion 3 makes it easy to build and manage even complex Web sites using techniques such as automatic navigation creation and update. For individual Web pages, Fusion takes a "page layout program" approach, enabling you to creatively lay out a page (i.e., it works more like PageMaker than like a word processor). Moreover, Fusion 3 creates DHTML with easy controls rather than wizards or timelines. No scripting required. This richly endowed software covers a lot of

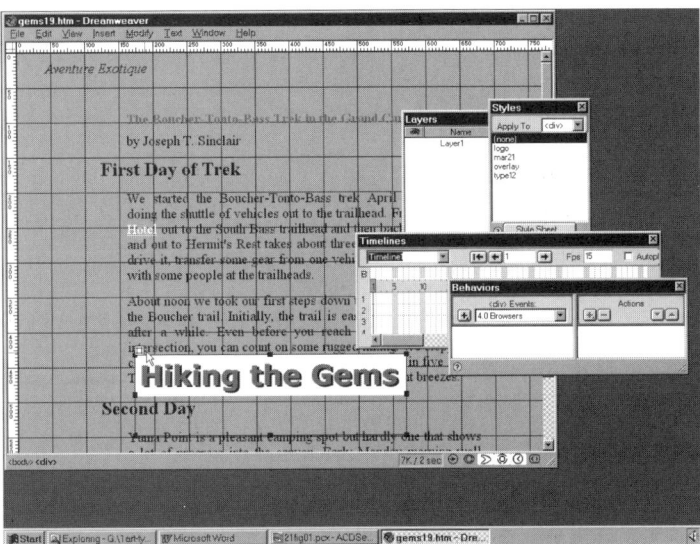

Figure 16.4 *Macromedia's Dreamweaver DHTML authoring program.*

ground for Web work and is one easy way for you to use DHTML if you are not a programmer. Like Dreamweaver, it does not interfere with your HTML, and it bundles Allaire's HomeSite as an HTML editor.

Summary

Where does DHTML fit in? Will it compete with XML? Does it have any limitation? DHTML is a way station on the road to XML. Just as CSS may be absorbed by XSL, DHTML may eventually be absorbed by XML as soon as the Web switches to XML. Therefore, time and energy invested in DHTML will help you prepare for the XML–XSL future.

Nonetheless, DHTML can help you build better Web pages today. You don't have to wait for anything else. As this chapter indicates, you can use DHTML even though you are not a programmer. The question is not whether you can use DHTML. The question is how you can use it to enhance the readability of your Web pages.

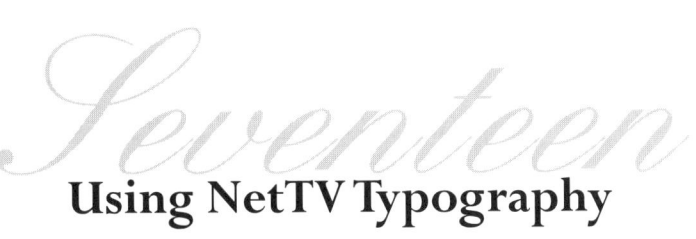

Using NetTV Typography

S ony and Phillips sell set-tops (network computers that sit on top of a television) that use WebTV as an Internet service provider (ISP). RCA sells set-tops that use NetChannel as an ISP. WebTV and NetChannel are not normal ISPs. They are television service providers (TVSPs) that provide browser interfaces and gateway Web sites to enable NetTV viewers (people who access the Web via a set-top and a television) to use the Internet and the Web very easily. Indeed, both WebTV and NetChannel do a superb job of making things effortless for NetTV viewers. Because televisions have inherently low resolution compared with computer monitors, however, the TVSPs must make some dramatic typographic adjustments.

TVSPs and Software Vendors

The TVSP are not ISPs in the normal sense. They do not own modems and routers to provide network services and local dial-up access to their subscribers. They contract with the normal ISPs to provide such services to their subscribers. The TVSPs exist only to provide interface software and gateway Web sites to their subscribers, and they aggregate content at their gateway Web sites for the convenience of their subscribers. In this regard, they are much like America Online except that they serve their specialty audience, television viewers, and do not create very much of their own content.

The interface software is a critical component of TVSP systems. It is essentially Web browser software, but it does not display like a PC Web browser. It displays more like a robust Web site but still provides all the basic functions of a

Operating System and Browser The operating systems for NetTV software are lightweight, about 1 MB, and Unix based. The browsers are also lightweight at about 1 MB. The operating systems reside in flash ROM in the set-tops and are updated via the Internet so as to always be current. The log-in takes place automatically, and NetTV viewers do not have to do anything even for the initial log-in.

Web browser. Indeed, it is difficult to determine where a TVSP's browser ends and its gateway Web site begins. It is all seamless (see Figure 17.1).

One important function of the interface software is that it renders Web pages into a format that televisions can display with maximum sharpness and with a rational layout. This special rendering directly affects TVSP typography. How do the TVSPs do it? The WebTV and NetChannel TVSP systems require the use of both special browsers and special servers, but all network connections are routed through the networks of the normal ISPs with which the TVSPs have contracted.

In addition to WebTV and NetChannel, three software vendors sell software that enables anyone to become a TVSP, whether on an intranet or the Internet. Network Computers Inc. (NCI, a subsidiary of Oracle—the TVSP software was developed by Netscape as Navio and sold to Oracle), Sun Consumer Technologies Group (Sun CTG—started as Diba and merged into Sun), and Spyglass (licenses the browser technology of the University of Illinois which invented the Mosaic multimedia browser) all sell inexpensive browsers and servers that enable

Figure 17.1 *A screen from NetChannel, a TVSP.*

wannabe TVSPs to create interfaces and gateway Web sites that provide service comparable to WebTV and NetChannel.

The software used by the TVSPs and software vendors renders Web sites in a special way so as to look good on television. This special rendering is crucial to the success of this new Web service. NCI and Sun CTG do all the special rendering in the browsers (see Figure 17.2). Spyglass does its television rendering in its special Prism server. Spyglass also plans to introduce a TVSP system in which the browser does the special rendering. A primary component of the special television rendering is the special treatment of typography.

Special Rendering

The special rendering done for NetTV viewers by TVSP interface software (browsers and servers) is different than for computers. The rendering does one or more of the following:

- Increases the size of the text and renders it in a sans serif font.
- Rearranges the text and graphics.
- Reduces the size of the graphics.
- Rescales the entire screen to a smaller size.

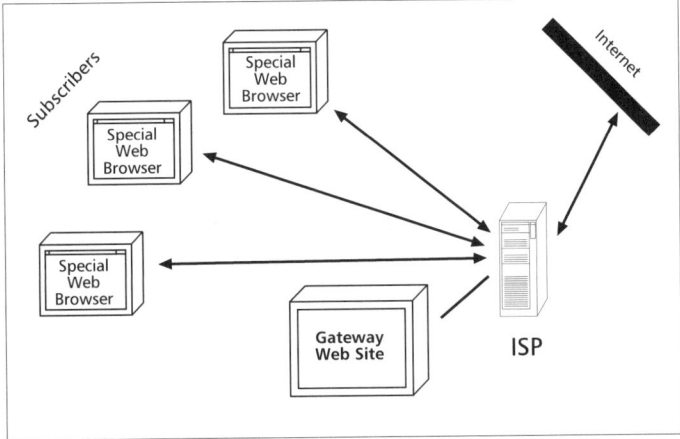

Figure 17.2 *TVSP system using browsers to render for television.*

The goal is to overcome the limitations of the lower-resolution television display and present an appealing screen with maximum sharpness. This special rendering is the prime feature of the interface software, whether it be browser or server software.

Resolution

Both the digital resolution and physical resolution are lower for NetTV than for computers. Characters must be larger and more distinctly defined in order to display with reasonable sharpness. Fine lines (less than 2 pixels in height) on a television cause twitter (visual vibration), and the serifs on characters are sometimes fine lines. Consequently, NetTVs display only sans serif type and in larger sizes than for a computer monitor. Because television viewers sit 8 to 12 feet away from the screen, the slightly larger sans serif letters look sharp to NetTV viewers in spite of the low resolution.

Digital resolution varies between systems but is always below the lowest for computer monitors (640×480). Develop your Web pages for 522×378 (WebTV), the lowest, and you will meet the requirements of the other TVSPs and software vendors, too (see Figure 17.3).

Font Substitutions

Can you substitute your fonts for the ones that the TVSPs use? No. The TVSPs and software vendors render everything into their standard sans serif fonts (see Figure 17.4). It's out of your control. The near future, however, is likely to bring greater capability. Spyglass may adopt TrueDoc or font embedding. NCI will adopt one or both as soon as the market demands it. Others are likely to meet the competition if the use of custom fonts proves desirable. Whatever the situation, however, you must take special care with your typesetting and layout to appeal to NetTV viewers.

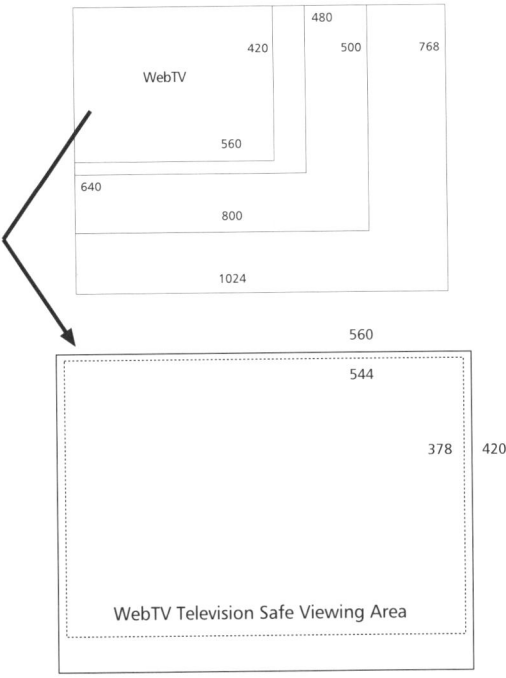

Figure 17.3 *Four resolutions.*

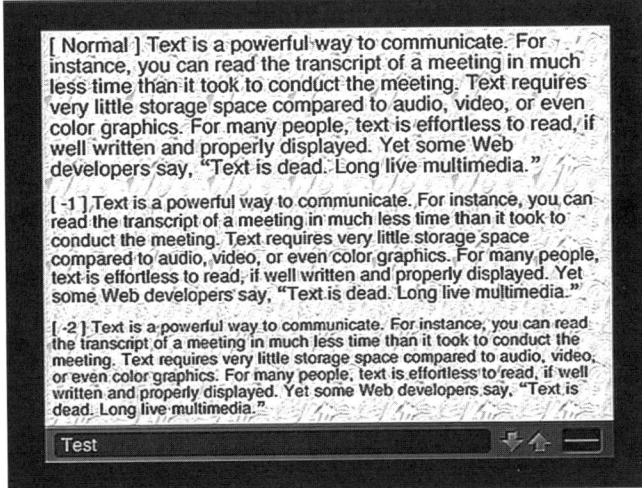

Figure 17.4 *Text on NetTV.*

HTML Extensions

Generally speaking, the TVSP and software vendors support HTML 3.2. However, there are some HTML markups that each does not support. In addition, each provides its own extensions to HTML just like Netscape and Microsoft do. As a result, there is no uniformity in HTML for NetTV. Each TVSP and software vendor is a little different. But they are similar enough that the differences may not be significant for most webmasters.

Special Effects

Some of the TVSP extensions to HTML introduce special effects. For instance, WebTV enables embossed, engraved, and shadowed type (see Figure 17.5). Check out WebTV's HTML Guide at the WebTV Web site (http://www.webtv.com). Televisions have problems displaying functional HTML forms as adeptly as do PCs. Therefore, each TVSP and software vendor usually offers HTML extensions to make forms more palatable to NetTV viewers. If you use a lot of forms on your Web site and you care about the NetTV audience, you will want to research the various TVSP HTML guides to ascertain what they contain in the way of HTML extensions affecting forms.

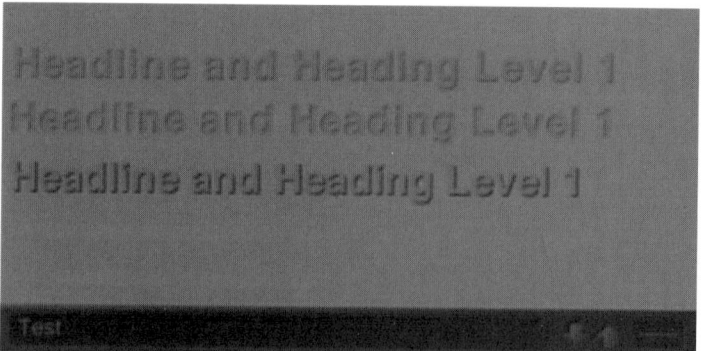

Figure 17.5 *Special effects for type.*

Although you will find it helpful to review and understand the extent and limitations of the TVSP's HTML, not many significant differences will affect your normal Web development. In fact, the treatment of typography is one of the most significant differences, and you have no control over NetTV typography yet, which doesn't leave much to fret about. However, you will want to take into account NetTV's crude but uniform treatment of typography when you plan your Web pages.

Developing for NetTV

This section offers some issues to keep in mind when developing for NetTV that one does not worry about for normal Web development.

Color

Color presents a problem for television displays. Pure primary colors tend to blush and bloom, particularly red. White, being the ultimate saturated color, is especially troublesome and should be avoided. Reduce the saturation on your colors to about 90 percent. Most people will not notice the difference, and you will avoid blushing, blooming, and shimmering. Below 90 percent saturation, the colors starts to look washed out.

Use color contrast in your Web page layout. Colors close together lose much of their communication effectiveness. This is particularly true of typography. The type must contrast with the background to achieve adequate readability. The research reported in Chapter 18 shows that this is true for print, and the research of the TVSPs shows that this is true for NetTV viewers.

The research of the TVSPs indicates that reverse type works well for readability, just the opposite of what's true for print. Consequently, the TVSPs seem to love black backgrounds with light-color text for typography (see Figure 17.6). Some people may find a constant diet of black backgrounds a little oppressive and may prefer other dark colors. In any event, a dark background with light-color text appears to be quite suitable for NetTV and better than a white background, which does not do well on television. Note that TVSP software may change your colors if they are not satisfactory. Such changes may not support the effect you intended.

One way to keep control over your color for NetTV is to use the National Television Systems Committee (NTSC) palette. If that is unpalatable, you can use a program like Equalibrium's Debablizer (http://www.equalibrium.com) to optimize your palettes for NTSC display. With the batch processing of images that programs like Debablizer enable, you can reduce saturation and optimize palettes efficiently.

Control Device

NetTV viewers use a channel-changer-like control device to navigate the Web (see Figure 17.7). This has been inaugurated by the TVSPs to make television viewers comfortable in the new Web medium. However, it works somewhat awkwardly

Figure 17.6 *A screen from NetTV.*

and requires navigation aids (hyperlinks) that run horizontally or vertically on the screen. Random placement of hyperlinks makes navigation difficult for NetTV viewers. NetTV viewers also find most image maps difficult to use. In other words, a set-top does not enable a mouse for navigation. Consequently, navigating the Web via a set-top is more like using keystrokes for navigation on a PC.

Twitter

Television, besides having low resolution and a color problem, also has a low interlaced refresh rate. The consequence is that lines less than 2 pixels in height twitter (visually vibrate). This causes a serious problem for NetTV. All graphical elements and all type elements must be at least 2 pixels in height. In small type, the serifs on serif type may be only 1 pixel in height, thereby causing twitter. To avoid such twitter, all TVSPs convert all fonts to a standard sans serif font slightly larger than the standard for computer monitors. Consequently, the only control you have over fonts for NetTV is size (e.g., +1).

Gyro Mouse Eventually the NetTV control device will be augmented by a gyro mouse, a mouse which does not require a flat surface. Until then, navigation will continue to be awkward for NetTV viewers.

Figure 17.7 *A NetTV control device.*

The TrueDoc system for NetTV antialiases the type, preventing 1-pixel serifs, and enables normal typesetting for NetTV. How soon it will be adopted and by which TVSPs are the questions. But expect the NetTV development environment to become richer soon.

Layout

Simple layouts work best on NetTV. Television doesn't have enough resolution (granularity) to support complex layouts. In other words, there's not much room to work in. Keep images separate from text as much as possible. Keep text blocks short. A little bit of text fills a huge amount of screen on a television. NetTV viewers have difficulty scrolling with their channel-changer-like control devices, so you don't want to make them scroll too much. Also keep in mind that NetTV viewers read text from 8 to 12 feet away, which requires larger fonts. Simpler and shorter are definitely better on television.

Does that mean that television cannot be a reading medium? Absolutely not. In spite of television's technological obstacles to readability and in spite of the digital pundits' predictions that reading on a television would be impossible, the TVSP and software vendors have done an amazing job of making NetTV work for text. Make no mistake: Text is readable on a television. Nonetheless, your job is to understand the shortcomings of the technology and plan and execute your NetTV typography with care so as to maximize readability. If you are careless in this regard, you are going to see some strange things on your Web site via television.

Does television technology mean that aesthetically attractive and interactive Web sites are unlikely for NetTV? Not necessarily. As you can imagine, some of the high-budget, high-glitz Web sites that appeal to the masses have already adapted their Web pages for NetTV. Such Web sites are attractive and functional for NetTV, yet have been able to maintain their appeal to computer users as well. See the Fox Web site at http://www.fox.com which has been adjusted for NetTV.

Design makes the difference. NetTV adds some considerations to the design process but does not disable the development process.

Many of television's technical problems in regard to text will go away with high-definition television (HDT). In the biggest giveaway since it gave land to the railroads in the 19th century, the federal government recently gave away the high bandwidth for HDT to the existing television stations (without even reserving air time for political campaigning). HDT is now in place. How soon the television stations will implement it remains to be seen, but, with its 1920 x 1080 resolution, HDT will certainly upgrade readability on television screens.

HoTMetaL PRO

SoftQuad's robust HTML author and Web site builder (see Chapter 7) includes a specially adjusted HTML DTD for Web-TV's HTML. This can be handy if you develop *only* for WebTV. Otherwise, don't use it. Keep in mind, too, that WebTV has a substantial competitor in NetChannel which uses its own slightly different version of HTML.

Testing

Unfortunately, no amount of information in a book can substitute for actually experimenting with this new technology. You will have to obtain a set-top and NetTV service in order to experiment. (Presumably, you already have a television.) Because of the smaller electronic display, typography for NetTV is cumbersome at best. You will not be able to achieve the highly refined Web typesetting that you can for PCs using CSS, and CSS will not work yet for NetTV. Unfortunately, each TVSP and the TVSP software sold by the software vendors works a little differently. To have 100 percent assurance that your Web site will work well for all NetTV software, you would have to experiment with all the software. However, sticking to basic HTML and keeping things simple will go a long ways toward making your Web site work on all NetTV platforms. Read *Developing Web Pages with TV HTML*, by Joseph T. Sinclair (Charles River Media, 1998), for further details that will help you maximize your Web site for television viewers.

Predictions

Find/SVP (http://etrg.findsvp.com) estimates that a third of the households (12.2 million of 36.5 million) that access the Internet in 2000 will do so through Internet appliances rather than PCs. Most of those Internet appliances are likely to be NetTVs. Other comparable estimates have been made regarding this quickly growing market. Consequently, you will want to give this new Web market increasingly serious consideration in regard to how you design your Web site.

Summary

NetTV today is the forerunner of tomorrow's huge mass market, and it brings a whole set of typography problems of its own. Although many of the problems will disappear with HDT, many experts expect HDT to take 10 years to become popular. This is a market that can't wait for HDT. You will undoubtedly soon feel compelled to adjust your Web site for NetTV. When you do, you will want to pay particular attention to the unique considerations required by typography on television.

Forging a Web Development Strategy

T his chapter rounds out the book with some information that will help you forge a sound strategy for developing Web pages and in particular for using Web typography. First, the chapter covers some interesting research on readability. Second, the chapter features a summary of the Web technologies that a webmaster needs to know. Third, the chapter offers useful tips on how you can use good typography in your Web pages. Fourth, the chapter romanticizes a bit about the third, fourth, and fifth dimensions of Web typography.

Research and Comments

This section features some interesting research relevant to the book. Even though the research was done for typesetting and layout in the print medium, much of it has direct application to typography on the Web.

Mr. Wheildon's Book

Up to this point in the book, I have tried to illustrate the principles of good typography as generally proclaimed by typography gurus, with some of my own opinions thrown in regarding typography on the Web. But a little empirical evidence never hurts; it is potentially more accurate than the opinions of gurus, and it might present a few surprises. Colin Wheildon, in his book *Type & Layout* (Berkeley: Strathmoor Press, 1995), reports on 9 years of quantitative research (1982–1990) regarding the effectiveness of printed text communication. For instance, he did a study that showed that about five times more readers comprehended a magazine page typeset in Garamond than the identical page typeset in Helvetica.

Mr. Wheildon's empirical research involved over 200 people. The participants originally numbered 300, but the number declined over the long period of the research through attrition due to death and people moving to distant cities. The research reinforces many of the notions we have about typography and challenges others.

Author's Comments on the Wheildon Book

Most of us who use digital typography do not have the opportunity to do empirical research and must make unscientific judgments based on our own experience. I would not step up to the plate to challenge Mr. Wheildon's conclusions regarding type and layout in the print medium. In fact, I feel comfortable with his research. The big question is, of course, how can we use his research (done for print) to achieve the highest level of readability in the digital media? To attempt to answer that question, I have followed each section of reporting on a topic of Mr. Wheildon's research with my own commentary (Author's Comments). The thoughts expressed in these comments are strictly my own and do not necessarily reflect anyone else's opinion.

The Law of Gravity

Mr. Wheildon tested Edmund Arnold's (typographer) theory of *reading gravity*; that is, the eye wants to start in the upper left-hand corner and go to the lower right-hand corner, and any typographical practice that interferes with the eye's inclination disrupts readability and comprehension (see Figure 18.1).

Mr. Wheildon found that, indeed, if you defy the law of *reading gravity*, comprehension is reduced by at least half. This means simply that a reader will move from the upper left-hand corner to the lower right-hand corner, and you cannot

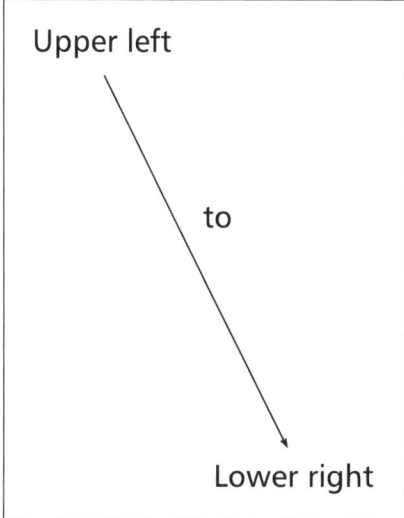

Figure 18.1 *Reading gravity illustrated.*

do anything to distract the reader from that path, or make the reader jump off the path, without the risk of losing her.

Author's Comments on Gravity

Does the law of reading gravity operate on a computer monitor screen? Each screen is a static presentation analogous to a page in print. It seems reasonable to make the leap of faith to say yes, the law of reading gravity works on screens, too. The validity of the law of reading gravity was pretty well substantiated by Mr. Wheildon's research. Keep it in mind for your Web typography.

Serif or Sans Serif?

Mr. Wheildon ran tests to compare serif typefaces to sans serif typefaces. The study showed that about five times as many people comprehend text typeset in serif type than the same text typeset in sans serif type. Note that this was not a close contest. In fact, his study reinforces scientific research done in Britain in 1926 (cited by Mr. Wheildon) that concluded that serif type is easier to read.

Author's Comments on Serifs

Serif or sans serif? That is the question. And indeed, many have come to the conclusion that sans serif type is better for the low-resolution cathode ray tube (CRT) monitors that everyone uses. This issue is clouded by the wide disparity in screen presentations across different digital and physical resolutions, different size physical displays, and different viewing distances. It is also compounded by the fact that, at low resolutions, some high-quality serif fonts display much better on the screen than other high-quality serif fonts, while in print they all perform equally well.

It is my opinion that serif fonts that display well on the screen have a considerable edge over sans serif fonts in providing readability. Whereas it is true that few serif fonts display well on the screen, nonetheless, the ones that do display well create a superior reading environment to that of sans serif fonts.

It turns out that Times New Roman displays very well on the screen. The fact that both Netscape and Microsoft have made Times New Roman the default font for their browsers appears to add credence to my view. Although this cannot be considered scientific evidence, it does seem to suggest that I am not alone, at least, in my opinion. Consequently, I recommend to you that if you don't like Times New Roman—or are tired of it—find another serif font that displays well, and use it with confidence for text. See Chapter 21 for more information on choosing fonts.

The TVSP (television service providers) and TVSP software vendors have all done research in regard to television viewer preferences. They all, without exception, use sans serif type. Indeed, they convert all Web text to sans serif text. However, there is a special reason for this. Television has very low resolution. As a result, serifs on type are sometimes as small as 1 pixel in height. Television cannot tolerate 1-pixel lines. Because of the nature of television, 1-pixel lines cause twitter (visual vibration) which is anathema to the TVSPs. One way to avoid twitter caused by text is to use sans serif type. So, that's what they do.

Regardless of the twitter problem, some of the TVSPs have licensed a version of Bitstream's TrueDoc programmed for NetTV. Presumably, in the future, we will be seeing serif type on the Web accessed via television. For more information on NetTV see *Developing Web Sites with TV HTML*, by Joseph T. Sinclair (Charles River Media, 1998).

Watch out for pure white, full-page-width technical writings on the Web typeset in sans serif fonts explaining Web style sheets and typography to you; there's no shortage of them. What can you do when you have to read this stuff? Take control of the page look via your browser under *Preferences* or *Internet Options*. Change the background color if white is too bright for you. Choose the fonts. And make your browser window tall and narrow to squeeze the text into a column. I made my browser one-third of a screen wide to read one nearly illegible Microsoft FAQ on a topic relevant to this book.

Headlines

When it comes to headlines, serif and sans serif provide about equal readability, according to Mr. Wheildon's research. The distinguishing difference for headlines was whether they were in lowercase or all caps. The study was conducted using a variety of oldstyle, modern, sans serif, decorative, script, cursive, and blackletter typefaces. Comprehension of lowercase headlines turned out to be significantly higher than headlines using all caps. An overall percentage could not be calculated because each typeface was tested individually. It is interesting, but not surprising, to note that the decorative, script, cursive, and blackletter headlines did not fare well in the study.

An Unscientific Observation My observation is that, the more technical a writing is on the Web, the more likely it is to be typeset with a sans serif font. Of course, technical writings often tend to be tedious to read, and sans serif type makes them almost unreadable, especially in page-width text blocks (i.e., text that runs all the way across the page without any margins). Throw in a pure white background, also common for technical writings, and the writings become illegible for many people. On the other hand, many Web pages use serif fonts for typesetting with ergonomic color backgrounds and with text in columns. Such Web pages are quite readable but seem more likely to feature nontechnical content.

Author's Comments on Headlines

It seems quite likely that lowercase headlines are easier to read on a computer monitor just as they are in print. Large type appears sharper and more readable on a CRT than text-size type, and therefore it is more like print than text-size type (see Figure 18.2). Mr. Wheildon's research should apply in this case.

Colored Text and Headlines

The studies regarding colored text were complex. The general conclusion was that the closer the text is to black (i.e., the darker it is), the more readable it is. The color combination that was the most readable was black type over a light-color tint.

Of particular interest was the study regarding reverse type (white type on a black background). Reverse type is just not very readable. In fact, Mr. Wheildon concludes that reverse type is virtually impossible for readers to comprehend.

What about colored headlines? Mr. Wheildon found that colored headlines attracted more readers, but the number of readers comprehending the text was lower than for black

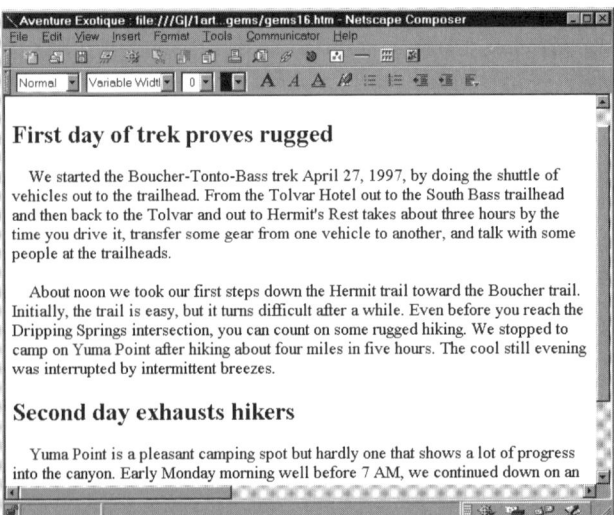

Figure 18.2 *Headlines on a screen.*

headlines. The colors were tested separately. High-chroma (more brilliant) colors attracted more readers but had lower readability. Low-chroma colors attracted less readers but had higher readability. Black attracted less readers but performed significantly better, with about four times the readability of high-chroma colors.

Author's Comments on Color

Both color text and color headlines are different for CRT monitors than they are for the print medium. Color is more likely to provide readability, properly used. A pure white background may prove a little harsh for many people. A printed page works on reflected light. A CRT blasts light. A light background color or even a medium color with black text can provide suitable reading, assuming maximum contrast. Active matrix LCD monitors don't blast light, but they do emit light; and you can consider them closer to CRTs than to paper. Experiment with background and foreground colors. We can productively use color combinations, I believe, that would undoubtedly fare poorly in print and in Mr. Wheildon's studies.

Given that using a color combination conducive to reading on a CRT is a reasonable choice, how do you handle different-color headlines? If your response to this question is, "different from what?", you may have an answer. One can extrapolate from Mr. Wheildon's studies that, if a Web document is composed in two colors, those colors set the base to which all else must be compared. Thus, the fact that a Web page is set in navy text with a cream background presumably makes navy headlines standard—just like black headlines are standard to the black-and-white print medium. If you made a headline purple instead of navy on such a Web page, presumably Mr. Wheildon's research would indicate that readers would find the nonstandard purple less readable than the navy. Whether this analysis will hold up in a scientific study is unanswered, but it seems an intelligent approach with which to experiment. The problem is that there is no standard set of colors for typography. Perhaps the moral of the story is: Keep it simple. Too much color can clutter, just like too many typefaces or typestyles can clutter.

Keep in mind too that a different text color from the base text on a Web page is a signal that such text is a hyperlink. In other words, wanton use of color text can interfere with navigation. This is another reason to keep your use of color backgrounds and text simple.

Color is laden with cultural meaning. A color combination that seems to work perfectly for reading may ultimately fail miserably for cultural reasons. Dark red text on a mint green background may read well, but how long can you read it without thinking of Christmas? This is another variable that complicates color choices.

The TVSPs seem to favor black backgrounds with light-color text (see Chapter 17). Their research has show that this is readable for NetTV viewers. Whether this research applies to computer users is unanswered, but there is no shortage of Web sites with black backgrounds and light-color text. I have found this combination to be quite readable and often attractive. Whether this combination or other dark background/light-color text combinations are culturally palatable for a steady diet of long documents is another question.

Are Italics Readable?

One of Mr. Wheildon's studies sought to determine whether italics are readable. Only serif italics were tested. He found them to be as readable as regular (roman) type except for a few typefaces that have fancy italics with a lot of flourishes. Thus, you may find it useful to note that clean-cut italics for serif type have a high level of readability in print. This provides a solid basis for potentially expanding your use of italics and generating greater creativity in your typesetting. Unfortunately, digital italics are different.

Author's Comments on Italics

Regular characters have mostly vertical and horizontal lines, which a digital device displays well. However, digital devices display slanted lines with less definition (see Figure 18.3). Hence, a computer monitor does not display italics well. The fact that, in print, serif italics are as readable as regular characters seems to be an observation that will not hold up on a CRT. Italics on a CRT do not have enough definition for people to read easily. Therefore, avoid the use of italics for text blocks, and use them only where appropriate according to common usage. Keep in mind that this recommendation applies to text-size print only. Note, however, that TrueDoc PFRs render italics better than normal digital fonts render italics.

Justified Text

Mr. Wheildon found that justified text is simply more readable. About twice as many readers comprehended justified text as comprehended flush left (ragged right, left justified). When

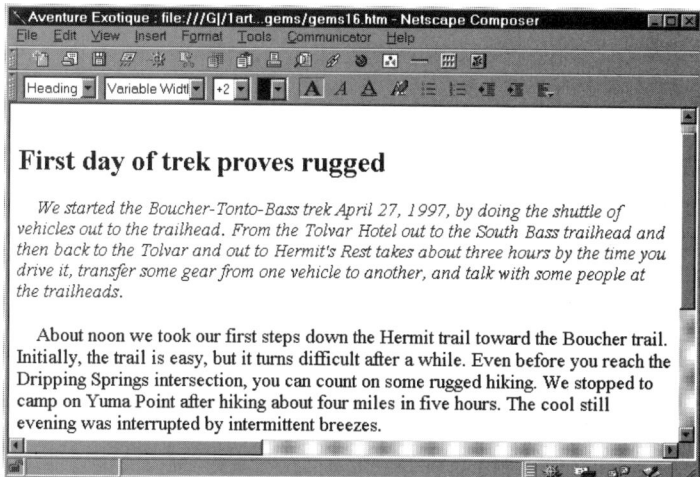

Figure 18.3 *Italics on the Web.*

it came to ragged left (flush right), he referred to it as "ragged right's sinister offspring." Indeed, ragged left fared very poorly in the study.

Author's Comments on Justified Text

Until now, whether to justify text on the Web has been a moot point. You couldn't do it, even if you wanted to. But CSS now enables fully justified text (see Figure 18.4), and according to Mr. Wheildon's study, we need to start using it. The party line has long touted flush left (ragged right) as being more readable than justified. Apparently, the party line is erroneous. But effective justification requires hyphenation and tight word spacing. Without the hyphenation, justified columns may not be ready for the Web yet, at least not for long text passages. Nonetheless, with the arrival of CSS, the time has come to *experiment* with justified text on the Web. You may find wide columns of justified text typeset with certain fonts suitable for long passages. The last word is not in yet regarding justified text on the Web.

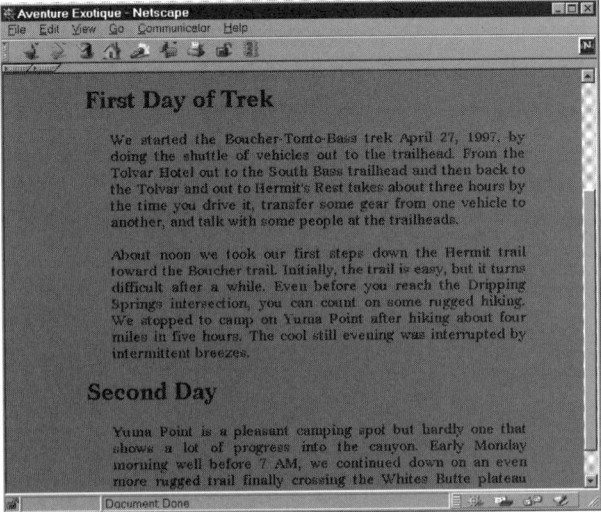

Figure 18.4 *Justified text on the Web.*

Jumps

Jumps? You know, when the text starts to absorb you and then asks you to jump to another place in the newspaper or magazine (e.g., continued on page 43). Mr. Wheildon found that readers find jumps annoying. Over 80 percent of the readers said that they disobeyed jumps. Disobeyed? Oh, my. What implications does that have for hyperlinks?

This was part of a larger study that explored annoyances to readers. The conclusion was that readers are easily annoyed with layout. Almost anything that disrupts the flow of reading is annoying. Text that is too narrow or too wide, lack of captions for illustrations, long headlines, all caps, and jumps are not favored. Subheadings, however, are appreciated.

Author's Comments on Jumps

Mr. Wheildon's research on ancillary annoyances indicates that a jump is not a pause that refreshes. That seems disquieting information for Web developers. The Web provides interaction, one of its great strengths as a medium. Much of the interaction occurs via hyperlinks. And what is a hyperlink but a jump? It appears that this research does not bode well for Web surfing and reading.

Rather than try to argue an exception for the Web, I find Mr. Wheildon's observations in this regard to not only be creditable but to be directly applicable to Web sites. In an interactive media like the Web, one of the risks is making your presentation *too* interactive (see Figure 18.5). People can get lost in endless labyrinths of interactivity, and the golden rule of interactive multimedia development is to keep interactivity shallow and simple. In addition, the purpose of the Web is not necessarily to be interactive. An equally valid use is for static online publishing where a Web site visitor's experience is strictly that of a reader, not an interactor. Thus, whether the Web might be a jumpy medium according to Mr. Wheildon's research depends on how you use it.

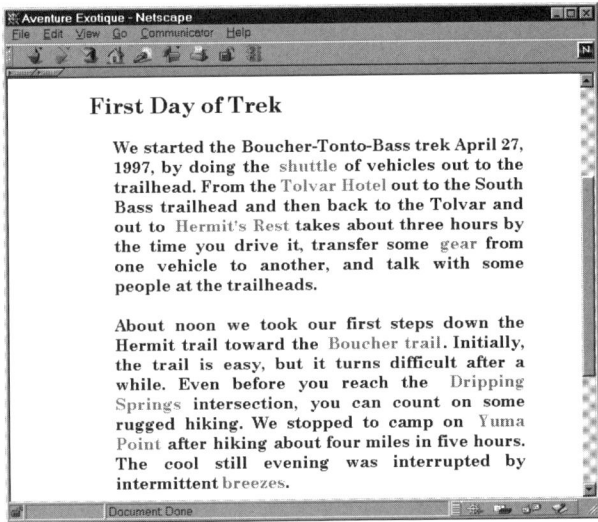

Figure 18.5 *Is this Web page readable with all the hyperlinks?*

In the case where your purpose is simply to post documents for reading, it would appear that Mr. Wheildon's research indicates that you should keep hyperlinks to a minimum or even eliminate them inside text blocks, if possible. The less disruptions, potential jumps, or jumps, the better the readability. On the other hand, where interactivity is appropriate but reading remains important, Mr. Wheildon's research would indicate the use of hyperlinks in moderation inside text blocks. Interestingly, most interactive consultants with whom I've discussed such matters would, I believe, find themselves in agreement with the general thrust of Mr. Wheildon's research.

In any event, it is very important that you design your text hyperlinks so that they are very easy to read through. This means giving them a color that is similar to the text color so that a reader can read through them with the least distraction. On the other hand, the color of the hyperlinks must be distinctive enough from the text so as to be noticeable (see Figure 18.6). Both the unvisited hyperlink color and the visited hyperlink colors should adhere to this principle. In short,

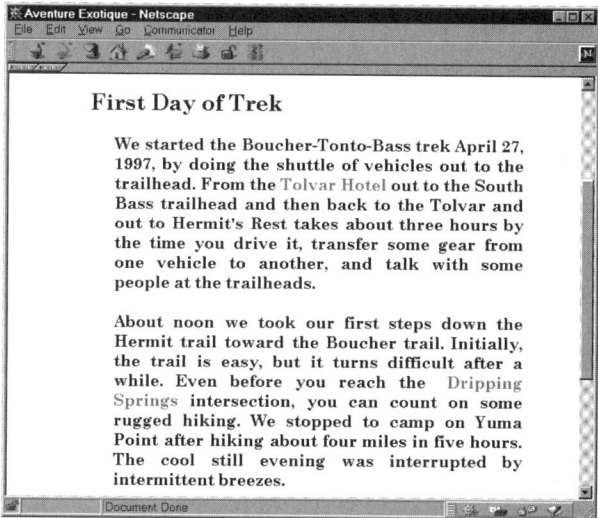

Figure 18.6 *Less disruptive hyperlinks.*

hyperlinks can be valuable links to valuable information resources, but they can be annoying too. When you create a Web page, you need to keep this in mind.

At least one well-known Web typographer has recommended red for hyperlinks—to catch visitors' attention. I don't think it takes quite so much to get attention, and Mr. Wheildon's research suggests that people might like to read through the hyperlinks. There is nothing in Mr. Wheildon's research to indicate that people don't return to the jumps later (i.e., after they have finished reading the main body of text).

Pamphlets

Mr. Wheildon did an interesting study regarding the readability of pamphlets which is worth your consideration. Perhaps the conclusion most relevant to the Web is the one regarding type size. He found that the most readable range of type was between 10-point type with 1 point of leading and 12-point type with 2 points of leading. Another conclusion was that a pamphlet should include an illustration.

Author's Comments on Pamphlets

Many Web pages are similar to pamphlets, and Mr. Wheildon's findings seem relevant. His conclusions regarding type size coincide with normal typesetting practices. However, for the Web, slightly larger type is appropriate. People view their CRTs from a greater distance than they read print. Leaning forward to read on a CRT is not comfortable. Leaning backward to read is more relaxing. Therefore, it's up to you to provide type that is large enough to enable Web visitors to lean back a little and read comfortably.

It is interesting to note Mr. Wheildon's conclusion that adding an illustration to the text engenders more interest and also improves readability. With all the bells and whistles available to us to use at our Web sites today, none is more powerful than an attractive graphic. Indeed, when the Web was with us in text mode only, it was not particularly popular. Then the Mosaic multimedia browser came into widespread use, enabling graphics to propel the Web to its present popularity. Color photographs, illustrations, design graphics, and even heading (text) graphics all contributed to fuel the Web's growth frenzy. Images are unquestionably the spice of the Web. Hence, remember to add some images to your Web pages, particularly to any long, dry Web pages that you have at your Web site. However, do not interpret this recommendation to include gratuitous graphics (i.e., graphics just for the sake of graphics). Use relevant graphics that enhance or none at all.

Read It Yourself

I found Mr. Wheildon's studies quite interesting. I have tried to relate his research to the digital typographical environment in which we must work to build Web sites. But I think Mr. Wheildon's book is important enough for you to read and form your own opinions. My report on his research is superficial and undoubtedly colored by my own point of view and understanding. Read his book yourself, and you will be better able to predict how many Web site visitors you will *lose* when you break the guidelines for typography established by his research.

The Other Shoe Drops

Having presented an *empirical* study, it seems appropriate to present the other end of the cultural spectrum, the *aesthetic* ideal. Is typography art or science? The aesthete would say that good typography is a matter of discovering the true typographical forms and formats, the ones that most elegantly display and arrange type on a page. But typography is not art in the sense that it does not simply provide an aesthetic experience. It exists to enable reading. Consequently, typography is always tied to its function: producing readable text. No matter how beautiful it is, a specific typeface or text arrangement is not good typography unless it's readable.

An admired typographer, Jan Tschichold (1902–1974), represents the aesthetic point of view in his book *The Form of the Book—Essays on the Morality of Good Design* (Hartley & Marks, 1991). He writes (on page 5), "Comfortable legibility is the absolute benchmark for all typography. . ." Thus, he squarely places himself well within the guidelines that typography must produce readable text. But the complete quote brings another attitude to light. "Comfortable legibility is the absolute benchmark for all typography—yet only an accomplished reader can properly judge legibility." The complete quote clearly establishes Mr. Tschichold's aesthete's point of view. Taking into account the context of his book, he seems to be saying that, yes, type must provide functionality, but it must have beauty as well, a beauty that only the cognoscenti can appreciate. He writes about good typography being founded on *good taste*. If asked whose good taste, he would undoubtedly answer: his.

Mr. Tschichold's many writings on typography, his career in typography, and his crafting of the Sabon typeface establish his credentials. He considered many typographical problems at great length with great intelligence and reached—no sur-prise—some rather precise and strongly held opinions. (Of course, strongly held views can change. Early in his career, Mr. Tschichold favored the use of sans serifs, a position from which he later retreated.) He has been a considerable influence on typographers in the 20th century. As an aesthete, he is well grounded in the craft of typography and cannot be considered an artist unconnected to the realities of reading.

The dilemma is: If science and aesthetics conflict, which are we to believe? Hypothetically, if Mr. Wheildon's research and Mr. Tschichold's views conflict, whom are we to believe? The point here is not to compare Mr. Wheildon's research with Mr. Tschichold's views and look for conflict. There may not be any. The point is to understand that, when science and the aesthetic meet and clash, there are choices to be made. Do we believe the 224 laypeople in Mr. Wheildon's study, or do we believe a typographer with strongly held views? Do we dismiss Mr. Wheildon's science as not being applicable to craftsmanship or art? Do we dismiss typographers like Mr. Tschichold as trying to make an art out of a craft?

Science provides one of the great problem-solving tech-niques of the 20th century and cannot be ignored, even for typography. At the same time, we know that science alone has not provided all the answers in any sphere of human activity, least of all in the aesthetic spheres. As Mr. Tschichold wrote in his book (page 31), "Typography is both art and science." Thus, we must balance the traditional, the aesthetic, the scien-tific, and the limitations of new technology to create a digital-display typography that provides both the functionality and the aesthetic quality that embody the typographic ideal.

Indeed, the contemporary problem is typography online. The people who move text successfully from paper to the Web will not be whiz kids from cyberspace. They will be people who are steeped in the traditions of typography, yet who also keep an open mind in solving new problems that arise. To develop a valid online typography, we need new experiments, opinions, respect for tradition, and empirical studies.

- **Experiments.** Experiments are more than people try-ing new ideas in Web pages. Experiments test new ideas and attempt to measure or otherwise evaluate the effec-tiveness of such ideas; that is, they evaluate readability.

- **Opinions.** Today, we need more opinions by accom-plished typographers that are based on experimentation with, and careful consideration of, the new digital-display media. Naturally, those opinions should be tempered by the 500-year history of typography in providing readable text, but such history should not necessarily take prece-dence. What we don't need is the digerati promulgating a new typography based on digital considerations, a pseudotypography.

- **Empirical studies.** Studies featuring (in part) typo-graphical inquiry have been done, primarily by busi-nesses that have a stake in online endeavors. Unfortunately, such research is often proprietary and thus available to only a small group of people. Although reality dictates that business entities need to keep such research secret for a period to be competitive, it does not dictate that they need to keep such research secret forever. If businesses more often make their research regarding readability public, it will benefit the entire Web publishing industry. And as we all know, what goes around comes around.

Therefore, to those who might object to the inclusion of Mr. Wheildon's research in this book, I submit that more readabil-ity studies are needed just for print typography; and certainly all the studies we can muster are needed for the new digital-display typography. Nonetheless, empirical studies are not the only valid source of reliable typographical knowledge. Experienced but open-minded typographers must intelligently apply typography traditions to the new digital media.

The scope of this task is staggering. For instance, Mr. Tschichold in his book provides very precise technical infor-mation on the size and proportions of text blocks and paper pages (e.g., a ratio of 1:1.618—the Golden Section, which is one of several proportions recommended; see Figure 18.7). This is valuable information to consider for printing books.

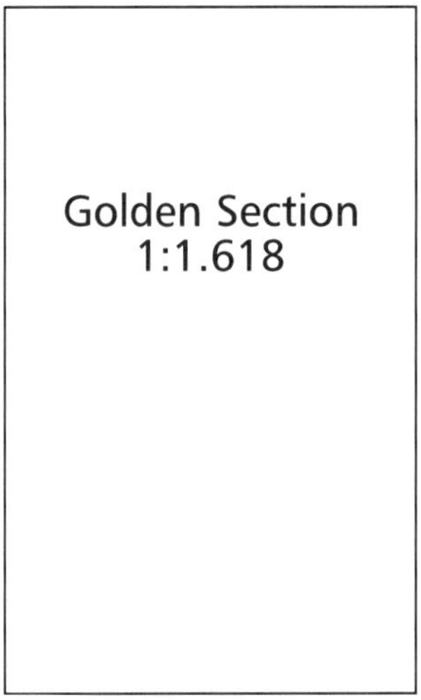

Figure 18.7 *The Golden Section (a ratio of 1:1.618).*

Yet, how do you translate the Golden Section, or any other proportion, into a Web page that might be any size and any proportion? Even with CSS, you have no assurance that an absolute size and proportion for a page will display uniformly cross-media the way you would like it to. Thus, forging a strategy from going from the paper page to the Web page will not be easy.

Chart of Technologies

This book covers CSS, TrueDoc, and font embedding as three new software technologies essential to professional Web development. DHTML has already come into vogue, and XML and XSL are just around the corner. Where does this leave webmasters? How much do we have to learn?

Tables 18.1 and 18.2 assume that the readers of this book are nonprogrammer webmasters. This includes me, and I believe that it includes the vast majority of people doing Web work. Recall that, in the introduction I defined a webmaster as being a nonprogrammer. Table 18.1 shows what a webmaster can be expected to know and what is outside the body of knowledge that he can be expected to have. Table 18.2 shows what software is available to help webmasters accomplish necessary tasks and also programming tasks that they cannot do without some kind of software assistance.

Table 18.1 *Technologies That a Webmaster Needs to Master*

Technology	Comments
HTML	HTML is basic for a webmaster. But make your life easy. Use only the markups common to both computer browsers (Netscape and Microsoft) and to NetTV.
TV HTML	Television is a future mass market for the Web. Learn what makes television technology different. So far, the differences are small, but they may grow. Use only HTML common to NetTV and to the two computer browsers.
CGI Scripts	Forget it. This is the realm of programmers. Look for CGI scripts available on the Web that you can put to use on your server without alteration, if you have the appropriate access to your Web server for installing such scripts.
SQL	If you need to use databases over the Web, you need to have an overview of SQL. Simple and even moderately complex queries are not difficult. Simple Web-database application projects can be fun if you use appropriate authoring software. But get a database programmer to build comprehensive Web-database applications.
Java scripts	Don't think about it. This is the realm of programmers. Look for Java scripts available on the Web that you can put to use in your Web pages without alteration.
Java applets	Forget about creating applets. This is the realm of programmers. Look for Java applets available on the Web that you can use in your Web pages. And you need to know how to install them in a Web page and set the parameters, if required.

(continued)

Table 18.1 *(continued)*

Technology	Comments
Java servlets	Ignore servlets. This is the realm of programmers who run Web servers.
CSS	CSS is now basic for a webmaster. Learn it—it's easy. But don't wait: CSS 2 is more difficult, and you don't want to eat the whole tamale in one bite. Like HTML, you don't have to hand code, but if you know enough to refer to the right place in the CSS guide, you can often tune up code that authoring programs just can't handle well.
CSS positioning	Just a little bit more CSS. Learn it well enough to get an overview of DHTML. You can also use it for normal layout without DHTML. It is now part of CSS 2.
DHTML	DHTML is the realm of programmers. But the creativity for DHTML presentations, which will become routine on the Web soon, will come primarily from webmasters or other creative people, not necessarily from programmers. Thus, you need to have an overview of DHML.
SGML	Get a good overview of SGML as a basis for understanding XML and even for understanding HTML better.
XML	Get a good overview of XML. Only with a good overview will you be able to determine when and why you might need XML. If you do need XML, you will find it similar to HTML. XML is the realm of programmers, but the creativity for XML systems will come primarily from webmasters or other people who want to establish special functions in Web publishing.
XSL	You don't need XSL unless you use XML. If you learn to use CSS 1 and 2, XSL will be easier to learn when you need it. Again, you will use an authoring for XSL, but it doesn't hurt to have a good overview.
TrueDoc	TrueDoc is now basic for a webmaster. Learn it and use it.
MS font embedding	MS font embedding is now basic for a webmaster. Learn it and use it. An option may be to use only TrueDoc and ignore MS font embedding.

Table 18.1 *(continued)*

Digital images	Get a good overview of digital images and digital color. Many webmasters create and manipulate images themselves, but even if others do it for you, you will need to have a basic understanding.
Streaming media	Streaming media such as RealAudio and RealVideo will gradually but steadily come into widespread use on the Web. Learn each streaming protocol as you find a need to use it.
Operating system	You need to know a few basic commands for the operating system (e.g., Unix, Windows NT) on which your Web server runs, but only if you have access to the operating system.

Table 18.2 *Authoring Programs for Various Web Technologies.*

Technology	Authoring Program
HTML	There are many authoring programs available that work well and can save you time, energy, and money. HTML editors can also save time.
TV HTML	Some of the HTML editors now include TV HTML (usually WebTV) markups.
CGI scripts	There are a few authoring programs that do general scripts, but they're expensive and haven't caught on.
SQL	There are many Web-database authoring programs. A few are easy to use; the rest are for programmers. You have to have an understanding of databases and SQL to use a database authoring program. However, you can create simple, and even moderately complex, Web-database applications as a nonprogrammer.
Java scripts	A few HTML authoring programs do light scripting on a limited basis.
Java applets	There are many Java authoring programs. A few are easy to use; the rest are for programmers. The few general authoring programs that nonprogrammers can use have limited capability. Some highly specialized Java authoring programs are easy to use, but they're only useful if you need what they can do.

(continued)

Table 18.2 *(continued)*

Technology	Authoring Program
Java servlets	You can program these only with a Java authoring program designed for Java programmers.
CSS	CSS has been integrated into many HTML authoring programs. A few easy-to-use standalone CSS authoring programs exist.
CSS positioning	CSS positioning has been integrated into HTML authoring programs that feature DHTML authoring.
DHTML	DHTML has been integrated into a few HTML authoring programs. Eventually, the best HTML authoring programs will have robust DHTML capability, but they will be more difficult to learn than normal authoring programs.
SGML	SGML authoring programs are generally easy to use. They create documents. They require DTDs. Soon, most will export an XML document. Don't confuse them with SGML development or publishing programs that create DTDs and style sheets. Such programs may not be so easy to use.
XML	Right now, the only way to create an XML document is to use an SGML authoring program (with a DTD) and export the document as an XML document. In the future, easy-to-use XML authoring programs will be widely available. Keep in mind that there are two aspects to XML authoring: designing the XML document and filling the document with content. Presumably, future XML authoring programs will enable you to do both.
XSL	You will use an XSL authoring program to create an XSL style sheet. Don't expect it to be as easy to use as CSS authoring programs.
TrueDoc	TrueDoc is incorporated into some HTML authoring programs. Stand-alone TrueDoc conversion programs are easy to use.
MS font embedding	You use Microsoft Web Embedding Font Tool (WEFT) to do embed fonts in Web pages. It's easy to use, or presumably will be when it gets out of beta.
Digital images	Image manipulation programs abound, and many are quite easy to use. Regardless, there's a lot to learn about digital color.

Table 18.2 *(continued)*

Streaming media	Streaming media converters (compressors) convert normal multimedia assets into streaming media. The conversion process is not necessarily difficult but requires special software, usually provided by the vendor for the streaming media.
Operating system	Operating system commands, if needed, are often provided transparently by authoring programs.

An important part of forging a Web development strategy is deciding what technologies you will master and what technologies you will leave to someone else.

Author's Best Tips

This is the place in the book where you will find my best tips for Web typography. They are listed in random order.

Tips for Better Web Typography

- Consider using color combinations other than black and white.
- Use serif type that is a little larger than you'd use for print.
- Put long text blocks in a continuous column not exceeding 60 characters in width. An ideal width is about 9 to 12 words.
- Use screen-tuned fonts that look sharp on the screen but also look good when rendered in TrueDoc.
- Keep layout simple. Keep text from wrapping around Web page objects such as images and Java applets wherever possible.
- Experiment with justified text for wide text columns but not for narrow columns.
- Use plenty of headings and subheadings.

- Use images where appropriate and useful.
- Where Web site visitors have choices, provide recommendations on how visitors can maximize the readability of Web pages (i.e., provide instructions).

Tips for the Future

- Learn TrueDoc, font embedding, and CSS now and start experimenting.
- Be ready to learn XML and XSL when they come into widespread use. Learning CSS will help you prepare. Learn enough to use an XML or XSL reference manual when your XML authoring program can't quite get it right.
- Take an ongoing interest in the current screen resolutions of CRTs, active matrix LCDs, and other digital display devices.
- Become thoroughly familiar with the capabilities of computer display devices and how they work with PCs and software.
- Experiment with creating Web pages that are readable on the screen but that also print well.

New Dimensions in Typography

Digital technology has transformed typography already but will continue to do so for a long time to come. The new dimensions described here may give you some insight about what is yet to come and assist you in conceiving a more forward-looking development strategy.

The Third Dimension

If you agree that normal typography has two dimensions (width and height, or black and white, or type and space), it's not much of a stretch to imagine color as the third dimension of Web typography.

Color adds enough complexity to typography to merit a lot of attention. Is color a new dimension? It is for most people. Some professionals have used color in typography for a long time but more for artwork than for text. Even desktop publishing has always been a primarily a black-and-white endeavor. Now, with the exciting new digital publishing media of the Web, everyone must learn to use color in typography. Moreover, with the recent rapid proliferation of inexpensive high-resolution color ink jet printers, color typography on paper has fallen into the hands of virtually everyone who wants to use it. Color is, indeed, a new and important dimension in popular typography—keeping in mind, of course, that popular typography didn't exist until the PC and desktop publishing came along in the 1980s.

Of course, you can make text look 3D by treating it with color. This 3D treatment also qualifies as part of the typography third dimension. 3D has been quite popular on the Web but is not for everyone. However, if you're making text GIFs, a very slight drop shadow can often give better definition to characters in some color combinations without creating a 3D effect.

Color on the Web In lieu of a book specifically on the principals of digital color typography, you might try Lynda Weinman's book on Web color, *<coloring web graphics.2>* (New Riders, 1997). It has plenty of ideas on the usage of color and includes hundreds of text-background color-combination examples.

The Fourth Dimension

If color is the third dimension of typography, dynamic digital text is the fourth dimension. Dynamic digital text, in my definition, encompasses anything that changes, manipulates, animates, or moves text on the screen. I see dynamic text being enabled by the digital environment in a variety of ways, specifically the following:

- **HTML hyperlinks.** Hyperlinks provide the ability to instantly move from one section of text to another or from text to a multimedia object (e.g., an image) and vice versa. It's more than analogous to a footnote or to turning a page in a book. It's a method with which a reader can manipulate a publishing product, primarily text, in a number of different ways to bring information immediately into view.

- **CGI scripts.** Server-side computing can provide a full range of text manipulation and other publishing effects. You can use scripting or a full-fledged programming language for CGI programming. You can do just about anything you want to do. CGI scripts tap the power of the server computer. The magic of computing is no longer relegated to computer programs. It can be right in the middle of the text in a way that barely disrupts reading.

- **HTML animation.** HTML currently includes the capability of animating GIFs. Since animated images can be text or include text, HTML animation brings movement capability to text.

- **Frames.** Frames enable you to do different things in different parts of one Web page. One part can be scrollable, but essentially static, text, while another part changes periodically or provides interactivity.

- **Java scripting.** Java scripting enables you to use programming, albeit light programming, right in a Web page. The possibilities for the creative use of Java Script in manipulating text are expanded by DHTML and XML.

- **Java applets.** Java applets bring the power of the client computer into the Web page. Java applets can be anything from floating frames with text to calculators embedded in the text of a Web page. The magic of computing is no longer relegated to computer programs with massive interfaces. The magic can be right in the middle of the text in a way that barely disrupts reading. Unlike CGI scripts which must be integrated into the server computer, however, Java applets can be more easily integrated into Web pages by Web publishers who have limited control over their Web servers.

- **Dynamic HTML.** DHTML subjects all HTML elements to being manipulated by scripting. This enables you to manipulate text and other HTML elements in any way that enhances publishing. This means a wide range of movement, periodic changes, and interactivity for text.

- **XML.** XML carries the idea of text publishing into new realms of creativity. Not only can you manipulate text more agilely, but you can create your own markup system as well.
- **XML metainformation.** Metainformation in XML documents enables the documents to change by themselves to accommodate readers. A publication in English can turn into a custom Japanese version (including translation).

Indeed, dynamic text is the future of typography, and it's here today. Of all the technologies listed here, only XML is not yet in the mainstream, and it's just around the corner. What does all this mean to typography? We stand at the beginning of the fourth dimension and we see a little of the future, but we don't see much. Yet one thing is certain. Typography is text; text is meant to be read; and reading is communication. Any one of these new capabilities amounts to naught unless it provides or enhances readability. Text in whatever form is only an effective communicator when it is easily readable.

Seize the day (if this were a Web document, the first three words of this sentence would flash back and forth between English and Latin: Carpe diem) and experiment with this new technology. The advances in typography were made by pragmatic persons whose aspirations were always tempered by practicality and the ultimate need for functionality (i.e., readability). Perhaps you will be the person to make the next significant advance in the new craft of digital typography.

The Fifth Dimension

What is the fifth dimension of typography? One can argue that it's digital multimedia. The hiss of a raging storm as a Web site visitor does a mouse-over on a headline about the bad weather. The ring of a church bell as a visitor clicks for more information about a Sunday service on a caption below the image of a steeple. A dramatic white flash as a visitor clicks on a hyperlink

What Would They Think? One wonders what Mr. Garamond, Mr. Baskerville, and Mr. Tschichold would think about a typography that moves, a typography that shouts, or a typography that you can feel.

to an magazine article on a terrorist bombing. And get this! The rough feeling of running a mouse pointer over digitally embossed text. No kidding! Check out the FEELit mouse at http://www.immerse.com. It really works. You can feel tactile sensations from ice to corduroy through your mouse. Can Web smell be many years away?

Does typography really have a fifth dimension? If so, it may not be a digital one. It may be a human dimension. You can argue that typography and publishing fell into the hands of the masses with the invention of the typewriter in the late 19th century. Certainly, you can strengthen your argument by claiming that the combination of the typewriter and the copier gave real publishing capability to the masses, albeit limited typographic capability. But it wasn't really until the digital desktop publishing explosion of the early 1990s that full-fledged typographic capabilities fell into the hands of the masses. Almost immediately afterward, the Web, the easy and inexpensive publishing medium of the Internet, materialized to provide an outlet for the new typographic and publishing capabilities enjoyed by anyone interested enough to buy a PC. Indeed, anyone who wants to be a competent typographer and publisher today will find few barriers except the learning curve.

Envisioning mass participation in typography as a fifth dimension, however, doesn't help much to anticipate or understand the changes that will take place just due to the mass participation. In fact, it seems to me much more difficult to predict how mass participation will affect typography than to predict how color and movement will affect it. Mass participation does not simply mean that more people will be using competent typographic techniques. It means that typography will change significantly in the future just due to the fact that it has become a mass medium, not only on the consumer side as it always has been, but on the creative side as well. As Paul Levinson says in *The Soft Edge: A Natural History and Future of the Information Revolution* (Routledge,

1997), "… decentralization in the generation and organization of knowledge will likely be one of the defining characteristics of the next century" (page 77).

Summary

In summary, you can see that the principles of the old typography are with us yet, according to Mr. Wheildon's research. For instance, the relatively new sans serif typefaces have not displaced the serif typefaces for text yet, nor do they show any indication that they will do so in the future. Yet, we are on the threshold of several new dimensions in typography: color and movement. There are few guidelines. You will be making up the rules as you go along. Regardless, there remains one unifying principle: readability. Test everything you do against a standard of easy readability (Tschichold's, "comfortable legibility"), and your Web typography will excel.

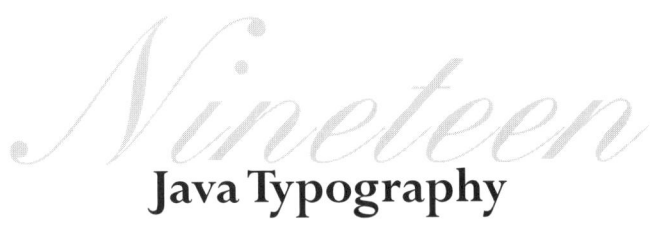

Java Typography

Java applets have the same problem as Web pages: no way to use professional typesetting effectively. Consequently, Bitstream has developed a font engine for use with Java. The Java programming language has only abbreviated typography capabilities. This is the realm of programmers, so this will be a short chapter. But it's relevant for webmasters who want to use Java documents at their Web sites (i.e., documents in the form of Java applets).

JET

Bitstream's Java-based Extendible Typography (JET) is a font rendering engine that accompanies a Java applet that makes use of it. It is a class library (i.e., a collection of Java programs). A programmer obtains the JET Software Development Kit (SDK) and uses the JET engine as either a stand-alone program to be downloaded with a Java applet or as a font engine integrated into a Java applet. As a stand-alone program, once downloaded, it can remain on a Web site visitor's computer so that it doesn't have to be downloaded again.

Because Java is font stupid, JET augments its font handling capabilities considerably. Although this proves to be important for many types of programs, it proves particularly important for those Java applets that display documents (Java documents). JET consists of several components.

- **Context.** The Context organizes and stores the fonts. Think of it as a warehouse. Bitstream offers several vector graphic fonts for use in Context. A font reader will also become available that converts TrueType and Type 1 fonts via TrueDoc technology into a format suitable for Context.

- **Composer.** The Composer enables the applet to typeset text prior to display.

- **Scaler.** The Scaler sizes the type.

- **Renderer.** The Renderer renders the font into a readable display on the screen.

JET resides between the applet and the Java virtual machine. Its various components include plug-ins for extended capability. Some of the possibilities for plug-ins are: new font formats such as OpenType, shape filters such as those that create 3D type, special text treatments such as gradient fills, and the like.

Permission Java security requires permission from a Web site visitor to have Java code remain permanently in the client computer. Web site visitors can verify that the code is legitimate via a digital signature.

Why Java?

Why the interest in typesetting for Java? Isn't Java just used for glitzy programs or functional programs that don't necessarily have to have sharp fonts? The answer is: yes and no. Many Java applets are glitz which do not use text, or they are functional programs that use text primarily for control labels. Nonetheless, Java is a general purpose programming language. As such, it must have the capability to provide typesetting features just as the C programming language has the capability to provide typesetting features for desktop publishing software. In fact, who is to say that an online desktop publishing program cannot be written in Java for the purpose of creating Java documents? At least three authoring programs, EZ Designer (http://www.ionwebproducts.com), Coda (http://www.randomnoise.com), and Net-It (http://www.net-it.com) are the Web equivalents of desktop publishing programs. They create Java applets that are documents.

One of the benefits for publishers of Java documents is that applets evaporate; that is, they disappear after a user either closes his or her browser or shuts off the computer. So, Java documents make a good publishing vehicle. The Java document applets disappear, giving a user no opportunity to copy and redistribute them.

Ion

Ion Systems markets several software programs that create Java applet documents: EZ Text, EZ HTML, and EZ Designer. Ion got its start making custom electronic documents called E*News for online distribution, a service popular with corporations. As this book went to press, Ion was seriously considering using JET with some of its products and has a relationship with Bitstream to evaluate the JET technology.

Ion's products distinguish themselves because they focus on readability. Ion tunes every aspect of their product to ergonomic reading comfort and has done some interesting research on digital reading problems. Although Ion wrestles with the low-resolution CRT like everyone else, they have provided some remarkable features with their documents. See Figure 19.1 for a look at an EZ Text article (Java document).

EZ Text

EZ Text is easy for authors to use. You simply place the markups for the applet in a Web page and set a few simple parameters. One of the parameters is a reference to a plain text file (ASCII file) that contains the text of the presentation (e.g., article5.txt).

```
<applet codebase="ez_class"
code="ez_text.class" width=300
height=200>
<param name="fileName" value="arti-
cle5.txt">
</applet>
```

HTML Documents Are ASCII Files Note that EZ Text can use an HTML file too. EZ Text ignores the HTML markups. You still have to apply the simple EZ Text markups to the text.

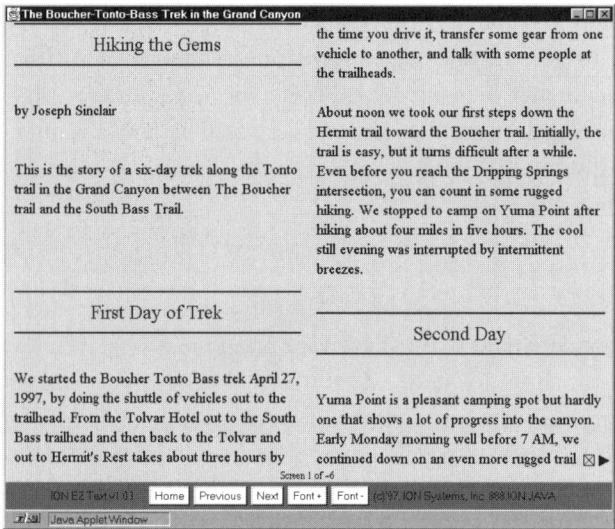

Figure 19.1 *EZ Text article.*

The applet renders the text from the text file into a comfortably readable format. This allows the text to be stolen quite easily, but Ion will soon market an upgraded system that encrypts the text file, thus making the system secure.

Inside the text file, you mark up the text with a few simple markups to prepare it to be used by the applet. That's about all there is to it. When you're ready to roll, you upload the Web page that contains the applet, the applet class files, and the ASCII text file to your Web site for your Web site visitors to start using (see Figure 19.2). This is a simple but effective system for providing easy-to-read text on the Web. It uses page flipping and even displays inline color graphics. With the addition of JET typography, this system may be the answer for publishing text products to sell on the Web.

From the Web site reader's point of view, the EZ TEXT applet is easy to use. It features columns coordinated with font size. The reader can change the size of the font, click on an inline graphic to see it full size, access a table of contents, and use a page-turning system rather than scrolling.

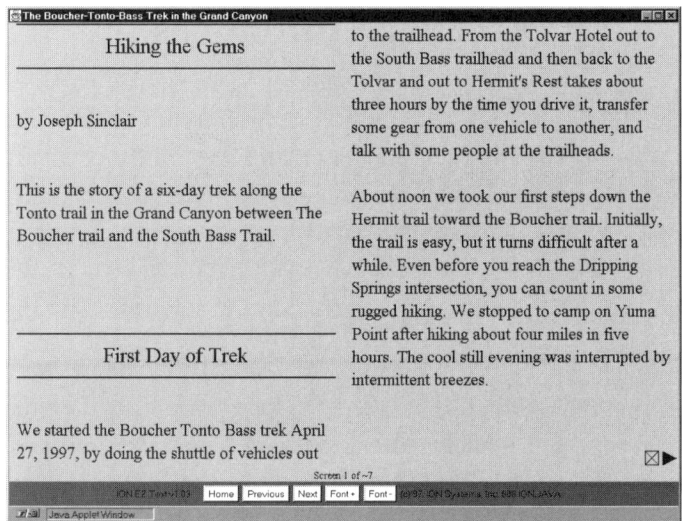

Figure 19.2 *A Web site visitor can change the size of the text.*

EZ HTML

Ion's EZ HTML works similarly to EZ Text except that it requires an HTML document. It publishes the document with the HTML functionality intact. Thus, you can have inline graphics, hyperlinks, frames, and the like. It operates as a sort of *super* EZ Text and sells for a higher price.

EZ Designer

Designer is a full-fledged desktop publishing program that cranks out Java documents with a variety of media. It includes capability that goes beyond ergonomic readability and is Ion's most expensive software.

If you have a compelling interest in publishing articles, reports, newsletters, and books to sell on the Web, Ion provides software that enables you to do that with typographical finesse. With the addition of JET, Ion will be able to provide even better online typography.

Internet Appliances

JET will be popular for Internet appliances like Personal Digital Assistants (PDAs) that access the Internet, pagers that operate via the Internet, and the like. They are likely to use Java and have bare-bones operating systems or Java operating systems that require a lightweight font engine.

Summary

Although it's a little premature to cover Java typography, I mention it nevertheless because it's close at hand. By the time you read this, it's likely that several Java typography software products that use JET will have been announced. The potential for Java documents to serve online publishing is huge, as the success of a small company like Ion attests. Java document systems that focus on ergonomic reading and offer professional typography may become the commercial publishing workhorses of the near future.

Cross-media Publishing

When you have an endless number of pages of text to publish, large-volume publishing techniques become important. Volumes of reports, procedure or equipment manuals, rules and regulations, treatises, books, legal briefs, and the like often have a standard format that enables efficiencies in publishing. Today, many companies have found that publishing is less expensive on the Web, yet they must continue publishing in print or other media until all employees, customers, and vendors are online. SGML provides the capability to organize and handle large-volume, standardized publishing. It is also the premier cross-media system that enables you to author once and publish in print, on the Web, on CDs, on NetTV, and in any other media. Read Chapter 6 for an introduction to SGML and XML and how they relate to HTML.

Style sheets play an important role in both large-volume publishing and cross-media publishing. For large-volume publishing, one style sheet can serve many documents, and a few style sheets can serve a whole system of documents. Writers can create and structure content without wasting time on styling each document. For cross-media publishing, the content and structure stay the same for multiple media; it is the style sheets for each media that generate the different formats appropriate for each media. Again, authors don't have to worry about different media and different styles; they just create and structure the content. Thus, style sheets play a key role in making SGML and XML work.

This chapter shows how to author an SGML document using a DTD and how to use the resulting document to publish in print and in XML. It's really quite easy. As this book went to press, SoftQuad, which developed the award-winning

HoTMetaL PRO HTML authoring program, was considering bringing a more robust HTML authoring program to market that would include XML authoring or both XML and SGML authoring for a low price. SoftQuad has marketed a moderately priced SGML authoring program, Author/Editor, for years (see Figure 20.1). If SoftQuad proceeds to market a low-cost combined editor, such a product will put SGML/XML/HTML capability into the hands of anyone who desires to gain efficiencies in large-volume and cross-media publishing. Perhaps other software companies like ArborText will bring competing products to market at a competing price point.

Using an SGML-XML Authoring Program

This chapter features ArborText's Adept Editor, a moderately priced SGML authoring program with the necessary capabilities for easy cross-media publishing. Adept Editor provides an example of a robust SGML authoring program that does what you need it to do while remaining easy to use.

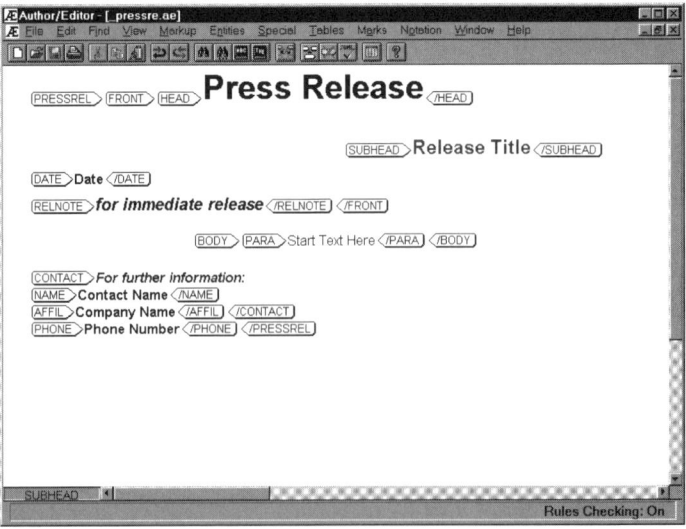

Figure 20.1 *SoftQuad's Author/Editor SGML authoring program.*

It Starts with a DTD

Before you start authoring, you must choose a DTD to use. Adept Editor comes with the following DTDs:

Memo	For memos
Letter	For correspondence
Report	For reports
Document	For general documents
Article	For magazines and professional journals
Book	For books
DocBook	For documentation
Press Release	For news releases
HTML	For Web pages
CALS	For military contracting

You can obtain other DTDs from:

• Software vendors
• Freeware or shareware sources
• Industry associations
• Colleagues who have created them

You can also create a DTD yourself, although the expense of doing so varies widely (see Chapter 6). Typically, a SGML authoring program will compile a DTD into a binary file before using it. This enables the authoring program to operate faster. The compiling process is a simple one-time task you perform the first time you use a new DTD.

When you start to use an authoring program, it will prompt you to specify a DTD, much as a word processor might prompt you to specify a document template. The DTD determines the tags that you can use and the rules for structuring a document. For instance, a simple letter DTD might contain the following sections:

\<date\>	Date of letter
\<addressee\>	Addressee's name
\<letterbody\>	Text of letter
\<author\>	Signature name

Moreover, the letter DTD would contain additional rules for structure. For instance, it would require that the date comes first, followed in order by the remaining sections. If you added tags to the letter, you would enclose the date with the *\<date\>* tags and so forth. Within the *\<letterbody\>* tag, you would use such tags as the *\<p\>* tag, the *\<i\>* tag, and so forth. In other words, the document would have the look and feel of HTML. That's no surprise, because HTML is a DTD of SGML. The preceding structure, however, just shows what will be printed. The document can contain any additional structure and metainformation necessary for a particular industry, a document archive system, or a software application. The metainformation would not be printed in the letter, of course, but it would be part of the document. You might have the following pieces of metainformation, each with its own attribute:

\<addressee relation=" "\>	Permitted entries: customer, vendor, or colleague
\<product upc=" "\>	Permitted entries: UPC product number
\<doc control=" "\>	An assigned number for document

The metainformation can be as much as you want it to be. With the appropriate software, you can use such information with a software application such as a database system.

Keep in mind that you use the DTD to provide structure and metainformation. The resulting SGML document is simply a structured document. In order to publish the document, you must combine the document with a style sheet appropriate to the publishing medium. For instance, if you used an

SGML authoring program, together with the letter DTD, to create a letter, you could use a style sheet to print the document on a laser printer with attractive and readable type. You use an SGML style sheet editor to create the style sheets for your DTDs. Perhaps, in the future, you will be able to obtain ready-made style sheets from the same source that provided your DTDs.

If you publish cross-media, you need to convert your documents to fit other DTDs. For instance, suppose you use the preceding letter DTD to do your correspondence, which will be sent on 8.5 × 11 letterhead after being laser printed. You can use ArborText's Adept Publisher to do the laser printing. But you also need to publish some of the letters on the Web for private access and review by your sales force in the field. You will use a conversion program to convert the SGML documents (made with the letter DTD) into HTML documents, as if they had been made with the HTML DTD.

Note, however, that HTML does not contain the proper tags to accommodate the letter DTD. In a conversion program, you would map the letter tags like <*letterbody*> to HTML tags like <*p*> which would structure the HTML documents properly. But why not convert the letters to XML instead? With XML, you can preserve the tags; that is, the <*letterbody*> tag does not have to be converted to the <*p*> tag. A browser with XML capability (e.g., the 5.0 browsers) can display the letters. ArborText Adept Editor will easily save SGML documents as XML documents (i.e., convert them).

Authoring with a DTD

An article DTD makes a good demonstration for using the Adapt Editor SGML authoring program. The editor shows the structure of the article DTD (see Figure 20.2). Notice that the title of the article, the name of the author, and an abstract of the article go in the *front* portion of the article document. The chapters (sections), chapter titles (section headings), and paragraphs go in the *body* portion of the article document.

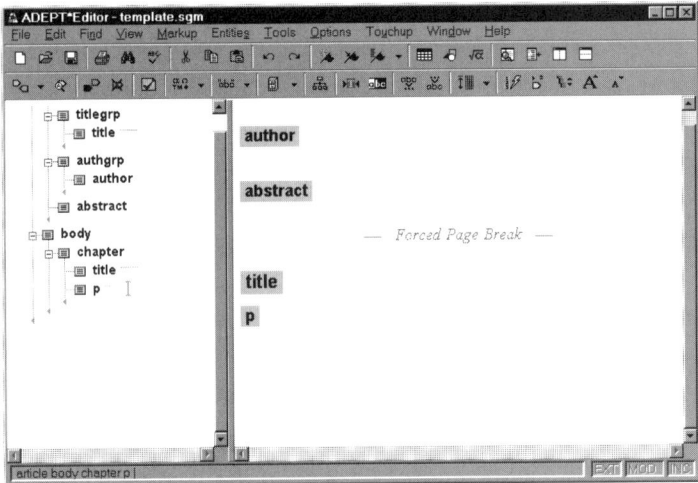

Figure 20.2 *The structure of the article DTD outlined.*

This makes a little more sense when you write the content. You do it one element at a time (see Figure 20.3).

It's easy to write the content, creating additional structure as you go (see Figure 20.4). You can also add tags for graphics and other documents elements, just as you do with HTML.

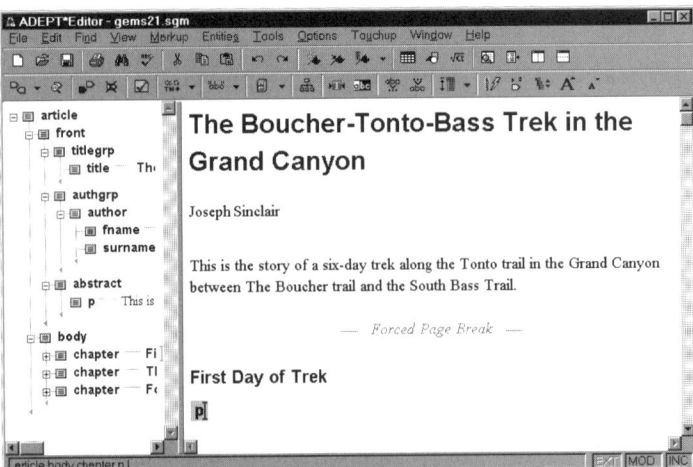

Figure 20.3 *Entering the content.*

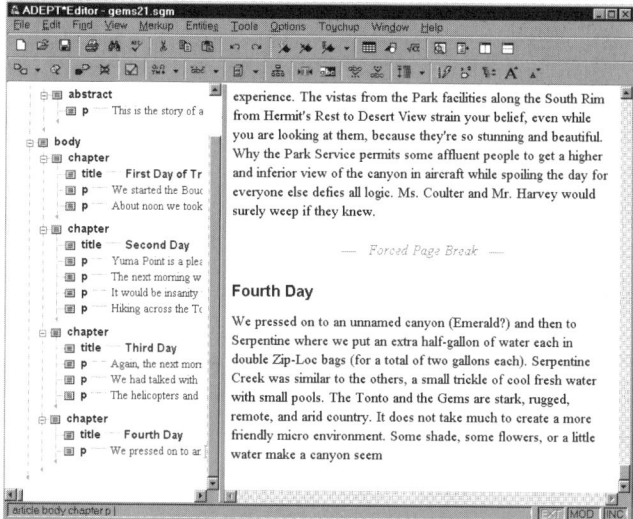

Figure 20.4 *The structure shows on the left while you create the content on the right.*

When you finish, you can save the document as an XML document. In other words, Adept Editor automatically converts the SGML document to an XML document. See the first few paragraphs of the following XML document.

```
<article>
<front>
<titlegrp>
<title>The Boucher-Tonto-Bass Trek
in the Grand Canyon</title>
</titlegrp>
<authgrp>
<author><fname>Joseph</fname><sur-
name>Sinclair</surname></author>
</authgrp>
<abstract>
<p>This is the story of a six-day
trek along the Tonto trail in the
Grand Canyon between The Boucher
trail and the South Bass Trail.</p>
```

```
</abstract>
</front>
<body>
<chapter>
<title>First Day of Trek</title>
<p>We started the Boucher-Tonto-
Bass trek April 27, 1997, by doing
the shuttle of vehicles out to the
trailhead. From the Tolvar Hotel
out to the South Bass trailhead and
then back to the Tolvar and out to
Hermit's Rest takes about three
hours by the time you drive it,
transfer some gear from one vehicle
to another, and talk with some peo-
ple at the trailheads.</p>
<p>About noon we took our first
steps down the Hermit trail toward
the Boucher trail. Initially, the
trail is easy, but it turns diffi-
cult after a while. Even before you
reach the Dripping Springs inter-
section, you can count on some
rugged hiking. We stopped to camp
on Yuma Point after hiking about
four miles in five hours. The cool
still evening was interrupted by
intermittent breezes.</p>
</chapter>
<chapter>
<title>Second Day</title>
<p>Yuma Point is a pleasant camping
spot but hardly one that shows a
lot of progress into the canyon.
Early Monday morning well before 7
AM, we continued down on an even
more rugged trail finally crossing
the Whites Butte plateau and
descending the Redwall. By the time
we got to Boucher Creek in early
afternoon, we were quite tired.</p>
```

```
</chapter>
</body>
</article>
```

It's not so much different from an HTML document, is it?

Again

It can't be said too many times. SGML relieves writers of the trouble of inventing structure or applying style, a very important concept for document systems. Writers write the content and apply the structure of the DTD. Although they have to learn the structure of the DTD, that's often easy; and most authors will use the same DTDs repetitively. Style sheets apply the style, a different style sheet for each medium. Thus, SGML provides both a large-scale document system, and a cross-platform document system. XML is the versatile online (Web) implementation of SGML.

Applying Style with Style Sheets

To publish the preceding article on the Web, you create a style sheet for it using XSL, and then embed it or link it to the document (see Chapter 10 on CSS). The XSL style sheet will be similar to a CSS but will have advanced capabilities. For instance, in the article DTD above, the *<title>* tag is used both for the title of the article and the titles (headings) of the chapters (sections). How does that work? In XSL, the context can give meaning to the style. XSL knows that when *<title>* appears in the *<title-grp>* section, it is styled one way. When *<title>* appears in the *<chapter>* section, it is styled another way.

Like CSS, once you have created the style sheet, you can reuse it for other articles to be published in the same style. You can create your typography once and have it serve multiple documents.

As XSL is not a standard yet, a demonstration of XSL styling is beyond the scope of this book (everything was in beta as this

The 4.0 Browsers The Microsoft 4.0 browser with an ActiveX add-on will process XML. The Netscape 4.0 browser will not. Presumably, both the 5.0 browsers will handle XML.

book went to press). Nonetheless, ArborText offers a program called XML Styler (beta) for downloading from its Web site (see Figure 20.5). It's worth a look to get acquainted. It provides XSL styling to your XML documents.

XML Styler enables you to create an XSL style sheet four ways (see Figure 20.6):

- Manually
- By collecting tag names from an existing document
- By collecting tag names from a list
- By collecting tag names from a DTD

You start with a default font typeface, weight, and size (see Figure 20.7).

Then you add XSL style to the tags for the XML document (see Figure 20.8).

XML Styler is the type of tool that you can use without being an XSL programmer, but you need to learn about XSL first. XML was set as a standard in February, 1998, and XSL isn't far behind. These few screen shots of XML Styler show that this is technology that can be made easy for webmasters to use.

Word Processing and SGML

Recognizing the importance of SGML, Corel has incorporated robust SGML capability into WordPerfect 8. Microsoft offers

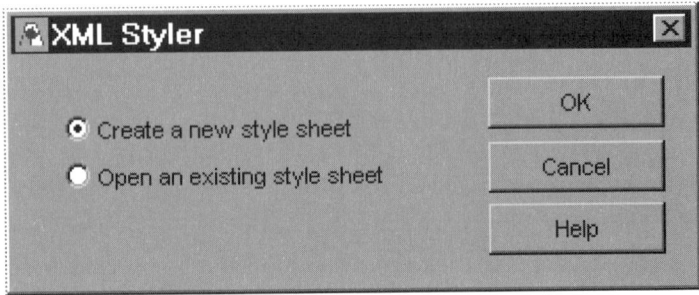

Figure 20.5 *ArborText XML Styler.*

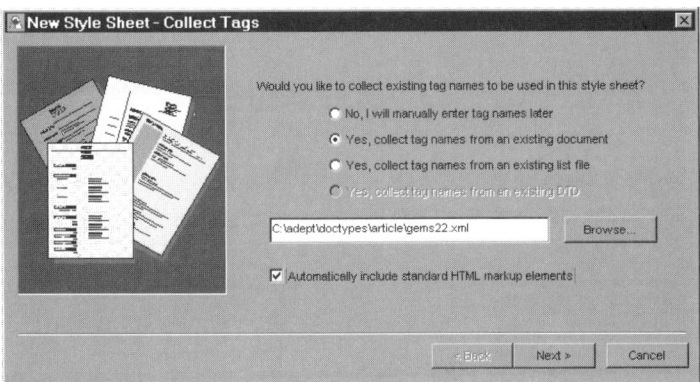

Figure 20.6 *Using XML Styler.*

SGML Author, an add-on for Word for Windows that incorporates similar capability into Word. These should not be mistaken for SGML authoring programs which can use DTDs easily. Note that someone has to map a DTD to a word processor template (a week's work, perhaps more) before people can use the word processor to create documents that conform to the DTD. But that's a one-time task, and premapped templates for the most popular DTDs may eventually materialize. However, these SGML capabilities may be supplemented or replaced soon by adding XML capabilities (see Chapter 6).

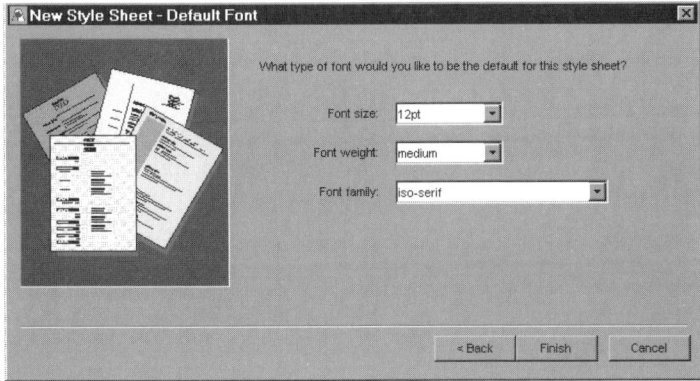

Figure 20.7 *Setting the default font in XML Styler.*

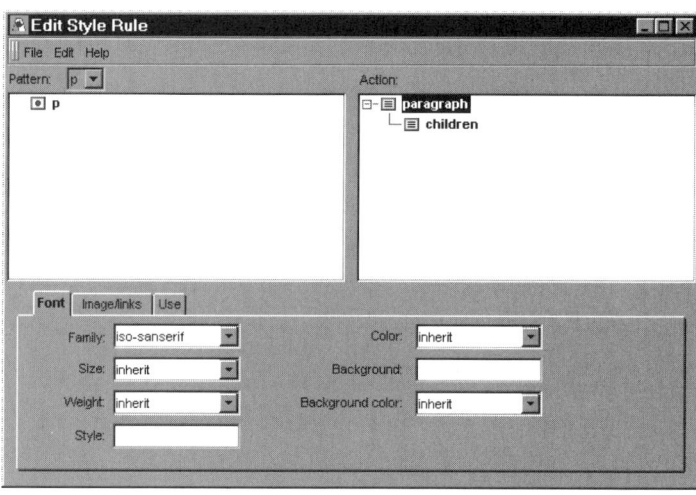

Figure 20.8 *Add style to the tags in an XML document with XML Styler.*

HTML Word Processor

The Xanthus iWrite software mentioned in Chapter 8 is a hefty HTML word processor. When CSS 2 provides precise pagination, you might look to it and software like it to provide cross-platform documents: attractive Web documents for a Web site that also print well in the office on a computer printer.

Adobe Acrobat

Adobe Acrobat technology (http://www.adobe.com) is paper replication technology. The promise of the digital environment is to free human activities from floating on paper. The new SGML, XML, and HTML documents are the harbingers of the future, with their multimedia and interactive capabilities. It appears that eventually paper and paper replication will fade away. For that reason, this book doesn't cover Acrobat.

Nonetheless, Adobe has done amazing things with a technology designed to handle paper. It has adapted Acrobat to the Web, complete with hyperlinks. You can use any fonts for an Acrobat document. Adobe has made Acrobat a document standard that competes with Word documents and ASCII documents. It has also made Acrobat an excellent cross-platform printing system (its primary purpose). But if Adobe wants to make Acrobat more digitally oriented and less paper oriented, ironically it will have to enable more reader controls over its digital display typography.

Webmasters (Web developers) create Web pages for Web sites and should be well versed in future typography now that the typographic capability is there to use. That means the migration of typographic control from Web site visitors to webmasters. On the other hand, business people who cannot be expected to be typographers create most of the Acrobat documents. For that reason, for Acrobat, more typographical control should be in the hands of readers who can adjust documents to be more readable, if necessary.

Compared with HTML documents, Acrobat documents are substantially larger. Web site visitors need the Acrobat reader to view them, which is inconvenient even though there is an Acrobat browser plug-in. But Acrobat documents print nicely and precisely, a feature that HTML documents won't have until CSS 2 is incorporated into the 5.0 browsers.

Acrobat will replace Postscript print-to-disk files that you take to a prepress service bureau. It also wouldn't surprise me to see a few more tricks come along in the Acrobat technology: a Java version of the Acrobat client (i.e., alleviating the need for a browser plug-in and a separate reader); a more favorable implementation for screen reading (e.g., some controls in the hands of readers); and some clever typographical innovations (Adobe is a master of innovation). Paper will still be with us for a long time to come regardless of how hard we try to get rid of it. But at the end of the day (as they say in Washington, DC), Acrobat is paper replication technology, and the world is going to convert to digital documents. The MLs (SGML, XML, and HTML) will provide the digital documents of the future.

Don't confuse Adobe Acrobat with Adobe FrameMaker + SGML, which is a robust SGML authoring system that will support XML soon and competes with ArborText and SoftQuad software for cross-media publishing.

And What about Web Printing?

What about printing Web pages? How does that work? Actually, it works quite well. Web pages print nicely on high-resolution computer laser and ink-jet printers. Even the

Why the Web? Why will the Web outdistance Adobe Acrobat in paper replication? It won't. But if you're talking about dual documents—made for Web publication and Web print publication both—the Web will dominate the market. People need no special reader, just a browser. They will need no separate authoring software. Most Web authoring software will incorporate the Web precision print publishing capabilities introduced by CSS 1 and CSS 2. The coming boom in Web print publishing, however, is likely to be only an interim phenomenon. It may last only until high-resolution flat-panel readers make reading on a digital device more attractive than reading on paper.

graphics look good. People do a considerable amount of publishing on the Web this way. Nonetheless, it has a few drawbacks. First, you have no control over what fonts and font sizes are set in a Web site visitor's browser. CSS 1, together with TrueDoc and font embedding, put more control in your hands to remedy this problem. Second, it's difficult to tell where the pages will break or to control the page breaks for layout purposes. CSS 2 with pagination will put the control in your hands to remedy this. With precise typesetting, layout, and pagination, there's no reason the Web won't *explode* soon as a super printing press, albeit a printing press with a significant twist.

For the Web, being a super printing press does not mean one printing machine cranking out hundreds or thousands of copies of printed documents. Instead, it's hundreds or thousands of copies, with each copy printed by a different computer printer. This type of publishing effectively transfers the cost of paper, ink, and production from vendor to customer (i.e., from publisher to reader). Up until now, lack of printing precision has retarded the growth of the Web as a printing press. With the new CSS 1 and CSS 2 capabilities, Web print publishing will grow quickly. Look for software such as Xanthus iWrite, a full-fledged Web word processor (see Chapter 8), to lead the way.

CSS 2 pagination is no trivial technique. It even includes heads and footers. It seems likely to be the kind of code that will require tweaking to make it work. You may not be able to leave pagination completely to an authoring program. In any event, CSS 2 pagination is a new technology that you will certainly use soon. It enables print on demand—documents with professional typography and correct pagination delivered via the Web. CSS 2 pagination will illustrate how a small bit of innocuous and mundane software technology can make an enormous difference in the way people do things. Although unfortunately beyond the scope of this book, CSS 2 pagination will certainly merit considerable attention in the next edition.

Summary

Because SGML has been around for a while, it won't take a long software development cycle to provide capable tools for XML. Already ArborText Adept Editor incorporates SGML to XML conversion, as easy as *Save As*. ArborText's XML Styler enables a nonprogrammer to apply style to XML documents. ArborText is ready for the Netscape and Microsoft 5.0 browsers (with XML). SoftQuad will be ready to provide tools, too, designed for its HoTMetaL PRO customers. Other software vendors will also have comparable software ready. This new Web technology is ready to go now, and ready to style.

Twenty-One

What's Your Type?

Choosing a typeface is not as simple as asking, "What's my favorite?" You must also ask, "For what?" Different typefaces evoke different feelings. Some are formal; some are informal; some are energetic; some are lazy; and some are even comic. You must match the typeface to both the occasion and your taste. You don't want to use a comic typeface for text that treats a serious topic. Likewise, you will probably feel it's out of place to use an elegant typeface for text that treats trivial matters. For every project, you must make a choice. Go to Esperfonto (http://www.will-harris.com) for some online assistance in choosing fonts.

You can best choose a readable type for text by looking at text passages, not alphabets. Unfortunately, text passages are seldom available. Catalogs usually do not have enough room for them. The best way to find text passages is to accumulate them. Save the periodicals from font vendors which often include extensive typesetting examples. Save old catalogs that feature text samples. And save articles and books for which you have identified the fonts used to print them.

The primary purpose of the first part of this chapter is to help you get a feeling for *printed* text. This book cannot provide extensive text passages for every popular typeface. As a compromise, it does provide a paragraph each for a selection of widely used typefaces, and some not so widely used. These text passages will give you a feeling for the typefaces beyond trying to project from alphabets how the typefaces will look. Most paragraphs feature 11-point type.

But, of course, the chapter and the book cannot end on a demonstration of *printed* fonts. After all, this book covers Web typography. Consequently, starting with the Microsoft Windows Fonts section, the chapter goes on to feature the

429

fonts that Microsoft provides free to Windows users: that is, the fonts that many people use on their screens. The chapter ends with information on fonts that have been tuned to the screen and fonts that render well in TrueDoc, all of which directly relate to your Web typography.

Traditional Text Favorites

These serif typefaces represent the traditional workhorse fonts for presenting readable text. Note that the next section presents a variety of Garamond typefaces, and therefore, this selection does not include Garamond.

Aldine 401

(Bitstream, comparable to Bembo)

We hiked on around two unnamed canyons (Jasper and Jade?) to Ruby Canyon. Although there are few trees anywhere, the sparse plant life on the Tonto, mostly blackbrush and cactus, looked healthy. Many plants bloomed with colorful flowers. The cactus bloomed too, mostly red flowers with infrequent yellows. An occasional Utah Agave (Century Plant) towered above the landscape with a heavy collage of pale flowers. Some places Agaves were abundant. Once in a while, a humming bird flew by. For lack of trees, the only place to find shade is in the shadow of a large boulder or under a rock ledge. The views from the Tonto, of course, are fabulous everywhere. It was always very rewarding to stop, rest your feet, and take in the view. So, we stopped a lot to rest on the trail.

ITC New Baskerville

We hiked on around two unnamed canyons (Jasper and Jade?) to Ruby Canyon. Although there are few trees anywhere, the sparse plant life on the Tonto, mostly blackbrush and cactus, looked healthy. Many plants bloomed with colorful flowers. The cactus bloomed too, mostly red flowers with infrequent yellows. An occasional Utah Agave (Century Plant) towered above the landscape with a heavy collage of pale flowers. Some places Agaves were abundant. Once in a while, a humming bird flew by. For lack of trees, the only place to find shade is in the shadow of a large boulder or under a rock ledge. The views from the Tonto, of course, are fabulous everywhere. It was always very rewarding to stop, rest your feet, and take in the view. So, we stopped a lot to rest on the trail.

Bodoni

We hiked on around two unnamed canyons (Jasper and Jade?) to Ruby Canyon. Although there are few trees anywhere, the sparse plant life on the Tonto, mostly blackbrush and cactus, looked healthy. Many plants bloomed with colorful flowers. The cactus bloomed too, mostly red flowers with infrequent yellows. An occasional Utah Agave (Century Plant) towered above the landscape with a heavy collage of pale flowers. Some places Agaves were abundant. Once in a while, a humming bird flew by. For lack of trees, the only place to find shade is in the shadow of a large boulder or under a rock ledge. The views from the Tonto, of course, are fabulous everywhere. It was always very rewarding to stop, rest your feet, and take in the view. So, we stopped a lot to rest on the trail.

Caslon 540

We hiked on around two unnamed canyons (Jasper and Jade?) to Ruby Canyon. Although there are few trees anywhere, the sparse plant life on the Tonto, mostly blackbrush and cactus, looked healthy. Many plants bloomed with colorful flowers. The cactus bloomed too, mostly red flowers with infrequent yellows. An occasional Utah Agave (Century Plant) towered above the landscape with a heavy collage of pale flowers. Some places Agaves were abundant. Once in a while, a humming bird flew by. For lack of trees, the only place to find shade is in the shadow of a large boulder or under a rock ledge. The views from the Tonto, of course, are fabulous everywhere. It was always very rewarding to stop, rest your feet, and take in the view. So, we stopped a lot to rest on the trail.

Century Schoolbook

We hiked on around two unnamed canyons (Jasper and Jade?) to Ruby Canyon. Although there are few trees anywhere, the sparse plant life on the Tonto, mostly blackbrush and cactus, looked healthy. Many plants bloomed with colorful flowers. The cactus bloomed too, mostly red flowers with infrequent yellows. An occasional Utah Agave (Century Plant) towered above the landscape with a heavy collage of pale flowers. Some places Agaves were abundant. Once in a while, a humming bird flew by. For lack of trees, the only place to find shade is in the shadow of a large boulder or under a rock ledge. The views from the Tonto, of course, are fabulous everywhere. It was always very rewarding to stop, rest your feet, and take in the view. So, we stopped a lot to rest on the trail.

Linotype Didot

We hiked on around two unnamed canyons (Jasper and Jade?) to Ruby Canyon. Although there are few trees anywhere, the sparse plant life on the Tonto, mostly blackbrush and cactus, looked healthy. Many plants bloomed with colorful flowers. The cactus bloomed too, mostly red flowers with infrequent yellows. An occasional Utah Agave (Century Plant) towered above the landscape with a heavy collage of pale flowers. Some places Agaves were abundant. Once in a while, a humming bird flew by. For lack of trees, the only place to find shade is in the shadow of a large boulder or under a rock ledge. The views from the Tonto, of course, are fabulous everywhere. It was always very rewarding to stop, rest your feet, and take in the view. So, we stopped a lot to rest on the trail.

ITC Galliard 1

We hiked on around two unnamed canyons (Jasper and Jade?) to Ruby Canyon. Although there are few trees anywhere, the sparse plant life on the Tonto, mostly blackbrush and cactus, looked healthy. Many plants bloomed with colorful flowers. The cactus bloomed too, mostly red flowers with infrequent yellows. An occasional Utah Agave (Century Plant) towered above the landscape with a heavy collage of pale flowers. Some places Agaves were abundant. Once in a while, a humming bird flew by. For lack of trees, the only place to find shade is in the shadow of a large boulder or under a rock ledge. The views from the Tonto, of course, are fabulous everywhere. It was always very rewarding to stop, rest your feet, and take in the view. So, we stopped a lot to rest on the trail.

Goudy Old Style

We hiked on around two unnamed canyons (Jasper and Jade?) to Ruby Canyon. Although there are few trees anywhere, the sparse plant life on the Tonto, mostly blackbrush and cactus, looked healthy. Many plants bloomed with colorful flowers. The cactus bloomed too, mostly red flowers with infrequent yellows. An occasional Utah Agave (Century Plant) towered above the landscape with a heavy collage of pale flowers. Some places Agaves were abundant. Once in a while, a humming bird flew by. For lack of trees, the only place to find shade is in the shadow of a large boulder or under a rock ledge. The views from the Tonto, of course, are fabulous everywhere. It was always very rewarding to stop, rest your feet, and take in the view. So, we stopped a lot to rest on the trail.

Adobe Janson

We hiked on around two unnamed canyons (Jasper and Jade?) to Ruby Canyon. Although there are few trees anywhere, the sparse plant life on the Tonto, mostly blackbrush and cactus, looked healthy. Many plants bloomed with colorful flowers. The cactus bloomed too, mostly red flowers with infrequent yellows. An occasional Utah Agave (Century Plant) towered above the landscape with a heavy collage of pale flowers. Some places Agaves were abundant. Once in a while, a humming bird flew by. For lack of trees, the only place to find shade is in the shadow of a large boulder or under a rock ledge. The views from the Tonto, of course, are fabulous everywhere. It was always very rewarding to stop, rest your feet, and take in the view. So, we stopped a lot to rest on the trail.

Minion

We hiked on around two unnamed canyons (Jasper and Jade?) to Ruby Canyon. Although there are few trees anywhere, the sparse plant life on the Tonto, mostly blackbrush and cactus, looked healthy. Many plants bloomed with colorful flowers. The cactus bloomed too, mostly red flowers with infrequent yellows. An occasional Utah Agave (Century Plant) towered above the landscape with a heavy collage of pale flowers. Some places Agaves were abundant. Once in a while, a humming bird flew by. For lack of trees, the only place to find shade is in the shadow of a large boulder or under a rock ledge. The views from the Tonto, of course, are fabulous everywhere. It was always very rewarding to stop, rest your feet, and take in the view. So, we stopped a lot to rest on the trail.

Aldine 720

(Bitstream, comparable to Plantin)

We hiked on around two unnamed canyons (Jasper and Jade?) to Ruby Canyon. Although there are few trees anywhere, the sparse plant life on the Tonto, mostly blackbrush and cactus, looked healthy. Many plants bloomed with colorful flowers. The cactus bloomed too, mostly red flowers with infrequent yellows. An occasional Utah Agave (Century Plant) towered above the landscape with a heavy collage of pale flowers.

Some places Agaves were abundant. Once in a while, a humming bird flew by. For lack of trees, the only place to find shade is in the shadow of a large boulder or under a rock ledge. The views from the Tonto, of course, are fabulous everywhere. It was always very rewarding to stop, rest your feet, and take in the view. So, we stopped a lot to rest on the trail.

Kuenstler (Bitstream, comparable to Trump Medieval)

We hiked on around two unnamed canyons (Jasper and Jade?) to Ruby Canyon. Although there are few trees anywhere, the sparse plant life on the Tonto, mostly blackbrush and cactus, looked healthy. Many plants bloomed with colorful flowers. The cactus bloomed too, mostly red flowers with infrequent yellows. An occasional Utah Agave (Century Plant) towered above the landscape with a heavy collage of pale flowers. Some places Agaves were abundant. Once in a while, a humming bird flew by. For lack of trees, the only place to find shade is in the shadow of a large boulder or under a rock ledge. The views from the Tonto, of course, are fabulous everywhere. It was always very rewarding to stop, rest your feet, and take in the view. So, we stopped a lot to rest on the trail.

Berthold Walbaum

We hiked on around two unnamed canyons (Jasper and Jade?) to Ruby Canyon. Although there are few trees anywhere, the sparse plant life on the Tonto, mostly blackbrush and cactus, looked healthy. Many plants bloomed with colorful flowers. The cactus bloomed too, mostly red flowers with infrequent yellows. An occasional Utah Agave (Century Plant) towered above the landscape with a heavy collage of pale flowers. Some places Agaves were abundant. Once in a while, a humming bird flew by. For lack of trees, the only place to find shade is in the shadow of a large boulder or under a rock ledge. The views from the Tonto, of course, are fabulous everywhere. It was always very rewarding to stop, rest your feet, and take in the view. So, we stopped a lot to rest on the trail.

Garamond Versions

Typefaces by Claude Garamond (1480–1561) were among the earliest and remain popular even today for text. Many contemporary versions of Garamond exist, and each has a slightly different feel. This book provides the following paragraphs specifically to enable you to experience the subtle differences in feeling conveyed by various versions of one basic typeface.

Adobe Garamond

We hiked on around two unnamed canyons (Jasper and Jade?) to Ruby Canyon. Although there are few trees anywhere, the sparse plant life on the Tonto, mostly blackbrush and cactus, looked healthy. Many plants bloomed with colorful flowers. The cactus bloomed too, mostly red flowers with infrequent yellows. An occasional Utah Agave (Century Plant) towered above the landscape with a heavy collage of pale flowers. Some places Agaves were abundant. Once in a while, a humming bird flew by. For lack of trees, the only place to find shade is in the shadow of a large boulder or under a rock ledge. The views from the

Tonto, of course, are fabulous everywhere. It was always very rewarding to stop, rest your feet, and take in the view. So, we stopped a lot to rest on the trail.

Simoncini Garamond

We hiked on around two unnamed canyons (Jasper and Jade?) to Ruby Canyon. Although there are few trees anywhere, the sparse plant life on the Tonto, mostly blackbrush and cactus, looked healthy. Many plants bloomed with colorful flowers. The cactus bloomed too, mostly red flowers with infrequent yellows. An occasional Utah Agave (Century Plant) towered above the landscape with a heavy collage of pale flowers. Some places Agaves were abundant. Once in a while, a humming bird flew by. For lack of trees, the only place to find shade is in the shadow of a large boulder or under a rock ledge. The views from the Tonto, of course, are fabulous everywhere. It was always very rewarding to stop, rest your feet, and take in the view. So, we stopped a lot to rest on the trail.

ITC Garamond

We hiked on around two unnamed canyons (Jasper and Jade?) to Ruby Canyon. Although there are few trees anywhere, the sparse plant life on the Tonto, mostly blackbrush and cactus, looked healthy. Many plants bloomed with colorful flowers. The cactus bloomed too, mostly red flowers with infrequent yellows. An occasional Utah Agave (Century Plant) towered above the landscape with a heavy collage of pale flowers. Some places Agaves were abundant. Once in a while, a humming bird flew by. For lack of trees, the only place to find shade is in the shadow of a large boulder or under a rock ledge. The views from the Tonto, of course, are fabulous everywhere. It was always very rewarding to stop, rest your feet, and take in the view. So, we stopped a lot to rest on the trail.

Berthold Garamond

We hiked on around two unnamed canyons (Jasper and Jade?) to Ruby Canyon. Although there are few trees anywhere, the sparse plant life on the Tonto, mostly blackbrush and cactus, looked healthy. Many plants bloomed with colorful flowers. The cactus bloomed too, mostly red flowers with infrequent yellows. An occasional Utah Agave (Century Plant) towered above the landscape with a heavy collage of pale flowers. Some places Agaves were abundant. Once in a while, a humming bird flew by. For lack of trees, the only place to find shade is in the shadow of a large boulder or under a rock ledge. The views from the Tonto, of course, are fabulous everywhere. It was always very rewarding to stop, rest your feet, and take in the view. So, we stopped a lot to rest on the trail.

Elegant Garamond

(Bitstream's version of Granjon)

We hiked on around two unnamed canyons (Jasper and Jade?) to Ruby Canyon. Although there are few trees anywhere, the sparse plant life on the Tonto, mostly blackbrush and cactus, looked healthy. Many plants bloomed with colorful flowers. The cactus bloomed too, mostly red flowers with infrequent yellows. An occasional Utah Agave (Century Plant) towered above the landscape with a heavy collage of pale flowers. Some places Agaves were abundant. Once in a while, a humming bird flew by. For lack of trees, the only place to find shade is in the shadow of a large boulder or under a rock ledge. The views from the Tonto, of course, are fabulous everywhere. It was always very rewarding to stop, rest your feet, and take in the view. So, we stopped a lot to rest on the trail.

American Garamond

We hiked on around two unnamed canyons (Jasper and Jade?) to Ruby Canyon. Although there are few trees anywhere, the sparse plant life on the Tonto, mostly blackbrush and cactus, looked healthy. Many plants bloomed with colorful flowers. The cactus bloomed too, mostly red flowers with infrequent yellows. An occasional Utah Agave (Century Plant) towered above the landscape with a heavy collage of pale flowers. Some places Agaves were abundant. Once in a while, a humming bird flew by. For lack of trees, the only place to find shade is in the shadow of a large boulder or under a rock ledge. The views from the Tonto, of course, are fabulous everywhere. It was always very rewarding to stop, rest your feet, and take in the view. So, we stopped a lot to rest on the trail.

Classical Garamond

(Bitstream's version of Jan Tschichold's Sabon)

We hiked on around two unnamed canyons (Jasper and Jade?) to Ruby Canyon. Although there are few trees anywhere, the sparse plant life on the Tonto, mostly blackbrush and cactus, looked healthy. Many plants bloomed with colorful flowers. The cactus bloomed too, mostly red flowers with infrequent yellows. An occasional Utah Agave (Century Plant) towered above the landscape with a heavy collage of pale flowers. Some places Agaves were abundant. Once in a while, a humming bird flew by. For lack of trees, the only place to find shade is in the shadow of a large boulder or under a rock ledge. The views from the Tonto, of course, are fabulous everywhere. It was always very rewarding to stop, rest your feet, and take in the view. So, we stopped a lot to rest on the trail.

Original Garamond
(Bitstream's version of Stempel Garamond)

We hiked on around two unnamed canyons (Jasper and Jade?) to Ruby Canyon. Although there are few trees anywhere, the sparse plant life on the Tonto, mostly blackbrush and cactus, looked healthy. Many plants bloomed with colorful flowers. The cactus bloomed too, mostly red flowers with infrequent yellows. An occasional Utah Agave (Century Plant) towered above the landscape with a heavy collage of pale flowers. Some places Agaves were abundant. Once in a while, a humming bird flew by. For lack of trees, the only place to find shade is in the shadow of a large boulder or under a rock ledge. The views from the Tonto, of course, are fabulous everywhere. It was always very rewarding to stop, rest your feet, and take in the view. So, we stopped a lot to rest on the trail.

New Typefaces for Text

This section includes some relatively new digital typefaces designed for print that enjoy widespread use today. It seems likely that the next generation of widely used typefaces will include some typefaces specifically designed for the Web rather than print.

Lucida

We hiked on around two unnamed canyons (Jasper and Jade?) to Ruby Canyon. Although there are few trees anywhere, the sparse plant life on the Tonto, mostly blackbrush and cactus, looked healthy. Many plants bloomed with colorful flowers. The cactus bloomed too, mostly red flowers with infrequent yellows. An occasional Utah Agave (Century Plant) towered above the landscape with a heavy collage of pale flowers. Some places Agaves were abundant. Once in a while, a humming bird flew by. For lack of trees, the only place to find shade is in the shadow of a large boulder or under a rock ledge. The views from the Tonto, of course, are fabulous everywhere. It was always very rewarding to stop, rest your feet, and take in the view. So, we stopped a lot to rest on the trail.

Stone Serif

We hiked on around two unnamed canyons (Jasper and Jade?) to Ruby Canyon. Although there are few trees anywhere, the sparse plant life on the Tonto, mostly blackbrush and cactus, looked healthy. Many plants bloomed with colorful flowers. The cactus bloomed too, mostly red flowers with infrequent yellows. An occasional Utah Agave (Century Plant) towered above the landscape with a heavy collage of pale flowers. Some places Agaves were abundant. Once in a while, a humming bird flew by. For lack of trees, the only place to find shade is in the shadow of a large boulder or under a rock ledge. The views from the Tonto, of course, are fabulous every-where. It was always very rewarding to stop, rest your feet, and take in the view. So, we stopped a lot to rest on the trail.

Slab Serif Favorites

Most slab serifs are not as elegant as traditional typefaces, but they are readable. Use them particularly in situations where the line of text is short with large type, and you want it to be readable. Slab serifs display text well on the Web.

Clarendon

We hiked on around two unnamed canyons (Jasper and Jade?) to Ruby Canyon. Although there are few trees anywhere, the sparse plant life on the Tonto, mostly blackbrush and cactus, looked healthy. Many plants bloomed with colorful flow-ers. The cactus bloomed too, mostly red flowers with infrequent yellows. An occa-sional Utah Agave (Century Plant) towered above the landscape with a heavy collage of pale flowers. Some places Agaves were abundant. Once in a while, a humming bird flew by. For lack of trees, the only place to find shade is in the shadow of a large boulder or under a rock ledge. The views from the Tonto, of course, are fabu-lous everywhere. It was always very rewarding to stop, rest your feet, and take in the view. So, we stopped a lot to rest on the trail.

Egyptian505 BT

We hiked on around two unnamed canyons (Jasper and Jade?) to Ruby Canyon. Although there are few trees anywhere, the sparse plant life on the Tonto, mostly blackbrush and cactus, looked healthy. Many plants bloomed with colorful flowers. The cactus bloomed too, mostly red flowers with infrequent yellows. An occasional Utah Agave (Century Plant) towered above the landscape with a heavy collage of pale flowers. Some places Agaves were abundant. Once in a while, a humming bird flew by. For lack of trees, the only place to find shade is in the shadow of a large boulder or under a rock ledge. The views from the Tonto, of course, are fabulous everywhere. It was always very rewarding to stop, rest your feet, and take in the view. So, we stopped a lot to rest on the trail.

Geometric Slabserif 703

(Bitstream, comparable to Memphis)

We hiked on around two unnamed canyons (Jasper and Jade?) to Ruby Canyon. Although there are few trees anywhere, the sparse plant life on the Tonto, mostly blackbrush and cactus, looked healthy. Many plants bloomed with colorful flowers. The cactus bloomed too, mostly red flowers with infrequent yellows. An occasional Utah Agave (Century Plant) towered above the landscape with a heavy collage of pale flowers. Some places Agaves were abundant. Once in a while, a humming bird flew by. For lack of trees, the only place to find shade is in the shadow of a large boulder or under a rock ledge. The views from the Tonto, of course, are fabulous everywhere. It was always very rewarding to stop, rest your feet, and take in the view. So, we stopped a lot to rest on the trail.

Traditional Italics

These italics represent the oldstyle, transitional, and modern periods. Mr. Wheildon's research shows that one can read clean-cut italic type as easily as regular type.

American Garamond italic (an oldstyle typeface)

We hiked on around two unnamed canyons (Jasper and Jade?) to Ruby Canyon. Although there are few trees anywhere, the sparse plant life on the Tonto, mostly blackbrush and cactus, looked healthy. Many plants bloomed with colorful flowers. The cactus bloomed too, mostly red flowers with infrequent yellows. An occasional Utah Agave (Century Plant) towered above the landscape with a heavy collage of pale flowers. Some places Agaves were abundant. Once in a while, a humming bird flew by. For lack of trees, the only place to find shade is in the shadow of a large boulder or under a rock ledge. The views from the Tonto, of course, are fabulous everywhere. It was always very rewarding to stop, rest your feet, and take in the view. So, we stopped a lot to rest on the trail.

ITC New Baskerville italic (a transitional typeface)

We hiked on around two unnamed canyons (Jasper and Jade?) to Ruby Canyon. Although there are few trees anywhere, the sparse plant life on the Tonto, mostly blackbrush and cactus, looked healthy. Many plants bloomed with colorful flowers. The cactus bloomed too, mostly red flowers with infrequent yellows. An occasional Utah Agave (Century Plant) towered above the landscape with a heavy collage of pale flowers. Some places Agaves were abundant. Once in a while, a humming bird flew by. For lack of trees, the only place to find shade is in the shadow of a large boulder or under a rock ledge. The views from the

Tonto, of course, are fabulous everywhere. It was always very rewarding to stop, rest your feet, and take in the view. So, we stopped a lot to rest on the trail.

Bodoni italic (a modern typeface)

We hiked on around two unnamed canyons (Jasper and Jade?) to Ruby Canyon. Although there are few trees anywhere, the sparse plant life on the Tonto, mostly blackbrush and cactus, looked healthy. Many plants bloomed with colorful flowers. The cactus bloomed too, mostly red flowers with infrequent yellows. An occasional Utah Agave (Century Plant) towered above the landscape with a heavy collage of pale flowers. Some places Agaves were abundant. Once in a while, a humming bird flew by. For lack of trees, the only place to find shade is in the shadow of a large boulder or under a rock ledge. The views from the Tonto, of course, are fabulous everywhere. It was always very rewarding to stop, rest your feet, and take in the view. So, we stopped a lot to rest on the trail.

Other Serif Favorites

These typefaces are not as formal, perhaps, as the preceding but are still easy to read. Use them for variety in appropriate situations.

ITC Bookman 1

We hiked on around two unnamed canyons (Jasper and Jade?) to Ruby Canyon. Although there are few trees anywhere, the sparse plant life on the Tonto, mostly blackbrush and cactus, looked healthy.

Many plants bloomed with colorful flowers. The cactus bloomed too, mostly red flowers with infrequent yellows. An occasional Utah Agave (Century Plant) towered above the landscape with a heavy collage of pale flowers. Some places Agaves were abundant. Once in a while, a humming bird flew by. For lack of trees, the only place to find shade is in the shadow of a large boulder or under a rock ledge. The views from the Tonto, of course, are fabulous everywhere. It was always very rewarding to stop, rest your feet, and take in the view. So, we stopped a lot to rest on the trail.

Zapf Calligraphic 801

(Bitstream, comparable to Palatino)

We hiked on around two unnamed canyons (Jasper and Jade?) to Ruby Canyon. Although there are few trees anywhere, the sparse plant life on the Tonto, mostly blackbrush and cactus, looked healthy. Many plants bloomed with colorful flowers. The cactus bloomed too, mostly red flowers with infrequent yellows. An occasional Utah Agave (Century Plant) towered above the landscape with a heavy collage of pale flowers. Some places Agaves were abundant. Once in a while, a humming bird flew by. For lack of trees, the only place to find shade is in the shadow of a large boulder or under a rock ledge. The views from the Tonto, of course, are fabulous everywhere. It was always very rewarding to stop, rest your feet, and take in the view. So, we stopped a lot to rest on the trail.

ITC Souvenir 1

We hiked on around two unnamed canyons (Jasper and Jade?) to Ruby Canyon. Although there are few trees anywhere, the sparse plant life on the Tonto, mostly blackbrush and cactus, looked healthy. Many plants bloomed with colorful flowers. The cactus bloomed too, mostly red flowers with infrequent yellows. An occasional Utah Agave (Century Plant) towered above the landscape with a heavy collage of pale flowers. Some places Agaves were abundant. Once in a while, a humming bird flew by. For lack of trees, the only place to find shade is in the shadow of a large boulder or under a rock ledge. The views from the Tonto, of course, are fabulous everywhere. It was always very rewarding to stop, rest your feet, and take in the view. So, we stopped a lot to rest on the trail.

ITC Tiffany

We hiked on around two unnamed canyons (Jasper and Jade?) to Ruby Canyon. Although there are few trees anywhere, the sparse plant life on the Tonto, mostly blackbrush and cactus, looked healthy. Many plants bloomed with colorful flowers. The cactus bloomed too, mostly red flowers with infrequent yellows. An occasional Utah Agave (Century Plant) towered above the landscape with a heavy collage of pale flowers. Some places Agaves were abundant. Once in a while, a humming bird flew by. For lack of trees, the only place to find shade is in the shadow of a large boulder or under a rock ledge. The views from the Tonto, of course, are fabulous everywhere. It was always very rewarding to stop, rest your feet, and take in the view. So, we stopped a lot to rest on the trail.

Sans Serif Favorites

Sans serif typefaces do not support reading nearly as well as serif typefaces, but you may want to use them for special reading situations. They make good headings, headlines, and titles. Use them also for advertising collateral that has short reading passages.

ITC Avant Garde Gothic 1

We hiked on around two unnamed canyons (Jasper and Jade?) to Ruby Canyon. Although there are few trees anywhere, the sparse plant life on the Tonto, mostly black-brush and cactus, looked healthy. Many plants bloomed with colorful flowers. The cactus bloomed too, mostly red flowers with infrequent yellows. An occasional Utah Agave (Century Plant) towered above the landscape with a heavy collage of pale flowers. Some places Agaves were abundant. Once in a while, a humming bird flew by. For lack of trees, the only place to find shade is in the shadow of a large boulder or under a rock ledge. The views from the Tonto, of course, are fabulous everywhere. It was always very rewarding to stop, rest your feet, and take in the view. So, we stopped a lot to rest on the trail.

Square 721
(Bitstream, comparable to Eurostile)

We hiked on around two unnamed canyons (Jasper and Jade?) to Ruby Canyon. Although there are few trees anywhere, the sparse plant life on the Tonto, mostly blackbrush and cactus, looked healthy. Many plants bloomed with colorful flowers. The cactus bloomed too, mostly red flowers with infrequent yellows. An occasional Utah Agave (Century Plant) towered above the landscape with a heavy collage of pale flowers. Some places Agaves were abundant. Once in a while, a humming bird flew by. For lack of trees, the only place to find shade is in the shadow of a large boulder or under a rock ledge. The views from the Tonto, of course, are fabulous everywhere. It was always very rewarding to stop, rest your feet, and take in the view. So, we stopped a lot to rest on the trail.

Futura

We hiked on around two unnamed canyons (Jasper and Jade?) to Ruby Canyon. Although there are few trees anywhere, the sparse plant life on the Tonto, mostly blackbrush and cactus, looked healthy. Many plants bloomed with colorful flowers. The cactus bloomed too, mostly red flowers with infrequent yellows. An occasional Utah Agave (Century Plant) towered above the landscape with a heavy collage of pale flowers. Some places Agaves were abundant. Once in a while, a humming bird flew by. For lack of trees, the only place to find shade is in the shadow of a large boulder or under a rock ledge. The views from the Tonto, of course, are fabulous every-where. It was always very rewarding to stop, rest your feet, and take in the view. So, we stopped a lot to rest on the trail.

Humanist 521
(Bitstream, comparable to Gill Sans)

We hiked on around two unnamed canyons (Jasper and Jade?) to Ruby Canyon. Although there are few trees anywhere, the sparse plant life on the Tonto, mostly blackbrush and cactus, looked healthy. Many plants bloomed with colorful flowers. The cactus bloomed too, mostly red flowers with infrequent yellows. An occasional Utah Agave (Century Plant) towered above the landscape with a heavy collage of pale flowers. Some places Agaves were abundant. Once in a while, a humming bird flew by. For lack of trees, the only place to find shade is in the shadow of a large boulder or under a rock ledge. The views from the Tonto, of course, are fabulous every-where. It was always very rewarding to stop, rest your feet, and take in the view. So, we stopped a lot to rest on the trail.

ITC Goudy Sans

We hiked on around two unnamed canyons (Jasper and Jade?) to Ruby Canyon. Although there are few trees anywhere, the sparse plant life on the Tonto, mostly blackbrush and cactus, looked healthy. Many plants bloomed with colorful flowers. The cactus bloomed too, mostly red flowers with infrequent yel-lows. An occasional Utah Agave (Century Plant) tow-ered above the landscape with a heavy collage of pale flowers. Some places Agaves were abundant. Once in a while, a humming bird flew by. For lack of trees, the only place to find shade is in the shadow of a large boulder or under a rock ledge. The views from the Tonto, of course, are fabulous everywhere. It was always very rewarding to stop, rest your feet, and take in the view. So, we stopped a lot to rest on the trail.

Lucida Sans
(the mate to Lucida)

We hiked on around two unnamed canyons (Jasper and Jade?) to Ruby Canyon. Although there are few trees anywhere, the sparse plant life on the Tonto, mostly black-brush and cactus, looked healthy. Many plants bloomed with colorful flowers. The cactus bloomed too, mostly red flowers with infrequent yellows. An occasional Utah Agave (Century Plant) towered above the landscape with a heavy collage of pale flowers. Some places Agaves were abundant. Once in a while, a humming bird flew by. For lack of trees, the only place to find shade is in the shadow of a large boulder or under a rock ledge. The views from the Tonto, of course, are fabulous everywhere. It was always very rewarding to stop, rest your feet, and take in the view. So, we stopped a lot to rest on the trail.

Zapf Humanist 601
(Bitstream, comparable to Optima)

We hiked on around two unnamed canyons (Jasper and Jade?) to Ruby Canyon. Although there are few trees anywhere, the sparse plant life on the Tonto, mostly blackbrush and cactus, looked healthy. Many plants bloomed with colorful flowers. The cactus bloomed too, mostly red flowers with infrequent yellows. An occasional Utah Agave

Readable Notice how readable Optima is due to its quasi serifs.

(Century Plant) towered above the landscape with a heavy collage of pale flowers. Some places Agaves were abundant. Once in a while, a humming bird flew by. For lack of trees, the only place to find shade is in the shadow of a large boulder or under a rock ledge. The views from the Tonto, of course, are fabulous everywhere. It was always very rewarding to stop, rest your feet, and take in the view. So, we stopped a lot to rest on the trail.

ITC Stone Sans
(mate to ITC Stone Serif)

We hiked on around two unnamed canyons (Jasper and Jade?) to Ruby Canyon. Although there are few trees anywhere, the sparse plant life on the Tonto, mostly blackbrush and cactus, looked healthy. Many plants bloomed with colorful flowers. The cactus bloomed too, mostly red flowers with infrequent yellows. An occasional Utah Agave (Century Plant) towered above the landscape with a heavy collage of pale flowers. Some places Agaves were abundant. Once in a while, a humming bird flew by. For lack of trees, the only place to find shade is in the shadow of a large boulder or under a rock ledge. The views from the Tonto, of course, are fabulous everywhere. It was always very rewarding to stop, rest your feet, and take in the view. So, we stopped a lot to rest on the trail.

Univers

We hiked on around two unnamed canyons (Jasper and Jade?) to Ruby Canyon. Although there are few trees anywhere, the sparse plant life on the Tonto, mostly blackbrush and cactus, looked healthy. Many plants bloomed with colorful flowers. The cactus bloomed too, mostly red flowers with infrequent yellows. An occasional Utah Agave (Century Plant) towered above the landscape with a heavy collage of pale flowers. Some places Agaves were abundant. Once in a while, a humming bird flew by. For lack of trees, the only place to find shade is in the shadow of a large boulder or under a rock ledge. The views from the Tonto, of course, are fabulous everywhere. It was always very rewarding to stop, rest your feet, and take in the view. So, we stopped a lot to rest on the trail.

Scripts

Scripts are beautiful but not very readable. Use them occasionally, but don't use them for text that people must read.

Shelley

We hiked on around two unnamed canyons (Jasper and Jade?) to Ruby Canyon. Although there are few trees anywhere, the sparse plant life on the Tonto, mostly blackbrush and cactus, looked healthy. Many plants bloomed with colorful flowers. The cactus bloomed too, mostly red flowers with infrequent yellows. An occasional Utah Agave (Century Plant) towered above the landscape with a heavy collage of pale flowers. Some places Agaves were abundant. Once in a while, a humming bird flew by. For lack of trees, the only place to find shade is in the shadow of a large boulder or under a rock ledge. The views from the Tonto, of course, are fabulous everywhere. It was always very rewarding to stop, rest your feet, and take in the view. So, we stopped a lot to rest on the trail.

Kaufmann

We hiked on around two unnamed canyons (Jasper and Jade?) to Ruby Canyon. Although there are few trees anywhere, the *sparse plant life on the Tonto, mostly blackbrush and cactus, looked healthy. Many plants bloomed with colorful flowers. The cactus bloomed too, mostly red flowers with infrequent yellows. An occasional Utah Agave (Century Plant) towered above the landscape with a heavy collage of pale flowers. Some places Agaves were abundant. Once in a while, a humming bird flew by. For lack of trees, the only place to find shade is in the shadow of a large boulder or under a rock ledge. The views from the Tonto, of course, are fabulous everywhere. It was always very rewarding to stop, rest your feet, and take in the view. So, we stopped a lot to rest on the trail.*

Fun but Useful Too

Use the kind of typefaces represented in this section for informal publishing where quick reading is not the primary requirement for the text.

Fritz Quadrata

We hiked on around two unnamed canyons (Jasper and Jade?) to Ruby Canyon. Although there are few trees anywhere, the sparse plant life on the Tonto, mostly blackbrush and cactus, looked healthy. Many plants bloomed with colorful flowers. The cactus bloomed too, mostly red flowers with infrequent yellows. An occasional Utah Agave (Century Plant) towered above the landscape with a heavy collage of pale flowers. Some places Agaves were abundant. Once in a while, a humming bird flew by. For lack of trees, the only place to find shade is in the shadow of a large boulder or under a rock ledge. The views from the Tonto, of course, are fabulous everywhere. It was always very rewarding to stop, rest your feet, and take in the view. So, we stopped a lot to rest on the trail.

Graphite

We hiked on around two unnamed canyons (Jasper and Jade?) to Ruby Canyon. Although there are few trees anywhere, the sparse plant life on the Tonto, mostly blackbrush and cactus, looked healthy. Many plants bloomed with colorful flowers. The cactus bloomed too, mostly red flowers with infrequent yellows. An occasional Utah Agave (Century Plant) towered above the landscape with a heavy collage of pale flowers. Some places Agaves were abundant. Once in a while, a humming bird flew by. For lack of trees, the only place to find shade is in the shadow of a large boulder or under a rock ledge. The views from the Tonto, of course, are fabulous everywhere. It was always very rewarding to stop, rest your feet, and take in the view. So, we stopped a lot to rest on the trail.

Regeneration X

We hiked on around two unnamed canyons (Jasper and Jade?) to Ruby Canyon. Although there are few trees anywhere, the sparse plant life on the Tonto, mostly blackbrush and cactus, looked healthy. Many plants bloomed with colorful flowers. The cactus bloomed too, mostly red flowers with infrequent yellows. An occasional Utah Agave (Century Plant) towered above the landscape with a heavy collage of pale flowers. Some places Agaves were abundant. Once in a while, a humming bird flew by. For lack of trees, the only place to find shade is in the shadow of a large boulder or under a rock ledge. The views from the Tonto, of course, are fabulous everywhere. It was always very rewarding to stop, rest your feet, and take in the view. So, we stopped a lot to rest on the trail.

Poetica

We hiked on around two unnamed canyons (Jasper and Jade?) to Ruby Canyon. Although there are few trees anywhere, the sparse plant life on the Tonto, mostly blackbrush and cactus, looked healthy. Many plants bloomed with colorful flowers. The cactus bloomed too, mostly red flowers with infrequent yellows. An occasional Utah Agave (Century Plant) towered above the landscape with a heavy collage of pale flowers. Some places Agaves were abundant. Once in a while, a humming bird flew by. For lack of trees, the only place to find shade is in the shadow of a large boulder or under a rock ledge. The views from the Tonto, of course, are fabulous everywhere. It was always very rewarding to stop, rest your feet, and take in the view. So, we stopped a lot to rest on the trail.

Present

We hiked on around two unnamed canyons (Jasper and Jade?) to Ruby Canyon. Although there are few trees anywhere, the sparse plant life on the Tonto, mostly blackbrush and cactus, looked healthy. Many plants bloomed with colorful flowers. The cactus bloomed too, mostly red flowers with infrequent yellows. An occasional Utah Agave (Century Plant) towered above the landscape with a heavy collage of pale flowers. Some places Agaves were abundant. Once in a while, a humming bird flew by. For lack of trees, the only place to find shade is in the shadow of a large boulder or under a rock ledge. The views from the Tonto, of course, are fabulous everywhere. It was always very rewarding to stop, rest your feet, and take in the view. So, we stopped a lot to rest on the trail.

Serpentine

We hiked on around two unnamed canyons (Jasper and Jade?) to Ruby Canyon. Although there are few trees anywhere, the sparse plant life on the Tonto, mostly blackbrush and cactus, looked healthy. Many plants bloomed with colorful flowers.

The cactus bloomed too, mostly red flowers with infrequent yellows. An occasional Utah Agave (Century Plant) towered above the landscape with a heavy collage of pale flowers. Some places Agaves were abundant. Once in a while, a humming bird flew by. For lack of trees, the only place to find shade is in the shadow of a large boulder or under a rock ledge. The views from the Tonto, of course, are fabulous everywhere. It was always very rewarding to stop, rest your feet, and take in the view. So, we stopped a lot to rest on the trail.

Willow

We hiked on around two unnamed canyons (Jasper and Jade?) to Ruby Canyon. Although there are few trees anywhere, the sparse plant life on the Tonto, mostly blackbrush and cactus, looked healthy. Many plants bloomed with colorful flowers. The cactus bloomed too, mostly red flowers with infrequent yellows. An occasional Utah Agave (Century Plant) towered above the landscape with a heavy collage of pale flowers. Some places Agaves were abundant. Once in a while, a humming bird flew by. For lack of trees, the only place to find shade is in the shadow of a large boulder or under a rock ledge. The views from the Tonto, of course, are fabulous everywhere. It was always very rewarding to stop, rest your feet, and take in the view. So, we stopped a lot to rest on the trail.

Willow I picked Willow out of a catalog featuring only alphabets. It turned out to be much less readable than I had imagined. Bad choice.

Decorative Typefaces

The typefaces in this section came from the SynFonts digital type foundry (http://www.synfonts.com) which offers a creative collection. This collection represents the explosion of creativity now taking place in typography, and you will find many more new digital type foundries and individual typographers offering their fonts for modest prices, many via the Web.

Some of these new fonts have been created only for use on the Web, where they look great. They may look terrible in print. Consequently, you must be careful when you purchase fonts to match them to your particular use.

Guilty

ABCDEFGHIJKL
MNOPQRSTUVWXYZ
abcdefghijkl
mnopqrstuvwxyz
1234567890

Human Condition

ABCDEFGHIJKL
MNOPQRSTUVWXYZ
abcdefghijkl
mnopqrstuvwxyz
1234567890

Liquid Sex

ABCDEFGHIJKL
MNOPQRSTUVWXYZ
abcdefghijkl
mnopqrstuvwxyz
1234567890

Nude

ABCDEFGHIJKL
MNOPQRSTUVWXYZ
abcdefghijkl
mnopqrstuvwxyz
1234567890

Nurse Ratchet

ABCDEFGHIJKL
MNOPQRSTUVWXYZ
abcdefghijkl

mnopqrstuvwxyz
12,34567890

SkannerZ
ABCDEFGHIJKL
MNOPQRSTUVWXYZ
abcdefghijkl
mnopqrStuvwXyz
1234567890

Microsoft Windows Fonts

Microsoft provides a small variety of fonts for everyone to use. Even though everyone has the three normal fonts, you cannot count on everyone having the remainder.

Normal

These typefaces comprise the standard for Windows. You can count on everyone having them. But overuse has made them a little boring.

Times New Roman

We hiked on around two unnamed canyons (Jasper and Jade?) to Ruby Canyon. Although there are few trees anywhere, the sparse plant life on the Tonto, mostly blackbrush and cactus, looked healthy. Many plants bloomed with colorful flowers. The cactus bloomed too, mostly red flowers with infrequent yellows. An occasional Utah Agave (Century Plant) towered above the landscape with a heavy collage of pale flowers. Some places Agaves were abundant. Once in a while, a humming bird flew by. For lack of trees, the only place to find shade is in the shadow of a large boulder or under a rock ledge. The views from the Tonto, of course, are fabulous everywhere. It was always very rewarding to stop, rest your feet, and take in the view. So, we stopped a lot to rest on the trail.

Times New Roman ABCDEGHIJKLMNOPQRSTU VWXYZ abcdefghijklmnopqrstuvwxyz 1234567890

Times New Roman ABCDEFGHIJKLMNOPQRSTU VWXYZ abcdefghijklmnopqrstuvwxyz 1234567890

Arial (comparable to Helvetica)

We hiked on around two unnamed canyons (Jasper and Jade?) to Ruby Canyon. Although there are few trees anywhere, the sparse plant life on the Tonto, mostly blackbrush and cactus, looked healthy. Many plants bloomed with colorful flowers. The cactus bloomed too, mostly red flowers with infrequent yellows. An occasional Utah Agave (Century Plant) towered above the landscape with a heavy collage of pale flowers. Some places Agaves were abundant. Once in a while, a humming bird flew by. For lack of trees, the only place to find shade is in the shadow of a large boulder or under a rock ledge. The views from the Tonto, of course, are fabulous everywhere. It was always very rewarding to stop, rest your feet, and take in the view. So, we stopped a lot to rest on the trail.

Arial ABCDEFGHIJKLMNOPQRSTUVWXYZ abcdefghijklmnopqrstuvwxyz 1234567890

Arial ABCDEFGHIJKLMNOPQRSTUVWXYZ abcdefghijklmnopqrstuvwxyz 1234567890

Courier

We hiked on around two unnamed canyons (Jasper and Jade?) to Ruby Canyon. Although there are few trees anywhere, the sparse plant life on the Tonto, mostly blackbrush and cactus,

looked healthy. Many plants bloomed
with colorful flowers. The cactus
bloomed too, mostly red flowers with
infrequent yellows. An occasional
Utah Agave (Century Plant) towered
above the landscape with a heavy collage of pale flowers. Some places
Agaves were abundant. Once in a while,
a humming bird flew by. For lack of
trees, the only place to find shade is
in the shadow of a large boulder or
under a rock ledge. The views from the
Tonto, of course, are fabulous everywhere. It was always very rewarding to
stop, rest your feet, and take in the
view. So, we stopped a lot to rest on
the trail.

Courier ABCDEFGHIJKLMNOPQRSTUVWXYZ
a b c d e f g h i j k l m n o p q r s t u v w x y z
1234567890

Courier ABCDEFGHIJKLMNOPQRSTUVWXYZ
a b c d e f g h i j k l m n o p q r s t u v w x y z
1234567890

Additions

Microsoft makes the following typefaces available at its Web
site for a free download. Microsoft also distributes them with
certain software products. For instance, with the 4.0
browser, Microsoft distributes Verdana, Comic Sans, Arial
Black, and Impact.

Georgia, Verdana, and Trebuchet MS were created from
scratch for the screen; that is, like Bitstream's Prima, they are
screen built and screen tuned. Consequently, they make excellent fonts for the Web.

Text

Georgia makes an excellent choice for serif text for the Web.

Georgia

We hiked on around two unnamed canyons (Jasper and Jade?) to Ruby Canyon. Although there are few trees anywhere, the sparse plant life on the Tonto, mostly blackbrush and cactus, looked healthy. Many plants bloomed with colorful flowers. The cactus bloomed too, mostly red flowers with infrequent yellows. An occasional Utah Agave (Century Plant) towered above the landscape with a heavy collage of pale flowers. Some places Agaves were abundant. Once in a while, a humming bird flew by. For lack of trees, the only place to find shade is in the shadow of a large boulder or under a rock ledge. The views from the Tonto, of course, are fabulous everywhere. It was always very rewarding to stop, rest your feet, and take in the view. So, we stopped a lot to rest on the trail.

Georgia ABCDEFGHIJKLMNOPQRSTUVWXYZ abcdefghijklmnopqrstuvwxyz 1234567890

Georgia ABCDEFGHIJKLMNOPQRSTVWXYZ abcdefghijklmnopqrstuvwxyz 1234567890

Sans Serif

Both Verdana and Trebuchet MS make excellent choices for sans serif fonts for the Web.

Verdana

We hiked on around two unnamed canyons (Jasper and Jade?) to Ruby Canyon. Although there are few trees anywhere, the sparse plant life on the

Using Microsoft Fonts

How can you use Microsoft fonts cleverly at your Web site? Put in a hyperlink to Microsoft's Web site. Instruct your Web site visitors who don't have Georgia (or another Microsoft font that you use in your Web pages) to click on the hyperlink that will take them directly to Georgia at the Microsoft Web site. From there, they can download and install Georgia.

Although this sounds good and may work well in many cases, it's not a universal solution. Some people will think it's too much trouble. Others will not know how to install a font. Still others will not know how to download. TrueDoc or Microsoft font embedding are the only ways to be sure that people will see your Web site as you intend; and they work only for the 4.0 browsers.

Tonto, mostly blackbrush and cactus, looked healthy. Many plants bloomed with colorful flowers. The cactus bloomed too, mostly red flowers with infrequent yellows. An occasional Utah Agave (Century Plant) towered above the landscape with a heavy collage of pale flowers. Some places Agaves were abundant. Once in a while, a humming bird flew by. For lack of trees, the only place to find shade is in the shadow of a large boulder or under a rock ledge. The views from the Tonto, of course, are fabulous everywhere. It was always very rewarding to stop, rest your feet, and take in the view. So, we stopped a lot to rest on the trail.

Verdana ABCDEFGHIJKLMNOPQRSTU VWXYZ abcdefghijklmnopqrstuvwxyz 1234567890

Verdana ABCDEFGHIJKLMNOPQRSTU VWXYZ abcdefghijklmnopqrstuvwxyz 1234567890

Trebuchet MS

We hiked on around two unnamed canyons (Jasper and Jade?) to Ruby Canyon. Although there are few trees anywhere, the sparse plant life on the Tonto, mostly blackbrush and cactus, looked healthy. Many plants bloomed with colorful flowers. The cactus bloomed too, mostly red flowers with infrequent yellows. An occasional Utah Agave (Century Plant) towered above the landscape with a heavy collage of pale flowers. Some places Agaves were abundant. Once in a while, a humming bird flew by. For lack of trees, the only place to find shade is in the shadow of a large boulder or under a rock ledge. The views from the Tonto, of course, are fabulous everywhere. It was always very rewarding to stop, rest your feet, and take in the view. So, we stopped a lot to rest on the trail.

Trebuchat MS ABCDEFGHIJKLMNOPQRSTUVWXYZ abcdefghijklmnopqrstuvwxyz 1234567890

Trebuchat MS ABCDEFGHIJKLMNOPQRSTUVWXYZ abcdefghijklmnopqrstuvwxyz 1234567890

Display

For headings and short text passages, try these typefaces.

Comic Sans
A B C D E F G H I J K L M N O P Q R S T U V W X Y Z abcdefghijklmnopqrstuvwxyz 1234567890

Arial Black
ABCDEFGHIJKLMNOPQRSTU VWXYZ abcdefghijklmnopqrstuvwxyz 1234567890

Impact
ABCDEFGHIJKLMNOPQRSTUVWXYZ abcdefghijklmnopqrstuvwxyz 1234567890

Screen-Tuned Fonts for Embedding

This section includes representative digital type foundries that offer screen-tuned fonts.

Bitstream

Bitstream doesn't offer a separate list of screen-tuned fonts. Nonetheless, it has tuned many of its fonts to the screen. It calls its excellent font tuning delta editing. If you bought a Bitstream font before it was delta edited for the screen, you may want to repurchase it or upgrade it before using it for Microsoft font embedding. If you buy a Bitstream font today, inquire whether it has been delta edited for the screen. But, if you use TrueDoc exclusively, it probably doesn't matter whether it has been delta edited.

Monotype

Monotype offers Enhanced Screen Quality (ESQ) fonts tuned to the screen. The current list follows. By the time you read this, Monotype may have added more to the list.

Albertus

Andale

Amasis

Andy (formerly Mead)

Apollo

Arial

(Regular, Rounded, Narrow, Cyrillic, Monospaced)

Arial Black

Monotype Baskerville

Bell

Bembo

Binner Gothic

Blueprint Web

Book Antiqua

Bodoni Book

Bookman Old Style

Century Gothic

Century Schoolbook

Monotype Clarendon

Courier

Courier Line Draw

Courier CE

Courier Cyrillic

Creepy

Curlz

Eraser Dust

Facade

Felix Titling

Footlight

Forte

Franklin Gothic Extra Bold

French Script

Monotype Garamond

Gill Sans

Ginko

Gloucester Old Style

Glowworm

Imprint Shadow

Kidprint

Letter Gothic

Lydian

MICR

OCR-A

OCR-B

Nimrod

News Gothic

Onyx

Pepita

Perpetua

Plantin

Rockwell

Sabon

Sassoon Infant

Sassoon Sans

Script Bold

Monotype Sorts

Swing Bold

Times New Roman

Times New Roman Cyrillic

Twentieth Century

Adobe Web Type

This is a 12-font package that includes Minion Web and Myraid Web in various type styles, together with Caflisch Script Web, Mezz Web bold, Penumbra Serif Web, and Giddyup Web, all tuned to the screen.

Text Fonts Created from Scratch for the Web

These are Bitstream Prima fonts created from scratch to be used on the Web. Thus, they are more than just screen tuned. Bitstream purposely created them for the Web rather than for print (see Figure 21.1). You might want to consider adding a little extra leading to your text when using Prima.

Prima Serif

We hiked on around two unnamed canyons (Jasper and Jade?) to Ruby Canyon. Although there are few trees anywhere, the sparse plant life on the Tonto, mostly blackbrush and cactus, looked healthy. Many plants bloomed with colorful flowers. The cactus bloomed too,

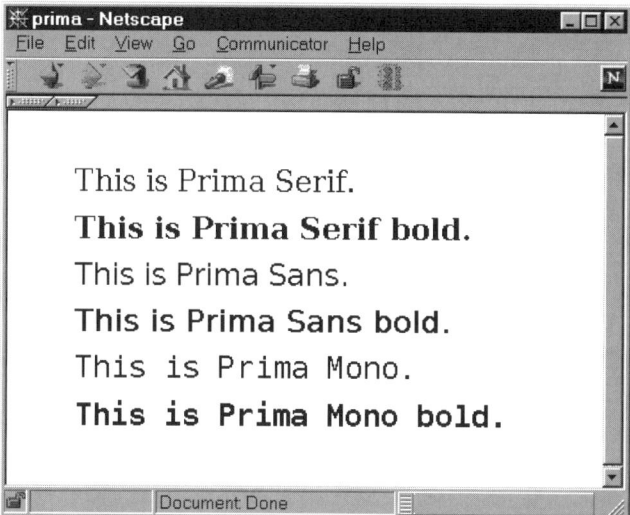

Figure 21.1 *Bitstream's Prima screen fonts.*

mostly red flowers with infrequent yellows. An occasional Utah Agave (Century Plant) towered above the landscape with a heavy collage of pale flowers. Some places Agaves were abundant. Once in a while, a humming bird flew by. For lack of trees, the only place to find shade is in the shadow of a large boulder or under a rock ledge. The views from the Tonto, of course, are fabulous everywhere. It was always very rewarding to stop, rest your feet, and take in the view. So, we stopped a lot to rest on the trail.

Prima Serif ABCDEFGHIJKLMNOPQRST UVWXYZ abcdefghijklmnopqrstuvwxyz 1234567890

Prima Serif ABCDEFGHIJKLMNOPQRST UVWXYZ abcdefghijklmnopqrstuvwxyz 1234567890

Prima Sans

We hiked on around two unnamed canyons (Jasper and Jade?) to Ruby Canyon. Although there are few trees anywhere, the sparse plant life on the Tonto, mostly blackbrush and cactus, looked healthy. Many plants bloomed with colorful flowers. The cactus bloomed too, mostly red flowers with infrequent yellows. An occasional Utah Agave (Century Plant) towered above the landscape with a heavy collage of pale flowers. Some places Agaves were abundant. Once in a while, a humming bird flew by. For lack of trees, the only place to find shade is in the shadow of a large boulder or under a rock ledge. The views from the Tonto, of course, are fabulous everywhere. It was always very rewarding to stop, rest your feet, and take in the view. So, we stopped a lot to rest on the trail.
Prima Sans ABCDEFGHIJKLMNOPQRSTUVWXYZ abcdefghijklmnopqrstuvwxyz 1234567890
Prima Sans ABCDEFGHIJKLMNOPQRSTUVWXYZ abcdefghijklmnopqrstuvwxyz 1234567890

Also, consider Georgia, Verdana, and Trebuchet MS in the Microsoft Windows Font section (above). They are all screen built and screen tuned just like Bitstream's Prima.

Fonts That Work Well for Font Embedding

This small selection of Bitstream fonts resulted from my modest effort to find some fonts in a portion of Bitstream's large font library that read well for text on my monitor. I recommend that you do your own search. These serve as examples of the quality you can find in high-quality font collections.

Caslon 540	
Cheltenham BT	
Geometric Slabserif 712	(Rockwell)
Egyptian 505 Medium	
Prima Serif	
Transitional 551	(Caledonia)
Zapf Calligraphic	(Palatino)
Zapf Elliptical	(Melior)

This small selection of fonts resulted from my modest effort to find some fonts in my miscellaneous collection that read well for text.

Century Schoolbook	(Monotype)
Georgia	(Microsoft)
Rockwell	(Monotype)
Times New Roman MT	(Monotype)

Fonts that Work Well with TrueDoc

This small selection resulted from my modest effort to find some fonts in my Bitstream collection that look good on my monitor when rendered in TrueDoc. I again recommend that you do your own search and experimentation.

Cheltenham BT	
Geometric Slabserif 712	(Rockwell)
Egyptian 505 Medium	
Imperial BT	
Prima Serif	
News 701 BT	

This small selection resulted from my casual effort to find some fonts in my miscellaneous collection that look good in TrueDoc.

Georgia   (Microsoft)
Rockwell   (Monotype)
Times New Roman   (Monotype)

In addition, I found a few fonts in a casual search through some large brand-name, but low-quality font collections (which I acquired over the years but have seldom used) that read well in TrueDoc.

Searching for the Ultimately Useful Fonts

Because many webmasters will develop for both the Microsoft browser and the Netscape browser, the trick is to find readable serif fonts that look good both as screen-tuned fonts and as TrueDoc fonts. It's difficult to find fonts that look good on a CRT even among screen-tuned fonts. But when you find them, they look good and are easy to read. Use them for Microsoft font embedding. Likewise, it's difficult to find fonts that look good when rendered by TrueDoc. But when you find them, they look especially good and are very readable. Use them for TrueDoc typography. Again, the goal is to find the rare readable fonts that look good on the screen and also look good when rendered by TrueDoc.

Keep in mind that it's not hard to find fonts that look good in larger sizes (i.e., 15 points and over). Generally, the larger the font, the better it looks on a CRT. The trick is to find text-size fonts that are readable. Also keep in mind that different fonts look different in different color schemes. A font that looks great in yellow on black may not be as readable in navy on cream.

My choices for the best fonts are:

Cheltenham BT

Geometric Slabserif 712   (Rockwell)

Egyptian 505 Medium

Imperial BT

Prima Serif

Other Than Bitstream

Georgia   (Microsoft)

Rockwell   (Monotype)

Times New Roman MT   (Monotype)

This is not a very large selection, but it was not an exhaustive search. I wanted to save some fun for the future. More importantly, I didn't want to preempt readers' efforts to find their own best screen/TrueDoc fonts. So, see what you can come up with to compare with my choices.

Keep in mind that I had over 500 Bitstream fonts of which I experimented with only a percentage. I had a few Monotype fonts and the standard Microsoft fonts. Thus, my experimentation was not extensive. A few of the great type foundries not included are ITC, Agfa, Adobe, and Monotype (very limited). So do not consider this a definitive study even for the Bitstream collection.

Finally, I should mention that the fonts I have chosen for the Web are not necessarily my favorites. Far from it. They represent simply the best I have found in my limited search for readable fonts for *both* TrueDoc and font embedding. My favorite fonts comprise a much different list. Yes, I can still appreciate how fonts look in print. Most of my favorites don't make the grade for the screen today, but as computer monitors grow sharper, it will be interesting to see which of my favorites do make the grade eventually.

Appendix

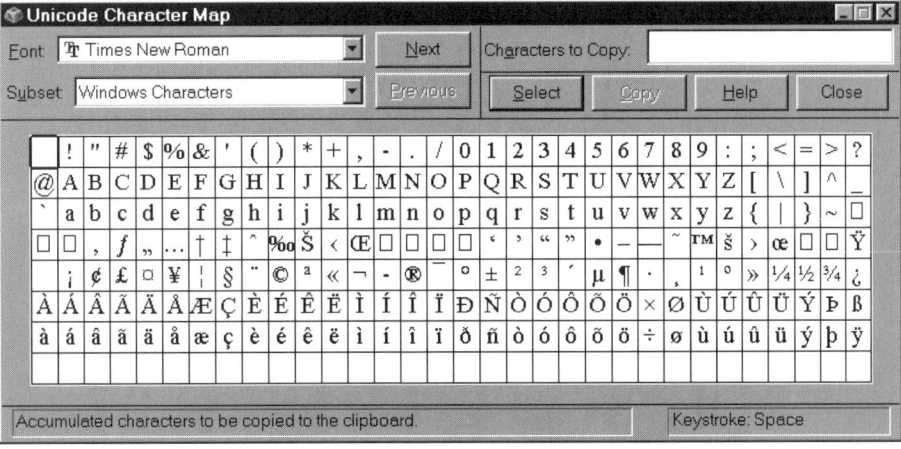

Figure A.1 *The Windows character set.*

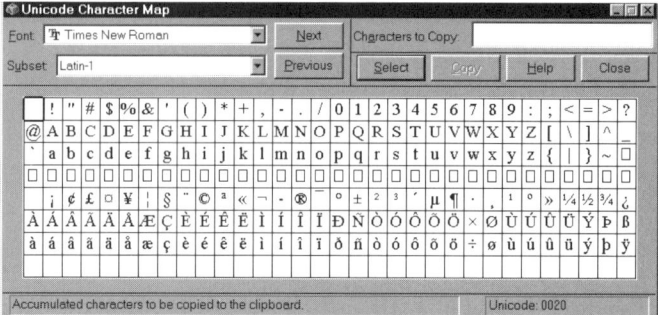

Figure A.2 *The Latin-1 character set.*

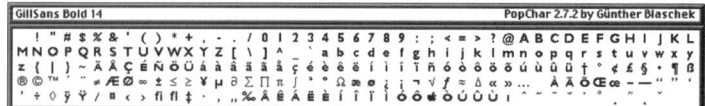

Figure A.3 *The Mac character set.*

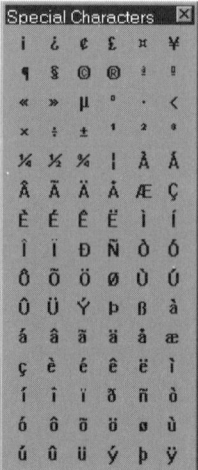

Figure A.4 *The HTML character set.*

Glossary

antialiasing A digital technique using interim colors to smooth the jagged appearance of alphanumeric characters and other graphic elements with diagonal or curved lines.

applet See Java applet.

ASCII American Standard Code for Information Interchange. A widely used standard for a plain text file with minimal formatting.

attribute A programming control within an HTML markup.

authoring program Software used by a nonprogrammer to create a typeset or multimedia document or presentation.

background Background image or color.

bitmap An image created by the mapping of dots in a matrix.

cascade A series of software components (style sheets), the output of each of which serves as the input for the next.

cathode ray tube (CRT) An electronic display tube that displays a video image.

cell A one-row entry in a column in an HTML table.

CGI See Common Gateway Interface.

CGI scripts The code used to tap the power of a server computer via an HTML page. A script can run a program on the server computer or can itself be a program.

character set The set of characters included with a font.

Character Shape Player (CSP) The TrueDoc software inside a browser that plays back the shape of the characters in a Web page using a PFR.

Character Shape Recorder (CSR) The TrueDoc software inside an authoring program or other program that records the shape of characters in a Web page and places them in a PFR.

child A characteristic or set of characteristics that deviates from a basic set of characteristics (parent).

clarity The characteristic of being easy to see and identify in regard to the individual characters of a typeface.

class (CSS) A CSS declaration invented by a user to define a special HTML markup or a new selector.

class (Java) A single Java program.

class libraries See Java class libraries.

client A computer on a network that receives digital services from a server computer.

client-side Computing by a client computer.

Common Gateway Interface (CGI) The Application Program Interface (API) that provides the means to tap the power of a server computer with CGI programs, with a Web page as the interface.

content The information in whatever form, intended for people, that a digital system conveys, presents, or processes (e.g., the story).

content provider A person, company, or other source that provides content on the Web (e.g., Time Warner).

control device A channel-changer-like device designed to control NetTVs from across the room. Also doubles as a channel changer.

CRT See cathode ray tube.

CSP See Character Shape Player.

CSR See Character Shape Player.

declaration A CSS instruction. A map between a selector and a property.

degradability The capability of using advances in Web markup and style technologies while continuing to adequately serve browsers based on prior versions of the technologies.

deprecated Regretful disapproval. A deprecated HTML markup is one on its way to being eventually eliminated.

Document Type Definitions (DTD) Define SGML documents.

dot pitch The distance between the center lines of holes in the aperture screen in a cathode ray tube. The smallest dot pitch for a computer monitor is currently .22 mm.

dpi Dots per inch, a measurement of physical resolution expressed as one dimension of a square.

electronic resolution An electronic image measured in pixels.

elements Multimedia items in a Web page such as text blocks and images.

embedded program Programming expressed in a Web page, or the links expressed in a Web page to outside programming that is used via the Web page.

ergonomics The science of how people function efficiently, comfortably, and safely in a work environment.

event An action that triggers a software reaction.

extended character set That portion of a character set not usable by the execution of individual keystrokes on a standard computer keyboard.

Extensible Markup Language (XML) A subset of SGML intended for online use that provides more functionality than HTML.

Extensible Style Language (XSL) A more robust style sheet language than CSS, to be used with XML.

font One size of one typestyle of one typeface for lead type. One typestyle of a single typeface in digital type. Often used generically to denote all the typestyles and variations of a digital typeface.

foreground Text or line color.

gateway Web site A Web site that a TVSP sets up and operates to make things easy for its subscribers. The TVSP browser takes subscribers immediately to the gateway Web site upon booting.

Graphics Interchange Format (GIF) An 8-bit (256-color) compressed color graphic file.

High-Definition Television The new high-resolution television system. It's a digital system.

hinting The adjustment of digital fonts below 15 points to trick the eye into perceiving them to be sharper.

Hypertext Markup Language (HTML) Used to create Web pages.

HTML document A plain text (ASCII) document marked up with HTML to create a Web page, an attractive publishing document viewed with a browser.

hyperlinks Active navigation mechanisms in an HTML page that take a viewer from one multimedia element to another.

inheritance Characteristics inherited by one HTML element (child) from another (parent).

interactivity Digital activities that involve participants and provide choices and controls over the activities (e.g., dialog between a computer and a user).

Internet Service Provider (ISP) A business with a network connected to the Internet that sells connections to its network to subscribers to enable such subscribers to use the Internet.

Java A programming language specifically designed to create applications for use on a network.

Java applet A Java program embedded in an HTML document.

Java class libraries A group of commonly used Java programs that software developers use to build common functionality into Java applications.

Java virtual machine Converts bytecode into machine language.

JavaScript An easy-to-use (for programmers), limited-function computer language (scripting language) for use in HTML documents.

Java-based Extendable Typography (JET) A Bitstream typography enhancement for Java.

Joint Photographic Experts Group (JPEG) A standard for compressing true color digital images with loss of image quality, although compression of up to 10:1 or even 20:1 shows little noticeable loss of sharpness.

jumps Distractions that interrupt the smooth flow of reading.

layer A means of giving display priority to elements occupying the same place on a Web page at the same time.

layout The arrangement of media on a Web page.

legibility The characteristic of smooth and easy reading in regard to the design of a typeface and how groups of characters read.

length A CSS measurement expressed in various standard measurements such as pixels and points.

licensing Licensing is used to describe two opposite actions: when the licenser licenses the right to use an intellectual asset to a licensee (usually to collect a fee) or when a licensee licenses the right to use an intellectual asset from a licenser (usually by making payment).

markup For HTML, characters between the < > marks used to provide structure to an ASCII document (e.g., an HTML page).

metainformation Information about the information.

multimedia Various digital media (e.g., audio bites, video clips, text, graphics) used in the same digital presentation.

Musical Instrument Digital Interface (MIDI) A protocol for music synthesized digitally. A set of instructions that run a digital synthesizer. A MIDI file is about 1/1,000 the size of an audio file of comparable duration.

NC See network computer.

NetTV A set-top or built-in NC for a television. Also the system for accessing the Web via television.

NetTV viewers People who gain access to the Internet by using a set-top and a television.

network computer (NC) A computer (client) without a hard disk or other physical storage device, used on a TCP/IP network, which gets most of its software from a server computer on the network.

objects Multimedia elements in a Web page, such as text blocks and images.

obsolete No longer useful. An obsolete HTML markup is one about to be eliminated.

page flipping An HTML structure that enables a user to see successive screens without scrolling.

palette A computer uses a palette of 4 (2-bit), 16 (4-bit), or 256 (8-bit) colors to generate a digital image. For denser graphics files (e.g., 64,000 colors, 16-bit or more), a palette is not necessary.

parent A basic generic set of characteristics.

Personal Java A subset of Java designed for Internet devices such as NetTVs.

PFR See Portable Font Resource.

physical resolution The physical resolution of a digital image as measured for the device that displays the image (e.g., dot pitch for a CRT).

pixel The smallest unit (monochrome) or cluster of units (color) in a video display. The unit is usually a rectangle.

plug-in A program that provides an add-on function to a browser or other program.

point A unit of measurement for type size (1/72 inch).

Portable Font Resource (PFR) A file of characters recorded by a CSR. This is essentially a font that accompanies a Web page uploaded to a Web site.

positioning The CSS capability to place an element precisely in a specific place on a Web page.

property The style description portion of a CSS declaration.

pseudoclass A differentiation of the same HTML markup used as a selector.

rasterizing Changing a vector graphic into a bitmap for publication on a device such as a CRT or printer.

readability The characteristic of being easy and comfortable to read, taking into account the total reading environment.

reading gravity The propensity of readers to read from upper left to lower right.

rendering The process of transforming digital information into a presentation to be viewed with a specific combination of hardware and software.

resolution The sharpness of an image.

safe viewing area That space within the television display in which you can be sure an image will display as intended.

sans serif Type that has no serifs. See serifs.

screen tuning The fine tuning of a digital font for display on a display device rather than for print.

scripts Lines of programming code. They can be relatively simple, or they can comprise a substantial application program.

Software Development Kit (SDK) A package of information, source code, and other digital assets, intended for programmers, regarding a software product.

selector The HTML portion of a CSS declaration.

serif Small horizontal elements on type.

server A computer on a network that provides services for a client computer on the network.

server-side Computing by a server computer.

set-top A network computer built to use a television as a display rather than a computer monitor.

spacer GIF A GIF 1 pixel wide of one color made transparent. An invisible image used to create space in a Web page.

Standard Generalized Markup Language (SGML) A general cross-media markup language that uses DTDs to define documents. HTML is a DTD of SGML.

structure The placement on the page of various word groups (text blocks) and other media elements.

style Typesetting and layout. See Typography.

Super VGA (SVGA) A video display standard that supports at least 640 × 480, 800 × 600, and 1024 × 768 in 256 colors (8-bit color) or more.

text block A group of words such as a paragraph or heading.

Television service provider (TVSP) An ISP specializing in providing service to those who access the Internet via a television and a set-top.

twitter Visible vibrations caused by graphic elements one pixel high in a video display.

typography Typesetting and layout. See Style.

typography definitions See Chapters 2 and 3.

Unicode A character set system providing for 65,000 characters to accommodate the languages of the world.

value A variable input for an HTML attribute.

vector graphic An image created by a set of curves defined by mathematic equations.

Video Graphic Array (VGA) The basic video display standard. See Super VGA.

virtual machine See Java virtual machine.

Web developer Someone who develops a system of Web pages (i.e., a Web site).

Web page An HTML page. An ASCII document structured up with HTML markups.

Web print A Web page printed on a computer printer.

webmaster Someone who creates, updates, refurbishes, and otherwise operates a Web site. A generic term for knowledgeable Web workers.

WEFT Web Embedding Font Tool, a Microsoft program that embeds fonts in a Web page.

wrapping Line breaks caused by the size of the display for text on a display device. The text block adjusts itself to fit inside the size of the display.

XML See Extensible Markup Language.

XSL See Extensible Style Language.

Bibliography

Book design & production for the small publisher. Malcolm E. Barker. Londonborn, 1990.

<coloring web graphics.2>. Weinman & Heavin. New Riders, 1997.

Creating Cool Web Databases. Sinclair and McCullough. IDG, 1996.

Creating Killer Web Sites. David Siegel. Hayden, 1996.

Desktop Publishing Type & Graphics. McClelland & Danuloff. Harcourt Brace Jovanovich, 1987.

Developing Web Pages with TV HTML. Joseph T. Sinclair. Charles River Media, 1998.

Dynamic HTML a Primer. Simon St. Laurent. MIS Press, 1997.

Dynamic HTML for Webmasters. Tom Dell. AP Professional, 1998.

The Form of the Book. Jan Tshichold. Hartley & Marks, 1991.

A History of Reading. Alberto Manguel. Penguin, 1996.

HTML Web Magic. Ibanez & Zee. Hayden, 1997.

Intranets vs. Lotus Notes. Sinclair & Hale. AP Professional, 1997.

Java Web Magic. Sinclair and Callister. Hayden, 1997.

Presenting XML. Richard Light. Sams Net, 1997.

Printing Types: an Introduction. Alexander Lawson. Beacon Press, 1971.

Printing Types Vols I & II. D.B. Updike. Harvard University Press, 1927.

Release 2.0. Esther Dyson. Broadway Books, 1997.

Thames and Hudson Manual of Typography. Ruari McLean. Thames and Hudson, 1980.

Type & Layout. Colin Wheildon. Strathmoor, 1995.

Web Designer's Guide to Style Sheets. Steven Mulder. Hayden, 1997.

Web Designer's Guide to Typography. Leary, Hale, & Devigal. Hayden, 1997.

Web Publishing with XML in Six Easy Steps. Bryan Pfaffenberger. AP Professional, 1997.

Index

Typography on the Web was set in Adobe Perpetua on the
Macintosh by Benchmark Productions, Inc. The Perpetua typeface was designed in
1925 by Eric Gill (1882–1940) for the Monotype Corporation.
This book was designed by Barbara Northcott. The cover was designed by Monty
Lewis in QuarkXPress on the Macintosh. The book was printed on 60-pound Domtar
Vellum paper and bound by InterCity Press, Inc.

Defy the limits of Web production. With Macromedia.

Fireworks

Flash 3

Dreamweaver 1.2

Introducing three ways to take the Web further, faster.
Macromedia® announces a major leap in Web production:
a powerful set of design tools, made for the Web, that
dramatically push the boundaries of what you can do.
All, while supporting the standards that make the Web
the world's most perfect open forum for ideas.

Leap graphical barriers with a single tool. With Fireworks.
Creating powerful Web graphics used to require an unholy
shuffling of applications, utilities, filters, and add-ons. Now, it
simply means Macromedia Fireworks®. The first comprehensive
graphics tool designed expressly for the Web. Create JPEG,
GIF, animated GIF, and PNG files and rollovers; preview for
quality and optimize for size–all in one place. Once created,
your graphics remain editable all the time.

Challenge the conventions of interactive design. With Flash.
Flash™ 3 takes the possibilities for riveting Web content even
further. Create compact, yet dramatic vector graphics, text,
sound, animation, and morphing effects that download instantly.
Even at 28.8. Preview at varying modem speeds. Reach a
worldwide audience–with or without plug-ins. Cool was never
so practical.

Draw it all together with pristine code. With Dreamweaver.
It all comes together in Dreamweaver™ 1.2. Compose your site
visually. Use Roundtrip HTML™ to stay in control of your live
source code. Drop in optimized Fireworks graphics. Add Flash
animations. Add JavaScript™ behaviors without coding. And
send it all to the Web, to view in old and new browsers. In a
fraction of the time. For a fraction of the budget.

Download a FREE trial at www.getmacromedia.com/mw
It's your Web. Your rules. Our tools. See Macromedia Fireworks,
Flash 3, and Dreamweaver 1.2 in action. Visit our site to
down-load FREE trial versions of all three, or to order a demo
CD. But whatever you do, jump to it.

macromedia®